Romans

Romans

An Exposition of Chapter 5
Assurance

D. M. Lloyd-Jones

THE BANNER OF TRUTH TRUST

THE BANNER OF TRUTH TRUST
3 Murrayfield Road, Edinburgh EH12 6EL, UK
P.O. Box 621, Carlisle, PA 17013, USA

*

First published 1971
Reprinted 1974
Reprinted 1976
Reprinted 1998
Reprinted 2003
Reprinted 2008
Reprinted 2013
Reprinted 2017

ISBN: 978 0 85151 050 7

*

Typeset in 11/13 pt Monotype Garamond

Printed in the USA by
Versa Press, Inc.,
East Peoria, IL

To the faithful and enthusiastic Friday-nighters at Westminster Chapel 1955-68

Contents

Contents

Preface

This volume consists of 26 sermons preached on chapter 5 of the Epistle to the Romans.

What was said in general by way of introduction to the previous volume (which consisted of sermons on chapters 3: 20—4: 25) is equally applicable here.

These are sermons, not lectures, and for the reasons given there.

As I explain in the text, I have long since regarded the fifth chapter of this great Epistle as the key chapter – absolutely essential to any true understanding of chapters 6–8.

At the same time it is one of the most difficult chapters, and especially in verses 12–19. Yet nothing can be more rewarding than a careful and patient following of the Apostle's argument.

Two of the great themes in connection with the Christian life are dealt with here, namely, assurance of salvation and our union with Christ. In many ways this chapter provides the essential basis for the enjoyment of our 'so great salvation'.

These sermons were delivered on consecutive Friday evenings in Westminster Chapel from 25 October 1957 to 30 May 1958 (apart from short breaks at Christmas and Easter).

Once more I offer my profoundest thanks to those who have helped me most in the production of this volume – Mrs E. Burney, Mr S. M. Houghton, and my wife.

August 1971 D. M. LLOYD-JONES

One

*

Therefore being justified by faith, we have peace with God through our Lord Jesus Christ:
by whom also we have access by faith into this grace wherein we stand, and rejoice in hope of the glory of God. Romans 5 : 1, 2

This fifth chapter of the Epistle to the Romans not only introduces a new section, but is in many ways the key to the understanding of the remainder of the letter. At the same time it contains comforting and exhilarating teaching of the highest order. It therefore demands careful and detailed study.

The Apostle has finished his great statement of the doctrine of Justification by Faith only. He has dealt with every objection, he has considered every conceivable argument that can ever be brought against it; and having dealt with them all, he has stated the great doctrine once again and, at the end of the fourth chapter, has shown that it is a message that is to be preached to all: 'It was not written for Abraham's sake alone, that it was imputed to him, but for us also, to whom it shall be imputed if we believe on him that raised up Jesus our Lord from the dead; who was delivered for our offences and was raised again for our justification.'

The Apostle starts the new section in characteristic fashion by using the word 'Therefore'. I sometimes think that the whole secret of the Christian life is to know how to use the word 'Therefore'. The Christian life is in many ways a matter of logic, a matter of deduction. The Christians who have shined most brightly throughout the centuries have always been those who have been able to use this 'Therefore'. Correspondingly most failures in the Christian life are to be traced to an inability to use this word, and to deduce what we should and what we ought, from this great doctrine we have been studying.

In other words the Apostle is now going to show us that in the light of what he has been saying there are certain inevitable deductions which can be drawn, and should be drawn. What are the deductions and the conclusions at which the Apostle arrives? It seems to me that the best approach to that is to consider his teaching in general, by making a general analysis of chapters 5, 6, 7 and 8. It is important that we should do this as we start this new section, because, as is well known, these chapters, and especially chapters 6, 7 and 8, have long been the subject of controversy and much misunderstanding.

A commonly accepted classification and sub-division of these chapters runs something like this. We are told that in the first eleven verses of this fifth chapter the Apostle draws out the results of justification by faith. Then, we are told, in verse 12 he starts with the great question of sanctification, and goes on dealing with that until the thirteenth verse of the eighth chapter. From there on, and until the end of chapter 8, he shows certain other results and consequences of this doctrine of justification, leading up to our final glorification and triumph over all trials and tribulations. There are those who say that the Epistle to the Romans is quite simple: first four chapters, justification; chapters 5–8, sanctification; and then chapters 9–11, the problem of the Jews; then the remainder, practical instructions and exhortations.

It seems to me that such a classification is quite wrong. I reject it for many reasons – as I hope to show – but particularly because, by adopting that classification, we rob ourselves of some of the greatest riches of this section which we are now about to examine.

I suggest that that analysis is quite untenable and inadequate were it only for the reason that it misses the real significance of the first eleven verses of this chapter. Paul's real business in these verses is not merely to draw out certain results of justification. They do that, but they do much more than that. The results are almost incidental; there is something much bigger here. Indeed, one popular 'Bible' does not hesitate to say that there are seven results of justification in these eleven verses. It does not tell us what the seven results are. I have tried to work them out, but I have completely failed to find them.

Furthermore, that classification, it seems to me, does not deal at all adequately with the tremendous doctrine that is introduced in the twelfth verse of this chapter, the doctrine of our union with Christ. In the same way it certainly fails to do justice to chapter 6 which starts with the question 'What shall we say then?' Surely, in chapters 6 and 7 the Apostle is dealing with objections and difficulties. He is not so much setting forth a positive doctrine as dealing with objections and difficulties that people bring forward against the doctrine. We are compelled therefore to reject that classification as being too artificial and superficial. Of course, in a sense the doctrine of sanctification is going to be dealt with in these chapters, but not in that way. It is introduced in an entirely different manner.

What, then, do I suggest is the business of these chapters? My suggestion is, that the Apostle is concerned primarily, from this point onwards, to show us the absolute character, the fullness and the finality of the salvation which comes to us in the way he has already described, namely, as the result of justification by faith. Having put before us that doctrine of justification by faith only, he goes on to show that if we really believe on him who raised up Jesus our Lord from the dead, 'who was delivered for our offences and was raised again for our justification', our salvation is absolute, complete and final, and that nothing can ever rob us of it. That, I suggest, is the true approach to the right analysis of these chapters.

Let me substantiate my contention. I maintain that Paul states this immediately in the first two verses: 'Therefore being justified by faith, we have peace with God through our Lord Jesus Christ; by whom also we have access by faith into this grace wherein we stand, and rejoice in hope of the glory of God.' There he leads us at once to the ultimate, the final end of salvation – 'the glory of God'. That is what he is anxious to teach us, that our salvation – if we really see and believe this doctrine of justification by faith, and if we thus rest our faith upon Christ –

that our ultimate complete salvation is certain, is guaranteed, is absolute. He states it immediately in the first two verses.

Then, in verses 3, 4 and 5 Paul goes on to show us that nothing can ever shake us out of it; the greatest tribulations that may come cannot rob us of this, if we are truly in this position. Whatever tribulations may come will make no difference to us. He goes on in verses 6–11 to show why this our salvation is so unshakeably certain. He is not just drawing out the results of justification, he is showing how it makes our salvation absolutely sure and final. In verses 6–11 he says it is so for the reason that it is all of God, that it is based upon God's love, upon God's character. Not only that; he shows that it is based upon God's action and God's love towards us while we were utterly weak and without strength, while we were, indeed, even enemies. But, he argues, that is the most powerful argument of all; God has sent His only Son to die for us and our sins, and if He did so even when we were enemies, then it is quite certain that He will never allow us to fall. That is the great argument of the tenth verse: 'If, when we were enemies, we were reconciled to God by the death of His Son, much more, being reconciled, we shall be saved by His life.' In other words, the argument is this. If you know that you stand justified before God through the death and resurrection of Christ, your whole salvation is guaranteed. If God has done that, the greatest thing of all, while we were enemies, He cannot fail to do the lesser things necessary to the securing of our ultimate complete deliverance from sin in every shape and form, and our final glorification. There, I suggest, is the analysis of the first eleven verses – all dealing with this finality, this absolute certainty of our salvation.

In verses 12–21 he is not dealing primarily with sanctification, but still with the same subject of certainty. His argument is that the greatest proof of our final salvation, and the guarantee of it, is our union with Christ; it is the fact that we are 'in Him' as we were once in Adam. The other explanations are of necessity in trouble at this point. Their problem is, Why does the Apostle begin to talk about Adam here? What is the point of doing so? From their standpoint there is really no answer. It is interesting to look through the various commentaries at this point and to notice how they are in obvious difficulties. Some do not attempt any classification at all; they merely give the impression that the Apostle brings in a number of unrelated subjects, and at this point suddenly brings in our being in Adam formerly and our now being in Christ. They fail to see the continuous argument. But there is a continuous argument here; it is this fact that we are incorporated into Christ as we were once in Adam, that finally guarantees our ultimate salvation. The man who is justified by faith is a man who is 'in Christ', and because he is there his final salvation is guaranteed.

In chapters 6 and 7 Paul deals with objections to this teaching, and especially to the teaching in verses 20 and 21 concerning the Law. The Apostle's teaching concerning grace, and justification by faith only, seems to suggest that the more we sin the more grace we shall receive, and that in any case the Law seems to be useless and unnecessary. He takes up the first objection in chapter 6 with the question, 'Shall we continue in sin that grace may abound?' That was the objection that was in the mind of the Jew particularly, leading him to ask, 'If you say that it is all so certain that it does not matter what we do, we can sin as much as we like; we are "in Christ", you say, and therefore eternally saved whatever we may do or not do; if you are saying that the Law is not vital to our salvation, then you are opening the flood gates to antinomianism, you are encouraging people to sin; and they can argue that the more they sin the more will grace abound towards them and shine before the world'. In chapter 6 the Apostle deals with this, saying, 'Not at all. If you really understand this doctrine of the Christian's union with Christ you will see that it will have precisely the opposite effect. Any man who is really convinced of this truth will strive with all his might and main to perfect himself for the coming of the final glory. As John puts it, "He that hath this hope in him purifieth himself, even as he is pure" [1 *John* 3:3]. The man who really understands the truth of justification does not say, "Because I am in Christ and because I am safe, therefore I can go and sin"; he says the exact opposite.' In chapter 7 he takes up the other objection which has reference to the real object and purpose of the Law. He shows that it was never meant to save us in respect of either justification or sanctification. Its object was simply to show us our need of salvation, our utter inability to achieve it; indeed, as he says in Galatians 3:24, its main purpose was to be 'a school-master to bring us to Christ'. In other words, chapters 6 and 7 are a parenthesis, an interruption of the main argument, to deal with two major difficulties and objections.

Having dealt with these difficulties, Paul returns in chapter 8 to the great theme he had left off at the end of chapter 5 and resumes it with the words, 'There is therefore now no condemnation to them that are in Christ Jesus' – 'in Christ Jesus', the theme of chapter 5, verses 12–21. 'Let me come back to my theme' he seems to say; then proceeds to do so. The great business of chapter 8 is to show us in yet clearer terms the absolute certainty and finality of our salvation – how everything conspires to that end in God's great plan and scheme. It ends on a glorious triumphant note with the great question, 'Who shall be able to separate us?' which he answers with his mighty affirmation, 'I am persuaded, that neither death, nor life, nor angels, nor principalities, nor powers, nor things present, nor things to come, nor height, nor depth, nor any other creature, shall be able to separate us from the love of God, which is in Christ Jesus our Lord.' 'Justified by faith' we are 'in Christ' and nothing can separate us from the love of God.

Let me produce what I regard as the strongest proof that this is the true analysis. Have you noticed that the Apostle does exactly the same thing in the first two verses of chapter 5 as he does in the thirtieth verse of chapter 8. Look at them, 'Therefore being justified by faith, we have peace with God through our Lord Jesus Christ, through whom also we have had our access into this grace wherein we stand, and rejoice in hope of the glory of God.' Notice what he does there. He goes straight from justification to glorification. He does not say a word about sanctification. Then look at verse 30 of chapter 8 – 'Moreover, whom he did predestinate, them he also called; and whom he called, them he also justified; and whom he justified, them he also glorified.' Once more he jumps straight from justification to glorification – from the beginning to the end. His point is that if you are in this place and scheme of salvation at all, the whole is guaranteed to you. Once you are in this, you are in it until you are glorified. So he jumps from justification to glorification. He does it at the beginning of chapter 5, and he does it as he begins to wind up his great argument in chapter 8 in verse 30, and he goes on with it until the triumphant outburst at the end of the chapter.

It is vital that we should understand these crucial chapters, and get out of the bog of confusion into which we have been brought by that other analysis with its various theories as to the way of sanctification, the endless arguing about 'the man in Romans 7', and the glib teaching about going over from chapter 7 to chapter 8. How mechanical it all is, and how it misses this tremendous element of certainty and of glorification! It is surely significant that there has been virtually no emphasis on glorification, especially during the past century; and yet this is the thing to which the Apostle directs attention at the very beginning of chapter 5 and which he unfolds to us in such glowing terms in chapter 8, and especially the certainty of it all.

That, then, being a general outline of the content of these four chapters we must now proceed to go through them step by step, as the Apostle himself does. We must allow ourselves to be led by him and expound his great statements in detail.

'Justification by faith' he tells us in verses 1 and 2 does three things for us at once. It gives us peace with God; it puts us firmly in the place of all blessings; and it enables us to exult at the prospect of our future final glorification. That is the statement which he then proceeds to expound. How does he do so?

In verse 1 he deals with the first consequence of justification. 'Being justified by faith', or 'Having been justified by faith' – a better translation – 'we have peace with God through our Lord Jesus Christ'. We must pause for a moment. You notice that he mentions again, 'through our Lord Jesus Christ'. How many times he has said that in the first four chapters! He constantly brings in the Name of our Lord, and reminds us of His death and of His resurrection. He has just been doing so at the end of chapter 4, and you would have thought that he had laboured it so much that he need not say it again. But he says it again. 'Therefore being justified by faith we have peace with God.' We would probably stop there: but not so the Apostle Paul. 'Through our Lord Jesus Christ.' He feels that he can never say that too frequently; he can never mention the blessed Name too often.

What a wise teacher he is! He knows how ready we are to forget; so he is determined that we shall not forget this. Every time he mentions these glorious blessings he persists in telling us that we get them 'through our Lord Jesus Christ,' that they cannot be obtained apart from Him, and that any man who thinks he knows God, or is blessed by God, except in and 'through our Lord Jesus Christ', is deluding and fooling himself. There is no other way. He is the only way. And if we but saw it as the Apostle saw it, we, too, would delight as he does in the mentioning of the Name of 'our Lord Jesus Christ'. Let us note this as we pass – not that the Apostle will ever allow us to forget it, as a matter of fact. But let us not foolishly fail to take notice of what he does, and skip over it. Let us underline it, let us look in amazement at it; and let us ask ourselves whether we are as fond of the Name as the Apostle Paul was, whether we like to repeat it as he did. And note, not just 'Jesus', but 'our Lord Jesus Christ'. Do you like repeating it? This is one of the best tests of our whole position as Christians. There is nothing without Him. It is all in Him. He is the Alpha and the Omega, the beginning, the end, the All and in all. Let us give Him the glory – 'our Lord Jesus Christ'.

What is it that we get through Him? The first thing is, 'peace with God'. 'Being justified by faith, we have peace with God through our Lord Jesus Christ.' This is the thing he puts first. He goes on to tell us of the blessings we get from God through the Lord Jesus Christ. But that is only put in the second position. This is put first – 'peace with God'. Why am I emphasizing that? I do so for this reason, that there are many people today who put the blessings first, and invite people to 'Come to Jesus' in order that they may get this or that or the other blessing, without saying a word about 'peace with God'. 'Do not worry about repentance now,' they say, 'that will come later.' 'Do you want a Friend? do you need help? do you need comfort? do you want happiness, peace and joy?' These are the things they put forward and emphasize, and so Christianity is made to look like the cults and to appear to be in competition with them. They start with us and our various needs and troubles and problems and our various desires, and then invite us to 'Come to Jesus' as the One who can satisfy such needs. The cults say much the same thing, the only difference being that their particular teaching is, they claim, the thing that produces the desired result.

It should ever be one of our objects to show the uniqueness of the Christian message, and so the first thing we must emphasize is 'peace with God'. Why? For the simple reason that we can have no blessings from God until we first of all have an access into God's presence and are reconciled to Him. We cannot pray to God as we are, and if we desire God to bless us, the first question we have to face is this – How can I have an entry, how can I have access to God, how can I have an audience with God? If you are anxious to obtain some benefit from the Queen of England, the first thing you have to discuss is, How can I get into Buckingham Palace? What have I to do to gain admission? Then, how do I approach this great personage? It is all so obvious in that realm. And yet we pay no attention to this when we seek blessings from God. We go to God and expect to get all we ask for at once. But that is not possible. All blessings come through our Lord Jesus Christ; and we must first be at peace with God.

Let me illustrate what I mean. You remember the incident in the ninth chapter of the Gospel according to John, of the healing of a blind man. That blind man said a thing of deep importance which many a modern evangelist seems to be forgetting. You remember that after he had been healed the authorities were trying to persuade him first of all that he had not been healed at all, and then, when they had to admit that he had been healed, that the One who had done this for him was a sinner. The man made a very profound reply; he said, 'God heareth not sinners'. His purpose was to prove that our Lord could not be a sinner because of what He had done to him. The man was right – right in this sense, that the sinner, as he is, cannot be heard of God. The first thing the sinner has to discover is the way back to God, how to get access to God.

So we start with 'peace with God'. Before we come to consider any blessings we must always consider the whole question of our standing and status and position before God. It is almost baffling to understand how anyone can miss this. We are all interested in blessings, and in our future in this world, but we should start with the realization that we may not be alive tomorrow. There is nothing wrong in seeking blessings, and we should thank God that He gives us such glorious blessings; but a man who starts with the blessings is a fool, for the reason that he may not be here to enjoy the blessings he is seeking. Our whole position is uncertain. 'Your life is but a vapour', as James reminds us, and the first question is our standing before, our relationship to God. I am bound to start there for every reason. How can I ask God for anything if I do not know how to approach Him? Before I begin to think of what I may do when I have obtained blessings, I should surely face the possibility that I may suddenly die and have to stand before God in the judgment? What then? I must start with that. The first thing, for every reason, is my relationship to God. Everything else follows that, and is dependent upon that.

Are we quite clear about this? The primary business of the Christian Gospel is not to give us blessings. I emphasize the *primary* purpose. Its primary function is to reconcile us to God. It is 'to bring us to God'. It is to put us into the place in which we can ask God for blessings, and God can bless us. Nothing must ever be put before that. All this teaching that repentance does not matter, and that it does not matter whether you have a sense of sin, and whether you realize your need of forgiveness, and that all you have to do is to 'Come to Jesus as you are' is utterly unscriptural. Indeed it is illogical. You can go to your bed at night and sleep soundly as the result of some teaching you may have espoused – 'the power of positive thinking', Christian Science, or what you will. You may have lost all your worries and be no longer troubled. The tragic delusion in following such teachings lies in the fact that they do not help you in the most vital matter of all; indeed they conceal it from you and encourage you to forget it. They do not help you if you should suddenly die. They will not help you in the Day of Judgment. You will have been lulled into a false sense of peace, and your position will actually be worse than it was before, because, thinking that you have got all you need, you will no longer be seeking. What a dangerous thing it is to fail to notice the order and the arrangement in which things are stated in the Scriptures, and to reverse them! 'Being justified by faith', the first result is that 'we have peace with God through our Lord Jesus Christ'.

Let us look at this. There is disagreement as to whether we should take it, as I have been doing, from the AV or whether we should follow the Revised Version translation. In the latter you have 'Being therefore justified by faith, let us have peace with God through our Lord Jesus Christ.' The difference is due, once more, to the variations in the ancient manuscripts of the New Testament. Some of the manuscripts have, 'Let us have peace', others have 'We have peace'. But surely, there is no real difficulty here if we take the context into consideration. What is the Apostle doing here? I have already stated that, in my opinion, he is proceeding to remind us of the certainty of our complete and final salvation. If that is right he is certainly not exhorting us to have peace with God; he is reminding us that we already have it. Then, in this next statement he goes on to say, 'By whom also we have access' – 'we have had our access' is the correct translation. We already have it. It is not an exhortation; he is simply urging us to realize what we have already. At this point, the Revised Standard Version is in agreement with the Authorized, and it is certainly more consonant with the trend and the run of the argument of the whole of this great passage. It is not an exhortation. Thank God it is not! It is the Apostle's way of getting us to see what we have already, and to rejoice in it.

What is meant by this 'peace with God?' Let us start with the negatives. What we have here is not just 'peace'; it is 'peace with God'. The world is crying out for peace. People are miserable and unhappy and what they are seeking and longing for is peace, peace of mind. They are in a turmoil, and unhappy. They are looking for peace, and they do not care very much how they may get it as long as they get it. Some turn to drink, some take drugs, some rush into pleasure, some turn to the cults – they are all out for 'peace'. That is not your primary need, says Paul, as does the Christian Gospel everywhere. What you need is 'peace with God', and it is by this method of justification by faith, and by this alone, that you can get that peace. The Christian Church is not one of a number of, or in competition with, the many agencies that are offering people an end to their frayed nerves, and various other ills. This is theology, this is doctrine, this is God's eternal truth. It is interested, not in peace as such, but in 'peace with God'.

The second negative is most important. What Paul says is not that we have 'the peace OF God', but that we have peace WITH God. We can see the difference by turning to the statement in Philippians 4:7, 'In nothing be anxious, but in all things with prayer and supplication and thanksgiving let your requests be made known unto God. And the peace of God, which passeth all understanding, shall keep your hearts and minds in Christ Jesus.' 'The peace OF God.' I am emphasizing that that is not what is dealt with here. This is peace 'WITH God'. I take the trouble to emphasize this because, to my amazement, the two greatest commentaries on the Epistle to the Romans, namely, those by Charles Hodge and Robert Haldane, seem to confuse these terms, and speak about the 'peace of God' here. This does not mean that their interpretation here is not essentially right, but they should not introduce the expression, 'the peace of God' here. 'The peace of God which passeth all understanding' is something that pertains to an entirely different situation from the one with which the Apostle is dealing here. 'The peace of God which passeth all understanding' is something that a man needs when surrounded by problems and difficulties and trials. He is in grave danger of succumbing to anxious care and worry and anxiety. We are all often tempted in that way. The Apostle was then dealing with people who were well established in the Christian life, not with the entry into that life. But here we are considering something quite different; here we are not considering how we stand up to problems and trials and difficulties and tribulations; here the question is, How do we stand before God? What we need at that point is not the 'peace of God' but 'peace with God'.

We shall never know 'the peace of God' until we first have 'peace with God'. It is most important that we should understand that here the subject is not how we stand up to the trials of life, but rather, how do we stand up to the Law of God, and to the Judgment, and to the righteousness of God? Indeed, Charles Hodge himself very rightly points out that a better translation here would be, 'Therefore, being justified by faith, we have peace in regard to God', not peace with regard to trials and tribulations and difficult circumstances, but peace with regard to God. 'Peace with God' is mainly an objective matter of our relationship to God and our standing with Him. 'The peace of God' is entirely subjective, it is the way I overcome the fatal tendency to anxiety and anxious care. Here the subject matter is essentially theological; in Philippians 4 it is essentially practical and pastoral.

The Apostle is reminding us that through our Lord Jesus Christ, and by means of justification by faith, we have peace with regard to God. He means that by justification by faith those obstacles which exist between God and the sinner are removed, have ceased to be, and that there is an entirely new relationship. There was formerly a barrier, there was a state of enmity, there was a state of war and antagonism; but being justified by faith, all that has gone, and a condition of peace is established between God and the man who believes that God raised Jesus from the dead, 'who was delivered for our offences and raised again for our justification'. We shall proceed to look (before I come to work it out still more in detail) at the God-ward and the man-ward sides of this peace.

Here, then, we find ourselves at the beginning of this great section of the Epistle which extends from chapter 5 to the end of chapter 8. The theme is the absolute certainty of our salvation, of our final glorification. The first thing that enables me to know that certainty is that we have 'peace with regard to God'. There is peace between God and me, and me and God. And it is all 'through our Lord Jesus Christ'.

Two

*

Therefore being justified by faith, we have peace with God through our Lord Jesus Christ:
by whom also we have access by faith into this grace wherein we stand, and rejoice in hope of the glory of God. Romans 5: 1, 2

We now proceed to look at the 'peace with God', that results from justification by faith, from the two sides – the Godward, and the man-ward. Far too often it is taken even here in a purely subjective sense. While it is true that there are great subjective consequences of this peace, as I hope to show, it is essential that we should look at it first in a more objective manner. Peace of necessity involves two people, it is a relationship between two persons; and in this case it is peace between man and God. We must bear in mind that something has to happen on God's side as well as on our side before peace can obtain. We must remind ourselves again of the position under the Law. The Apostle has shown us at length that from the side of God the position was that God's wrath was upon us. He laid that down as a primary postulate as far back as the eighteenth verse of the first chapter where he says, 'For the wrath of God has been revealed from heaven against all ungodliness and unrighteousness of men'. He is 'not ashamed' of the Gospel because it deals with that and delivers us from it.

Here he is saying the same thing in a different way by asserting that we have 'peace' with God. Apart from justification, apart from that which has been done for us in and through the Lord Jesus Christ, there is no peace between God and man. There is no peace either on God's side or on man's side, 'for the wrath of God is against all ungodliness and unrighteousness of men'. We should never forget that, but mankind is always very ready to forget it. That is why so many by-pass the Lord Jesus Christ and all His work. That is why so many pray to God without ever mentioning the Lord Jesus Christ. They see no need of Him. They say, 'God is love' and believe that they can go to God directly just as they are. That is a complete denial of the Christian faith. It is the result of the failure to see that there is no peace between them and God even from God's side, and that the wrath of God is upon them because of their ungodliness and unrighteousness. Before there can be peace between God and man, and man and God, something has to happen with respect to the wrath of God, which is a revealed fact.

The Apostle has already told us what has happened, in chapter 3, verses 24–26: 'Being justified freely by his grace through the redemption that is in Christ Jesus, whom God hath set forth to be a propitiation through faith in his blood, to declare his righteousness for the remission of sins that are past, through the forbearance of God; to declare, I say, at this time his righteousness, that he might be just, and the justifier of him that believeth in Jesus.' As we have seen, the great problem confronting the mind of God was this – How can God at one and the same time forgive a sinner and yet remain just and righteous and eternally the same? The answer is that God has sent His Son into the world, and has 'set Him forth' as a 'propitiation' for our sins. That means that He laid our sins upon Him, and poured out His wrath against sin upon the Lord Jesus Christ. It is only because He has done that, that God can look upon us with favour, and pardon us and forgive us and reconcile us unto Himself. This had to happen before the wrath of God could be appeased and He could look upon us and deal with us in a new way. The Apostle asserts here that, in the light of what has happened in Christ, who was 'delivered for our offences and raised again for our justification', as far as God is concerned the wrath is no longer there, and He is at peace with all 'that believe in Jesus'.

But it was necessary also that something should happen from our side, for by nature we are all at enmity with God. As the result of the blindness caused by sin, and our being drugged by the devil, we imagine that all is well, and often believe that we are pleasing God. But this is because we are ignorant of God. We have conjured up a god out of our own imaginations, we have projected our own thoughts, and we have thought that that is God. The moment we realize the truth about God we are troubled and disturbed and our natural enmity to Him reveals itself. That is what happens to many people who have always thought that they were Christians, and have always been religious and godly. They suddenly awaken to the fact that the God whom they thought they were worshipping is not God at all, not the God revealed in the Bible, not the God who has revealed from heaven His wrath against all ungodliness and unrighteousness. The moment they see that, they hate God, they are no longer at peace with Him. They had a false peace arising out of their own imaginations, but they were not at peace with God.

The Apostle teaches in many places that 'the carnal mind is enmity against God' [*Romans* 8: 7] and that by nature we are all 'the children of wrath' [*Ephesians* 2: 3] and 'alienated from the life of God' [*Ephesians* 4: 18]. That is man by nature. He is afraid of God, he has a craven fear of God, a 'fear that hath torment'. He is afraid of the very idea of God. He feels that God is some great tyrant waiting to crush him. He dare not think about death and the grave because of the judgment that will follow it. As Paul teaches the Corinthians, 'The sting of death is sin, and the strength of sin is the law' [1 *Corinthians* 15: 56]. The moment a man realizes the truth about God this feeling rises within him, and he is fearful and alarmed. There is no peace between such a man and God; rather is he troubled and afraid, disturbed and unhappy. He tries to find peace but cannot. He is afraid of God, afraid of death, and afraid of the judgment. It is surely obvious that before there can be peace between such a man and God, man has to be dealt with. And what the Apostle teaches here is that as the result of the perfect work of the Lord Jesus Christ, and that alone, all causes of enmity have been dealt with, and man can be at peace with God as God is at peace with him. On both sides there is this reconciliation, and there is 'peace with God'. God at peace with us, we at peace with God. The communion between God and man, broken by sin and the Fall, is re-established.

That is the meaning of this statement that because we have been justified by faith we have peace with God. This is such a vital statement that we must examine ourselves in the light of it. The test of our profession of Christianity is whether this is true of us. Has our natural state of fearfulness with respect to God, our enmity with respect to God, been removed? The Apostle lays it down here that it is an inevitable consequence of justification. Notice that he does not say that the Christian is a man who is 'hoping' that this may be the case. 'Being justified – having been justified – by faith, we have peace.' We are not looking for it, we are not hoping to get it; we have it, we have got it, we are rejoicing in it. That is the statement, and that is why it becomes a test of our profession of the Christian faith. A Christian of necessity is one who is clear about this, otherwise he has not got peace. There is no more thorough test of our profession of Christianity than just this: are we enjoying this peace with God? There are many, alas, in the Church, as there have always been, who dispute this altogether. They say that a Christian is a man who is hoping that he is going to be forgiven, and that at the end he will go to heaven. But that is not the Apostle's teaching. We have peace, it is already a possession. He will say later on in chapter 8, 'There is therefore now no condemnation to them that are in Christ Jesus'. That is the same thing. It is clearly important therefore for us to make sure that we are in this state of 'peace with God'.

What does this mean experimentally or in experience? The first answer is that a man who has peace with God is a man whose mind is at rest about his relationship with God. He is clearly able to understand with his mind the doctrine of justification by faith only. This means that a change has taken place in his thinking concerning his relationship to God. When awakened to the truth about God and himself his thoughts would be something like this: Ah, there is God in His utter absolute holiness and here am I, a sinner and 'in sin'. There is God's holy Law and its pronouncements. I have sinned against it and cannot erase my past. How can I possibly stand in the presence of God? With Job he asks, 'How can a man be just with God?' He realizes that he cannot, and he is troubled and disturbed, and unhappy.

John Bunyan tells us in *Grace Abounding* that he was in that condition and in an agony of soul for eighteen months. The time element does not matter, but any man who is awakened and convicted of sin must be in trouble about this. How can he die and face God? He is aware that he cannot in and of himself, and therefore he is unhappy and troubled. There is no peace; he does not know what to do with himself; he is restless. Having 'peace with God' is obviously the opposite of that. It implies first and foremost that the man's mind is at rest, and he has that rest because he now sees that this way of God, as provided in Christ, is really a way that satisfies every desideratum. Now he can see how this satisfies the justice and the righteousness and the holiness of God. He can see how in this way God can justify the ungodly, as Paul has already put it in chapter 4. He thinks it out and he says, 'Yes, I can rest upon that; because God "justifies the ungodly" He can justify even me'.

You notice that I put this intellectual apprehension and understanding first. There is no peace between man and God until a man grasps this doctrine of justification. It is the only way of peace. And it is something that comes to the mind, it is doctrine, it is teaching. In other words we are not just told, 'All is well, do not worry. All will be all right in the end; the love of God will cover you.' That is not the Gospel. It is all stated here, in detail, in this explicit manner; and it comes as truth to the mind. The first thing that happens is that the mind is enlightened, and the man says, 'I see it. It is staggering in its immensity, but I can see how God Himself has done it. He has sent His own Son and He has punished my sin in Him. His justice is satisfied, and therefore I can see how He can forgive me, though I am ungodly and though I am a sinner.' The mind is satisfied.

You will never have true peace until your mind is satisfied. If you merely get some emotional or psychological experience it may keep you quiet and give you rest for a while, but sooner or later a problem will arise, a situation will confront you, a question will come to your mind, perhaps through reading a book or in a conversation, and you will not be able to answer, and so you will lose your peace. There is no true peace with God until the mind has seen and grasped and taken hold of this blessed doctrine, and so finds itself at rest.

Having said that, I go on in the second place to say that the man who believes this truth and grasps its import is a man who knows that God loves him in spite of the fact that he is a sinner, and in spite of his sin. He was troubled before by the wrath of God. His question was, How can God love me and bless me? But as he looks at Christ dying on the Cross, buried, and rising again, he says, 'I know He loves me. I cannot understand it but I know He does. He has done that for me.' It is not mere sentiment or feeling, he has solid facts of history to prove that God loves him. God does not merely tell us that He loves us, He has given the most amazing proof of it. The Apostle goes on to say that, and to prove it, in this very chapter, from verse 6 to verse 11. Nothing is more wonderful than to know that God loves you; and no man can truly know that God loves him except in Jesus Christ and Him crucified.

My third answer to the question of how we may know that we are justified is also a most practical test. The man who has been justified by faith, and who has peace with God, can answer the accusations of his own conscience. It is essential that he should be able to do so, because thoughts will arise within, which will suggest to him, 'This is impossible, how can you be at peace with God? Look at yourself, look at your heart, look at the plague of your own heart. How can it possibly be the case that God has forgiven you, and that God loves you?' These accusations arise within our minds and consciences. If you cannot answer them you are obviously not clear about being justified by faith, and if you cannot answer them as they try to shake your confidence, you will again be miserable and unhappy; and there will be no peace with God. But the truly justified man can answer them, and thus he retains his peace.

Not only that; in the fourth place I go on to assert that he can not only answer the accusations of his own conscience, he can answer with equal firmness the accusations of the devil. Nowhere has that been put so movingly as in a verse of that great hymn of John Newton's which begins with the words – 'Approach, my soul, the mercy-seat, Where Jesus answers prayer'. It is the following verse:

Be Thou my shield and hiding-place,
That, sheltered near Thy side,
I may my fierce accuser face,
And tell him Thou hast died.

Poor John Newton! Before his conversion he had been engaged in the slave trade and traffic. He had been a vile and a foul sinner. There was scarcely a sin that he had not committed. You can well understand therefore how the devil would rake up his past and hurl it at him. The devil would resurrect it all and cause it to pass as a horrible panorama before his eyes and then challenge him, 'Do you still claim to be a Christian, forgiven and at peace with God?' But John Newton had his answer, an answer that can silence the devil. He says in effect in that verse, 'What can I tell him? I cannot tell him that I am a good man, I cannot tell him about my past or even my present. There is only one way of silencing him; "I can my fierce accuser face, and tell him Thou hast died", for me and my sin.'

But it is only the man who believes in the doctrine of justification by faith who can do that. The man who believes vaguely in the love of God cannot do so, for the devil will not listen to him. The man who says 'I feel happy' will soon be made unhappy by the devil, for he is more powerful than we are. There is only one thing that the devil can never answer and that is the argument of 'the blood of Christ'. 'They overcame him', says the Book of Revelation, 'by the blood of the Lamb and the word of their testimony' [*Revelation* 12:11]. Their testimony was a testimony concerning the blood of the Lamb. It is the only way. Can you do that? Can you do so with confidence, and in spite of what you may feel momentarily? If you can, and do, the devil will have to be silent, he will leave you alone. He will come back again, but you will always be able to silence him, and thus continue in a state of peace.

Another test can be put in this way: when a man has a true grasp of the doctrine of justification by faith he no longer has a fear of death, no longer a fear of the judgment. This follows of necessity. The author of the Epistle to the Hebrews deals with that in the second chapter of his Epistle. He says that Christ has delivered all those who 'were all their lifetime subject to bondage'. What was the bondage? 'The fear of death', which was controlled by the devil. Christ has defeated the devil, and has therefore delivered them from this bondage of the fear of death. These are very practical matters. Have you visualized yourself lying on your deathbed? What are your feelings when you do so? Are you still afraid of death? Are you still afraid of the judgment of God? If you are, you cannot say 'I have been justified by faith and am at peace with God'. If your faith cannot stand up to these tests it is not truly Christian faith. The man who has been justified by faith has peace with God, and can say with Toplady:

The terrors of law and of God
With me can have nothing to do;
My Saviour's obedience and blood
Hide all my transgressions from view.

The last test I suggest is one which I find increasingly to be a most valuable test in my pastoral dealings with people about spiritual problems. It is this: can you do all that I have been describing even when you fall into sin? It is understandable that a man should be fairly untroubled in mind and conscience when he has been living a fairly good life; but what happens when he falls into some grievous sin? A sudden temptation overtakes him and before he knows what has happened he has fallen. Here is the question. When this happens to you, can you still employ the argument I have been describing? I find that many are caught by the devil at that point. Because they have fallen into sin they query and question their salvation, they doubt their justification, they wonder whether they have ever been Christians at all. They lose their peace and they are in a torment and an agony. They have gone back, and have started doubting their whole standing in the presence of God because of that one sin.

Any man in that position is just betraying the fact that, for the time being at any rate, he is not clear about the doctrine of justification by faith only. Because if he believes that one sin can put a man out of the right relationship to God, then he has never seen clearly that hitherto he has been in that right relationship, not because of anything in himself, but because of the Lord Jesus Christ and His perfect work. When a man says, 'Because I have sinned I have lost it', what he is really saying on the other side is, 'I had it because I was good'. He is wrong in both respects. In other words, if we see that our justification is altogether and entirely in the 'Lord Jesus Christ and Him crucified', we must see that, even though we fall into sin, that is still true.

'But', you may say, 'what a dangerous doctrine!' Every doctrine is dangerous, and can be, and has been, abused. But this is the doctrine of justification by faith only. We have already been told in chapter 4: 'But to him that worketh not, but believeth on him that justifieth the ungodly, his faith is counted for righteousness.' So we must never feel that we have lost everything because we have fallen into sin. If a man goes back over the whole question of his salvation, and his standing before God, and his relationship to God, every time he falls into sin, we must come to the conclusion that he has never clearly understood justification by faith. The Apostle surely makes it very plain to us here. 'Therefore being justified by faith', says the Authorized Version. But a better translation, the right translation is, 'Therefore having been justified by faith'. 'Having been.' It is in the Aorist tense, and the Aorist tense means that the thing has been done once and for ever. You do not have to go on being justified; it is one act. It is this declarative act of God that we have emphasized so frequently, in which He makes a declaration that because He has imputed Christ's righteousness to us, because He has already punished our sins in Christ, He pronounces us to 'be just' once and for ever. You cannot be just one day and not just the next, then again just the day after. That is impossible. This is a declarative, a forensic, a legal matter. It happens once and for ever; and therefore to query it because of sin is to display again some ignorance or uncertainty of the doctrine.

There, then, are six tests which, I suggest, we can easily and practically apply to ourselves.

Let me now make some comments. That is the statement, that is the position, but, again to be practical and helpful, certain comments are called for. Though what I have been saying is the truth with regard to justification by faith, and though it is true of everybody who is justified by faith, I still say that faith at times may have to fight. But I hasten to add that faith not only may have to fight, faith does fight, faith can fight; and faith always fights victoriously in this matter of justification. There is always the element of rest and of peace, and as we have seen, of certainty in connection with faith. Abraham we are told was 'fully persuaded that' – there is an element of knowledge and of certainty always in justifying faith. There must be, otherwise we cannot have peace with God. But at the same time faith may have to fight at times when the devil, as it were, brings up all his batteries. The greatest saints have testified that even to the end of their lives the devil would come and raise this question of justification with them and try to shake them. But faith can always deal with him, faith can always silence him. It may be a desperate fight at times, but faith can fight and faith does fight.

Let me use another illustration. Faith in this matter is remarkably like the needle of a compass, always there pointing to the magnetic north. But if you introduce a very powerful magnet at some other point of the compass it will draw the needle over to it and cause it to swing backwards and forwards and be most unstable. But it is certain that the true compass needle will get back to its true centre, it will find its place of rest in the north. It may know agitation, it may know a lot of violence, but it will go back to its centre, it always finds the place of rest, and the same thing is always true of faith. So the mere fact that we may be tempted to doubt, the mere fact that we may have to struggle and bring out all arguments, and go over the whole question again, does not mean that we have not got faith. In a sense it is a proof of faith, as long as we always arrive back at the position of rest. That is my first comment.

I am emphasizing that there is always an element of assurance of faith, but I do not mean by that, that there is always 'full' assurance of faith. There is a great phrase about the full assurance of faith in Hebrews 10, verses 19–22: 'Having therefore, brethren, boldness to enter into the holiest of all by the blood of Jesus, let us go in', he says, 'with full assurance of faith.' Now the assurance that I am talking about as a constant element in faith does not mean of necessity that 'full' assurance. There is a difference between assurance and full assurance. What I stipulate and postulate is that there is always some assurance. You can be a Christian, you can be justified by faith, and have an assurance of justification without knowing what Paul has in mind when he says, 'The Spirit beareth witness with our spirits that we are the children of God'. You can be a Christian without this full assurance of faith; but you cannot be a Christian without being justified by faith, and that always means an element of assurance, the ability always to come to a place of rest.

At times your faith may only just be able to get you to that place, but it does get there. That is assurance of faith though it is not the full assurance of faith. How many have been discouraged by that! The devil has got them into trouble because he has been able to prove to them they have not got the full assurance, and then he says, 'Well if you have not got that, you have not got anything'. Some of the Protestant Fathers were tempted to say that, but surely they were wrong; and the Puritans were certainly right at that point, as were the great leaders of the Evangelical Awakening of two hundred years ago. You can be a Christian without the full assurance of faith, but you cannot be a Christian at all without having justification by faith and the element of assurance that is involved in that doctrine.

Unfortunately I have to make a third comment. I wish that it were unnecessary. 'Being therefore justified by faith we have peace with God' – and I have described the peace. But alas, there is such a thing as a false peace; there are people who think they are at peace with God and who are not. What then are the characteristics of false peace? We have to consider this because it is in the New Testament. John says about certain people who had been in the Early Church, 'They went out from us, but they were not of us; for if they had been of us, they would no doubt have continued with us: but they went out, that they might be made manifest that they were not all of us' [1 *John* 2: 19]. Take also the people described in the sixth chapter of Hebrews; they had had certain experiences but finally they are lost, they were never regenerate at all. We have to test ourselves and prove ourselves and examine ourselves, say the Scriptures, whether we are in the faith or not [2 *Corinthians* 13: 5].

What are the characteristics of false peace? It generally results from thinking that faith simply means believing, and giving an intellectual assent to certain propositions and truths. That was the essence of the heresy known as Sandemanianism to which I referred earlier. It is based, as the Sandemanians based it, on Romans 10: 10, 'If thou shalt confess with thy mouth the Lord Jesus'. They taught, and teach, that any man who says, 'I believe Jesus is Lord, I believe He is the Son of God', is thereby saved and that all is well with his soul. But all may not be well. You can subscribe to the truth, and give an intellectual assent to it, and yet not really be saved by it. There are men who have 'a form of godliness but deny the power thereof'. Faith is not only a matter of intellect; it is deeper, as I have been trying to show in stressing the element of assurance.

Secondly, the person with a false peace is generally found to be resting on his or her faith rather than on Christ and His work. They really look at their own believing rather than at Christ and what He has done. They say, 'I now believe, therefore I must be all right'. They persuade themselves; a kind of Couéism. They are not looking to Christ; they are looking to their own faith, and they turn faith into a kind of work on which they rest.

Another characteristic of false peace is somewhat surprising and unexpected. The man who has a false peace is never troubled by doubts. But that is where the devil makes a mistake. The counterfeit is always too wonderful, the counterfeit always goes much further than the true experience. When the devil gives a man a false peace counterfeiting the true peace, he creates a condition in which the man is never troubled at all. He is in a psychological state. He does not truly face the truth, so there is nothing to make him unhappy. Let me put this in the form of a very practical question. Can you sit in an evangelistic service without being made to feel uncomfortable at all? If you can you had better examine yourself seriously. I am assuming, of course, that the Gospel is being preached truly, that it is the true evangel which starts with the wrath of God and man's helplessness. It matters not how long you may have been saved, if you are truly justified you will be made to feel unhappy, you may even be made to feel miserable temporarily, and you will thank God again for justification by faith and have to apply it to yourself. But the intellectual believers are never troubled at all, they are always perfectly at ease, without a doubt or any trouble. They say, 'Ever since I made my decision I have never had a moment's trouble'. Such talk is always indicative of a very dangerous condition, is always very suspicious because it is too good to be true.

To put it in another way, I say that this kind of person is always much too 'healthy'. The people who have this false, counterfeit peace are much too glib, much too light-hearted. Compare them with the New Testament picture of the Christian. The New Testament Christian is 'grave', 'sober', and he approaches God with 'reverence and godly fear'. But the people with the false peace know nothing of that; they are perfectly healthy, all is well, and they are supremely happy. Nothing like that is to be found in the Scriptures. Can you imagine the Apostle Paul speaking in that manner, with such glib clichés falling from his lips? His speech is, 'Knowing the terror of the Lord we persuade men', and 'I was with you in weakness and in fear and in much trembling', and 'Work out your salvation in fear and trembling'.

Another characteristic of false peace is that it is only interested in forgiveness and not in righteousness. The man who has the false peace is only interested in forgiveness. He does not want to go to Hell, and he wants to be forgiven. He has not stopped to think about being positively righteous, he is not concerned about being holy and walking in holiness before God, so he is negligent about his life, and does not pursue holiness. He does not heed that exhortation in the Epistle to the Hebrews, 'Follow peace with all men, and holiness, without which no man shall see the Lord' [*Hebrews* 12: 14]. He is an Antinomian, only interested in forgiveness, and negligent with regard to living the Christian life.

Another invariable characteristic of the man with the false peace is that when this man falls again into sin he takes it much too lightly. He is not like the person I have just been describing whose faith is shaken by Satan when he falls into sin. This man says almost as soon as he has fallen, 'It is all right, the blood of Christ covers me'. And up he gets and on he goes as if nothing had happened. You cannot do that if you have any true conception of what sin means, and what the holiness of God really is. This man with a false peace heals himself much too quickly, much too easily, much too lightly. It is because he takes sin as a whole too lightly.

What are the characteristics of true peace? They are the exact opposite of what I have just been describing. First, the man with true peace is never glib, never light-hearted. The man who is a true Christian is a man who has had a glimpse of Hell, and who knows that there is only one reason for the fact that he is not bound for it. That is always present with him, so he is never glib, never superficial, never light-hearted.

Secondly, he is a man who is always filled with a sense of wonder and amazement. He can re-echo the words of Charles Wesley:

And can it be, that I should gain
An interest in the Saviour's blood?
Died He for me, who caused His pain;
For me, who Him to death pursued?
Amazing love! how can it be
That Thou, my God, shouldst die for me?

This seems to me to be inevitable. The man who has true peace is a man who never ceases to be amazed that he has it, amazed at the fact that he has ever been justified at all, that God has ever looked upon him and called him by His grace.

Which leads to the next characteristic, namely, that he is humble. You remember that one of the characteristics of Abraham's faith was, 'he staggered not in unbelief at the promise of God, but was strong in faith, giving glory to God'. Go through the New Testament and you will always find that the most outstanding characteristic of the Christian is that he is humble, 'poor in spirit', 'meek', 'lowly'. Realizing the truth about himself and about God, and realizing that he owes all to Christ, he is a humble man, he is a lowly man. That is another way of saying that his sense of gratitude to God and to our Lord is always prominent. There is no better index of where we stand than the amount of praise and of thanksgiving that characterizes our lives and our prayers. Some people are always offering petitions or making statements; but this man, having realized something of what God in Christ has done for him, is thanking God, is always praising God, Father, Son and Holy Spirit. It is inevitable and incontrovertible. The man who realizes his position truly must be filled with a sense of 'wonder, love, and praise'.

Then, finally, he is a man who is always careful about his life. Not that he may be justified as the result of the carefulness; he is careful because he has been justified. Again this is quite inevitable. He does not fall back on works and try to justify himself; his position is that because of what Christ has done for him he wants to show his gratitude to Him. Realizing the terrible character of sin he wants to leave it, and in addition he is anxious to be holy and to go to Heaven. 'He that hath this hope in him purifieth himself, even as he is pure' [1 *John* 3: 3].

The Scriptures are full of this. Let me remind you of some great statements of this truth. 1 Timothy 1: 19, 'Holding faith and a good conscience'. You not only hold faith, you hold the good conscience as well, 'which some having put away, concerning faith have made shipwreck'. What a terrible statement! 'Of whom is Hymenaeus and Alexander; whom I have delivered unto Satan, that they may learn not to blaspheme.' Hymenaeus and Alexander claimed to have faith, and to hold faith; but they did not 'hold the good conscience' and so 'made shipwreck'.

Then 1 Timothy 3: 9, 'Holding the mystery of the faith in a

pure conscience'. Faith is something which you carry in a most precious, delicate vessel because it is such a wonderful thing. Carry it, says the Apostle, 'in a pure conscience' – 'holding the faith in a pure conscience'.

And then a final quotation from Titus 3, verses 8 and 9. 'This is a faithful saying.' What has he been talking about? 'Justified by his grace', etc. 'This is a faithful saying, and these things I will that thou constantly affirm, that they which have believed in God might be careful to maintain good works. These things are good and profitable unto men.' The man who is not careful to maintain good works is a man who is proclaiming that he has got a false sense of peace. The man who has the true peace is a man who is always careful to maintain good works. He carries his faith in a pure conscience, he holds not only the mystery of the faith but he also holds at the same time this conscience, this good conscience.

There, it seems to me, are the characteristics of true peace. Have you got it? How can one maintain it? There is only one way to maintain it; it is to be living a good deal of your life in the First Epistle of John, chapter 1 and the first two verses of chapter 2. That is how you maintain the peace. You have been given it: 'Having been justified by faith we have peace.' You have been given it once and for ever. The devil will come and tempt you, sin will make you shaky. Go back, go back to that section of John's First Epistle and you will find that you will be able to maintain, to preserve, and to keep your peace.

Three

*

Therefore being justified by faith we have peace with God through our Lord Jesus Christ:
by whom also we have access by faith into this grace wherein we stand, and rejoice in hope of the glory of God. Romans 5: 1, 2

We turn now to look at the second consequence and result of justification by faith, which the Apostle puts in the words, 'By whom also we have our access by faith into this grace wherein we stand'. Some translations leave out the expression 'by faith'; and surely it is quite unnecessary. The difference in the Versions is due to the difference in some of the early manuscripts, and it cannot be decided definitely whether it should be there or not. But as I say, it is quite unnecessary in any case, because the Apostle has already been saying that everything is the result of this faith. So we can read it: 'By whom also we have access into this grace wherein we stand.' We have it 'by Christ', because it is in Him we are justified by faith.

What does this mean exactly? The best way to answer that question is to observe carefully the exact translation. Take the expression 'we have' as found in the Authorized Version. That certainly does not give us the full meaning. It should read 'By whom also we have had' – 'we have had our access'. In other words Paul is emphasizing that it is something that has happened to us once and for all. There was a time when we did not have this 'access'. Now, he says, we have it. How is it that we have it? Because we have had it at a certain point in time, and therefore we have it now. In other words, the translation 'we have our access' does not bring out as it should the fact that there was this critical point, this moment, when we ceased to be outside and came inside. 'We have had our access.'

The significance and the importance of that particular emphasis should be obvious. It reminds us again that justification by faith is not a process; it is something that happens 'once and for ever'. Sanctification, on the other hand, is a process. We 'grow in grace and in the knowledge of the Lord'. We become progressively sanctified, but we do not become progressively justified. Justification is one act, and it is once and for ever. It is that act in which God declares (let us remind ourselves) that in Christ He regards us as if we had never sinned at all. He pronounces that we are just and righteous in and through the Lord Jesus Christ. Our sins are forgiven, we are clothed by the righteousness of Christ, and God declares that. That is justification. It is one concrete act. And what the Apostle is saying here is that the moment God makes the declaration we have had our access into this grace wherein we stand. We were outside grace before, we are now inside. So let us be very careful to give the exact translation here. 'By whom also' – by the Lord Jesus Christ – 'we have had our access' – we have had it, and we still have it – 'into this grace wherein we stand'.

We must also look at this word 'access'. In a sense the word access is quite accurate, but once more it is not quite strong enough. This is a word that is only found three times in the whole of the New Testament. It is here in this Epistle to the Romans, and it is also found twice in the Epistle to the Ephesians. It is in Ephesians 2: 18 where we read that 'through him we both have access by one Spirit unto the Father'. The other place is Ephesians 3: 12, where again you have this same idea, this entry into the presence of God – 'In whom we have boldness and access with confidence by the faith of him'. What exactly does this represent?

It is generally agreed, and I am certainly in full agreement, that a better word here would be the word 'introduction'. It is roughly the same idea as we have in the word which we use about people being 'presented' at Court. That helps to explain the access. You have no access to the Queen as you are. Certain formalities and procedures are essential before that becomes possible. There is a way whereby you can have access – you can be 'presented at Court', you can have an introduction. The Apostle is still working on the same idea. There was a time when we were in sin, when we had no right of entry, no entrée into the presence of God, no access. We had no introduction, we had not been presented, and we could not come into His presence. But now, he says, as the result of this justification by faith, and through the Lord Jesus Christ, we have our introduction, we are introduced into 'this grace wherein we stand'.

The value of giving that additional weight and meaning to the word which we have here translated as 'access' becomes clear at once. Nothing is more wonderful when we look at it in this way. What our Lord Jesus Christ does is to introduce us to God. We cannot go to Him as we are. We are sinful and vile and polluted. Our very righteousness is but as 'filthy rags', says the Scripture. We have nothing to commend us, our clothing is unworthy and unsuitable, and we have no right in our own name to ask to be allowed to enter in. But here comes One who has a right of access and entry Himself, who having dealt with our sins can take us and present us to God the Father. He introduces us. It is the Lord Jesus Christ who does it all – 'By whom also . . .'. The peace we have is through Him; and this introduction, this access, is also entirely and only in Him. He clothes us with His righteousness, He takes us by the hand. He is the great High Priest who is at God's right-hand. He is our Advocate. All these terms are simply explanations and elaborations, if you like, of this term used here concerning the 'introduction into this grace wherein we stand'.

What is 'this grace wherein we stand'? This again is a most interesting term. He means our state of justification. It is something that we enter into. We should always think of it as a state or a condition, and it is one in which we derive and receive all the benefits that are attached to this particular state. In other words the Apostle is teaching us that, having been justified by faith in the Lord Jesus Christ, He now brings us into a relationship with God in which we can receive benefits and blessings from God which we could not receive before.

Perhaps the best way of looking at this is to use the very method the Apostle himself uses later. In the sixth chapter and the fourteenth verse he uses a most important expression: 'For sin shall not have dominion over you, for ye are not under law but under grace.' We are now 'under grace', whereas formerly we were 'under law'. What that means is that before we believed in the Lord Jesus Christ, before we were justified by faith in Him, before we had this introduction, this entry, God looked upon us in a legal manner. We were 'under law'. God did not look upon us as children then; He looked upon us as rebels, because we had all rebelled against Him. The Apostle has proved that abundantly already: 'There is none righteous, no, not one. All have sinned and have come short of the glory of God.' We are all, he has said in the first chapter, 'under the wrath of God'. God looks at man in sin in that way, in a strictly legal manner. But that is no longer the case; we are no longer 'under the law' we are 'under grace'.

That is what the Apostle is saying here, although he is using slightly different language. We have entered, he says, into a position of grace, we have had our introduction to God and we stand before Him in an entirely new manner; and God now looks upon us with grace and in a gracious manner. God looks upon us favourably. The sinner has the frown of God upon him. That is the terrible thing about the position of the sinner. God cannot smile upon the sinner. God frowns upon sin, God hates sin. 'God is of such an holy countenance', says Habakkuk, 'that he cannot look upon sin.' But now that we have had this introduction, God looks upon us favourably, and He not only accepts us, He delights to receive us, and He delights to bless us.

This is the most marvellous thing of all about being a Christian; our whole relationship to God is different; it has been entirely changed. It is like the case of a man who has spent his whole life out on the street outside a great palace. Inside the palace there are endless riches and wealth and a great banquet is being given. He sees people enjoying themselves; but he is shivering out on the street and he cannot partake. He has no right of entry, he is not fit to enter. Suddenly, in a miraculous and marvellous way, he is approached and invited to enter, and provided with a festal garment. He is brought in and introduced, and he takes his place and begins to partake of the feast of the riches of God's grace.

That is what the Apostle is saying. We are 'standing in grace', he says. We are no longer prisoners at the bar with God as the Judge. No! God has become our Father, and He delights to see us coming to Him. He receives us, and He loves us, and He is ready and prepared to bless us, to shower His blessings upon us. It is not surprising that the Apostle refers to it as 'this grace wherein we stand'. He never forgets that he owes all to the grace of God. And we all need to be reminded of it. All the benefits and the blessings of God that we ever have enjoyed, or ever will, are utterly and absolutely undeserved. We deserve nothing but punishment. Man deserves nothing at the hands of God save retribution and punishment. Why? Because he rebelled against Him. When God made him perfect and put him in Paradise, man deliberately rebelled against Him. What does such a creature deserve? And he has continued to behave in the same manner. We are all the same, we are all rebels by nature against God. We have put our will before His, our likes and dislikes before His; we have ignored Him, we have insulted Him, we have forgotten Him. We deserve nothing at the hands of God but punishment and retribution. Therefore all the blessings we receive, and all we ever have received, and all we ever shall receive, is all of grace. It is in grace we stand, and by grace we stand.

Grace, let us never forget, means benefits given to the undeserving, favour shown to those who do not deserve any favour at all; favour shown to those who legally deserve the severest punishment conceivable. But instead of punishing us God forgives us, He blesses us, and showers favours upon us. It is all of grace. Nothing in us calls it forth. It is entirely because God is the 'God of all grace', the God of love. It is because of the 'exceeding riches' of His grace – entirely undeserved on our part, and entirely free on His part, and in spite of our being what we are.

This is now the position of the Christian, and nothing is more important for us than to realize this. We have had our access, says Paul; we are standing in this grace. This is a most amazing and astonishing thing. What does it mean for us? The Bible is full of the answers to that question. You find, for instance, some account of this in the Second Epistle of Peter in the first chapter, where the Apostle reminds the early Christians that 'all things that pertain to life and godliness' are already provided for us. Do we realize this? Are we finding the Christian life hard and difficult? Is it a constant struggle? Is it because we have forgotten that 'all things pertaining to life and godliness' have been provided for us? There are 'exceeding great and precious promises' made to us who have had this introduction, who have been justified by faith, who are the children of God. There is a line in a hymn that puts this very well; it refers to prayer, and it says:

Thou art coming to a King;
Large petitions with thee bring;
For His grace and power are such
None can ever ask too much.

Are we living in the light of that truth? Are we living as the 'children of the heavenly King?' Do we live as people who realize that we belong to One 'whose grace and power are such, none can ever ask too much?' Do we not rather appear to be but paupers and to be living in a state of spiritual penury? If so, we are very wrong indeed, we are most sinful.

The Lord Jesus Christ, when He was here in the days of His flesh, made perfectly plain what was possible for us when He said to the woman of Samaria, 'Whosoever drinketh of this water', pointing to a well, 'shall thirst again; but whosoever drinketh of the water that I shall give him shall never thirst; but the water that I shall give him shall be in him a well of water springing up into everlasting life' [*John* 4: 13–14]. He repeats it in the sixth chapter of the same Gospel, where He says, 'He that cometh unto me shall never hunger, and he that believeth on me shall never thirst' – never! [*John* 6: 35]. We are told of an experience in the life of Hudson Taylor, when he first realized the truth of that: he had been a remarkable man before, a man of prayer and a man of faith; but he tells us that when he came to the realization that our Lord said 'never' – 'shall never hunger, never thirst' – his whole experience was revolutionized.

That is what the Apostle is saying here. He says, we have been 'introduced into this grace wherein we stand'. God is our Father and all the riches of His glory and of His grace are at our disposal. The Lord Jesus Christ was constantly emphasizing this. He says to the disciples – and it is as true of us as it was of them – 'Fear not . . . the very hairs of your head are all numbered' [*Luke* 12: 7]. You remember the comparison. He tells us that it is true of sparrows that 'not one of them is forgotten before God'. Again He argues that if God so clothes the lilies and so cares for the birds of the air, how much more will He provide for you – 'O ye of little faith!' Looking at lilies He says, 'Solomon in all his glory was not arrayed like one of these'. His argument is that, if God does that for them, how much more is His care for us? So He tells us not to have 'anxious care'. 'Take no thought for the morrow.' Do not be always talking about what 'you shall eat or what you shall drink, or wherewithal you shall be clothed'. Why? Because God is your Father, because you are in this relationship of grace to Him and no longer under Law; and the God of all grace is able to provide for your every need. This is not theory; this is what is testified to repeatedly in the Scriptures, and verified in the subsequent history of countless numbers of God's people throughout the centuries.

The Apostle Paul repeats this in that great and lyrical statement in the fourth chapter of the Epistle to the Philippians, 'I rejoiced in the Lord greatly, that now at the last your care of me hath flourished again; wherein ye were also careful, but ye lacked opportunity. Not that I speak in respect of want; for I have learned in whatsoever state I am, therewith to be content. I know both how to be abased, and I know how to abound: everywhere and in all things I am instructed both to be full and to be hungry, both to abound and to suffer need. I can do all things through Christ which strengtheneth me' (verses 10–13). Then in verse 19 he says, 'But my God shall supply all your need according to his riches in glory by Christ Jesus.' That is the grace wherein we stand! That is what justification by faith does.

Instead of being outside and poor, we are now, as the children of God, standing before Him; and He looks upon us graciously. This is something that we have to work out, and to realize, and perhaps especially in the matter of prayer. I have already reminded you that the only two other places in which this word is used in the New Testament are both in connection with prayer. 'By him' – by Christ, says the Apostle – 'we both (Jew and Gentile) have access (introduction) by one Spirit unto the Father.' And in the third chapter of Ephesians, the twelfth verse, 'In whom we have boldness and introduction (entrée) with confidence by the faith of him.'

In other words, we are to test ourselves to know whether we do truly understand and realize that we have this introduction into this grace by the Lord Jesus Christ. The way to be sure that we do understand it, and are living by it, is to examine ourselves when we pray. Do we pray with confidence? Do we pray with assurance? Do we pray with boldness? Are we quite certain of our introduction, or do we spend most of our time wondering whether we really have a right or not, and whether God is listening? Now, says the Apostle, we have had our introduction; you must never think of yourself again in terms of that pathetic man on the street outside. You are not outside; you are inside. Do not bring those old memories with you. Realize that you have as much right to be in this banqueting chamber as anybody else who is there, because you have been introduced by the Son of the King. No higher introduction is possible.

This comforting, consoling teaching is to be found running right through the Scriptures. The author of the Epistle to the Hebrews puts it in his way in his fourth chapter. He has been reminding those people that 'we have a great High Priest who has passed through the heavens, Jesus the Son of God', that He is 'not an High Priest which cannot be touched with the feeling of our infirmities, but was in all points tempted like as we are, yet without sin'. Realizing that, he says, 'Let us therefore come boldly unto the Throne of Grace' – 'boldly', with confidence, with assurance, with certainty. We know we have the introduction, therefore we come to God and pray with this 'holy boldness'.

But the point is, we must go with boldness. 'In whom we have boldness and access with confidence by the faith of him' [*Ephesians* 3: 12].

Therefore, we must test ourselves by this. What is the character of our prayer life? Do we realize that not only do we have this entry, this introduction, but also that God is looking upon us with favour, smiling upon us? Do we remember that He is our Father? Do we remember that He delights to bless us, that He is much more concerned about our welfare than we are ourselves? That is what all this means. We have been introduced into this grace, and we are now surrounded by these 'exceeding great and precious promises'. We are 'partakers of the divine nature', and in our praying we should always remind ourselves of these things. Doubt must go; uncertainty must be banished. We must remind ourselves of what justification by faith means, what our being in Christ means, and that He is the High Priest who is introducing us and presenting us to God at His Throne of Grace. There is only one inevitable conclusion to draw; we must come with boldness, with full confidence. Or, as we have it again in the Epistle to the Hebrews, we must come with the 'full assurance of faith' [10: 22].

I emphasize this because I have an increasing conviction that it explains one of the great sources of our weakness and trouble at this present time. The masses of people are outside the Church because we who are Christian people are representing the Christian life so badly. We are living like spiritual paupers, whereas we are meant to be princes and children of the Heavenly King. We have got to realize that we are in this grace, that this is the relationship. We must act upon it, and go to God with confidence and assurance and certainty. 'We have had our access', our introduction, and we are in, we have been brought into the banqueting chamber. It is a state and condition. You do not go in and out of this. You are either in, or you are not in; you are either 'under law' or else you are 'under grace'. You cannot be half way; you cannot be sometimes one, sometimes the other. If God has pronounced that you are just and righteous, you are 'under grace', you are in the realm of grace, you are in the

Kingdom in which God deals graciously with all the citizens.

But we must add something even to this, because the Apostle does. Have you ever been enraptured, I wonder, by the peculiar way in which he describes our being in this state? 'By whom also we have had our access into this grace wherein we stand.' Why does he describe it as standing? Why did he not say, 'By whom also we have had our introduction into this grace in which we are'. That would be quite true. But he did not say that: he says that we 'stand' in it. Once more we must be careful to give the full weight and meaning to the word. What does this word 'stand' mean? The real meaning of the word – and this is not my idea, not my theory; you will find it in all the best dictionaries – all are agreed is, 'stand fast', 'stand whole'. 'We have had our introduction into this grace in which we stand fast', or 'in which we stand firm or firmly'. This fuller meaning shows that the Apostle is primarily concerned in these verses to emphasize what I have suggested is the main point and purpose of the early part of this fifth chapter. What he is talking about is the certainty, the finality, the absolute assurance of faith; so he is careful to remind us that we are not only in this grace, but that we are firmly set in it, that we stand in it.

We can bring this out by means of a negative. There is nothing uncertain about this. Not only are we admitted or introduced into this grace, but we are confirmed in it; if you like, we are planted in it, we are set in it, we are established in it. The word implies stability and security. It means, therefore, continuance and establishment. It is a very strong word. Paul is anxious to say not merely that we are in this grace, but that we are secure in it. In other words our position is not that we are just allowed to stand for a few hours in this grace and then find ourselves again out on the street. No! We stand in it, we are secure in it, we are certain in it. There is no falling from grace. What an utter contradiction of the teaching of the whole of Scripture that notion is! 'But what about Galatians 5 : 4', says someone, 'where you get the very phrase "fallen from grace"?' The answer is, that the Apostle is dealing there with a hypothetical argument. What he is saying is this: 'If you talk like that, well then you have left the whole ground and standing of grace, you are thinking in a false manner.' He is concerned there about teaching and thinking, not experience, and he shows them their self-contradiction. We stand in grace. There is nothing uncertain about this. It is not a temporary procedure or arrangement or provision. It is the opposite of the staggering and the falling and the weakness to which he contrasted the faith of Abraham at the end of the previous chapter.

This is so important that I must prove that it is a vital part of the Apostle's teaching. Take, for instance, the way in which he says it as he winds up his mighty argument at the end of the eighth chapter. 'For I am persuaded' – which means 'I am absolutely certain' – 'that neither death, nor life, nor angels, nor principalities, nor powers, nor things present, nor things to come, nor height, nor depth, nor any other creature, shall be able to separate us from the love of God which is in Christ Jesus our Lord.' If you are in grace, you are in, and you will never be out. But take again 1 Corinthians 15: 1, 'Moreover, brethren, I declare unto you the Gospel which I preached unto you, which also ye have received and wherein ye stand.' Paul is obviously very fond of this idea of 'standing'. Look at it again in 2 Corinthians 1: 24, 'Not for that we have dominion over your faith, but are helpers of your joy: for by faith ye stand.' Then there is a great classic statement of it in the Epistle to the Ephesians, in chapter 6 beginning at verse 11: 'Put on the whole armour of God that ye may be able to stand' – keep on standing – 'against the wiles of the devil.' God has enabled you to stand, and given you a standing; and if you use what He provides you will be able to continue standing against the wiles of the devil. He repeats it again in verse 13: 'Wherefore take unto you the whole armour of God, that ye may be able to withstand in the evil day, and having done all, to stand.' And yet again in verse 14, 'Stand therefore, having your loins girt about with truth, and having on the breastplate of righteousness', etc.

In other words, it is what he means also in the Epistle to the Philippians in the first chapter and the sixth verse, where he says, 'He that hath begun a good work in you will perform it until the day of Jesus Christ.' But this is not only Paul's idea. The Apostle Peter says precisely the same thing in his First Epistle, chapter 5, verse 12: 'By Silvanus, a faithful brother unto you, as I suppose, I have written briefly, exhorting and testifying that this is the true grace of God wherein ye stand.' This is a tremendous idea. We do not shuffle into this grace; we are introduced and presented, standing erect upon our feet. 'Ah but', you say, 'I have been a vile sinner, I have been a terrible sinner, how can I possibly go into the presence of God with boldness?' My reply to that is, that if you do not go in with boldness you do not enter by faith. Realize that you go in Christ's hand, that His righteousness is upon you and that He leads you in. You should hold up your head with boldness. You stand in grace; you do not slink into it; you do not creep into it; you do not crawl into it! Christ justifies us and we walk into this grace, and we stand in it.

This is an idea that is to be found even in the Old Testament. You remember the contrast drawn in the first Psalm in verse 5: 'Therefore the ungodly shall not stand in the judgment, nor sinners in the congregation of the righteous.' The ungodly will not be able to stand. When the last Assize is held and their names are called, and the account is brought and the charge is read, they will collapse. They will not be able to stand. But the child of God, the godly and the righteous man, will be able to stand. This is just another way of describing the boldness that characterizes the believer. We must realize it in two ways. We must realize that, being in this position of grace in Christ, we are safe. The final perseverance of the saints is guaranteed by their relationship to the Lord Jesus Christ. The Apostle does not use his words haphazardly, he does not use terms like this incidentally. He and the other New Testament writers agree in saying that we stand in grace firmly fixed, firmly established, secure. It is because we are not looking at ourselves and have no righteousness of our own. It is because it is all 'in Christ'.

Let me work this out a little. We have got to realize this great truth and we have got to act upon it in our prayer life. And not only in our prayer life, but also in our testimony. By that, I do not of necessity mean standing in a pulpit to give a testimony;

I mean in our conversation with people. The Christian is a humble man, and yet in Christ he makes his boast. He knows where he stands, and he must not be afraid to say so. It is not presumption, it is faith; and anything less than this is dishonouring to God's great salvation. Or let me put it like this. We must be perfectly certain of our position in the sense that we take the advice given to the man who is depicted by James in the first chapter of his Epistle. This man, if he lacks wisdom, is urged to 'ask of God, that giveth to all men liberally, and upbraideth not'. James goes on to say: 'But let him ask in faith.' He must not be double-minded, he must not be a waverer. He says, 'Let him ask in faith, nothing wavering. For he that wavereth is like a wave of the sea . . .' If this man really wants wisdom, says James, then he must go and ask in faith, believing – 'nothing wavering'. How can he possibly do this? He can only do so because of his relationship to the Lord Jesus Christ who introduces him; and if he realizes that, he will pray without wavering at all. He is not asking in his own name. His prayer is 'in the Name of the Lord Jesus Christ', 'for the sake of Christ'; and as long as he prays in that Name there is no need to waver. 'In Christ' he has a right to pray with all this confidence and assurance; and he must never waver or be doubtful or hesitant.

That brings us to my last word under this heading. The Christian is a man who should have assurance; it is the business of every Christian to have assurance. The Apostle wrote these words in order to give us this assurance. He says to these Roman Christians, 'I want you to know that you are standing in grace'. That is the peculiar glory of our Protestant faith and our Protestant emphasis. The Roman Catholic Church not only does not teach the doctrine of Assurance of Salvation, it preaches and teaches against it. Why? The explanation is quite simple. As long as you are uncertain, you are dependent upon the Church, you are dependent upon the priests. If you have assurance of salvation you do not need a priest, you do not need the help of the Virgin Mary, or the works of super-erogation of the saints; you go directly to God through Christ. Assurance of salvation militates against the whole policy and activity of that Church with its teaching about purgatory and need of indulgences and so on; so they denounce that doctrine. That is, of course, because they put their own tradition before the Scripture, indeed because they here deny the plain teaching of the Scripture. They are thoroughly un-scriptural and they can only establish their whole system, and keep it going, in defiance of the Scriptures.

This was the grand discovery of Martin Luther. Almost as soon as he saw the doctrine of justification by faith clearly he saw the whole error of the Roman Church and her tyrannical priesthood. There is only one great High Priest. 'There is one God and one Mediator (only) between God and men, the man Christ Jesus' [1 *Timothy* 2: 5]. I do not depend slavishly on the Church, I do not need any human priesthood, I do not rely on some magical belief in transmissible grace received through the sacraments. I go boldly through my great High Priest. I am sure, I am certain, I stand in His grace. As we grasp this great and blessed truth we shall be filled with this glorious consciousness of assurance of salvation. We shall know that we are in the hands of the Lord Jesus Christ, who Himself said, '. . . neither shall any man pluck them out of my hand' [*John* 10: 28].

There is nothing more wonderful than this, to be introduced into this grace by Christ, to be set there by Him, to be established there by Him, to be made to stand in it by Him, and to know that we are eternally secure. May God by His Spirit enable us to understand this! We must never be apologetic Christians again, we must never be doubtful and hesitant and uncertain. We must look to Him, and make our boast in Him, and declare that in Him we are standing in grace. We must go to God with confidence, knowing that He is our loving Heavenly Father who now delights to see us, and to receive us, in a way beyond our highest imagination. He is 'the God of all grace'. Never forget 'the exceeding riches of his grace', remember that there is no end to His grace. What right have we to be so poor, and to live so much as paupers in the spiritual realm, while the truth about us is that we are standing in grace?

Four

*

Therefore being justified (or, *having been justified*) *by faith, we have peace with God through our Lord Jesus Christ:*
by whom also we have had our access by faith into this grace wherein we stand, and rejoice in hope of the glory of God.

Romans 5: 1, 2

We come now to look at the third result and consequence of justification by faith which the Apostle emphasizes, namely, the words found in the last phrase of the second verse: 'and rejoice in hope of the glory of God'. Once more, the first thing we have to do is to bring out the full meaning of the words we have before us. Take this word 'rejoice' which is the translation found in the Authorized Version. In a sense it is quite right, it is true; but it is not adequate, it is not strong enough. The word the Apostle used is the word that is generally translated elsewhere in the Scriptures, 'boast', or 'glory'. Take, for instance, the statement found in the last verse of the first chapter of the First Epistle to the Corinthians where the Apostle says, 'He that glorieth, let him glory in the Lord'. That is exactly the same word as is used here. It is more than rejoicing, it is boasting. Obviously a man who boasts does rejoice, but a man may rejoice without boasting.

What the Apostle is concerned to say here is that, because of this doctrine of justification by faith, because of our faith in Him whom God has 'delivered for our offences and raised again for our justification', because of that we boast, we exult, we glory in this 'hope of the glory of God'. The word used here carries that idea as a part of its essential meaning. It means to congratulate oneself. You congratulate yourself upon something that you have succeeded in doing, or something that you have received, some favour that has been shown you. You congratulate yourself on it and then you boast of it, and exult in it, and glory in it. That is the word the Apostle uses here, and it is important that we should give it its full weight and meaning, because it is a very special part of the Apostle's argument at this point.

This word is one of the most characteristic words of this Apostle's literary style; it can even be described as a favourite word of his. I entirely agree with those who suggest that it is a word which tells us a great deal about the Apostle's character and temperament. He was a man who always gloried in what he believed; he had done so before he was converted. The Apostle Paul was never a half-hearted man. When he persecuted the Church he did so with all his might and main, and in the day when he thought that his righteousness 'after the law' was blameless he made his boast in that. It is certain, therefore, that he is not going to use a weaker term when he comes into the Christian life. As he used to boast of his own righteousness he now boasts of his position in Christ; and he boasts and exults in this 'glory of God' to which he now looks forward 'in hope'.

That brings us to the next question. What does he mean by 'glorying in hope of the glory of God?' He is looking forward to it with confidence, he is looking forward to it with assurance. The very prospect of it is something that thrills his very being. That makes it incumbent upon us to enquire what exactly he means by this. Let me put it as a question. Here we are; we are believers in the Lord Jesus Christ; we believe that we are justified by faith. Very well, says the Apostle, if you realize what you are saying, you should be boasting in hope of the glory of God. Are we doing so? But what does that mean?

What is it to glory in, and to boast in, the hope of the glory of God? First of all, it means that he was looking forward in a spirit of exultation and of joy and of pride to seeing the glory of God. You remember the words of our Lord in one of the Beatitudes: 'Blessed are the pure in heart, for they shall see God'. It means what it says, 'they shall see God'. This 'rejoicing in hope of the glory of God' includes that. The Apostle was looking forward to that, the Beatific Vision, the Vision of God. This is the ultimate end of our faith; this is the final goal of it all. The real object of redemption and of salvation is to bring us eventually to that place where we shall stand and behold the glory of God – the vision of God.

The expression also means that we look forward to seeing the glory of the Lord Jesus Christ. Our Lord Himself expressed His desire for this for His own people. In His High Priestly prayer, in the seventeenth chapter of John's Gospel we read in verse 24, 'Father, I will that they also, whom thou hast given me, be with me where I am, that they may behold my glory which thou hast given me; for thou lovedst me before the foundation of the world.' You remember how at the beginning of that prayer our Lord prayed, 'Father, the hour is come; glorify thy Son that thy Son also may glorify thee. As thou hast given him power over all flesh, that he should give eternal life to as many as thou hast given him; and this is life eternal, that they might know thee, the only true God, and Jesus Christ whom thou hast sent. I have glorified thee on the earth, I have finished the work which thou gavest me to do. And now, O Father, glorify thou me with thine own self with the glory which I had with thee before the world was.' And then at the end of the prayer He prays that we, His people, may see that glory. The apostles had only seen Him 'in the form of a servant', in the days of His humiliation, and He desires that they may see Him as He truly is, sharing the eternal glory with His Father. And not only the apostles but all who should believe in Him. So the Apostle Paul was looking forward to beholding this full glory of the Lord Jesus Christ, and he says that all Christians should do that because of the fact of justification by faith. We should not only look forward to it, we should make our boast in the prospect of this, and exult in it.

Well might the Apostle use such an expression because, as we know, he had had a glimpse of this already. And he was not the only one to have had such a glimpse. Perhaps I ought to mention first the case of Stephen, which the Apostle may well have had in his mind also. You remember what we are told about the martyr Stephen in Acts 7:55, 'But he, being full of the Holy Ghost, looked up steadfastly into heaven and saw the glory of God, and Jesus standing on the right hand of God'. What a tremendous statement! Here is this man who is about to be stoned to death, with his enemies gnashing their teeth at him and doing their worst, and all Hell, as it were, let loose upon him: but God does not forget him, and what Stephen was most conscious of was not the malignity of his enemies, or the suffering, or even death, but the sight of the glory of God, the Beatific Vision.

But the Apostle Paul himself knew what he was writing about when he uttered these words. You remember what happened to him on the road to Damascus. There he was going along 'breathing out threatenings and slaughter', when suddenly he saw that light in the heavens above the brightest shining of the sun. We know something of looking into the face of the sun; and we read today in our newspapers about the flash that is seen when they explode atomic bombs; we read about looking at these mighty flashes that are so bright that they are enough to blind a man. The Apostle saw something beyond and above the brightest shining of the sun, and he was blinded by it and fell to the ground. But he also saw a face, the face of Someone glorified; glory such as he had never seen before. He uttered his cry, 'Who art thou, Lord?'; and back came the reply, 'I am Jesus whom thou persecutest'. He saw the risen Lord and the glory streaming from His face.

You remember also how Peter and James and John had been given a glimpse of this, and some insight into it, on the Mount of Transfiguration. They had climbed the mountain with our Lord, and as they went up His appearance was what they had always known; but suddenly they saw Him completely transfigured, 'And his face did shine as the sun, and his raiment was white as the light' [*Matthew* 17:2]. What was this transfiguration? It was something of the glory that really belonged to Him, coming upon Him again just for a moment. The Apostle Peter never forgot that. That is why, in writing his Second Epistle, he says, While I am with you I want to remind you of these things,

'For we have not followed cunningly devised fables, when we made known unto you the power and coming of our Lord Jesus Christ, but were eye-witnesses of his majesty' [2 *Peter* 1:16]. 'We were with him in the holy mount when he received from God the Father honour and glory, when there came such a voice to him from the excellent glory. . . .' Peter was amazed at what he saw, and that was what made him say at the time, 'Master, let us make three tabernacles, one for thee and one for Moses and one for Elias'. He wanted to stay on in the glory; but that was not to be. They were only given a glimpse of it there.

The Apostle tells us that he is looking forward to this, to seeing this glory 'full displayed', as one of the hymns puts it. This same idea appears in other places also in his teaching. For instance, he says in 1 Corinthians 13:12, 'For now we see as through a glass darkly, but then face to face'. We already see something of this glory, but it is through a glass darkly, in a kind of mirror, a kind of enigma in a mirror; but it is nevertheless something of the glory. He says that he is looking forward to seeing it, not as in a glass darkly, but then 'face to face'.

We have a further reference to it in 2 Corinthians 3:18. He has been contrasting the believer with the unconverted Jew, over whose eyes there is still a veil, so that he cannot see the truth of the Scripture which he reads every Sabbath in the synagogue. The position of the Christian, he says, is entirely different from that: 'But we all with open face' – with the veil gone – 'but we all, with open face beholding as in a glass' (again, a mirror) 'the glory of the Lord.' We already see something of that, and it has the effect of changing us from glory to glory. Here, he tells us that he is looking forward to the day that is coming when it will not be 'as in a glass' but in all its fullness and effulgence.

Then there is the passage in the Second Epistle to the Corinthians, chapter 12, in the first 10 verses, in which the Apostle tells us that, some fourteen years before, he had a remarkable experience. He cannot tell 'whether he was in the body or out of the body', it was so marvellous and so glorious. He cannot analyse it and give us a detailed description of it. All he knows is that he 'was taken up into the third heaven' – that is, to the place where God dwells and God's glory is to be seen. He was taken up there somehow, he does not know how, and he heard things which cannot be repeated because of their glory and their wonder. Though still alive and still in the body, and though still limited in that way, he was given this sight, this glimpse of the glory, and heard something of the language of heaven and eternity. All this had created within him a deep longing and desire to see it without any hindrance and to enjoy it for ever and for ever.

I have quoted these passages because it is the only way in which we can have some dim perception of what the Apostle is teaching here. What this passage means, then, is that to all who are in Christ, to all who are justified by faith, there is coming for certain this Beatific Vision. We shall stand in the Presence of God, and see the glory of God and of Christ without a veil; no longer a pale reflection in a mirror, but 'face to face'. That is the first thing it means.

But it also means something further, and that is, that we ourselves shall be glorified. This is essential because without it we should never be fit or able to stand the glory of God which shall be revealed to us. This, again, is a part of the ultimate of salvation. For some remarkable reason it is something that is tragically neglected by us all, and by the Church in general. We talk much about sanctification, but how little do we talk about glorification. When did you last hear emphasis being placed upon it?

What does it mean? To understand this, we must look for a moment to the third chapter of our Epistle and the twenty-third verse. There, in showing the need of, and in introducing the doctrine of justification by faith, he says, 'For all have sinned and come short of the glory of God'. He meant that as the result of sin we have all fallen away from God, that we are not in that communion with God which we should be enjoying and which Adam had before the Fall. Adam communed with God directly. God came and spoke to Adam. Adam saw the glory of God, not in all its fullness, but he certainly saw it. He was in the state of innocence, but he fell and so lost his communion with God, that direct communion, that fellowship and friendship with God which he had been enjoying. Ever since then the whole of mankind has fallen short of the glory of God. We were meant for the glory of God, and we were meant to reflect the glory of God. God made man in His own image and likeness, and something of the glory of God was in man. He was made the lord of creation; there was a glory about him. But he has lost it, and none of us possess it because 'we have all sinned and come short of the glory of God.' But we are going to possess this glory again. That is what the Apostle is saying here.

He says it again more explicitly, in the eighth chapter in the thirtieth verse: 'Moreover, whom he did predestinate, them he also called; and whom he called, them he also justified; and whom he justified, them he also glorified.' This is something which the Apostle constantly teaches. Take for instance 1 Corinthians 1:30: 'But of him are ye in Christ Jesus, who of God is made unto us wisdom, and righteousness, and sanctification and redemption.' 'Redemption' there means glorification. All this wealth is ours in and through the Lord Jesus Christ.

Another of Paul's great statements of this is found in the eighth chapter of this epistle from verse 18: 'For I reckon that the sufferings of this present time are not to be compared with the glory which shall be revealed in us.' That not only means that we shall see the glory of God revealed to us, but there is a glory of God to be revealed in us and through us. In other words, it is a reference to glorification. The Apostle proceeds, 'For the earnest expectation of the creature waiteth for the manifestation of the sons of God'. The animals and the whole creation are waiting for this manifestation of the glorification of the sons of God. Yet further, 'For the creature was made subject to vanity, not willingly, but by reason of him who hath subjected the same in hope, because the creature itself also shall be delivered from the bondage of corruption into the glorious liberty (or, the liberty of the glory) of the children of God. For we know that the whole creation groaneth and travaileth in pain together until now. And not only they, but ourselves also, which have the firstfruits of the

Spirit, even we ourselves groan within ourselves, waiting for' – what? – 'for the adoption, to wit (that is), the redemption of our body.' There the same truth, quite explicitly.

What does it mean? It means that here and now we are justified, we are being sanctified; we indeed have, as Paul says, 'the firstfruits of the Spirit'. But there is one thing that we have not got, one thing we shall never have perfectly in this world, and that is the final redemption of our bodies. Our bodies have suffered as the result of the Fall. It was not merely man's spirit which fell. When Adam fell the whole man fell – body, mind, and spirit. Our very bodies are not what they were meant to be. Our bodies are weak and subject to illness and infections and coughs and colds and aches and pains and all these things. It is all the result of the Fall. And there is no real beauty. All the beauty of man, the most handsome man or woman, is only relative beauty, and there are seeds of decay in it. But when we are glorified our very bodies shall be perfect, every vestige of sin will be taken out of them, and all the results and consequences of sin will be entirely removed. There will be no trace of sin left, and every one of us will be glorious in beauty.

Another great statement of this is found in Philippians 3:21, where the Apostle says that we who are Christians are a 'colony' of heaven. 'Our citizenship', he says, 'is in heaven, from whence also we look for the Saviour, the Lord Jesus Christ, who shall change our vile body' – that is, 'the body of our humiliation' – 'that it may be fashioned like unto his glorious body, according to the working whereby he is able even to subdue all things unto himself.' What the Apostle is saying is that he is looking forward to that day, which is coming, when he shall be perfectly glorified, fully saved; not only his spirit and soul saved, but his body saved also.

It is an essential part of the Christian message to preach the redemption of the body. That is why we must never let go of the doctrine of the physical resurrection. We are to be raised, and we are to be changed, we are to be glorified. We shall be glorious in our bodies, even as He is in a glorified body now. That is what Paul saw on the road to Damascus. He had a glimpse of the glorified body of the Lord Jesus Christ. Now this, we are promised, is going to happen to us. The Apostle John puts it in this way in the First Epistle, third chapter and the second verse. He says, 'Beloved, now are we the sons of God, and it doth not yet appear what we shall be: but we know that, when he shall appear, we shall be like him; for we shall see him as he is.' We shall be like Him! That is John's way of saying what the Apostle Paul says in Philippians 3:20–21.

What the Apostle is telling us in our text is that he is rejoicing in hope of this: he is going to see God, he is going to see the Lord Jesus Christ without a veil, and he himself is going to be glorified. In that glorious body there will be 'neither spot nor wrinkle nor any such thing'. There will be no remnant of sin in spirit or in body or in any part of us. We shall be perfect and entire, glorified in a glorious body, in the Presence of 'the God of all glory'.

In the light of this we can understand the meaning of three words of our Lord recorded in the tenth chapter of Luke's Gospel, verse 20. He had sent out the disciples to preach and to cast out devils, and they had been very successful. They came back full of pride and in a spirit of exultation, and they said to Him: 'Lord, even the devils are subject unto us through thy name.' They were tending to boasting. Our Lord said to them: 'In this rejoice not, that the spirits are subject unto you.' That is surely something of which to boast, it is something to rejoice in. He is not telling them not to rejoice in it at all, but he is telling them not to lose their heads over it, not to think that this is the end. That is only the beginning, only a very small instalment – 'but rather rejoice that your names are written in heaven'. That is what really matters; because if your names are written in heaven, you are not only going to see Satan falling, you are not only going to have power over these servants of the devil, these emissaries of his; you yourselves are going to be glorified, you are going to see God, you are going to judge the world. 'Rejoice rather,' therefore, 'that your names are written in heaven.' The thing to rejoice in is, as the Apostle tells us here, this 'hope of the glory of God'.

This is something that is to begin now. I have already given examples and quotations to show how certain servants of God have been given some glimpse of the glory; but there is clear teaching to the effect that our ultimate glorification starts as a process in this world. This is clear in that great statement in 2 Corinthians 3:18, 'But we all, with open face, beholding as in a glass the glory of the Lord, are changed into the same image, (are being changed), from glory to glory, even as by the Spirit of the Lord.' The Apostle says that of all Christian people, – of himself and these Corinthian Christians to whom he was writing. Those of us, he says, who behold as in a glass the glory of the Lord, are being changed into the same image. A verse in a well-known hymn by Charles Wesley states it thus:

Changed from glory into glory,
Till in heaven we take our place;
Till we cast our crowns before Thee,
Lost in wonder, love, and praise!

While we are on our way to heaven we are 'changed from glory into glory'. That is 2 Corinthians 3:18.

If we are 'in Christ' this is happening to us now; we are being changed into the image of the Lord. What does regeneration mean? It means that a seed of divine life is in us. We have been born again, this principle of eternal life has been put into us; we have been created anew into the image of God's dear Son. We are 'created in righteousness and true holiness' after the image of Christ. That has already happened to us. If we have the life of Christ in us, something of this glory is in us. It may be very small, but we are 'being changed from glory into glory, even as by the Spirit of the Lord'. The work of glorification has already started in us, and we must not in our thinking postpone it entirely to the next world. It is because of this that we who are Christian people should be so heartily ashamed of ourselves that we are as we are, and live as we do, and often go through this world with our heads down. We seem to glory in what we have here, and what we are, less than the man of the world does in what he has and in what he believes. Turn to yet another statement of this wonderful truth by the Apostle in his Epistle to the Colossians, in the first chapter and verse 27: 'To whom God would make known what is the riches of the glory of this mystery among the Gentiles, which is Christ in you, the hope of glory.' Christ in us! If we are Christians He is in us. 'Christ in you, the hope of glory'. Isaac Watts is therefore quite right when he says,

The men of grace have found
Glory begun below;
Celestial fruit on earthly ground
From faith and hope may grow.

'The men of grace have found.' We are the 'men of grace', we are standing in grace, as we have seen. But do we realize that glory has begun below, and that 'celestial fruit' – the fruit of heaven – is to be found on earthly ground in this life as the result of 'faith and hope'? Isaac Watts reminds us in that same hymn that here in this world, 'We are marching through Immanuel's ground'. We have not yet arrived at 'the golden streets', but already the glory has begun in us.

What we must lay hold of is that all this is absolutely certain. I have already drawn your attention to the way in which the Apostle jumps from justification to glorification. He does it here, and he does it again in chapter 8:30. What is of vital importance is that we should all learn to make this jump. We must not stop at justification. If you are justified you are glorified. It is the God who has predestinated you who does everything; and if He has predestinated you to justification He has also predestinated you to glorification.

Do you rejoice in this jump? You cannot divide the Lord Jesus Christ. If you are in Christ you are in Christ; and if Christ 'has been made of God unto you wisdom, even righteousness and sanctification', He must be glorification to you also. You cannot divide Him and 'take' justification only, or sanctification only, It is 'all or nothing'. You must not divide these things. It is unscriptural, indeed it is impossible. It is the Person of Christ that matters. He is indivisible. We have all these in Christ, and the germ of my glorification is in me now as certainly as my sanctification, and as certainly as my justification in Him. It is our union with Christ that guarantees everything. That is why the Apostle tells the Ephesians that 'we are already seated with him in the heavenly places'.

That is why we must learn to make our boast in these things. That is why we have lingered over these two verses. How superficial it is for people to say glibly, 'Ah yes', verses 1 and 2 'the results of justification – peace with God, standing in grace, rejoicing in hope of the glory of God', and then rush on to the next verse. We have no right to go on to the next verses until we know these things thoroughly. I therefore ask again, Do you know this peace with God? Are you really standing in this grace as a child of God? Do you go with confidence to the Throne of Grace and pray with a holy boldness? Are you rejoicing in hope of the glory of God? There must be no uncertainty about these things. This is not a mere hope. Do not be misled by that word 'hope'. As the Apostle uses the word he means something which is absolutely certain. It is the 'blessed hope', 'the hope that is set before us; which we have as an anchor of the soul, both sure and steadfast, and which entereth into that within the veil; whither the forerunner is for us entered, even Jesus' [*Hebrews* 6:18–20].

In other words, to understand the doctrine of justification rightly means that we have assurance and certainty of salvation. That is what the Apostle teaches, and that is why I say once more that there is nothing more un-scriptural than the Roman Catholic teaching at this point. The same is true also of the Barthian teaching: that is, Professor Karl Barth denied and disputed the possibility of assurance. He spoke and wrote actively against it. That is because his theology, in spite of his many protestations, was more philosophical than biblical. If you are biblical you must take the same ground as the Apostle Paul. Paul says that we must boast of this, we must exult and glory in it. But how can you do so if you are uncertain about it? That is also the reason why any doctrine that teaches a possibility of falling away from grace is un-scriptural. You cannot boast and exult and glory in the ultimate of salvation if you may suddenly lose it all. The answer is that it is all of God, it is all in Christ, it is all of grace and by faith, 'in order that the promise might be sure unto all the seed' [4:16]. You and I, seeing this and believing it and understanding it, are meant to rejoice in hope of the glory of God. We are to say, 'We're marching through Immanuel's ground to fairer worlds on high'. We are to pay heed to the exhortations of John Cennick:

Children of the heavenly King,
As ye journey, sweetly sing,

and of Isaac Watts:

Come, we that love the Lord,
And let our joys be known;
Join in a song with sweet accord,
And thus surround the Throne.

Watts' argument is thoroughly sound scripturally:

Let those refuse to sing
That never knew our God;
But children of the heavenly King
May speak their joys abroad.

Then let our songs abound,
And every tear be dry;
We're marching through Immanuel's ground
To fairer worlds on high.

Let us be certain of these things, and lay hold of them. They are things that are inevitable because of justification by faith.

Let Henry Francis Lyte in one of his hymns reinforce the exhortation of Isaac Watts:

Haste then on from grace to glory,
Armed by faith, and winged by prayer;
Heaven's eternal day's before thee,
God's own hand shall guide thee there!
Soon shall close thy earthly mission,
Swift shall pass thy pilgrim days;
Hope soon change to glad fruition,
Faith to sight, and prayer to praise!

Do you know anything of this glory? Do you behold it with open face as Paul says in 2 Corinthians 3:18? Have you seen anything of the glory of the Lord in a kind of mirror? The church of today is as she is because we 'behold' these things so little, because we are so ignorant of them. We are concerned about getting the reluctant outsiders into the Church, but when you and I know something of the glory of God, and when those others see that we are being 'changed from glory into glory', they will come to us of their own accord as they have always come to such people. It is when a man like George Whitefield came to know something of this glory, saw it, and began to manifest it, and Wesley and others with him – it is when that happened to these men that they were used of God and attracted people like magnets. The churches then became too small, and they had to go and preach in the open air.

We must start with the Church if we are to evangelize the outsider. It is largely because we are lacking in this sense of the glory, and not boasting in it, that many are outside. Here we are in a world where 'men's hearts are failing them for fear', where they have lost their way or know not where they are, nor what to do, nor where to turn, and you and I, who ought to be able to help them, often seem to be as bewildered as they are. That is why they will not listen to us. But if they saw something of the radiance and the glory of God Himself and of Christ upon our faces, as those Israelites saw it in the face of Moses when he came down the mount with the Tables of the Law in his hands, they would begin to listen to us. They would say, 'Look at these people. In spite of their being in this world, in spite of the hydrogen bomb, in spite of the various "curtains", in spite of all that is happening – look at them, look at their peace, their equanimity, the wonder of their lives and personalities.' They would be drawn and attracted, and they would come to us and enquire of us the secret of our different type of life and outlook.

Are you boasting and exulting and glorying in hope of the glory of God? If not, and if you would like to, I can give you Paul's prescription as to how it becomes possible to do so. It is in 2 Corinthians 4, verses 17 and 18: 'Our light affliction, which is but for a moment, worketh for us a far more exceeding and eternal weight of glory; while (as long as we) look not at the things which are seen, but at the things which are not seen: for the things which are seen are temporal; but the things which are not seen are eternal.' 'I can say that these things that are happening are a light affliction, and but for a moment', says Paul, 'while – as long as – I look, not at what is round about me, but away to Him, as long as I look into His face as in a glass darkly by faith, as long as I see the glory there, that glory that awaits me, everything else becomes but a light affliction then.' For exactly the same reason he says in writing to the Colossians, 'Set your affections on things above, not on the things on the earth' [*Colossians* 3:1]. If you have not seen something of the glory of God and of Christ it is because you are looking too much at other things. You are looking too much at your newspapers, at your television, at the world and its gaudiness. Turn away from it all and begin to look at, to gaze upon, the things which are not seen, the things which are eternal. Set your affections there. It calls for an effort of the will, and discipline. It means diligence in your study of the Scriptures, and meditation upon them. Seek Him there; ask the Spirit to reveal Him to you. Ask Him to manifest Himself to you. Once you have caught a glimpse of Him and the glory that awaits you, then you will be very ready to join Paul and say that you boast and glory and exult in the hope of the glory of God.

Five

*

And not only so, but we glory in tribulations also; knowing that tribulation worketh patience;
And patience, experience; and experience, hope:
And hope maketh not ashamed, because the love of God is shed abroad in our hearts by the Holy Ghost which is given unto us.
Romans 5: 3–5

These three verses, as the opening words suggest, are a continuation of what the Apostle has already been saying in the first two verses. In them the Apostle has told us of the grounds on which we can be certain of our salvation as the result of justification by faith only. The three grounds are, 'Being (having been) justified by faith, we have peace with God through our Lord Jesus Christ'. Secondly, 'By whom also we have had our access into this grace wherein we stand'. And thirdly, 'We rejoice in the hope of the glory of God'.

Having said that, the Apostle continues by saying, 'And not only so'. What he has been saying is not the end, there is something further, something which in a sense is even stronger. Those three things are wonderful but, he says, I can go on to tell you something which is equally wonderful. Those, you would have thought, were sufficient grounds of assurance, and a guarantee of the finality of our salvation, but there is even more.

What is this further proof of the fact that we are saved, that we are the children of God, and that we are destined for that glory that awaits us? The answer is: the way in which our faith enables us to face the trials, the troubles, the problems, and the tribulations of life. That is the theme with which he deals in these three verses. Now it is not surprising that he should do this, because he knew very well from his own experience, and from the experience of others, that Christian people often had to endure very severe and sharp trials and tribulations. He knew, further, that there were those who were always ready to argue, as they are still ready to argue, that the fact that Christian people should be allowed to undergo such trials brings into question the whole of salvation. It is essential, therefore, that the Apostle should deal with this.

This is an extremely important subject. I am more and more impressed by the amount of space and attention which is given in the New Testament Scriptures to this one particular problem. There is no theme that is dealt with more frequently. Our Lord Himself began to deal with it at the very end of His ministry. When He was giving a number of messages to His disciples and followers this is one of the last things He said to them: 'These things I have spoken unto you that in me ye might have peace. In the world ye shall have tribulation; but be of good cheer, I have overcome the world' [*John* 16:33]. Our Lord turned to the disciples and warned them that in the world they were going to have tribulation. But at the same time He tells them to be of good cheer because He has overcome the world. The Apostle Paul warned his young converts, his young followers, in almost exactly the same way. He reminded them that it is 'through much tribulation that we must enter into the Kingdom of God' [*Acts* 14:22]. He was going on a round of the churches with Barnabas and that is what he impressed upon them. He warned them not to be surprised when persecutions and tribulations came, but at the same time assures them that this would not interfere with their final salvation.

That, then, is our theme, and we can lay down this proposition. There is no more important, and no more subtle test of our profession of the Christian faith than the way we react to the trials and the troubles and the tribulations of life in this world. There is no test which is more delicate, more sensitive than this particular test. I have sometimes ventured to describe it as the acid test of a man's profession of the Christian faith. Let me show what I mean.

It is in particular the way to differentiate between the Christian faith and the various cults. The claim we can make for this message, for this way of life, is that it is a life that never fails us, never lets us down. Now that cannot be said of any false teaching, whether it is false religion or a false philosophy. Indeed the cults generally betray their spurious character at the very outset by promising far too much. It is the cults that say, 'Believe this teaching and you will never have any more troubles. You will not know yourself, you will not know the world. You will walk with a fresh step and a bright outlook, and you will never have any troubles again.' This is always the language of the cults, but it is never the language of the New Testament. On the contrary it says, 'In the world ye shall have tribulation'. Indeed I could make out a case for saying that the New Testament teaches us that the Christian is more likely to have troubles than anybody else. That will come later. But the cults make these great claims, and then, in the moment of crisis, when men need them and their help most of all, they are unable to give it.

There is an excellent illustration of this in the Old Testament. It is that great scene on Mount Carmel, which is described in the First Book of Kings, chapter 18, where the solitary, lonely Elijah stands alone facing some 850 false prophets, and challenges them and their god Baal in the Name of the living God. That produced a great crisis. The false prophets were given the first opportunity, to pray for fire from heaven to fall on the altar, and they pleaded with their god. They scarified their flesh, they cried, they prayed, they pleaded; but nothing happened, there was neither a voice nor any that answered. They were utterly discomfited, disappointed, and left to themselves in the agony of the crisis. Then Elijah, you remember, prayed to God, and God answered by fire, and Elijah's faith was vindicated. The way to test between the true and the false is to observe what happens in the hour of crisis, in the time of real need. A faith that does not help us when we need it most of all is not the Christian faith; for this never fails.

To be more practical, let me put it like this. This is a very good way of testing between a true belief and some merely emotional or psychological experience. There are people who think that they have become Christians because they have had some strange feeling, some new experience, perhaps in a meeting. It was marvellous, it was wonderful, and they tell everybody about it, almost making some of us feel that we have never been Christians at all. But we have seen the same people sometime afterwards, when something had gone wrong, or when there had been difficulties and trials, and find that they have renounced all they had claimed to believe. Why? Because they never had a true belief. They had had an emotional experience, they had had, perhaps, a psychological experience; there are such things. They had thought that now everything was going to be perfect; so the moment a trial comes they lose everything. Salvation to them meant being happy, living on your feelings; and, of course, when things go wrong you become unhappy, and so everything goes. Trials and tribulations soon put an end to a mere emotional or psychological experience.

Or let me put it like this. Trials and tribulations always differentiate between what we can describe as 'believism' or 'fideism' and true faith. Here again is a terrible danger that we must never forget, the danger of thinking that merely to subscribe to the Christian teaching means true faith. True faith includes that, but it is more than that, as we have seen already many times in working out the doctrine of justification by faith. It is not a mere believism; and it is important to realize that, because trials and tribulations test mere believism. The man who merely has this kind of believism is found to fail altogether when the trials and the tribulations come. He has got nothing to fall back upon.

Our Lord teaches this in the Parable of the Sower. He says that some of the seed fell on stony ground. It sprang up very quickly but, because there was no depth of soil, it had no root and it did not last. He goes on to say, 'He hath not root in himself, but endureth for a while; for when tribulation or persecution ariseth because of the Word, by and by he is offended' [*Matthew* 13:21]. This is often the kind of man who has some trouble or problem in his life. He has tried everything. He then comes to a Christian meeting and is told that he has only to believe this message, and accept it, and all will be well. 'All right,' he says, 'I will believe it.' He is told to say, 'I believe in the Lord Jesus Christ' and he does so. He is then assured that he is saved. But his trouble is still with him and his problem unsolved; he finds that trials and tribulations still come, and he says, 'But I thought that, if I believed this, I would never get this kind of trouble again.' As our Lord puts it, 'When tribulation or persecution ariseth because of the Word, by and by he is offended'. He says, 'I did not think it was going to be like this. Why does God allow this sort of thing to happen? I thought that once I believed I would never again be in such a position.' So you see that trials and tribulations and troubles do indeed constitute a most vital and thorough-going test of our Christian profession.

What, then, is to be the Christian reaction to these things when they come? 'Tribulations' means afflictions, pressures, stresses, difficulties, illnesses perhaps or persecutions; they can take almost any form. What is to be the reaction of the Christian to trials of every conceivable type and kind? We need scarcely say that it is not enough that he does not grumble and complain, does not feel he is being dealt with harshly, and does not query his faith altogether, and fail. In the second place, it is not that he merely puts up with adversities in a philosophical manner. To put up with them is better than to fail, but that is not the Christian reaction. The Christian, says the Apostle, does not merely resign himself in a negative spirit to his tribulations.

This is a most important distinction, especially today. Christianity is not Stoicism which is mere resignation. Stoicism puts up with things, bears them, just manages not to give in. With courage and a tremendous effort of the will Stoicism goes on and just gets through. That is Stoicism; bearing it, putting up with it, not failing, not breaking down. That is not the Christian's reaction. This is a most important point. It often seemed to me in the last war, and, indeed, since the last war, that there was much confusion between Stoicism and Christianity. The 'firm upper lip', and 'sticking it', or 'taking it' is not a description of the Christian. A Christian is not merely a man who exercises courage.

What he has is not merely a passive resignation. It is this: 'Not only so, but we glory in tribulations also.' Once more we have the same word that we found at the end of the second verse, translated, 'Rejoice in hope of the glory of God', and which we saw means, to 'boast in it', 'exult in it', 'glory in it'. This is the Christian's reaction, his response, to these tribulations; he boasts, he exults, he glories in them.

Here again we must bring out a meaning which may well be missed. You notice how Paul puts it. 'And not only so,' he says, 'but we glory in tribulations also.' Now that word 'in' is most important. He is not saying that we glory in spite of them. People have often thought that it means that; that though these things are happening, we will still go on glorying; we glory in spite of them. No! Neither does it mean that we glory in the midst of them. It does mean that, but it means more than that. It is a very good thing that we are able to glory in the midst of our tribulations, but the Apostle goes well beyond that. He says we glory on account of them, because of them. That is the meaning of the word 'in' here. Not in spite of, not in the midst of, but on account of, because of – we glory because of our tribulations.

How do we interpret this? Perhaps the best procedure is to consider this kind of teaching as we find it elsewhere in the New Testament. I am concerned to show that it is typical and characteristic New Testament teaching. This is not just something said by the Apostle Paul when he happened to be in a good mood and was carried away by his own eloquence. It is the universal teaching of the New Testament. Look at the Lord Jesus Christ stating it in Matthew 5:10–12. 'Blessed are they which are persecuted for righteousness' sake; for theirs is the Kingdom of heaven.' 'Blessed are ye when men shall revile you and persecute you, and shall say all manner of evil against you falsely, for my sake. Rejoice, and be exceeding glad; for great is your reward in heaven; for so persecuted they the prophets which were before you.' Our Lord is exhorting us in the midst of these things to 'rejoice and be exceeding glad'. Nothing could be stronger than that.

Or take it again in Acts 5:41. Here are the apostles being persecuted, put into jail, and threatened with death, but this is what we read of them, 'And they departed from the presence of the council, rejoicing that they were counted worthy to suffer shame for his name.' Rejoicing that they had been put into prison! Rejoicing that they had been counted worthy to suffer shame for His Name! See Paul saying it to the Corinthians: 'Our light affliction, which is but for a moment, worketh for us a far more exceeding and eternal weight of glory' [2 *Corinthians* 4:17]. That is exultation. Again in that same epistle, in the twelfth chapter, verses 9 and 10, he repeats that with regard to his own 'thorn in the flesh'. Three times he prays that it might be removed, and the answer comes back, 'My grace is sufficient for thee, for my strength is made perfect in weakness'. 'Very well', says Paul, 'most gladly, therefore, will I rather glory in my infirmities that the power of Christ may rest upon me. Therefore I take pleasure in infirmities, in reproaches, in necessities, in persecutions, in distresses for Christ's sake; for when I am weak, then I am strong.' To the Philippians he says, 'Unto you it is given in the behalf of Christ, not only to believe in him, but also to suffer for his sake' [1:29]. It is 'given' unto you. It is something for you to glory in therefore.

Or take James – for all the writers are unanimous about this, there is no contradiction – 'Count it all joy, my brethren, when ye fall into divers temptations (trials) . . .' [1:2]. Or, again, in the twelfth verse of that same chapter, 'Blessed is the man that endureth temptation, for when he is tried he shall receive the crown of life'. Then turn to the First Epistle of Peter, chapter 4, verses 12-14: 'Think it not strange', he says, 'concerning the fiery trial which is to try you, as though some strange thing happened to you: but rejoice, inasmuch as ye are partakers of Christ's sufferings; that, when his glory shall be revealed, ye may be glad also with exceeding joy. If ye be reproached for the name of Christ, happy are ye; for the spirit of glory and of God resteth upon you.' This is sufficient evidence to prove that the New Testament is full of this teaching. The Christian's reaction is not merely to put up with trial, it is not just to be happy in spite of it, it is not to be happy in the midst of it: it is to rejoice on account of it, because of it.

How does this work out in practice? It does not mean, of course, that we should actually be glad when these things happen to us. It does not mean that the moment these things happen to us we begin to praise and to thank God thoughtlessly, still less automatically. You notice how the author of the Epistle to the Hebrews puts it: 'No chastening for the present seemeth to be joyous, but grievous' [12:11]. When a Christian is taken ill, or when things go wrong with him, of course he does not like these things. The Christian is not meant to be unnatural or a psychological oddity. The Apostle is not teaching a kind of masochism; that is not what we have here. There are people, and there have been people in the Church in the past who have thought that and taught it. In a sense they have only been happy when they have been miserable. They have almost been troubled when things were going well with them. They have courted trials. That is not the teaching at all. Immediately, and at first, these things are not pleasant, and nobody likes them. The Apostle does not say that we should like these things; what he says is that we should glory in them – which is a very different thing.

How then does this work out? We can glory in tribulations because our faith enables us to view them in such a way as to realize that, far from working against our hope, they actually promote it, and, indeed, further it. In other words the reaction of the Christian to tribulations is not an automatic one. It is not a case of 'Come what may, I'm always happy'. He is enabled to glory in them as the result of the application of his faith. Because he is a man of faith he is able to do certain things. Trials and tribulations come, and at first he is troubled, he is made unhappy. But he does not stop at that; he proceeds to deal with them. How does he do this? The Apostle gives us the answer. 'Not only so, but we glory in tribulations also.' How? 'Knowing': it is because of something we know. It is this knowledge, and the application of this knowledge, that enables us to exult and to glory and to rejoice. What is the knowledge? It is a knowledge of, and an insight into, God's purposes and methods with respect to us. Or, if you like, what our faith does is to enable us to follow the argument which the Apostle now proceeds to work out. That is always the real test of our faith. Are we able to follow this reasoning, this argument that the Apostle works out here?

Paul says that we are enabled to rejoice in these things, and to boast in them, because we know that 'tribulation worketh patience'. Clearly the important word here is the word 'worketh'. It is a word that the Apostle uses elsewhere. There is an example of it in a passage we have already quoted in 2 Corinthians 4:17, 'Our light affliction, which is but for a moment, worketh for us'. He obviously has a process in his mind, or a kind of treatment which does something to us. It is a process that works out certain results, works them out in detail from step to step, and produces a final product, namely patience. What is patience? Patience means constancy. Patience means the ability to go on patiently enduring. In other words, it means steadfastness.

The Apostle says that tribulations produce, or work, this kind of endurance, this patient continuing. How do they do that? We can all surely draw on our own experience to see exactly how it happens. The moment these trials and tribulations come we realize a new and a fresh need of our Lord. We had been going on in the Christian life rather thoughtlessly, thinking that we knew everything, and that we had everything. But suddenly we are confronted by these trials and tribulations and problems; and at first we are taken aback and do not understand. But if we have true faith, that will make us turn back to Him. That is the test. We will not just look at the problems, we will remember what He has said and what He has promised. So we go to Him about them. The man who has not got real faith says, 'Ah, my feelings were all imagination, there was nothing in it.' He gives it up and goes out, and goes back. Not so the Christian! The new condition makes him realize the need of a fresh supply of grace and strength. In other words, the trials and tribulations make him think of the Lord Jesus Christ again, the One he is always liable to forget. They do more, they send him to Christ, they make him pray to Him, they make him spend more of his time with Him, they make him plead with Him and ask Him for greater strength and understanding. To put it in another way, the trials are doing something that is very good for him, they are driving him back to the Lord Jesus Christ. They do not drive the man of the world to Him; but rather away from Him. But tribulations always drive the man of faith back to Christ Himself.

But not only that, trials and tribulations are very good for us in that they help us to know ourselves better than we knew ourselves before. We are always over-estimating ourselves, and we always tend to think things are better with us than they are. That is why we always need to be exhorted to self-examination. We are all on good terms with ourselves, and we balance things up very cleverly. It is only when a trial or a tribulation comes that we are forced to see our true condition, and how perhaps we have been drifting away from our Lord. So trials are good for us in that they bring us not only to a better knowledge of Him but to a better knowledge of ourselves also. We thought we could stand, but we find that we are shaking. We thought we had faith that could meet anything, and here we are, badly shaken maybe by something comparatively small.

That is very good for us because it gives us a true picture of ourselves, and we realize that we are not as strong as we thought we were. It drives us back to a sense of dependence upon Him, and that results in our having a much better conception of the Christian life than we had before. It was superficial before, it is now much deeper. We realize our weakness and the strength of the enemy, but above all, we realize His strength. We thus have a more balanced view, a deeper view, a larger and a truer view. The result is that, when further trials come, we do not get flustered and excited; we are steadier: '. . . tribulation worketh patience'. Having had this experience we now have a truer picture of the Christian life. It is no longer, 'they all lived happily ever after'. In this world we shall have tribulations, and they help to steady us because 'tribulation worketh patience'.

But it does not stop there: – 'and patience, experience'. Unfortunately this is not a good translation. In a sense it is right, but it does not bring out the better meaning. 'Experience' here means 'proof', 'trial', 'approvedness'. If you like, it means this–experience as the result of an experiment, the experience that is the consequence of a trial or an experiment. It is a proof, a trial, it is an approvedness. In other words, what the Apostle is saying here is that this 'patient endurance' leads to a proof that we are really and truly Christian. We have been able to pass the test.

Our Lord brings out this aspect also, as we have already seen, in the Parable of the Sower. The seed is sown and it springs up quickly, and there is marvellous joy. But persecution comes and there is a falling away, or the cares and the affairs of this world choke the Word. The result of the sowing seemed to be excellent but it is not so. It does not last. The parable indicates that these trials test us and show what we really have. Now that is what the Apostle says here. This patient endurance is a wonderful test; and the man who passes the test is giving proof that he is a true Christian.

James also says all this in his own characteristic way: 'My brethren, count it all joy when you fall into divers temptations, knowing this': 'Knowing' – the same word again – 'that the trying of your faith worketh patience'. 'The trying' of your faith, the testing of your faith works patience. The same words exactly! Again in verse 12 he says it once more: 'Blessed is the man that endureth temptation, for when he is tried (when he has been tried or tested) he shall receive the crown of life, which the Lord hath promised to them that love him.' What the patience does is to try and to test our faith. Peter has precisely the same idea in his First Epistle, 'Wherein (in the salvation) you greatly rejoice, though now for a season, if need be, you are in heaviness through manifold temptations: that the trial of your faith (the trial, the testing of your faith), being much more precious than of gold that perisheth, though it be tried with fire, might be found unto praise and honour and glory at the appearing of Jesus Christ' [1:7]. This patient endurance provides a test and a trial which determine whether we are truly approved as Christians and children of God and not what the Puritans used to call mere 'false professors'.

How do trials and tribulations do this? The very fact that God is trying us ought to be a proof in and of itself that we are God's children. That is the argument used in Hebrews 12. That is why the Christian ought to rejoice when he is tried. There is nothing more suspicious for a Christian than never to have any trials. 'Woe is unto you', said our Lord, 'when all men speak well of you.' There is something seriously wrong with the man who is praised by everybody. There are certain preachers who are praised by evangelicals and praised by liberals – everybody praises them. I always feel concerned about such men. 'Woe is unto you when all men speak well of you.'

So trials are good in many ways. They give me an assurance that God is interested in me. 'Whom the Lord loveth he chasteneth; he scourgeth every son whom he receiveth'. 'If you are not chastened', says Hebrews 12, 'you are bastards, you are not sons.' How terribly wrong it is to picture the Christian message as saying that you will never have trials any more! It is more likely to be the exact opposite of that. The Christian who is not experiencing some kind of trial or chastisement had better examine himself seriously again.

Tribulations also work in this way, that they not only bring out God's love to me, but at the same time test my love to God, and prove it. If I only love God when everything is going well, I am not truly Christian. It is the man who can say with Job, 'Even though he slay me, yet will I trust in him', who is truly Christian. When you are down, as it were, and everything is against you, and the devil says to you, 'Where is your God, where is the love of God?', if you can turn to him and say, 'Get thee behind me, Satan; you do not understand. This is God's method of perfecting me and of bringing me to glory. I need it. There are angles and corners that need to be rubbed off, there is so much impurity in me still. I have not responded to His Gospel as I ought, and He is doing this for my good. My earthly parents chastened me and punished me to satisfy themselves because they loved me; how much more does the Father of spirits do this for those who belong to Him!' – if you can say that to the devil, all is well with you. Given this spiritual understanding, even in the midst of trials and tribulations, my love to God becomes greater than ever. I can see now that He is so concerned about me, that He loves me so much, that He wants me to be perfect.

'Your faith', says Peter, 'is much more precious than gold' [1 *Peter* 1:7]. How do you purify gold? By putting it into a furnace, and the fire burns away the alloy and admixture and all that is impure. You put this mass of metal into the crucible and everything that is dross is burnt away, and you are left with nothing but the pure gold. That is what tribulations and trials do. They test us, they prove us, they get rid of everything in us except that which is true. Everything else has gone, but this true faith comes out brighter and more glorious than ever.

The scientists have to test the steel before they put it into an aeroplane or into a bridge. Can it stand the stress? Can it stand up to varying atmospheric pressures when you are at variable heights? They test it to see if it is true. That is what tribulations do. And after you have passed the test you know that your faith is better than you ever knew it to be. It comes out purified and stronger. 'Tribulation worketh patience, and patience worketh testing, proof' – it makes us approved.

We know that God loves us, and we have had a proof of our true love to God. That in turn leads to hope once more – 'and experience (or proving), hope'. What is this hope? It is the same hope that the Apostle spoke of in verse 2, 'and rejoice in hope of the glory of God'. He starts with hope and he ends with hope. What has been happening? It is nothing but that great argument of Hebrews 12. We started with this hope; because of justification by faith we do indeed rejoice (or glory) in hope of the glory of God. We say that we understand that. Then these trials come, and they seem to be leading away from such a hope and contradicting it. But they do not; they bring us back to it. They not only bring us back to it, they make us much more certain of it than we were at the beginning. Having gone through all this we are much more certain that we belong to God. We saw that we rejoice in this hope of the glory of God because we are God's children, and because He has started the process. But having passed through the furnace of affliction, through the trials and the tribulations, I am much more certain of that than I was before.

So my hope is greater than it was at the beginning. It is the same hope, but I am more certain of it.

That is why we glory in these things. They strengthen the hope, they make us more certain of the hope, and they do it in the way I have been indicating. God has already told me in His Word that I am His child, His son, in Christ who bore my sins. I believe that, I have been given the assurance of that. But now He has given me this further proof. He is so concerned about me that he is perfecting me, He is going on with this treatment of me. He takes pride in me, and He wants to bring me to that perfect image of His own dearly beloved Son. By driving us back to the Lord Jesus Christ, by showing us God's love to us, by giving us fresh experiences of God's strength and grace and power, sufficient for every trial and for every need, these things give us absolute proof of God's purpose with respect to us. We never knew that He had such a loving interest in us. We thought we did, but it was all theoretical; we really did not know. There are aspects and phases of it that we never imagined for a moment, but now we have known them, we have experienced them, and we are more certain of God than we ever were before. We therefore glory because of these tribulations, on account of them; we thank God for them. We say with the writer of Psalm 119, 'It is good for me that I have been afflicted' (verse 71). I am better than I was before, I am more certain of God, I am more certain that I am His child, I am more certain of His love, I am more certain of the love of the Lord Jesus Christ.

Indeed, as a quaint expositor put it, 'Christian hope is both the parent and the child of patience'. Christian hope is both the parent and the child of hope at one and the same time. How so? Well, start with the hope – there is the parent. And it is because we have that hope that we are able to be patient in the endurance of the tribulations. So the hope is the parent of the patience. Yes, but as I have been able to show, the patience in turn leads to a yet further grasp of the hope. So the patience also leads to the hope and is therefore partly its parent. Hope is both parent and child of patience at one and the same time. In the first instance the patience is the child of the original hope but in the second instance it is the parent of this larger, deeper, bigger, more certain and more solid hope that we have.

Thus the Apostle has shown us how it is that we can glory in tribulations, because we know that 'tribulation worketh patience; and patience, experience; and experience, hope.'

Six

*

And hope maketh not ashamed, because the love of God is shed abroad in our hearts by the Holy Ghost which is given unto us.
Romans 5:5

This is obviously a part of the statement that the Apostle has been making from the beginning of the chapter. His primary object is to show the certainty and the finality of our salvation as the result of justification by faith only. He shows that we have that in three ways; it gives us 'peace with God'; it enables us to 'stand in grace'; and it enables us to 'rejoice and to glory in hope of the glory of God'. He then goes on in verses 3 and 4 to show that the trials and tribulations that come to us, far from shaking that hope, make it yet more sure. He does that by means of the great circular argument concerning hope which we have worked out.

However, he has not quite finished even yet; he still has to bring out his climax, and the climax is what we have in the fifth verse. In a sense he has completed the argument, but he adds to it, he says something which underlines it. Having arrived back at 'hope' he adds, 'and hope maketh not ashamed'. What does that mean? The first thing we have to understand is that he is referring to the present and not to the future. Some expositors seem to me to have missed the point completely by imagining that what the Apostle is saying here is that the man who has this hope in him will not be disappointed in the great Day of Judgment, that he will not be put to shame then when the final and the last test comes. That, of course, is perfectly true, but here, surely, the Apostle is not referring to the future but to the present, to the actual experience of the believing Christian while he is in this life in this world. What he means, therefore, is that we shall never be put to shame in this life, neither shall we be put to shame on the great Day of Judgment. But, primarily, we shall never be put to shame in this life. It does not matter what happens. There will be trials, there will be problems, there will be tribulations, there will be difficulties, but if you have this hope you will never be put to shame, you will never feel ashamed, you will never be disappointed, you will never feel that you are let down. 'Hope maketh not ashamed.'

The best way to understand this is to turn to the first chapter of the Second Epistle of Timothy where the Apostle puts it very clearly in the twelfth verse. He is talking about this selfsame thing there. He was a prisoner when he wrote that letter to Timothy, and to be in prison is very discouraging. He was feeling old, 'Paul the aged' he calls himself, and he had become a sick man, and here he is in prison, in a condition and in circumstances which are calculated to depress anyone. But he is not depressed; he says, 'for the which cause I also suffer these things: nevertheless I am not ashamed'. That is it! I am in the midst of these trials and troubles and tribulations, but I am not ashamed. I am not ashamed of my position or of my calling, I am not in any sense disappointed, 'for I know whom I have believed, and am persuaded that he is able to keep that which I have committed unto him against that day'. His hope does not put him to shame; he is not disappointed, he is not let down by his faith and by his belief. He says in effect: I am in these circumstances, but all is well with me.

Let us remember that he is writing to a young man, Timothy, who was not as clear about these matters as was the Apostle, and who seems to have been given to depression. The Apostle says to him in verse 8, 'Be not thou therefore ashamed of the testimony of our Lord, nor of me his prisoner'. He is dealing with the same idea of not being 'ashamed'. A man who is not clear about the Christian faith is liable to be put to shame by circumstances; and the temptation assailing Timothy was that of being ashamed of the Apostle and of the Christian life. He was not quite clear as to what answer to give to people who said, 'Well now, here is this Apostle who makes tremendous claims. We remember his assured preaching. But look at him now, a prisoner and facing death – how do you explain this? Why does God allow this? Why does the Lord Jesus Christ allow a special servant of His to go through all this if your Gospel is true?'

The moment we become doubtful, and cannot answer people who say things like that, we are ashamed or put to shame. So the Apostle exhorts Timothy, 'Be not thou therefore ashamed of the testimony of our Lord'. Notice also how he returns to this again at the end of the chapter in referring to the case of Onesiphorus, 'This thou knowest, that all they which are in Asia be turned away from me, . . . the Lord give mercy unto the house of Onesiphorus, for he oft refreshed me, and was not ashamed of my chain:'. In other words, Onesiphorus was so strong in faith, and had such an understanding that, far from being put off or disappointed, and turning away from the Apostle feeling that there was nothing in the Gospel after all, he was not ashamed of Paul's imprisonment but went to the Apostle often and ministered to him there.

That is the idea and the meaning of this expression, 'hope maketh not ashamed'. But we must take the meaning a little further, and we do so by realizing that here the Apostle is using a figure of speech, which is not uncommon in his epistles, and which is known as 'litotes'. That is a way of asserting a positive by using the negation of its opposite. There is a notable example of this in the first chapter of this Epistle in verse 16 where the Apostle says, 'I am not ashamed of the Gospel of Christ'. What he means is, 'I am very proud of it. I make my boast of it. It is to me the greatest thing in the whole world'. But he puts it negatively. This is said to be the favourite figure of speech of the English. They do not like positives, they prefer to speak in negatives and understatements! 'I am not ashamed of', instead of saying, 'I am very proud of'. The Apostle on another occasion said that he was a citizen of 'no mean city'. What he means is a very great city. Sometimes this form of speech adds force to the statement; and we have an instance of this here in, 'hope maketh not ashamed'. What he really means is that hope far from making us ashamed, or producing a tendency to be ashamed, rather does the exact opposite; it leads to glorying.

Thus we are back again to what he said at the beginning – 'Not only so, but we glory in tribulations also'. And here he says that that is what hope always does. Hope does not make you feel ashamed. The man who really has got this hope, and who sees it, is a man who is not only going to overcome these trials and tribulations, he is going to boast in them, he is going to glory in them. But here he puts it in this very strong form; not only does it never let you down, it really puts you on your feet. He says it again in the eighth chapter in verse 37: 'Nay in all these things we are more than conquerors through him that loved us.' 'Hope maketh not ashamed' is just another way of saying that we are 'more than conquerors'. Not only do we endure the trial, not only do we go through with it, but we go further; we are enabled to rejoice and to exult and to glory in it all.

This is a most important statement, and it is not surprising therefore that the Apostle went on to this addition. This has been the universal testimony of the saints and the martyrs throughout the centuries. It is this hope which was there before them, and which they saw so clearly, that enabled them to die such glorious deaths. The record starts with Stephen, and it has been continued ever since. That is the glorious thing in the history of the martyrs. What enabled them to die so gloriously? The answer is that they were sure of the hope; being justified by faith they rejoiced in hope of the glory of God. They knew it, they were certain of it, and so they could smile in the face of the cruel men who were putting them to death.

It is a wonderful story! Read the story of the martyrs in every age throughout the centuries, and in each case you will find that their secret was that they knew exactly where they were going. They had had such views of the glory to which they were going, such glimpses of it, that they were certain of it. 'Hope maketh not ashamed'; rather it makes us certain. It makes us 'more than conquerors', and as we are enabled to look steadfastly at it we can even glory in the things that normally produce depression, the things that normally defeat us.

That is the Apostle's great assertion. But what is it exactly that enables us to do this? How can we ever come to this position? What is it that gives us this final kind of certainty about the hope that is set before us? What is it that gives us an ultimate assurance of the blessed hope which will never fade away? The Apostle answers that question in his next assertion, which is a very great statement indeed. 'Hope maketh not ashamed, because the love of God is shed abroad in our hearts by the Holy Ghost which is given unto us'. 'Because' says the Apostle. This is partly the explanation, then, of what he has been saying. His 'Because' means 'for this reason'. Or if you like, you can take it as a kind of additional and further reason. It does not matter which; both are true.

As this great statement seems to me not to be grasped and understood as it should be, and as I have a feeling that its full content and meaning is not even brought out in the expositions of Charles Hodge and Robert Haldane, we must look at these words very carefully. The first thing we must look at is the expression 'the love of God'. Here there is no need for argument, because most are agreed that 'the love of God' here means, not our love to God, but God's love to us. That is of course, vital. The Apostle is not talking about our love to God – that follows – he is talking about our knowledge of God's love to us.

Then we come to the expression, 'shed abroad', which is the really important one. What does it mean? It really means to be 'poured out'. It is the same expression that is found in connection with the coming of the Holy Ghost on the day of Pentecost as described in the second chapter of the Acts of the Apostles. In verse 17 we read: 'And it shall come to pass', says Peter quoting Joel, 'that in the last days, saith God, I will pour out of my Spirit upon all flesh'. Again in verse 33, 'Therefore being by the right hand of God exalted, and having received of the Father the promise of the Holy Ghost, he hath shed forth this' – poured it out. That is the meaning of the expression used here. It carries the idea of profusion, a kind of gushing forth, a 'shedding abroad' of the Spirit, as it is translated here in the Authorized Version.

The next word is the word 'in'. Here it does not mean 'upon', and it does not mean 'into', but it means 'in', as the translation has it. It means that it is permeating every part, it is filling it until it is overflowing.

The last expression is 'our hearts'. What does 'heart' mean here? It undoubtedly means the very centre of our being and personality. It certainly does not mean the mind only, or the understanding only; it includes the emotions and feelings, and the sensibilities. The Apostle chooses his words carefully. He says that the love of God is shed abroad in our hearts 'by the Holy Ghost which is given unto us'. The Holy Ghost is given unto us all as Christians, and it is the Holy Ghost, who is given unto us as Christians, who sheds abroad in the heart this love of God. And when He has done that to a man, such a man glories in tribulations, and he glories in the hope of the glory of God.

It is very important that we should give their full weight and meaning to these terms. The whole idea of 'shed abroad', meaning 'poured out', is one of profusion and of abundance and of overflowing – torrents. The implication of this should be obvious. If the love of God is thus shed abroad in our hearts, there can be no doubt about it, there is no uncertainty concerning it, because the whole idea is one of a superabundance and of a great profusion. What Paul says here, therefore, is that the Holy Ghost in this way gives us an abundant assurance of God's love toward us. The Holy Ghost, then, makes us abundantly certain and assured of the love of God to us in Jesus Christ our Lord.

We shall find later that the Apostle repeats this in the eighth chapter in verses 14–16: 'For as many as are led by the Spirit of God, they are the sons of God. For ye have not received the spirit of bondage again to fear; but ye have received the Spirit of adoption, whereby we cry Abba, Father. The Spirit itself (or himself) beareth witness with our spirit, that we are the children of God.' It is the same idea. The Apostle John says the same thing in his First Epistle in the fourth chapter verse 16: 'And we have known and believed the love that God hath to us.' Someone has translated that like this: 'We know the love that

God hath to us and we confide in it'. We know, and have believed, and are certain of it and therefore trust ourselves to it. And again it is in the context of the work of the Holy Spirit.

What is the nature of this certainty concerning the love of God to us? This is not merely something that we believe; this is not merely something that we deduce: this is certainly not something that we argue out. It is not that at all, because beliefs and deductions are indirect; and this is direct. He does not say that as the result of our faith and the working out of this argument we come to the conclusion that God loves us. He has already dealt with that aspect. That is not what he says here. He says, 'the love of God is shed abroad in our hearts'. It is something that the Holy Spirit does, not something that we arrive at as the result of an argument. Let me show you the difference between these two things.

Up to this point the Apostle has been deducing, and he has taken us through the steps of the argument. We go through life, and adverse things happen to us and we learn to say, 'Well now then, the very fact that God is allowing this to happen to me is the proof of the fact that I am a son, because "whom the Lord loveth he chasteneth" it must be for my good'. We work out the argument. All that is deduction. In that way I am deducing the love of God. By means of my faith I am working out the argument, and I can arrive at that kind of assurance and certainty in that way. That is good and right, but, says the Apostle, there is something that goes beyond that. Over and above your intelligent apprehension of it, over and above your intelligent and intellectual deduction of it, there is a direct and immediate assurance given by the Holy Ghost who sheds abroad the love of God in your heart. You are overwhelmed by it, it is poured out in your heart, and there is no uncertainty any more.

This is surely something that is of the greatest importance and the greatest value. I am convinced that there is no aspect of the Christian truth that has been so sadly neglected in this century as this particular teaching. That is one of the direct consequences of the pernicious teaching of 'Take it by faith'. Nothing has so militated against this glorious, experimental, immediate knowledge of the love of God in our hearts. This is not something that you take by faith; it is something that the Holy Spirit does to you. He sheds abroad in the heart the love of God, and this leads to certain inevitable results, as the Apostle has been showing us in this chapter. Peter says that the relationship of Christians to the Lord Jesus should be, 'Whom having not seen, ye love; in whom, though now ye see him not, yet believing, ye rejoice with joy unspeakable and full of glory'.

In other words, this is the highest form of assurance possible to the Christian. It is a form of assurance, I repeat, that you do not deduce. There are forms and types of assurance that can be deduced. You can argue, Scripture tells us, 'Whosoever believeth is not condemned'. I believe, and therefore I am not condemned, therefore I can be sure. That is quite right. You can go further and say, 'I go to the First Epistle of John and I read there the tests of life and of sonship. I examine myself in the light of these tests, and finding evidence of these things in me I deduce that I am a child of God'. That also is good; it is another form of assurance and a higher and better one than the first. But the highest form of assurance is the one we have here. You do not deduce the love of God here; the Holy Spirit sheds it abroad in your heart. The same thing is described in this Epistle in chapter 8: 16, 'The Spirit itself (himself) beareth witness with our spirits that we are the children of God.'

Let me give you some testimonies to support what I am saying. Here is a statement made by Henry Venn, a saintly, godly Church of England vicar who lived about two hundred years ago and died in 1797. Venn was a great help to Charles Simeon of Cambridge when the latter was a young man. He was first of all a vicar in Huddersfield and then went to a little place called Yelling, on the borders of Cambridgeshire and Huntingdonshire. He was a powerful influence in the so-called 'Clapham Sect'. I am going to quote from a letter written by Henry Venn to the Countess of Huntingdon. He writes this letter just after the death of his wife who had been taken from them, leaving five young children. The position was tragic; but this is how he writes to the Countess of Huntingdon. 'I am now a living witness of the truth you so strenuously maintain, and of the necessity of that truth in our miserable condition here below. Did I not know the Lord to be mine, were I not certain His heart feels even more love for me than I am able to conceive, were not this evident to me, not by deduction and argument, but by consciousness, by His own light shining in my soul as the sun's doth upon my bodily eyes, into what a deplorable situation should I have been now cast?' Do you notice what he says? he emphasizes that it was evident to him 'not by deduction and argument, but by consciousness', 'by His own light shining in my soul as the sun's doth upon my bodily eyes'. He continues: 'I have lost all that I could wish myself to have been, in the partner of my cares and joys, and lost her when her industry and ingenuity and tender love and care of her children were all just beginning to be perceived by the two eldest girls, and to strike them with a sense of the excellency of such qualities. I have lost her when her soul was as a watered garden, when her mouth was opened to speak for God, and He was blessing the testimony she bore to a free, full and everlasting pardon in the blood of Jesus. Nevertheless I can say, *all is well;* Hallelujah! for the Lord God Omnipotent reigneth. At all times and in everything pertaining to me, let Him do what seemeth Him good.' Then, and yet more important: 'Were there no Holy Ghost now to strengthen me mightily, were there nothing more than a dependence on the Word of Promise, without an Almighty power and agent to explain, impress and apply it, how would my hands hang down, and my knees be so feeble that I should faint and fall under the pressure of my cross' (*Life and Times of the Countess of Huntingdon*, Vol. 2, page 7). Note again the distinction Venn draws between reading about the truths and the promises of God in the Word and reasoning from them to derive comfort, and the Holy Ghost Himself impressing these things upon him. He goes on: 'But on the contrary, I abound in hope through the power of the Holy Ghost given unto me. I rejoice in tribulation, from the experience I now have, more than I possibly could in a less severe trial, that the Man of Sorrows is as rivers of water in a dry place, and giveth songs in the night.' Is not that very wonderful?

Now let us turn to what Charles Simeon has to say about this truth. Here is Evangelicalism as it was towards the end of the eighteenth and the beginning of the nineteenth century. These men did not believe in the teaching of 'Take it by faith' that came in during the last quarter of the last century and has been so popular in this century. These men knew these things, knew them internally by the work of the Holy Spirit. They were as certain of them as they were that the sun was shining upon their bodies. This is how Simeon puts it: 'This is a blessing which, though not appreciated or understood by those who have never received it, is yet most assuredly enjoyed by many of God's chosen people. We scarcely know how to describe it, because it consists chiefly in an impression on the mind occasioned by manifestations of the love of God to the soul.' You see how he puts it: far from being something that you deduce as the result of an argument, he says, 'I can scarcely put it into words'. Any man who knows it can scarcely describe it, because it is something internal and experimental, something you are absolutely certain of, but so glorious that it is difficult to find words to express it. 'It is a blessing', he says, '. . . not appreciated and understood by those who have never received it.' They think that this is 'enthusiasm', of course; they think it is a false kind of subjectivism, but, says Simeon, 'it is yet most assuredly enjoyed by many of God's chosen people'.

You find exactly the same thing in a work by the saintly John Fletcher of Madeley, known as *Six Letters to a gentleman on the spiritual manifestations of the Son of God*, in which he demonstrates that this is clearly taught in the Church of England Homilies.

This is what our Lord is speaking about in the fourteenth chapter of John's Gospel, where he says, 'I will manifest myself unto you'. It is His promise concerning what is going to be true when the Holy Ghost comes. He had not yet come in that way, but He tells his unhappy disciples that He is going to come, this 'Other Comforter' whom He is going to send to them. This is what Paul calls elsewhere 'the sealing of the Spirit'. Another expression concerning it is 'the earnest of the Spirit'. It is God through the Holy Spirit giving us this absolute certain knowledge that we are His children, that we are heirs of the glory that is coming. He gives it in the form of an 'earnest', He gives us 'foretastes' of that glory, samples of it, instalments of it in order to make it real to us.

We do not 'take it by faith'; we know; we have tasted it, we have felt it. It is the love of God being made real by means of this impression upon the mind and the heart by the Spirit. It is a sensible something; it is experimental; it affects the emotions and the feelings; it is direct and immediate, not indirect and mediate. There is surely nothing more precious in the whole of Scripture, and yet how little we hear about it today. It seems to have dropped out of evangelical teaching. It is because of that 'psychological' teaching about 'taking it by faith and not worrying about your feelings'. What if Henry Venn had been in that position! He says himself that he does not know what he would have done, had not God made His love so plain and clear to him directly and immediately. He is so sure and certain of it in the depth of his soul. He was not 'taking it by faith'; he knew it had been given to him by God Himself to prepare him for the grievous trial that was to come to him. And he was able to shout 'Hallelujah!' No man has ever had the love of God 'shed abroad' in his heart without knowing it; and it always leads to the shout!

As Charles Simeon says, you can be a Christian without this ultimate form of assurance. You cannot be a Christian without the Holy Spirit, but you can be a Christian without having the love of God shed abroad in your heart. Let me put it in the form of a question. Can you say that the love of God is shed abroad in your heart? Can you speak like Henry Venn? Perhaps not, and it is for that reason I emphasize that you can be a Christian without this. As a Christian you have the Holy Spirit dwelling in you, because 'if any man have not the Spirit of Christ, he is none of his'. Unless the Spirit of God is in us we are not Christians. But you can be a Christian without this fuller additional experience. This is what Paul in a sense was praying for the Ephesians to experience. They had known it already in a measure, but he wants them to know it still more, this 'love of Christ that passeth knowledge' [*Ephesians* 3: 12]. It is beyond intellectual apprehension, but it is real. He wants them to know that in an experimental sense.

All Christians have not had this experience, but it is open to all; and all Christians should have it. It does not depend upon your natural greatness, the greatness of your intellect or anything else. Listen to what Henry Venn goes on to say: 'My blessed Lord sent to me two preachers, (messengers), immediately after my loss. The one was a poor and most afflicted widow, sick, very sick in body, with two helpless children, destitute almost of raiment; and upon my asking her how she did, "Oh Sir, since you have been gone," she answered, "I cannot tell you how much my Saviour has done for me. Though I have utterly lost the sight of one eye since you went, I have got better light than the sun can give me. I feel myself so sinful, and Him so full of love to me, that I am happy, and only beg of you that I may not be carried into the workhouse to be amongst so many people, because I feel by being alone as I am, I can enjoy the love and presence of the Lord more abundantly. But if you think it proper that I should go, I can go still in faith and cheerfulness." The weighty manner in which she spoke this, and the air of her countenance was, indeed, such as I think I never saw. It was as if she saw her Lord, and He was attending to every word that came out of her mouth. This was a sermon to my heart, and as seasonable as the rain upon the mown grass.'

Let me end with one further quotation. It comes from a man called Richard Robarts, a Minister of God who died of consumption at the age of thirty-six, much less well known than Venn and Simeon. 'Frequently', he writes, 'all around me thought me about to expire. My cough was dreadful, so were the pains I felt in my chest and side; and above all the languor which oppressed me for a while seemed almost overwhelming. But while I was thus sinking I felt more of the consolations and supports of religion than I ever had experienced before. Oh, with what strong and assured confidence was I enabled to look up to my Redeemer, and how gladly would I have resigned my soul into His hands! What glorious manifestations of His love and mercy did He make to my soul, and how did I rejoice to believe that in a few days more I should be with Him in glory eternal! For the sake of my dear wife and friends I was willing to live, and saw it my duty to use all proper means to promote my recovery which, however, I and everyone else, I believe, conceived to be impossible without a miracle; but for my own sake I had a desire to be with Christ. Thus I lay in sweet suspense, as it were, between earth and heaven, and, indeed, so I have remained in general ever since.'

Later on, a friend said to him: 'I should be glad to enjoy your happiness.' Richard Robarts at this stage could not speak it but he wrote this on a slate. 'Believe constantly on the Lord Jesus Christ, and you may be much happier than you are. Had I been more faithful in this respect I should have enjoyed more consolation and done more for the glory of God.' Then the report goes on: 'In the course of this day he experienced an ecstasy of heavenly joy. His eyes were bathed in tears, and he uttered words of praise, consolation and triumph; it appeared as if he was transported into Paradise. It was evident that he experienced a foretaste of heaven. Every one in the room thought him dying. He expressed a desire to see his sister whom he sincerely loved. "Oh," he said, "I am happy in my God, in His love. I am going to possess Him for ever. I shall enter into that City whose streets are of fine gold, yes, the New Jerusalem from above, the City of the Living God".' Here is the last quotation: 'Since my last attack three weeks ago the Lord has been near and has manifested His love to my soul in an uncommon degree. I have been deeply humbled under a sense of my unworthiness and past unfaithfulness, but I have felt myself firmly fixed upon the Rock of Ages, and have been enabled to anticipate my departure from the body with unspeakable delight. One thing has much occupied my mind, namely, the great proneness I have ever felt to rest short of all the fullness of God. Often it seemed within my grasp, often has my soul seemed to take possession of it, but never did I enjoy a constant sense of it, of all the great salvation of God. However, I never gave up the hope of possessing it fully, and I trust that I shall now obtain my heart's desire.' And so it goes on.

Let us draw certain conclusions from these quotations. This

is something given to one man like Robarts just before he died, given to Henry Venn before the great trial of the loss of his wife, given to that widow woman in her poverty. But according to the teaching of the Scriptures, as I understand it, this is something that is open to us all, something, as Robarts says, we always ought to be enjoying. It is only when some of us are brought to a deathbed that we turn away from the vain things of life and realize that nothing matters but this, and we seek it with the whole of our being, and we find it. So I end by quoting the words of Thomas Goodwin, the great Puritan: 'Sue Him for it! Sue Him for it! Ask Him for it! Don't give up!' That was his way of expressing what our Lord said in the words, 'If ye, being evil, know how to give good gifts unto your children, how much more shall your Heavenly Father give the Holy Spirit to them that ask Him?' [*Luke* 11: 13].

Can you say that the love of God has been shed abroad in your heart? The Apostle's assertion is that the man who can really rejoice and glory in tribulations is the man in whose heart the love of God has been shed abroad. He is so certain of that love, he does not merely believe in it and have to remind himself of it, he knows it experimentally. So if we feel that we cannot honestly say that we 'glory in tribulations' and 'glory in hope of the glory of God' which is coming, it is really because we do not know God's love to us as we ought; to know it as we should know it, and as we can know it. As Goodwin urges, go to Him and ask Him for it, ask Him to manifest Himself to you; plead with Him to do so, saying,

O Love Divine, how sweet Thou art!
When shall I find my willing heart
All taken up by Thee?
I thirst, I faint, I die to prove
The greatness of redeeming love,
The love of Christ to me.

Ask Him for it. Do not be content with less. He has promised to manifest Himself to those who keep His commandments, to those who really seek Him in this way. You will find that saints throughout the centuries have been able to testify to this 'immediate' knowledge, this 'shedding abroad' of the love as Henry Venn describes it. It is not the result of deduction or reasoning, but the action of the Holy Spirit in diffusing it throughout the whole of the centre of our lives, and making us as certain of it as we are of the shining of the sun in the heavens.

Has the love of God been shed abroad in your heart? Do you rejoice in Christ 'with a joy unspeakable and full of glory?' This, it seems to me, was given to the first Christians universally to start off Christianity and the Church, and to show us what is possible. It happened to the people on the Day of Pentecost, it has happened to countless others throughout the centuries, it has happened to those who have sought it truly. Why should you not know it, so that you may bask in the sunshine of His love, more sure of His love than of anything in the entire universe? Sue Him for it! 'Hope maketh not ashamed, because the love of God is shed abroad in our hearts by the Holy Spirit which is given unto us.'

Seven

*

And hope maketh not ashamed; because the love of God is shed abroad in our hearts by the Holy Ghost which is given unto us.
Romans 5 : 5

We return once more to this great verse because of the interesting statement that the Apostle makes at the end. He says, 'Because the love of God is shed abroad in our hearts by the Holy Ghost which is given unto us'. We have seen that there are different types of assurance, and that the assurance produced by the love of God shed abroad in our hearts is the highest of all. There is nothing higher than that. No Christian has ever had anything that surpasses that; and, thank God, that is possible to all of us, though not possessed by all of us. You can be a Christian without knowing that particular experience. But there are other types of assurance, and it is to another type of assurance in particular that I now call attention. There is an assurance short of that assurance that a man knows who has had the love of God 'shed abroad' in his heart, which latter we have illustrated from the case of Henry Venn and others.

We could illustrate it also from the life of George Whitefield and Jonathan Edwards. They describe how this love of God was 'shed abroad' in their hearts, and how it seemed to come in wave after wave until they were melted under the glory of it, and almost felt that their physical frames would collapse. But there is an assurance short of that supreme and final assurance which we should all enjoy, and that is the one introduced by this expression 'the Holy Spirit which is given unto us'. This is therefore an addition to what we have been considering. This must not be regarded as just a statement in and of itself. It is, I must emphasize, a part of the Apostle's whole argument in this section. It is a part of his argument with regard to the certainty of salvation. The man who knows what it is to be justified by faith should have assurance of salvation. That is the whole argument here. If we only understood it truly, he says, it would follow of necessity.

As we come to look at it we must turn aside for a moment to observe the great Apostle's method, and the way in which his mind proceeds in logical steps. What he does here is very characteristic of that method. He first makes a number of statements, such as we have in the first five verses. Then having done that, he takes them up in particular. We shall find when we come to verse 6 that he takes up in particular the love of God which is shed abroad in the heart by the Holy Spirit. He deals with that from verse 6 to verse 11. But, here, he introduces the doctrine of the Holy Spirit for the first time in this great Epistle; although we shall find that he does not deal with it really fully until the eighth chapter.

Why do I trouble to say this? I do so for the reason that it is because so many people forget that he introduces the Holy Spirit here in chapter 5, verse 5, that they go wrong in their interpretation of chapters 7 and 8. They have got into the habit of saying that the Holy Spirit is not mentioned until chapter 8. But He is mentioned here, though the doctrine concerning Him and His work is only elaborated and explained fully in chapter 8. As I say, this is Paul's method; he makes a comprehensive statement, then he takes up one of the particular statements and works it out, then takes up another and works it out, and yet another until he has finished. But here in these five verses we have a full statement concerning this great certainty. The particulars are not discrete and separate; they all belong together, they are all interlinked. Indeed that, as I understand it, is the real purport of his argument at this particular point in this epistle. Let us just remember it in passing, and note his method, and note particularly that here he introduces us to the doctrine concerning the Holy Spirit.

Why does he do that here? Why did he make this addition? Because it is an essential part of the whole. The statement would not have been complete if he had not added this about 'the Holy Spirit which is given unto us'. What is the teaching? I would divide it like this. First, the Holy Spirit is given to all Christians without exception. There need be no difficulty about that. We have the absolute proof of that in this very Epistle in chapter 8 verse 9, where Paul says, 'Now if any man have not the Spirit of Christ he is none of his'. You cannot be a Christian without having received the Holy Spirit. There is no question about that; it is impossible, it is inconceivable. That means that the Holy Spirit dwells within every Christian.

This is a most astonishing doctrine, but it is a part of the New Testament teaching. Here it is again in that same verse: 'But ye are not in the flesh but in the Spirit, if so be that the Spirit of God dwell in you.' Then this statement, 'Now if any man have not the Spirit of Christ he is none of his'. Then in verse 10, 'And if Christ be in you, the body is dead because of sin; but the Spirit is life because of righteousness'; and verse 11, 'But if the Spirit of him that raised up Jesus from the dead dwell in you, he that raised up Christ from the dead shall also quicken your mortal bodies by his Spirit that dwelleth in you.'

We must not think of the Holy Spirit merely as an influence upon us; the Holy Spirit has been 'given' to us, which means that the Holy Spirit dwells within us. That was the promise of our Lord as recorded in the fourteenth chapter of John's Gospel: 'He is with you and shall be in you.' We have a yet more specific statement with regard to it in the First Epistle to the Corinthians, in chapter 6, verses 19 and 20: 'What? know ye not that your body is the temple of the Holy Ghost which is in you, which ye have of God, and ye are not your own?' That is as specific and as explicit as anything can be. It is an astonishing doctrine. Who can understand it? Who can understand the fact that the Holy Spirit dwells within us in our bodies, tabernacles within us? Who can understand our Lord's statement when He says that He and His Father will come and take up their abode within us? Who can understand the real meaning of Revelation 3 : 20, 'Behold, I stand at the door, and knock; if any man hear my voice, and open the door, I will come in to him, and will sup with him, and he with me'? But there it is; this is the teaching, that the Holy Ghost dwells within us and in our bodies. Our bodies are the temple of the Holy Ghost.

Obviously this is a vital matter in this whole question of assurance. So I lay it down as my second principle that His being given to us is a guarantee of the finality of our salvation. That is what the Apostle is concerned to show at this point.

But how does that prove and establish the certainty of salvation? Let us pick out some of the answers to that question. One answer is that the fact that the Holy Spirit is in us is in itself proof positive that God has started to work in us, and that He is concerned about our ultimate glorification. It is the same argument as the Apostle uses in Philippians 1 : 6, 'Being confident of this very thing, that he who hath begun a good work in you will perform it until the day of Jesus Christ.' There is nothing more sure than that, as there is nothing more wonderful.

The work which His goodness began,
The arm of His strength will complete;
His promise is Yea and Amen,
And never was forfeited yet.

If the Holy Ghost is in you, you know that God is concerned about you. He has started working in you: and if God starts, God will continue. God never begins a work and then drops it. As certainly as God begins, He continues, He will end. It is an absolute certainty. We therefore can draw that deduction.

Then, in the same way, this is a proof of our rebirth, for that is always the work of the Spirit. You cannot say of a man that the Holy Spirit dwells within him unless he has been born again, unless he has the new nature. There is no receptacle in the natural man to receive the presence of the Holy Spirit. It is only the new nature that can receive Him. The work of regeneration is preliminary and preparatory to the coming of the Spirit to dwell within us.

We have to divide these things in thought. There is no division in time with regard to that particular matter, but we have to divide them in thought in order to get our conceptions clear. So the fact that He is in us is a proof of regeneration.

Again, the fact that we are given this new principle of life, that we are born of the Spirit, is a guarantee of our final perfection. It is inconceivable that this work of God in the soul should vanish and disappear or be destroyed. That is why you cannot fall from grace. What a monstrous suggestion that is, that a man can be a Christian one day, and that then he can sin and fall from grace, and cease to be a Christian; and then on a later day become a Christian again! Such an idea implies a most defective view of regeneration. A true understanding of regeneration as the work and action of God the Holy Spirit in the soul makes that utterly impossible. The regenerated man may sin and backslide, but he is still a child of God, he is still a partaker of the divine nature. The 'seed' is still in him, and always will be in him; it cannot disappear. There is no more powerful argument for the ultimate certainty of our complete salvation than that. It is here we should place our emphasis and not on our believing and our holding on. It is the fact that our salvation is the work of God that guarantees our final glorification; and the Holy Spirit within us is a guarantee of that work.

Another way of putting the matter is to say that the presence of the Holy Spirit within us is a guarantee that we shall continue in the faith, and be kept in the faith and in touch with God. That is clearly the teaching of Philippians 2, verses 12 and 13: 'Work out your own salvation with fear and trembling; for (because) it is God that worketh in you both to will and to do of his good pleasure.' What does that mean? It is really the answer to those who are constantly emphasizing our activity, our choice, and our decision and our willing, indeed our 'willing to be made willing'. In their scheme of salvation everything always depends upon us – our initial decision for Christ, our decision to 'surrender fully' later on, and our 'abiding' in Christ. And the logical conclusion is that we may lose all we may have had.

That is not the teaching of Scripture. If it were, and if we were left to ourselves, we would of course all be hopeless. If God merely did some initial work in us and then left the remainder to us, how could any man be sure of his salvation? We are all lazy, we are all forgetful, we are all influenced by the world, we are all weak, and we are all very frail. What guarantee have I that I shall go on, and ultimately stand perfect before God? It is the fact that the Holy Spirit is within me. He acts and He works in me 'both to will and to do'. In other words, He influences me constantly, He pulls me up, and upbraids me, He gives me a taste for the Word and a desire for it.

The Holy Spirit influences me in countless ways. He is at the back of my very willing and yearning towards good. 'It is God (through the Holy Spirit) that worketh in you both to will and to do.' Have we not all experienced this? Suddenly, perhaps, after an arid period in the history of your soul, or when perhaps you have even been guilty of sin and have become forgetful, suddenly, you are reminded of something – a verse of Scripture comes into your mind, or the verse of a hymn. What is this? It is the operation of the Holy Spirit that is within you. He is working within us both to will and to do. He creates holy desires. He guides and directs the mind and the heart of the Christian towards true godliness, and thus the fact that He is in me is a guarantee that I shall be kept in touch with God and that I shall go on to the end. What a wonderful thing this is! It is not I, it is not my faithfulness, it is not my frail grasp and hold on Him; it is 'His mighty grasp of me'.

God keeps His mighty grasp on us through the work of the Holy Spirit whom He has put within us. He is there always within us. As Paul will remind us in the eighth chapter, 'We know not what to pray for as we ought, but the Spirit himself maketh intercession for us with groanings that cannot be uttered'. At such times we do not quite understand what we are saying, but He does, and He works these prayers within us. It goes on endlessly in that way.

But let us look at it in another way. He guarantees our growth also. These things are, in a sense, all the same; but it gives us great comfort and encouragement to look at them from different aspects. The Holy Spirit guarantees my growth, and sees to it that I shall not remain stunted. How does he do this? He does it by revealing the truth. 'We have received', says the Apostle to the Corinthians, 'not the spirit of the world, but the Spirit which is of God, that we might know the things that are freely given to us of God' [1 *Corinthians* 2: 12]. What are these things? These are the things, as the Apostle goes on to explain, which the natural man does not receive because they are foolishness unto him. 'But God has revealed them unto us by his Spirit.' The princes of this world do not understand these things, but God has revealed them unto us; and He goes on revealing them, He opens them out, and so leads us on.

God, in the same way, enlightens our minds. That is why this Apostle prays so constantly the kind of prayer he prayed for the Ephesians. He says, 'I cease not to give thanks for you, making mention of you in my prayers; that the God of our Lord Jesus Christ, the Father of glory, may give unto you the spirit of wisdom and revelation in the knowledge of him: the eyes of your understanding being enlightened; that ye may know what is the hope of his calling, and what the riches of the glory of his inheritance in the saints, and what is the exceeding greatness of his power to us-ward who believe' [*Ephesians* 1: 16–19].

The Holy Spirit does all this and thus He is a guarantee of our growth and development. It is He who enables us to understand. John says the same in his First Epistle, chapter 2, 'But ye have an unction from the Holy One, and ye know all things' (verse 20). Thus did the Apostle John write to those early Christians. He was an old man and knew that he about to leave them. How could he be so happy about them in spite of those anti-christs and false teachers that were troubling the early Church? His own answer is, 'But the anointing which ye have received of him abideth in you, and ye need not that any man teach you: but as the same anointing teacheth you of all things, and is truth, and is no lie, and even as it hath taught you, ye shall abide in him' (verse 27). What a wonderful source of assurance and of certainty this is! God gives us His Spirit, and the Spirit dwells within us and guarantees our growth and development.

But, finally, the dwelling of the Holy Ghost within us is a guarantee of our becoming ultimately fit to enter into that glory that God has prepared for us. The Apostle has mentioned that at the beginning of the chapter. It is the third of the things that are inevitable if we truly know what it is to be justified by faith. It is that 'we glory (rejoice) in hope of the glory of God'; 'we boast in hope of the glory of God'. There, it is by faith, but here we are given the guarantee, and shown how it will happen.

How often do you think of your salvation in this way? 'The glory of God'! We shall see Christ as He is! 'Blessed are the pure in heart, for they shall see God!' Have you ever thought of that? But 'Who among us shall dwell with the devouring fire? Who among us shall dwell with everlasting burnings?' 'Who shall ascend unto the hill of the Lord?' What hope have we of ever getting there, and seeing Him, and entering into that glory, and living in that realm where there is no sin, and none of the things which surround us in this present world? We are told that nothing dark or impure or unclean shall enter in there; the 'dogs and sorcerers and adulterers' are outside. Who can conceive of that absolute purity? 'God is light, and in him is no darkness at all.' How can you or I or anyone ever get there? How can we glory and exult and boast of this hope of the glory of God? There is only one answer. It is because the Holy Spirit is in us, and it is His peculiar work to sanctify us, to rid us of sin. 'Sanctify them through thy truth: thy word is truth'.

The Holy Spirit is the great Sanctifier and He purifies and cleanses and purges us. He has His methods and His ways, and He is the guarantee that eventually we shall stand in the presence of God, 'faultless and blameless, without spot or wrinkle or any such thing'. And my only way of knowing for certain that I shall arrive there is the fact that the Holy Spirit has been given to me, and is in me. Let us never forget that the Apostle is dealing here with assurance. We must never take this fifth verse out of its context. It is a part of the great argument about assurance, and it is in some such way as this, including the work and process of sanctification, that this assurance is given to us.

But now let me be very practical. Let me in the third place put this question. How then may we know that the Holy Spirit has been given to us? It is a large subject and I can only give some headings. Take for answer, the statement that you will find in

1 Corinthians 12: 3. The Apostle is there dealing with the gifts of the Spirit, but before coming to that he says, 'Wherefore I give you to understand, that no man speaking by the Spirit of God calleth Jesus accursed; and that no man can say that Jesus is the Lord, but by the Holy Ghost'. No man can say 'Jesus is the Lord' but by the Holy Ghost. If the Holy Ghost is not in him, he cannot say that.

But what does that mean? Obviously it does not just mean uttering the words that 'Jesus is the Lord', for anyone can utter the words. It clearly means more than that. This is really the full Christian confession, and by that I mean that the man who says 'Jesus is the Lord' in the sense meant here is a man who is making certain statements about the Lord's Person. He is saying that Jesus of Nazareth is the Son of God and the Lord of glory. He is committing himself to the doctrine of the Incarnation and of the Person of Christ. He is saying that in Him there are two natures, but only one Person. He is asserting that He is fully God but at the same time fully man. Truly God, truly Man! Two natures in One Person, unmixed! That is a part of what is meant by saying that Jesus is Lord. The one who so speaks believes all we are told in the Scripture of what happened at Bethlehem, of how that Babe was born of the Virgin Mary, 'conceived by the Holy Ghost', and that that Babe is none other than the eternal Son of God. He is testifying to the uniqueness, the glory, the marvel, the wonder of His Person. That is a part of that confession.

But it does not stop at the Person, it also includes His work. Jesus is the Lord. In what way? He is the Lord of the universe. He is the Word through whom all things were made, and without whom nothing was made that was made. But it means more: it has reference to the work that He accomplished when He was here on earth. He is the Lord in this sense. Complete that quotation from 1 Corinthians 6: 19–20, 'Know ye not that your body is the temple of the Holy Ghost, which is in you, which ye have of God, and ye are not your own? For ye have been bought with a price . . .' He is my Lord because He has bought me, He has ransomed me, He has paid the price of my deliverance. I was a slave of sin and of the devil; he has bought me out, I belong to Him.

Paul describes himself as 'the bond-slave of Jesus Christ'. Christ is the Lord, Paul is the slave. A man who says 'Jesus is Lord' is saying that; he is confessing that he believes that the Lord Jesus Christ has died for him and for his sins, that He has purchased his pardon at the cost of His own blood. No man can say that, without the Holy Ghost. The man of the world does not believe that, neither does he believe in the Person. 'The princes of this world did not know him, for had they known him they would not have crucified the Lord of glory'. And they still ridicule the Atonement and His sacrificial death upon the Cross. They dismiss it with contumely and scorn and ignominy. Why? Because they have not received the Spirit. 'No man can say that Jesus is the Lord but by the Holy Ghost.' 'The natural man receiveth not the things of the Spirit of God because they are foolishness unto him; neither can he know them' – Why? – 'because they are spiritually discerned'. The Spirit alone enables a man to do this.

Do you believe in the Lord Jesus Christ? Do you believe that Jesus is the Son of God, and that He died for your sins on Calvary's hill, and that, because He did so, 'God hath highly exalted him, and given him a name that is above every name: that at the Name of Jesus every knee should bow, of things in heaven and things in earth, and things under the earth; and that every tongue should confess that Jesus Christ is Lord, to the glory of God the Father'? That is the content of saying that 'Jesus is the Lord'. It is one of the fullest statements you can ever make. It includes the whole doctrine of the Person and His work, His life, His death, His burial, His Resurrection, His Ascension, His Exaltation, His coming again. He is Lord of all. Are you anxious to know that the Holy Spirit has been given to you? Well, that is the way you may know it. Do you believe these things? Are they the most vital things in your life? Do you know that by nature you were a hopeless and condemned sinner, and that though you turn over new leaves and try to live a good life, and indulge in good works, you will never be a Christian, and never make yourself fit to see the glory of God? Do you believe, and know, that your only hope of ever getting to the glory is that Christ came down from heaven and took your sins upon Himself and died for you, and bore your punishment on the Cross, and rose again to justify you? Do you genuinely believe in justification by faith only, that God justifies the ungodly, the sinner, and that, only because of Christ and His sacrificial atoning work upon the Cross? Are you trusting yourself and your eternal future to that? Have you given up trusting to yourself and your good works and all your good thoughts? Have you finished with all that, and can you say that you have nothing but Christ? Can you say –

My hope is built on nothing less
Than Jesu's blood and righteousness;
I dare not trust the sweetest frame,
But wholly lean on Jesu's Name.
On Christ the solid Rock I stand,
All other ground is sinking sand?

If you can say that, the Holy Ghost is in you. No man can say that, and mean it, unless the Holy Spirit is in him, and has been given to him by God. It is an absolute proof.

But then there are other things. Take all the tests suggested in the First Epistle of John. 'Belief on him'. This is how we know that we believe in Him, says John, 'because of the Spirit which he hath given us'. Take the last verse of the third chapter of the same Epistle: And hereby we know that he abideth in us, by the Spirit which he hath given us'. But not only that! 'We know that we have passed from death unto life, because we love the brethren' [1 *John* 3: 14]. If you can say honestly that you would rather be in a company of God's people than in the greatest palace on earth, with the greatest earthly persons if they are not Christians, I assure you that you have the Holy Spirit in you. The world despises us, and is not interested in us, and regards us as fools. But if you 'love the brethren' you can be certain that the Holy Spirit is in you. If you like the fellowship and the conversation of the saints, if you like talking about the soul and salvation and God and Christ and Heaven and the glory that is coming, I tell you that the Holy Ghost is in you. You would not like such things otherwise.

Then what about God's commandments? John says that if the Holy Spirit is in us 'his commandments are not grievous' [1 *John* 5: 3]. They are very grievous to the man of the world who says, 'Your Christianity is very narrow, it prohibits all I like and enjoy, and commands what I find to be irksome and uninteresting'. The Christian says, 'His commandments are not grievous', he agrees with them. Why? Because he has a Spirit within him that makes him hunger and thirst after righteousness. He wants to be holy and clean and pure: and if that is your desire, the Holy Spirit is in you. Do you long to know the Lord Jesus Christ better? Do you long to love Him more? If you do I tell you again that the Holy Spirit is in you. It matters not how feeble your love may be, nor how feeble your desire. I would remind you of one of my favourite quotations from Blaise Pascal, 'Thou wouldst not be seeking Me unless thou hadst already found Me'. A man who wants Christ is a man who has Christ. The very fact that you want Him is a proof of the Spirit within you. The unregenerate man does not want Him; he is 'at enmity against God' and at enmity against Christ. Apply those tests from the First Epistle of John to yourself.

Then apply to yourself the test of the 'fruit of the Spirit'. 'The fruit of the Spirit is love, joy, peace, long-suffering, gentleness, goodness, faith, meekness, temperance' [*Galatians* 5: 22–23]. Are they in you? Are they manifest at all? If they are, there is good presumptive evidence that the Holy Spirit is in you. It is a sad and grievous thing that anyone should be uncertain as to whether or not he is a Christian, as to whether the Holy Spirit is in him. We are meant to enjoy these things. We are meant to be enjoying peace with God, we are meant to be enjoying the grace of God, and standing in it. We are meant to be boasting in anticipation of the glory of God to which we are going. We should know these things and be certain of them. If the Spirit is in you He will bring you more and more to an assurance of these things.

Let me add one further word. These five verses are wonderful and marvellous. Do we realize what they tell us? They tell us that the Three Persons in the Blessed Holy Trinity are interested in us, and interested in our salvation. We have peace with God the Father, through the Lord Jesus Christ, and the Holy Ghost is given unto us. Shame on us Christian people for being lethargic and cold and lifeless and so lacking in joy! Why do we not realize that these Three Blessed Persons in the Holy Trinity are interested in us and concerned about us, and have done amazing things in order to rescue and to redeem us, and to bring us into the Family? God the Father planned it and He sent His Son to do the work. He came on that first Christmas Day, lived a life in this world, died on a Cross, was buried, then rose again and went back to the Glory. The Son and His glorious work! And now the Spirit is given, and is within us in order to keep us and prepare us for the glory that is coming. The Three Persons in the Blessed Holy Trinity are engaged in the work, and are concerned about us, and are active in our salvation. How we should prostrate ourselves before God and offer our humble praise and adoration and worship!

The five verses remind us of the basic importance of faith. All this comes out of justification by faith. 'Being justified by faith' we have all these things. Faith is the foundation. Faith leads to hope. What is faith? 'Faith is the substance of things hoped for, the substantiating of things not seen' [*Hebrews* 11 : 1]. Faith produces hope, and the more clearly and consciously we have that hope, the more we shall know the love of God to us, and the more, in turn, we shall love God. Have you noticed the two groups of three? God the Father, God the Son, God the Holy Spirit. And in me, faith, hope, love. Are you exercising this faith? Have you got this hope? Is there just a flicker, if no more, of love in your heart for God the Father, God the Son, and God the Holy Spirit?

Eight

*

For when we were yet without strength, in due time Christ died for the ungodly.
For scarcely for a righteous man will one die; yet peradventure for a good man some would even dare to die.
But God commendeth his love toward us, in that, while we were yet sinners, Christ died for us. Romans 5 : 6–8

It is important that we should be clear about the connection and the setting of this great statement. Indeed, the Apostle himself, as is his invariable manner, compels us to pay attention to the context by beginning with the word 'For'. In other words, he is following on from something he has already been saying. He is going to introduce an argument to substantiate something that has gone before, namely, the certainty, the finality of our salvation in Jesus Christ. A man who knows that he is justified by faith only is a man who should enjoy great certainty; peace with God, standing in the grace of God, rejoicing in hope of the glory of God. And nothing can shake that, for the reasons Paul has given.

The whole object of this statement beginning at verse 6 and on to the end of verse 11 – and, indeed, beyond that, as we shall see – is to substantiate that, and to make it yet more certain. In the verses we are about to look at, verses 6 to 10, the Apostle works out in detail one line of argument which he had already introduced. In verse 5 he had referred to the love of God – 'the love of God has been shed abroad in our hearts by the Holy Spirit which is given unto us'. He is concerned that we should realize fully what this means, so that is what he takes up at the beginning of verse 6. He wants us to see, in other words, that nothing can give greater assurance of the certainty of our salvation, and its finality, than this very love of God.

We can divide the section in this way. In verses 6, 7 and 8 he makes a positive statement about God's love, he gives an exposition of it. Then, in verses 9 and 10 he draws what are inevitable logical deductions from that statement. The two sections together are designed to show how absolutely certain and final is our salvation. The moment we are justified, as we have seen, and as Paul is going to show us again in chapter 8, we can take that leap over to glorification. These things all go together because they are all 'in Christ'. The love of God in our hearts gives us great assurance of that, so the Apostle feels it is important for us to understand this love, its nature and its character. Then, having brought us to understand the truth of what God has done for us in His love, in verses 9 and 10 he will show us how it follows of necessity that God will provide everything else that is necessary to our final salvation.

Verse 6 is one of the greatest verses in the whole Bible. I do not hesitate to assert that there is no greater statement of the love of God than in that verse. We can describe it quite legitimately as the Apostle's exposition of John 3:16: 'God so loved the world that he gave his only begotten Son, that whosoever believeth in him should not perish but have everlasting life.' 'When we were yet without strength, in due time Christ died for the ungodly.' Verse 6 really says everything, it is the complete statement; and what the Apostle does in verses 7 and 8 is to elaborate it. Lest anyone might fail to understand how great it is, he opens it out.

There is a sense in which it is true to say that what the Apostle is saying here he has already told us in chapter 3 in the mighty statements beginning at verse 24: 'Being justified by his grace through the redemption that is in Christ Jesus: whom God hath set forth to be a propitiation through faith in his blood, to declare his righteousness for the remission of sins that are past, through the forbearance of God; to declare, I say, at this time his righteousness; that he might be just and the justifier of him which believeth in Jesus.' There it is; but here he says it again.

Why does he repeat himself? He does so not only because he is a good teacher – the essence of good teaching is repetition, because we are all so prone to forget – but also because he has a different object in mind at this point. There, in chapter 3, his object was to show that there was no method or way of justification apart from this. Here, what he is concerned to show is not so much the way of salvation as the love that ever devised such a way of salvation. It is the love of God he is anxious to expound here. Therefore, though he repeats what is virtually the same statement, his motive and object are different. The whole statement is designed to show us the love of God. It is because we do not know and realize that love as we should that we are what we are. The greatest characteristic of the greatest saints in all ages has always been their realization of God's love to them. That is what the Apostle expounds here. Not our love to Him, but His love to us. Our salvation, our assurance, depend not on our love to Him, thank God! Our outlook would be most precarious if such were the case. No, it is His love to us that matters, and that is what the Apostle unfolds to us here.

The first principle is, that our salvation is entirely of God and of His love. It is essential that I should put it like this. Sometimes, rather loosely, evangelical people are tempted – and it is the peculiar temptation of those who are evangelical – to put this whole question of the Atonement and of Salvation in this way, that it is something that the Son of God has done to affect the Father. The idea is that the Son, having done the work, as it were stands before the Father and pleads with Him, and has to persuade Him to forgive us in the light of what He has done for us. That is a wrong way of putting it, but it has often been put like that. There are hymns that are guilty of this very thing. I well remember a Welsh hymn which quite specifically and explicitly put it like that – that the Son was there pleading with the Father and saying, 'I have died for them, O, let them live!' That is surely a travesty of the teaching of Scripture.

Though we must always emphasize that the work was done by the Son, we must never forget that it was the Father who sent the Son to do it. 'God so loved the world, that he gave his only begotten Son'; 'God was in Christ reconciling the world unto himself'. It is always the action of God, God is the prime mover; salvation is of God the Father. It is wrong to represent God the Father as being passive, and as simply responding to the appeals and pleadings of the Son to grant us salvation and forgiveness on the basis of what He has done for us.

I stress this point for this good reason, that you will find that those who are not evangelical, and who do not believe the substitutionary doctrine of the Atonement, constantly charge us with being guilty of the very error which I have just been refuting. Because, of necessity, we have to emphasize the doctrine of the wrath of God, they say that your picture of God is of Someone who in His great wrath is opposed to man and that we hold that there is a kind of division in the Trinity, with the Son taking one side and the Father the other. But that is not our position. The fact that we proclaim and preach the doctrine of the wrath of God, as the Apostle does, does not mean that we teach any division in the blessed Trinity. The Apostle has told us that the wrath of God is against all ungodliness and unrighteousness of men, but then he goes on to say that the same God has sent forth the Son as a propitiation for our sins. So we must never allow it to be said that, because we preach the wrath of God, therefore we say that there is a conflict between the Father and the Son.

I remember being involved in a discussion on this precise matter some time ago when this very thing was said to me. One of the company put it like this. I apologize for his terms, but this is what he said. 'Your doctrine of the wrath of God, and your conception of propitiation in the Atonement, seems to me to involve a kind of schizophrenia in the mind of the Eternal God; it suggests that there is a kind of conflict between justice and love, between righteousness and compassion and mercy.' But there is no need to talk about a conflict, because in the same great and Eternal God there is a hatred of sin and at the same time this everlasting and eternal love to the sinner. There is no conflict, there is no incompatibility; the two things are there. We shall never really understand the love of God, until we see what sin is in the sight of this holy God whose wrath is upon it.

We start therefore with this principle, that salvation is entirely and altogether of God, and is the result of the great and eternal love of God. For you notice that the Apostle tells us that it is God who has planned it all. This is brought out in the words 'in due time'. 'For when we were yet without strength, in due time.' What does that mean? Another translation would be 'in the appointed time'; it even carries the suggestion of 'in the appropriate time'; but it carries especially the notion of the appointed time. What is this idea of an appointed time? It means that, away back before the foundation of the world, before the world was ever made, before man was ever created, before time had ever come into existence, God planned this mighty and glorious way of salvation. He planned it in detail; He planned that at a given point in time His Son should come into the world in order to make the Atonement, whereby alone salvation would be made possible. The Apostle often gives expression to this idea. He says exactly the same thing in the fourth chapter of the Epistle to the Galatians, verse 4: 'When the fullness of the time was come' – 'in due time' – 'God sent forth his Son, made of a woman, made under the law, to redeem them that were under the law.'

It is very important that we should understand this. Salvation is not an afterthought. Nothing is an afterthought where God is concerned. God sees the end from the beginning. He knows everything. The importance of all this from the standpoint of our salvation needs no demonstration. This is not something haphazard. God had planned it all before the foundation of the world. There is a sense in which our Lord can be referred to as 'the Lamb slain from the foundation of the world'. All that is brought before us in this expression 'in due time'.

In other words, we must not think of God's love in terms of our love. Our love is impulsive and changeable. God's love is unchangeable and eternal. And salvation was planned in Eternity. It is not accidental or contingent or haphazard. God has seen the whole from beginning to end. There is a plan of salvation, there is a scheme of salvation, and it was purposed before time. We must draw the right conclusions from this. The very planning and purposing of it is a glorious manifestation of the love of God. The Apostle is concerned to show us the love of God; and herein is a mighty demonstration of it, that even before the world was made, God knew about us and was interested in us, and our names were entered in His book of life. He is concerned about us, and He has loved us with an 'everlasting love'. That is the expression that is used in the Old Testament. There is no greater proof of the love of God towards us than the fact that He was aware of us, and had chosen us, before the foundation of the world. It was planned that Christ should die for us before we ever lived.

But we can take this term, 'in due time', in another sense. It shows that our salvation is not only altogether and entirely the result of God's love, but in particular the result of what God has done because of His love. 'While we were yet without strength, in due time Christ died for the ungodly.' When was this time? What is the significance of that particular point in history at which Christ came into the world? When exactly was this 'fullness of the time?' The same expression is found in Ephesians 1: 10, 'In the dispensation of the fullness of the times he might gather together all things in Christ'. What is this particular point of time?

The answer is that this particular point in history was the point when it had been proved beyond any doubt that man was incapable of saving himself. It was that point in history when the Law that God had given to the Children of Israel had had a full opportunity of doing its work. The Children of Israel had had this Law for nearly fourteen hundred years when the 'due time' arrived. Ample time had been allowed to prove that 'by the deeds of the law shall no flesh be justified in his sight'. We are always ready to argue that we have not had enough time, and that if only we were given further time or a further opportunity things would be different. Well, the Children of Israel, who claimed that they had sufficient moral power to put the Law into practice and thereby to save themselves, were given fourteen hundred years by God to prove their claim and completely failed to do so, as we saw in chapter 3.

But this 'due time' was also a point in time when Greek

philosophy had likewise had its opportunity. That great flowering period in the history of thought and the search for truth and ultimate reality had already passed. Oh the wisdom of God! He had given man every opportunity of saving himself by his own efforts and endeavours. 'For after that in the wisdom of God the world by wisdom knew not God, it pleased God by the foolishness of preaching to save them that believe' [1 *Corinthians* 1: 21]. Note the 'after that' – that is the 'due time'.

In the same way Roman civilization and law and culture had had their opportunity. The mighty civilization of Egypt had also risen and had waned. So had those of Assyria and Babylon and China. The world had had full opportunity and time to save itself but it had completely failed. So when God sent His Son it was in every way the 'due time'. Sufficient time had been allowed to prove that nothing else could save man. Man had failed, so salvation must be entirely the result of the grace of God and the love of God. That is what the Apostle is saying – 'When we were without strength, in due time'. But that is a great demonstration and proof of the love of God. 'God commendeth his love, he proves his love toward us', and that is how He does so.

If all that proves and commends and demonstrates the love of God, what God has actually done proves it and commends it still more. The fact that God ever thought of it, and conceived of it, and planned it, and purposed it, is, as I have been showing, a tremendous proof of the love of God. But look at what God has actually done in practice. Notice the terms: 'When we were yet without strength, in due time Christ'. Christ! Who is this?

I had almost said that there is no need to spend time in answering that. And yet there is something very wrong in saying that. Not spend time in talking about the Lord Jesus Christ! We can never spend too much time in preaching about Him. He is not to be taken for granted. It is because we do not realize the truth about Him that the Church is as she is. Who has been sent? Christ! How do I know about the love of God? I look at Christ. Who is He? He is the only begotten Son of God. Are you in doubt about the love of God? If so, go back and consider what happened at that 'due time', that due point in time. 'God sent forth his own Son, made of a woman, made under the law'. That is who Christ is. It is here we really begin to see the love of God.

Let us take Scripture to expound and to elucidate Scripture. John has a marvellous statement of this selfsame thing in his First Epistle, chapter 4, verse 9: 'In this was manifested the love of God toward us, because that God sent his only begotten Son into the world that we might live through him.' Or take the way in which it is put in that parable spoken by our Lord Himself as recorded in Matthew's Gospel, chapter 21, beginning at verse 33. It is the parable of workers in a vineyard. There was a man who owned a vineyard and left it in the charge of certain workers. In due season he sent a servant to gather the fruits, but those wicked men said, 'Let us kill this fellow and we can keep the fruits'. The owner sent another servant, and another, and they either beat or killed or stoned them. The man said to himself at last, 'I will send my son; they will reverence my son, they will honour my son'. What our Lord was telling them was really this: 'I am the Son. God has sent His servants; He sent you a succession of prophets, and you have killed the prophets. But God has now sent me, His own Son. I am the Son.' Christ Jesus, Son of God! That is where we see the love of God. This is how God recommends His love to us, this is how God proves His love, that He sent not only servants, such as Moses and Aaron, and the great prophets, but He has sent His own Son, His only begotten Son. Read into that the whole glory of the Incarnation – the coming of the Son of God out of the glory of Eternity into a world such as this, a world of sin and of shame, misery and sorrow.

Then we must go on to the other term. 'Christ', he says, 'died'. This is most important. Do you notice what he picks out? It is not the life, it is not the teaching, it is not the miracles; but 'Christ died'. This is what he emphasizes in order to show and to prove God's love towards us. This is how God commends His love toward us, in that Christ not only came, but that He died. How does that commend God's love? There are two main things here. The first thing we must grasp is that it is by His death that the Lord Jesus Christ saves us. He does not save us by His life; He does not save us by His teaching; He does not save us by His example. All those are glorious and of inestimable value; but He does not save us by them. In order to save us He had to die for us. Why did He come into the world? According to the Epistle to the Hebrews, chapter 3, verse 9, it was 'for the suffering of death' and 'to taste death for every man'. If He had not died He could not save any man. That is why the Apostle picks out His death.

We must be exact and careful in our exposition. We must not make too much of the word 'for' in our text: 'When we were yet without strength, in due time Christ died *for* the ungodly.' It is not the strongest term which is sometimes used in the Scripture in this connection. But it does tell us that He did die for us, and that by dying for us He saves us. There are other terms which are stronger and which say that He died in our place, in our stead, on our behalf. This 'for' does not actually say that, but it clearly says that He died in connection with our salvation, and in connection with our sin; He died in order to save us. It is not the strongest term, so you must not base your doctrine of the Atonement on this one verse. The statements in chapter 3, verses 25, 26 and 27, are much stronger where the word 'propitiation' is used; and there are stronger words still to come. But while we do not have the strongest word here, Scripture must be taken with Scripture. Here the Apostle is putting it in a very general form. He says, 'Christ died for the ungodly'. In other words, that is what saves the ungodly.

But what was uppermost here in the mind of the great Apostle – that is why the word translated 'for' is the more general term rather than the strong one – the thing he is most concerned to prove, is the love of God, and the supreme manifestation and demonstration of that love to us. The very coming of the Son of God into this world is a great demonstration of the love of God – that He should ever have humbled Himself; that the Father should ever have asked Him to do so, that He should have been born of a Virgin, that He should have lived in this world at all and grown up as a little boy and worked as a carpenter, using the fingers and the hands that, as it were, had made the universe, to make ordinary things – and so too all He said and all He did is a demonstration of that same love.

But we do not really see the love of God even in such facts. The love of God is seen in its fullness in Christ's death upon the Cross, in His giving Himself even unto death. The argument concerning that, follows in the subsequent verses. He says, 'For scarcely for a righteous man will one die, yet peradventure for a good man some would even dare to die'. Death is the last act, it is final, there is nothing beyond it. And not only that, there is also the particular form of the death, the death on the Cross, the shame, the insult, the ignominy connected with it and attached to it. It is here we really see the depth and the height of the love of God. The Apostle will say that again many times, and gloriously so, as in 8 : 32, 'He that spared not his own Son, but delivered him up for us all'. It is all, of course, in John 3 : 16, 'God so loved the world, that he gave . . .' The giving does not stop at sending His Son into the world; it includes 'giving Him over' to death. That is the content of the 'gave' in John 3 : 16; and that is the thing the Apostle is saying here: 'He delivered him up for us all.' 'Who was delivered for our offences', as the last verse of the previous chapter has already told us, 'and was raised again for our justification.'

Our Lord's death on the Cross is the supreme manifestation of the love of God. As you look at that Cross on Calvary's hill what do you feel? Isaac Watts has told us what he felt:

When I survey the wondrous Cross,
On which the Prince of glory died,
My richest gain I count but loss,
And pour contempt on all my pride.

. . . . . .

Were the whole realm of nature mine,
That were an offering far too small;
Love so amazing, so divine,
Demands my soul, my life, my all!

And in between those two verses he has taken us with him through the details of the suffering:

> *See from His head, His hands, His feet,*
> *Sorrow and love flow mingled down;*

– the crown of thorns and everything else. Look at it, he says, survey it. And that is the way to know the love of God. You do not wait for a feeling, or try to conjure up a feeling. You go to the Cross and look, and survey it, consider it, meditate upon it and all that was involved. Ask the Spirit to give you enlightenment and understanding. That is the way in which we can come to know and to understand the love of God. That is what God has done. He had purposed it before the foundation of the world; but it was at Calvary that the work was actually done. Christ, His only begotten Son, 'humbled himself, and became obedient unto death, even the death of the Cross', says Paul, descending step by step with the Lord in that great passage in Philippians 2, verses 5–8. 'Even the death of the Cross.' He did it because of His love. It was entirely gratuitous; it was all because of His grace and love, His mercy and compassion.

But if you are still not convinced, says the Apostle in effect, let me take you one step further, and this is the third principle. Consider the character of the people for whom this was done. If it had been done for good people and godly people and loving people, it would have been wonderful, but it was not for such, says the Apostle. Here he tells us something about ourselves, and you notice that he uses three terms. We were 'without strength'; we were 'ungodly'; we were 'sinners'. In other words, another way of measuring this love is to measure the depth of the deplorable condition of the people for whom He did it.

'Without strength.' What does this mean? It means 'total inability', it means that we were entirely devoid of any spiritual strength. The technical term used theologically is the one I have already used – man's total inability in a spiritual sense. Man is totally incapable, he is without any strength at all in the matter of his salvation.

In what respects is he incapable? He is not able to understand spiritual truth. 'The natural man receiveth not the things of the Spirit of God, for they are foolishness unto him; neither can he know them . . .' [1 *Corinthians* 2: 14]. The explanation of that inability is that these things 'are spiritually discerned'.

Are you clear about this? Do you feel that you do not know the love of God as you ought to know it? If so, perhaps it is because you have never realized your own condition, that you are without strength and totally incapable. We are all by nature entirely incapable of spiritual understanding. Another way of saying this is, that we are 'dead in trespasses and sins' – dead spiritually. This is not my theory. I have quoted the Apostle's statements.

Another respect in which we are 'without strength' is that we are totally unable to please God. Man as he is born into this world is totally unable to please God. His righteousness is but as 'filthy rags'. Man does not like to be told that, and he does not believe it. The Apostle himself did not believe it at one time. He tells us in Philippians, chapter 3, that there was a time when he was very proud of his own righteousness. He was a Jew, 'circumcised the eighth day, of the stock of Israel, of the tribe of Benjamin, an Hebrew of the Hebrews; as touching the law, a Pharisee; concerning zeal, persecuting the church; touching the righteousness which is in the law, blameless.' What a wonderfully good man he was, what righteousness he had, and how he had pleased God! A Pharisee giving his whole life to religion and to pleasing God! And he was very proud of himself. But he came to understand that it was all useless and that he was quite incapable of pleasing God. He looks later at all this marvellous righteousness that he had gloried in so much, and of which he had boasted so much, and he says that it is but 'dung', it is refuse, it is vile. 'Our righteousness is but as filthy rags'; for that which is highly esteemed among men is abomination in the sight of God' [*Luke* 16: 15]. Man by nature is totally unable to please God; he is 'without strength'.

In the same way he is unable to obey God. This need not detain us because the Apostle has taken most of the four chapters of this Epistle to prove that. And he has proved it, and he has come to mighty conclusions, such as, 'Therefore by the deeds of the law there shall no flesh be justified in his sight; for by the law is the knowledge of sin'. To have the knowledge of sin does not mean that you can deal with it, and before we can be saved we must deal with it. To know about the Law and its demands is not enough; 'it is the man who doeth these things who shall live by them', as he reminds us in chapter 10, verse 5. And by nature we are all incapable of doing these things.

What the Apostle says here is that, as we are by nature, we are totally, completely incapable of saving ourselves, of delivering ourselves from the just and righteous condemnation of God and His most holy Law; we are altogether and entirely without spiritual ability. Man can do nothing at all in the matter of his salvation – absolutely nothing.

This first term, 'without strength', is a very important one. It is to the extent to which we realize our inability and incapacity that we realize the love of God. The way to realize it, according to the Apostle, is to realize that 'while we were yet without strength, in due time Christ died for the ungodly'. Need I ask the question again? Are you trusting to anything whatsoever in yourself? Are you priding yourself on the fact that you believe the Gospel? For if you are, it is a false pride; and you are trying to claim that you have something that can justify you before God. Are you holding on in this way to anything at all? 'Without strength' means without any strength whatsoever. We have nothing at all whereof to boast; our boasting is entirely in Him. 'That no man should boast', 'that no man should glory'. 'Let him that glorieth, glory in the Lord.' Those are the scriptural terms. To glory in the Lord is the result of seeing that we are without strength, that we are totally incapable of anything spiritual, or of pleasing God in any way at all, that our nature as the result of sin is so polluted and vile and foul that our best actions are sinful, that man by nature can do nothing whatsoever about his own salvation; but above all seeing that our salvation is entirely of God, and due alone to God's everlasting and eternal love. What a love! What shows and commends it is that He should do anything for people who have got themselves into such a position of shame and utter helplessness. Originally they were made and created in the image of God, but they have become 'without strength', utterly incapable, in a state of total inability. And yet, in spite of that, God sent His only begotten Son, the Lord Jesus Christ, not only into the world, but even to die for us on the Cross on Calvary's hill.

Love so amazing, so divine. . . .

Nine

*

For when we were yet without strength, in due time Christ died for the ungodly.
For scarcely for a righteous man will one die; yet peradventure for a good man some would even dare to die.
But God commendeth his love toward us, in that while we were yet sinners, Christ died for us.
Much more then, being now justified by his blood, we shall be saved from wrath through him.
For if, when we were enemies, we were reconciled to God by the death of his Son, much more, being reconciled, we shall be saved by his life.
And not only so, but we also joy in God through our Lord Jesus Christ, by whom we have now received the atonement.

Romans 5: 6–11

We come back again to the third great proof of God's love to us, His people, and that is, the character of the people for whom all this has been done. As we have seen, we can look at the love of God in two ways – what has been done, and the people for whom it has been done. In the first we are, as it were, looking at the height of God's love; and we have considered that. We are now trying to measure the depths of His love. Christ had to come down so low in order to raise us up, and we are considering the depths out of which He has brought us, our condition before this mighty operation of salvation began to change us. The Apostle's argument is that nothing but the love of God can possibly account for this. We have looked at the first expression which says that we were 'without strength'. That is the biblical doctrine of the total inability of man to do anything whatsoever about his own salvation.

The second thing he tells us about ourselves as we were by

nature is that we were 'ungodly': 'For when we were yet without strength, in due time Christ died for the ungodly.' What does this mean? This means, first of all, that we are unlike God. To be ungodly is to be unlike God. The Apostle has already said this in the third chapter in the twenty-third verse, where he says, 'For all have sinned and come short of the glory of God'. We expounded that as meaning that we were meant for the glory of God, meant to live for the glory of God, and were meant to reflect the glory of God. In other words, to be ungodly means that God's image upon man has become defaced. In the first chapter of Genesis we are told that God said, 'Let us make man in our image, after our likeness'; and later that He made man 'in His own image'. Man was made in the image of God; and there was something of the glory of God upon him. But as the result of sin, says the Apostle, 'we have all come short of the glory of God'.

Another way of saying that is to say that we have become ungodly. This image of God which was put upon man, this imprint of God's own Being, consists partly in his intellect and understanding, his power to reason, to look at himself objectively, and his capacity for communion with God. That has been defaced. Not only that, man was made lord of the creation. But he has lost much of this as the result of the Fall, and because of sin, and he is no longer like God. The image of God is not totally destroyed, but it is terribly defaced; so much so that man is no longer recognizable as one that was made in the image of God. He is ungodly. Now that is the tragic truth about man; and it shows us very clearly the enormity of sin. God honoured man in this way by putting His image upon him. It was the greatest thing about man – not his various physical powers and faculties. They were wonderful, but what gave man his real dignity and glory above everything else was the image of God. But as the result of sin that has become defaced and man is ungodly.

The second thing it means is that man is without love to God. Not only is he unlike Him but he is without love to Him. Indeed the Apostle goes further in this Epistle and says explicitly that not only is man without love to God, but that he is actually an enemy of God. We find that in verse 10: 'If, when we were enemies'. Man by nature is actively opposed to God; he does not delight in God, neither does he delight in the Law of God. The Apostle puts this still more explicitly in chapter 8, verse 7, where he says, 'The carnal mind is enmity against God; for it is not subject to the law of God, neither indeed can be'. That is what he means by 'ungodly' – without love to God, without a desire for God, indeed hating God and His holy Law.

The Old Testament frequently teaches the same truth. 'God', says the Psalmist of the godless, 'is not in all his thoughts'; he lives as though there was not a God; he lives without God, apart from God. Nowhere perhaps does the Apostle Paul state this more clearly than in the second chapter of Ephesians where he describes the Ephesians before their conversion as 'aliens from the commonwealth of Israel, and strangers from the covenants of promise, having no hope and without God, in the world'. Such he says are the people for whom Christ died, these ungodly people.

But to whom does this description apply? There is only one deduction that we can draw from what the Apostle says, and that is, that the whole world is ungodly. Every man who is a Christian now was once ungodly. There are many who are not prepared to grant that. There are people who argue that you should not say that everybody by nature is ungodly, 'because, after all,' they say, 'there are people who are not Christians, who do not believe the Christian faith, but you can not say they are ungodly. They believe in God, and they say their prayers, they go to church and are members of a church. They may not believe that Christ's blood alone saves them, they do not believe in the Atonement, but they believe in God and they worship God.' The Apostle has only one answer to that, and that is, that these people are ungodly. All of us by nature are ungodly. 'All have sinned and come short of the glory of God.'

But let us press this still further. You may argue that if these people say that they believe in God, and pray to God, and are concerned to please God, and if they do a lot of good in order to honour God, then surely they cannot be described as ungodly. But they are ungodly, and for this reason, that the God they think they are worshipping is not God. He is a god of their own imagination, he is but a projection of their own thinking. 'No man cometh to the Father', said Christ. 'but by me'. No man has a true conception of God except in and through the Lord Jesus Christ and the revelation given by Him. That a man says he believes in God does not prove he believes in God; his idea of God may be all wrong.

You can soon discover whether a man really believes in God or not. Tell him what the God of the Bible has said about Himself. Take, for instance, the biblical statements about the 'wrath of God'. Take the statements that God made about Himself when He gave the Ten Commandments to Moses. Concerning that, many are saying today – alas, sometimes from Christian pulpits – that they do not believe in that 'tribal God of the Jews, that God who sits on the top of Mount Sinai'. They say that they do not believe in the God of the Old Testament. They thereby pronounce that they are ungodly, for the Lord Jesus Christ did believe in the God of the Old Testament. He believed the Old Testament fully. The God of the Old Testament is the God of the New Testament. He is the same God.

That is the way in which we justify the Apostle's statements. The mere fact that people think they believe in God, and that they are pleasing God, does not tell us anything at all. The test of whether a man is godly is whether he believes in the revelation of God and His ways which we have in the Scriptures. Does he submit to that? Does he see himself as lost and damned? Does he see the absolute, utter need of relying solely upon the work of the Son of God on his behalf? That is the test – 'Christ died for the ungodly'. He did not die for that Pharisee who stood forward in the Temple and said, 'I thank thee that I am not as other men are . . . or even as this publican' [*Luke* 18:11]. He did not die for people like that, for that man saw no need of Christ. He thought that all was well with him. But he was not worshipping God, he was worshipping himself. The Pharisee did not praise God, he praised himself. He thought he was very godly, but he was not. As the Apostle says later on in the tenth chapter of this Epistle concerning his fellow-countrymen, the Jews,

'They have a zeal of God but not according to knowledge. For, they being ignorant of God's righteousness, and going about to establish their own righteousness, have not submitted themselves to the righteousness of God.' 'They think they are pleasing God', he says, 'but they are not. I was once like that, a proud, self-satisfied, and, as I thought, godly Pharisee; but I was pleasing myself the whole time, I had no righteousness at all.'

Let us be clear about this. There is no such thing as a naturally godly person – 'all have sinned and come short of the glory of God'. 'The carnal mind is enmity against God', and when you hold before them the full revelation of God they will soon let you know that they are ungodly. They say, 'If that is God, I hate Him, I do not want Him'. Their god is a figment of their own imagination, a projection of their own ideas. They are ungodly. By nature we are all ungodly and opposed to God and at enmity against Him. Christ died not only for people who were without strength, but also for us when we were ungodly. That is the measure of the love of God.

But let us go on to consider the argument of verses 7 and 8, where in a sense he is just elaborating all this. 'For', he says – and here he is putting it to our reason and our experience and to our knowledge of life – 'For scarcely for a righteous man will one die; yet peradventure (possibly) for a good man some would even dare to die. But God commendeth his love toward us, in that, while we were yet sinners, Christ died for us'. We must be clear about the terms here, otherwise we shall not be able to follow the argument.

What, for instance, is the difference between a righteous man and a good man? Would you have assumed that a righteous man was even better than a good man? According to the Apostle he is not. What is a righteous man? A righteous man is an upright man; a righteous man is a man who keeps the Law, a man who honours the Commandments. He is a man who obeys the rules and regulations, and is very correct in his behaviour. What is a good man? A good man is a man who does all those things, but who goes further. The good man is not only a righteous man, he is also governed by love; he goes the second mile; asked for his cloak he gives his coat also. He is not merely correct, he goes beyond that.

Let me show the difference by means of an illustration. A man may play the piano correctly, strike the right note every time, and keep the right time, and yet all you can truthfully say about his playing is that it is just correct. But there is another man who plays the piano, and plays the same piece; yet you realize at once that there is something more. He is an artist, he puts life into the performance, he does it in such a way that it moves you and thrills you. The first man was quite correct, but he lacked this extra something that the second man has got. That is the kind of difference between a righteous man and a good man.

Let us see how the Apostle works it out. He says, 'Scarcely for a righteous man would anyone die', then he says, 'now possibly, possibly, for a good man some would even dare to die' – and people have died for good men. You do not find people laying down their lives for a man who is just righteous and correct; but people love a good man and are so attached to him that they say, 'I would die for him'. History has many illustrations of this. Yet even in this case, there is no guarantee that one would die for another; it is not certain, it is just a possibility. Paul is building up his case. 'But now', he says, 'God commends his love toward us', and by that he means, 'proves it', makes it conspicuous and plain. God makes it so clear that there can be no question about it, 'God proves his love towards us'. How does He do that? In that Christ died for us. What was the truth about us? We were certainly not good men; we were not even righteous, we were ungodly.

That is how the Apostle proves his case. He works upwards first of all from the righteous man to the good man. Then he comes to an end and works downward. Where are we? Certainly not 'good'. What about 'righteous'? Not even righteous. Well, what are we? Sinners! Nothing lovable about us at all. God shows His love and proves His love towards us in that Christ died for us, not because we were lovable and lovely and good. Well, although we may not have been lovable and lovely, we were correct at any rate, we were law-abiding? No! We were not even righteous. The truth about us was that we were sinners, and a sinner is the exact opposite of the good man and the righteous man. A sinner is an offender. A sinner is a man who has missed the mark; he has come short. There is no righteousness about him at all. The very term suggests moral turpitude; not moral excellence, but moral failure. Not only have we not kept the Law, we are guilty of transgressing the Law, we have broken the Law. That is what a sinner is. These are the terms that are used to describe him in the Bible. In other words, he is not only a man who is guilty of moral turpitude and trespasses, wrong actions and iniquities, and because of this, guilty in the sight of God; he is reprehensible before the Law, he is deserving of divine displeasure, he is deserving of the wrath of God.

That is the truth about a sinner. He is one who has deliberately flouted God's Law, he is not interested in God, he does not like God, he is a hater of God. Because of that he pits his own will against the will of God. He says, 'Hath God said? Very well, I will do the opposite. Is this the commandment? I will break it. He tells me not to covet, but I want this thing and I am going to have it.' He has therefore deliberately offended God, rebelled against Him, attacked Him, flouted His Law, spurned His voice, gone his own way deliberately, and made himself guilty in the sight of God.

That is the kind of person for whom Christ has died. 'Not the righteous – sinners Jesus came to call.' Not the good men and the lovable, but the vile and the hateful! Paul says the same thing in Ephesians 2:2, 'Wherein in time past ye walked according to the course of this world, according to the prince of the power of the air, the spirit that now worketh in the children of disobedience.' How did they walk? 'In the lusts of (our) flesh, fulfilling the desires of the flesh and of the mind; and were by nature the children of wrath, even as others' (verses 1–3). We have a similar description in the Epistle to Titus, chapter 3, verse 3, 'For we ourselves also were sometime foolish, disobedient, deceived, serving divers lusts and pleasures, living in malice and envy, hateful, and hating one another.' Sinners! Hateful creatures! Ugly, foul, vile, despicable, desperate! Hurl your epithets and still you have not said enough. The sinner is an abomination, he is a monstrosity in God's universe, he is altogether vile and hateful.

It is only as we realize this, that we are able to follow the Apostle's argument. The argument is this. God proves His love toward us in that, while we were like that, when we deserved the wrath of God in His justice, and punishment and perdition and banishment out of His sight, God actually sent His Son to die for us. If that does not prove the love of God to us, nothing ever will, nothing ever can. The people who have appreciated the love of God most have always been those who have realized their sinfulness most.

Let me remind you of how our Lord taught this truth in Luke, chapter 7, the last paragraph, in the incident concerning a sinful woman and Simon the Pharisee. The Pharisee had invited our Lord to a meal in his house. This woman came and fell at His feet and washed His feet with her tears, and then wiped them with the hairs of her head. Simon was amazed that our Lord allowed such a woman to do such a thing to Him, or, indeed, that he should have anything to do with such a person. Our Lord answered him, and here is His teaching.

He spoke a parable about two debtors and then applied it, first showing that it is those who have received much forgiveness who love much, and that those who are only conscious of a little forgiveness are those who love but a little. 'Her sins, which are many, are forgiven; for she loved much; but to whom little is forgiven, the same loveth little.' That is the test. The woman realized the depth of her sin and shame, and that this Person had power to forgive and to deliver her from her sin, so she wept tears of joy. Nothing was too good for Him, she would wash His feet or do anything to show her love and gratitude. She realized His great love and her indebtedness to Him. But the Pharisee was not aware of his sinfulness, so there was no love felt or love shown. When Christ entered his house, he did not give Him water to wash His feet, neither did he anoint His head with oil. Why not? Because he did not realize his debt, his need.

How important it is therefore that we should understand this argument of God's love toward unworthy sinners; and surely the Apostle puts it very plainly! Here is the proof of the love of God; we were without strength, we were ungodly, we were sinners, yet in spite of that, God sent His only begotten Son, the Lord Jesus Christ, not only into the world for us, but even to the Cross and its cruel, shameful death. His blood was shed that we might be reconciled to God.

Let us now sum up the whole argument of verses 6 to 8. The Apostle's argument is that there is nothing whatsoever in us to recommend us, nothing at all. Why did Christ come into the world? Was it in answer to some plea that came from mankind? Not at all! Was it in response to some good in man? Was it because of some divine spark still remaining, and some manifestations of that? Not at all! There was nothing in mankind to recommend it to God, nothing in human nature, nothing in any one of us to recommend us in any way to God and to His love. Indeed the truth about us was, and is, that there was everything in us that was wrong and vile and hateful, everything calculated to antagonize God towards us – enemies, hateful, vile, ungodly, sinners as we were. We must realize that our salvation is entirely gratuitous, and arises only and altogether from the love of God in His infinite grace. That is the Apostle's argument. He expresses it again most movingly in his Epistle to the Ephesians, chapter 2:4–10, 'But God, who is rich in mercy, for his great love wherewith he loved us, even when we were dead in sins . . . '. He talks about 'the exceeding riches of his grace' and His kindness towards us. There is nothing but sin in us; all good is from God. 'By grace are ye saved through faith; and that not of yourselves: it is the gift of God.' It is all of grace, 'lest any man should boast'. It has nothing to do with our works, nothing indeed to do with us in any way at all.

I end by putting a question: Do we realize how all this should be to us the greatest source of assurance, apart from the direct witness of the Holy Spirit? That is the Apostle's whole argument. He wants these people to rejoice in their salvation and 'the hope of the glory of God', and he shows that they will only rejoice in it as they understand and grasp God's great love to them.

That is why I say that this demonstration, this proof of the love of God, is one of the profoundest sources of assurance that one can ever have.

How does this gratuitous element in our salvation provide me with grounds of assurance? Let me put it like this. Imagine what the position would be if our salvation were not entirely of grace. If, for instance, I believed that Christ had died for me because I loved God, and because I was trying to please God, and because I was a good man who was striving to keep the Law, and who had succeeded up to a point, if I believed that my salvation was the result of the fact that I was such a good man, then the inevitable corollary would be, that I would say to myself, 'What if in the future, sometime or another, I should love God less, what if I failed to keep His Commandments, what if I failed to seek God and to please Him and to live for Him as I have been doing in the past? If my salvation depends upon what I am, and what I have done, and what I desire, if it in any sense depends upon me, what security have I got? I may change, I may falter, I may fail.'

If our salvation depended in any sense, or to any extent at all, upon ourselves, our position would always be precarious. We might fail at any moment and would then lose all. But, thank God, says the Apostle, that is not the position. Our salvation in no respect at all depends upon ourselves, it is entirely dependent upon the love of God. And because my salvation depends upon the love of God and on that alone, and on nothing in me, I am sure of it, I am certain of it. Why? Because God does not change, and cannot change, and if I am within the ambit and the scope of the love of God now, I always shall be. The love of God, the gratuitous character of my salvation, my realization that I was without strength, that I was ungodly, a sinner, and that it is entirely in spite of me that Christ died for me, these are the ultimate ground of my assurance. And on this ground I am assured, not only that I am saved now, but that I shall remain saved, that because I am justified I am also glorified, and therefore I rejoice in hope of the glory of God.

That is the statement of the Apostle's case. In verses 9 and 10 he goes on to draw a mighty deduction from it. He is so concerned that we should grasp this, and that we should be rejoicing in full assurance of hope, that he does not leave it even with this great statement. That ought to be enough, but the Apostle is not satisfied. He has knocked in the nail, as it were, and he now wants to clinch it. In verses 9 and 10 he does so in order that there can be no question at all about it.

But is the Apostle's great logic and argumentation plain and clear to you? Have you seen yourself as 'without strength', 'ungodly', a 'sinner'? Have you realized that your salvation does not depend in any sense upon yourself? Do you know God's love, this wondrous love that God Himself is commending, is proving, is establishing to you? It was because he had realized these things that Samuel Davies, that mighty and eloquent preacher in America, who succeeded Jonathan Edwards as President of what is now Princeton University, two hundred years ago wrote his great hymn,

Great God of wonders, all Thy ways
Are matchless, godlike, and divine;
But the fair glories of Thy grace
More godlike and unrivalled shine.
Who is a pardoning God like Thee?
Or who has grace so rich and free?

Such dire offences to forgive,
Such guilty, daring worms to spare,
This is Thy grand prerogative
And none shall in the honour share.

In wonder lost, with trembling joy,
We take the pardon of our God,
Pardon for sins of deepest dye,
A pardon bought with Jesu's blood.

O may this strange, this matchless grace,
This godlike miracle of love,
Fill the wide earth with grateful praise,

And all the angelic hosts above.
Who is a pardoning God like Thee?
Or who has grace so rich and free?

Study that hymn again. Samuel Davies has said it all – 'Such guilty, daring worms . . .' Such we were, but in spite of that, God sent His Son 'for us and for our sins'. Christ died for the ungodly, not only when we were without strength, but while we were sinners, vile, condemned, and under the wrath of God! There is only one thing to say: 'Who is a pardoning God like Thee, and who has grace so rich and free?'

Ten

*

Much more then, being now justified by his blood, we shall be saved from wrath through him.
For if, when we were enemies, we were reconciled to God by the death of his Son, much more, being reconciled, we shall be saved by his life. Romans 5 : 9, 10

To get the real force of these two verses we must remind ourselves of what the Apostle has just been saying. This expression 'much more then' at once reminds us of the connection between this statement and what has preceded it. The Apostle has been showing how God covenants His love to us, but he is so concerned about this that he goes yet further, and in these two verses, 9 and 10, he draws deductions from what he has just been saying. To put it another way, he works out an argument on the basis of his declaration concerning God's love. The argument of these two verses is, I suggest, the most powerful argument with respect to assurance of salvation, or the finality of our salvation, that can be found anywhere in the whole of the Scripture. There is only one way of assurance that goes beyond this and that is the direct and immediate witness of the Spirit Himself, which we have referred to in verse 5, and which the Apostle mentions in the eighth chapter verse 16 in the words, 'The Spirit itself beareth witness with our spirits that we are the children of God'. That is the highest form of assurance of all. There is nothing beyond that. But these two verses, from the standpoint of the argument, and reason, and logical deduction are the highest and mightiest statement with regard to this matter that can be found anywhere in the whole range of the Scriptures.

We are dealing here with two of the most glorious statements that are to be found anywhere. It is amazing to notice the way in which the Apostle can in this one paragraph go on saying the same thing, and yet say it in a different way. The reason is that this theme of the Cross and of the death of Christ is endless. Isaac Watts 'surveys it', and it is the only thing to do with it. To take a passing glance at the Cross or to think you have said the last word about it, means you have never truly seen it. The theme is endless; it is the theme that will occupy our attention throughout eternity. So Paul goes on writing about it in these different ways.

Let us, then, follow the Apostle's argument as he draws his mighty deductions beginning with the words, 'much more then'. If all I have been saying is true, he seems to say, then, certain other things follow of necessity.

I must call attention to a point which in a sense is just a mechanical one and yet is very important. You notice how he uses this expression, 'much more' in both these verses. Verse 9: 'Much more then, being justified by his blood, we shall be saved from wrath through him.' Verse 10: 'For if, when we were enemies, we were reconciled to God by the death of his Son, much more, being reconciled, we shall be saved by his life.' We shall find the same expression again in this chapter in verse 15 and verse 17: 'But not as the offence, so also is the free gift. For if through the offence of one many be dead, much more the grace of God, and the gift by grace, which is by one man, Jesus Christ, hath abounded unto many' (verse 15). And verse 17: 'For if by one man's offence death reigned by one, much more they which receive abundance of grace and of the gift of righteousness shall reign in life by one, Jesus Christ.' This is the employment of argument and of reason. This is a most important matter which I hope to deal with at a later stage. I simply point out in passing now that it is not unspiritual to reason and to be logical. Indeed, as I hope to prove, to be logical and to reason and to argue is to be highly spiritual.

This element of reason and of logic is particularly characteristic of the writings of this particular Apostle. He does not seem to have been much of a poet, but he was a brilliant logician, a master debater, an acute reasoner. These were the gifts that he used constantly, we are told in the Acts of the Apostles, when he went about preaching. He would go into the synagogue and he would 'reason with them out of the Scriptures, proving and alleging'. That was his method, and what a wonderful method it is! Now that is what he is doing here – 'much more then'. And we must learn to do this. The Christian is not to live on his feelings; he is essentially a man who grasps truth and knows how to reason from it. Let us learn from this great master how to do so.

What he is saying in effect is that this is something which should be obvious to us. It follows by a logical necessity, it follows as the night follows the day. It does not need to be argued about, it is so obvious; it is a matter of logic. So he puts it before us. But note the type of argument he uses in both verses 9 and 10. It is the argument from the greater to the lesser. If the greater is true, the lesser of necessity must be true. That is very good logic, sound logic. If the greater proposition can be established there can be no difficulty about the lesser. That is the point which he makes in both verses.

Let us look at the argument in verse 9 first of all. In verse 9 he states the deduction which he draws from verses 6, 7 and 8. Then having stated it in verse 9, he repeats it in verse 10 in greater detail and with still greater force. What a privilege, and I trust delight, it is to watch the working of this great mind. Here is the model for all teachers, here is the master teacher, and he illustrates perfectly the saying that the secret and the art of teaching is repetition. The true teacher says a thing, then says it again but with a slight variation and addition, and then works it out and elaborates it.

So we turn to the argument of verse 9. Here, he seems to be imagining someone raising a question and saying, 'You have been telling us about the love of God to us, and you have told us that the love of God is so great that Christ has died for us and that our sins are forgiven. But how can we be sure even now that we are not going to be lost finally and eventually? We still have to go on living in this world, and we are still very weak and fallible, many things may happen to us. How can we be sure that we are not finally going to be condemned and lost? Is it possible for us to have some kind of security, some certainty, that our position is established eternally, that our salvation is really a final one, and that we need have no fears and no doubts or forebodings at all?' That is the question he takes up; and he puts it, you observe, in terms of our being 'saved from wrath'. That is the crucial question and therefore we must be quite clear about it.

This is obviously a reference to the future. The wrath of which he speaks is the day of judgment, something which has yet to come. The Apostle has already referred to this in the second chapter in verse 5: 'But after thy hardness and impenitent heart treasurest up unto thyself wrath against the day of wrath and revelation of the righteous judgment of God'. There is a great day coming when the wrath of God against sin, when the righteous judgment of God upon sin and evil, will be manifest, will be revealed, will be pronounced. This is that tremendous day to which the Scripture continually refers – 'The day will declare it', 'the wrath to come'. That is what is meant here by 'wrath', and the question is, How can we be safe and know that we shall be safe on that great day of judgment which is coming?

At this point it is vital that we should remind ourselves that the term 'saved' is used in the Scripture in three different tenses and senses. We must not be in any confusion about this. There is first of all the fact that we have been saved. In what sense have we been saved? We have already been saved from the guilt of sin. That is something that has happened. 'Having been justified by faith we have peace with God.' That is in the past. We have been saved in that sense.

But there is another sense in which we are still being saved. We are being saved from the power of sin and from the pollution of sin. Our relationship to sin is not merely one of guilt; unfortunately there is something more than that. Our trouble and our problem is not merely that we have committed certain acts of transgression and are therefore guilty before God. The sin of Adam affected the very nature of man. It became polluted and man fell under the power and the dominion of sin. So we need to be saved in that respect also. It is not merely from the guilt of sin as we face the Law of God that we need to be saved; we need to be saved also from this terrible power that has tyrannized over us and still tends to do so; and beyond that, to be saved also from the pollution of sin, that effect of sin upon our very constitution which mars it and perverts it and makes it unclean. We need to be saved from that; and the Christian is being saved from that. That is sanctification, which is a process that is going on within us in the present.

There is, however, yet another tense in which we can think of salvation, and that is wholly in the future. This is the sense which the Apostle has chiefly in his mind here, because there is a day coming when we shall be finally and completely saved. This means that not only shall we be delivered from the power and the pollution of sin, but our very bodies shall be delivered from sin. This is our glorification. We saw in verse 2, and as we shall find again in chapter 8 verse 23: 'Not only they, but ourselves also, which have the first-fruits of the Spirit, even we ourselves groan within ourselves, waiting for the adoption, to wit, the redemption of our bodies.' That is the final aspect of salvation, and in that final aspect we shall be completely and entirely delivered from sin in every respect, and stand 'faultless before the presence of his glory with exceeding joy' [*Jude* 24].

The question the Apostle raises here is this, 'How can I be sure that I shall have that final and complete salvation? Over and above my forgiveness and my deliverance from guilt, how can I know that I am going to be entirely delivered, and that somehow or another I shall not lose my salvation somewhere between now and the day of judgment?'. That is the question; and here is his argument in reply: 'Much more then', he says, 'being now justified, having already been justified by his blood, we shall be saved from wrath through him'. 'We have already', he says, 'been justified by his blood'. That is the basis of the argument; and because of that we can be sure and certain that 'we shall be saved from wrath through him'.

Now in order to get the full force of the argument we must be clear in our minds as to the meaning of our terms. Once more we must be certain that we are clear as to what it is to be justified. We can take no risks in this matter.

To be justified means not only to be forgiven. It does mean that, but it means much more than that. To be justified means that God declares us to be righteous. It is a legal or a forensic term; it is something that God does and God alone does. He declares that He regards us as righteous, and He does so because He has attributed to us, put to our account, the righteousness of the Lord Jesus Christ. He clothes us with the righteousness of Christ, puts His robe upon us. So we stand in the presence of God clothed with the righteousness of Christ, as we have seen in verses 1 and 2.

Now we come to a most interesting point. He says, 'much more then, being now justified by his blood'. That is a new expression suddenly introduced. We have already found him saying in chapter 3, verse 24, 'Being justified freely by his grace'. In verse 28 of that chapter he says, 'Therefore we conclude that a man is justified by faith without the deeds of the law'. But here he says 'Being now justified by Christ's blood'. And in verse 10 he says, 'If, when we were enemies, we were reconciled to God by the death of his Son . . .'

It is interesting to notice how he varies his terms in this way; and unless we understand why he does so, we may well be in a state of confusion. How do these various terms fit into the teaching about justification? It is the grace of God that makes justification possible at all. Then justification comes to us through faith as the channel. That is *how* it comes to us. But – and this is the important point – what really procures it for us, the ground of our justification, is our Lord's righteousness and obedience to God's holy Law including His death, His blood shed on the Cross. This is the crucial, the focal point.

What makes justification possible, in the sense that God devised it as the means of saving us, is the grace of God. So we can say that we are justified by the grace of God. There it is as an idea, as a thought in the mind of God. The very idea of justification springs out of grace; that is the beginning of it. So it is right to say that we are justified by the grace of God.

But that is not the whole truth, because we know that this

grace of God comes to us through the channel or medium of faith. We must never lose sight of that. We can therefore say that we are justified by faith. But that still leaves the question of how it really has come to us. What has dealt with the problem of our guilt and provided this righteousness which we have, and which comes to us by faith? The answer is, it is the Lord Jesus Christ and especially His death on the Cross, the shedding of His blood, His life poured out. So the Apostle is entitled to say that we are justified by His blood, we are justified by His death. What is essential to our justification is that which happened on the Cross. 'Whom God hath set forth to be a propitiation through faith in his blood' [3:25]. Remember also what our Lord said about Himself as 'The good shepherd who lays down his life for the sheep'. That is what makes it possible. The grace of God thought of and planned the way, and then sent Him to carry it out. It becomes ours through the channel of faith. But let us understand clearly that it is not our faith that justifies us: It is His blood, His death that saves us, and His righteousness, and nothing else. The basis of all is our Lord Himself and His redeeming work on our behalf.

Let us be equally clear that it is not our regeneration that saves us. It is not the fact that we are born again that saves us. It is the righteousness of Christ that saves us. God justifies the ungodly, and the ungodly are not regenerate. It is while we are ungodly that we are declared righteous. Regeneration comes practically at the same time, but it is something different. God does not first regenerate us and then say we are justified because we are regenerated. No! He justifies the ungodly entirely by the righteousness of Christ. These distinctions are most important.

Let me go further: we are not justified, either, by our sanctification, our good works and our progressive deliverance from sin. This verse is a great sign-post at which we must always keep looking – 'Having been justified by his blood'. It is His blood that reconciles us, it is His death which is the basis and the foundation of it all. This verse is one of the most important verses in the whole of Scripture, because it stands against all those other false notions. Not our works, not our faith, not our regeneration, not our sanctification – nothing at all apart from Him in His active and passive obedience, and His righteousness which God imputes to us.

There, then, are the terms, and this is the argument the Apostle bases upon it. 'If God', he says, 'has so loved us as to do that for us, as to justify us by sending His Son to the death of the Cross on our behalf – if God has already done that for us, then – and surely there is no need to argue about this – He will save us from wrath also by the same Christ.' Why? Because He has already done the bigger thing, the greater thing. He has already taken the fundamental decision, and because He is God who cannot change, He cannot go back on it. The decision of God the Father was to justify all who 'believe in Jesus'. But that involved the sending of the Lord Jesus not only into the world but also to the death on the Cross and the shedding of His blood. God not only decided to do that, He has done it. And if He has done that, there is nothing He will not do for us.

The Apostle's argument is that this method, this way of salvation that God has planned, is a complete whole, and therefore, if we have been justified by Christ's blood we are joined to Christ, we are in Christ, and we shall therefore be saved by Him completely and perfectly. The Apostle obviously rejoiced in this argument. That is why he used it so frequently. Take, for instance, the way in which he expresses it in the First Epistle to the Thessalonians, chapter 1, verses 9 and 10: 'They themselves show of us what manner of entering in we had unto you, and how ye turned to God from idols to serve the living and true God; and to wait for his Son from heaven, whom he raised from the dead, even Jesus, which delivered us from the wrath to come.'

The Apostle states it there in that simple form. He was just summarizing his message to those people because he had not been able to stay very long with them. He puts it all, so to speak, in a nutshell. What Christ has done for us already, 'delivers us from the wrath to come'. All the particular parts and steps of salvation are parts of a complete whole. In other words, Paul is saying once more what he has said already in verses 1 and 2 of this chapter, that justification guarantees our final salvation. That is the thing he wants us to lay hold on, that if God has procured our justification by the blood of Christ, then we need have no worry and no concern at all about our final, eventual, complete salvation in the same Christ.

Our Lord Himself taught this very doctrine. Take for instance what He says in the Gospel according to John, chapter 5, verse 24: 'Verily, verily, I say unto you, he that heareth my word, and believeth on him that sent me, hath everlasting life, and shall not come into condemnation, but is passed (is already passed) from death unto life.' That is the most explicit statement imaginable. The man, says our Lord, who hears My words and who believes on Him that sent Me, already has everlasting life and he shall not come into judgment and condemnation. Why not? Because he has already passed from death unto life. Are we clear about this? Do we see that God has already decided our eternal fate and destiny in our justification? That is Paul's argument.

Here is the position. We were without strength, ungodly, sinners, and as the Apostle will say in the next verse, even 'enemies', and here is God in His eternal righteousness and holiness. Now the first thing that happens to us is that we are justified, and this, as we have seen, means not only that we are forgiven but that God declares us to be righteous in His sight. He clothes us with the righteousness of Christ and enables us to stand before Himself in that righteousness, and pronounces that He has nothing against us. Can you not see that that is already judgment? Our judgment has already taken place. God has already arrived at the fundamental decision with respect to us. When God as the Judge Eternal makes this pronouncement and promulgation in the Court that He regards us as righteous, He has pronounced His judgment on us, and God never goes back on His Word. It is final. We are justified, and therefore, as our Lord puts it, 'we have passed from death', from the whole realm of death, we have passed away from that 'into life'. So that we have already been judged, and therefore we can never come under condemnation.

Do we realize what a tremendous thing justification is? When God justifies a man He is really making a final pronouncement concerning him. The man who is justified is a man who is safe, and safe to all eternity. 'No man', says our Lord, 'shall be able to pluck them out of my hand' [*John* 10:28]. 'It is God that justifieth, who is he that condemneth?' says Paul in chapter 8, verses 33 and 34 of this Epistle. That is the argument. Because it is God that justifies, who can condemn? 'Who shall lay anything to the charge of God's elect' in the light of the fact that it is God that justifies? Justification is the most momentous, the most glorious thing we can ever grasp or experience.

That is why Martin Luther was so moved when he realized what it meant. That is why that realization led to the Protestant Reformation. It was no longer a matter of works, no longer a matter of penances, no longer a matter of confessing to priests, and priests doing various things for us, no longer a question of transubstantiation and depending on the so-called 'real presence' of Christ in the sacrament to build us up and to make us worthy of forgiveness. Salvation was no longer something uncertain, something contingent. No longer was there the dread possibility that we might not be finally saved after all, but would need the Church and her ministrations throughout life, and indeed even after death because of purgatory. No longer was there need for others to go on praying for us after our death, and lighting candles for us, and praying to the Saints to shorten our time in purgatory. All that was abolished.

But what abolished it? The realization of the truth of the doctrine of justification by faith only. Justification is final as regards our standing before God. Justification means that God makes the pronouncement, and the pronouncement He makes is that He has finally forgiven us and regards us as righteous in His most holy sight. There is nothing that you and I can ever know in this world that is in any way comparable to the knowledge that God has justified us and that we are just in His sight.

'How may I know that?' asks someone. I have already answered in discussing verses 1 and 2. But let me repeat it. 'Peace with God.' Peace with God, knowing that you are forgiven, able to answer the accusations of conscience and the Law and everything else that is against you! Standing in His grace and knowing Him as your Father, seeing something of that glory which is awaiting you, and rejoicing in anticipation of it! Being able to laugh at the world and its gaudy treasures and the glittering prizes and all that it has! Seeing through it all, seeing beyond it, seeing something of the glory that awaits you, and having within you a spirit which cries, Abba, Father! That is how one knows! But the argument here is that all this is in justification. And that is why the Apostle starts his eighth chapter by saying, 'There is therefore now no condemnation to them that are in Christ Jesus.' They are already out of the entire realm of condemnation. When we come to chapter 6 – indeed at the end of this chapter 5, he will already be introducing it – we shall find the Apostle arguing all this out in detail. He will tell us that we are 'dead to sin', 'dead to the law', and that they have nothing to do with us because we are justified.

Here, then, is the argument. If that is true of me now, if God has made that pronouncement with respect to me now, He will never go back on it. He cannot, for that would mean that He was contradicting and denying Himself. That is inconceivable of God. That is why Paul says, 'Much more then, having already been justified by his blood, we shall be saved from wrath through him'. It was because of his understanding and realization of this that Toplady was able to spell out the mighty argument in his great hymn,

The work which His goodness began,
The arm of His strength will complete;
His promise is Yea and Amen,
And never was forfeited yet.
Things future, nor things that are now.
Not all things below or above,
Can make Him His purpose forego,
Or sever my soul from His love.

My name from the palms of His hands
Eternity will not erase;
Impressed on His heart it remains,
In marks of indelible grace.

Yes, I to the end shall endure,
As sure as the earnest is given;
More happy, but not more secure,
The glorified spirits in heaven.

Note the statement, 'More happy, but not more secure, The glorified spirits in heaven'. That is the vital point. Their security is not greater, though their enjoyment of it is.

In verse 10 Paul will say all this again and add to and elaborate it. What matters, supremely, for each one of us is that we understand these things, and rejoice in them, and go on repeating them to ourselves every day of our lives: for it is as we are able to do so, that we shall be able to join the Apostle in saying what he says in verse 11: 'And not only so, but we also joy in God through our Lord Jesus Christ, by whom we have now received the atonement.'

Eleven

*

For if when we were enemies we were reconciled to God by the death of his Son, much more, being reconciled, we shall be saved by his life. Romans 5: 10

Here is another of those great and glorious statements which make the writings of this particular Apostle unique. We have seen that actually the Apostle is repeating in a sense what he has already said in verse 9; but he does it in such a way, and with such additional emphasis, that one is not conscious of repetition; one just thanks God that he has said it again and said it still more magnificently. This is something that happens frequently in Paul's writings: he seems to have stated something perfectly, but then he says it again and in a still more wonderful way. That is not because of his greatness as a man, great though he was; it is the greatness of the theme that accounts for it. Whatever one may say about the love of God in Christ Jesus there is always something more to be said. This is the theme of the angels in glory, it is the anthem, the song of all the redeemed. It is the theme that will occupy us throughout eternity.

Once more let us be quite clear in our minds about what we are doing. The Apostle's concern is that we should all have an assurance of salvation, that we should be clear and certain about the finality of our salvation, that we should realize that if we are justified by faith we are eternally safe. He has worked out his great argument in terms of God's love to us in Christ Jesus and has deduced that, if God has already sent His Son to the death of the Cross for us, all the rest must follow of necessity. But still he seems to feel that he can put it yet more clearly and forcibly.

He is so anxious that the Roman Christians should get hold of this truth that he puts again what is the same argument, in its essence, in these magnificent and moving words.

To get its full force we must analyse it, and we shall not be detracting from it in doing so. There are those who seem to think that, with a great statement like this, all you need do or ought to do is just to read it or recite it, and then pronounce the Benediction. But that would defeat the very object the Apostle has in view. We might be moved aesthetically or artistically, or emotionally by doing that, but it would end at that point. It is essential that we should examine and analyse it word by word to appreciate it truly; and, of course, in doing so we are simply doing what the great Apostle himself did.

There are foolish people who think that the moment you enter the realm of logic you have departed from eloquence. But that is not so. Here we have logic and eloquence wedded together. Indeed I would suggest that you can never be truly eloquent unless you are logical. You cannot be eloquent about nothing. You must have something to say if you would have true eloquence, and the greater the theme and the stronger the reasoning, the greater will be the eloquence.

We must never separate these two aspects, the intellect and the heart; they go together. You can be moved sentimentally, it is true, by very little. But we are not interested in sentiment, we are interested in true emotion, in the heart being moved. Sentiment is a pretence, emotion belongs to the realm of reality. We must never be satisfied with what just does duty for emotion, we should always desire to feel the profundity of the truth. This can only happen as we adopt the Apostle's own method and become logical and analytical. If at the end of our analysis we do not see the glory of this verse much more clearly and movingly than we did at the beginning, then we shall have done our work very badly.

The Apostle's method is again that of applying reason and logic to the situation, so he introduces it by the words, 'For if'. It is the same essential argument as in verse 9: If that is true, then this must be still more so. That is pure logic. He says, If God has already done the greater thing He cannot fail to do the lesser thing – for Him not to do so would not make sense. It is unthinkable. He puts it so strongly that to say anything else seems ridiculous. But the vital question is, Is it ridiculous to us? You test whether it is ridiculous to you in this way. Have you got a full assurance of salvation? If you have not, it is probably because you do not see the ridiculous position which follows if we do not accept the Apostle's argument.

The Apostle's argument divides itself into two parts. Let us look first at the greater thing which God has already done for us. It is only as we grasp that, that we shall see that the other follows inevitably. What is this great thing, the greater thing, that God has already done? We have but to examine his series of statements to discover the answer. 'When we were enemies' or 'while we were enemies' God has done something about us. That is a most important statement and a most significant one; and we must be very careful that we attach the right meaning to it. Does it mean when we were in a state of enmity against God? He certainly does include that, but to stop at that is to miss the real point of his argument altogether. It does not refer only to the fact that we were once in a subjective state and inward condition in which we felt enmity towards God. That is not the primary meaning of what he says here. What the Apostle is concerned to emphasize is our objective position in the sight of God. We can even describe it as a kind of technical, legal position. Our state and condition, our position, our relationship to God was that of enemies.

The terms 'technical' and 'legal' can be explained by an analogy. We talk about countries being 'at war' with one another or in 'a state of war'. Before they come to that, very often they break off diplomatic relationship; but still they are not technically in a state of war. They have to take another step before they are actually at war; they have to declare war. It is only then that the two countries are technically and legally at war. They are now enemies and in a state of war. That is the position which the Apostle is describing here. He is not so much concerned at this point – and I will be able to demonstrate this – with our feelings of enmity against God. What he is saying is that the mutual relationship and attitude is one of war and of enmity. We were in this position, this legal position, of being enemies of God. God looked upon us as enemies, and we were at enmity against God. The Apostle is concerned with the whole relationship and state and not with our subjective feelings.

I prove that in this way. Paul's whole argument is based upon this very fact that God has done something about us and for us, though we were in that position; and if He has done that for us, when we were in that state, how much more will He do for us now that we are in a new state! So let us get rid of the idea that a subjective state alone is intended, though that is included.

We can illustrate this further by quoting what the Apostle says later on in this Epistle in chapter 11, verse 28. Speaking of the Jews he says, 'As concerning the gospel, they are enemies for your sakes; but as touching the election, they are beloved for the fathers' sakes'. By that he means that the Jews as a people are now in the technical position of being enemies of God. That is one way of looking at them, he says, but you can look at them in another way – '. . . as touching the election, they are beloved for the fathers' sakes'. They are beloved for their fathers' sakes though in the outward position of enemies for the time being. It is clear, therefore, that the Apostle is thinking of a purely objective condition both in chapter 11 and also in this verse which we are analysing. There we were, enemies of God. That was the relationship between God and man, and man and God, when God did this amazing thing for us.

But let us go on. He says, 'When (or while) we were enemies, we were reconciled to God by the death of his Son'. Take first the phrase, 'reconciled to God'. He says that we have been reconciled to God. The meaning of 'reconciliation' or of 'being reconciled' is again of the profoundest importance to us. Are we to take this as referring to some subjective state in us? Is the Apostle saying that while we were enemies our attitude towards God was changed? Is he saying that while we were enemies we were reconciled to God in our minds, that we ceased to hate Him, and to feel enmity towards Him, and began to love Him and to desire to obey Him and to worship Him? Once more the reply is the same. That is included, but it is certainly not the chief thing, it is certainly not the only thing.

Again, if we are not clear about this, we cannot possibly follow the argument which the Apostle works out in this verse. Reconciliation means primarily a change in the relationship existing between God and man, and man and God. In other words, it involves and implies – and I say this deliberately and reverently – a change in God's attitude towards us before it leads to a change in our attitude towards God. That is the whole point. Reconciliation not only applies to us and what happens within us. It starts with God's attitude towards us.

This is a controversial matter, unfortunately, as we saw when we were dealing with the word 'propitiation' in chapter 3, verse 25. Many do not like this idea of 'propitiation', because they argue that surely nothing is necessary on God's side, and that the only change that is necessary is on our side. But this verse we are considering surely settles this matter once and for ever. If that argument is correct which says that all that is necessary is a change in us, that we need to be reconciled in mind and heart to God who is always the same, then the Apostle's argument here would have to read like this: 'For if when we were enemies our attitude to God was changed by the death of his Son, much more, in view of the fact that our attitude towards God has been changed, we shall be saved by his life'. But that deprives the Apostle's argument of its real force, the argument has vanished. It puts the entire emphasis on me, and on my subjective attitude towards God, as if that were the big thing.

But that is not the Apostle's argument. What he is saying is this: 'If, while you were an enemy in His sight, God's attitude towards you was such that He sent His Son to die for you, is it likely that His attitude towards you is going to change now that He regards you as His child?' Obviously it is not, for that would be absurd and mean that God is capricious. Since God has planned a way of so treating you, while you were an enemy in His sight, and under the Law, as to save you, even by the death of His Son, surely He can never reverse that, and especially since he has also adopted you as His child He can never go back on that!

In other words, if we take the subjective view of reconciliation and think of it as only something in ourselves, the whole value of this argument has gone. The greater and the lesser no longer obtain. But when you take it in its true meaning, and understand that reconciliation involves something in God as well as in man, then you see the point and the cogency of the argument.

Let me put it like this. The whole of this section is concerned about the love of God to us, not about our love to God. Can that be disputed? The exclusive theme from verse 5 onwards has been the love of God to us. Paul is not interested at this point in us and our attitude towards God, and our love to God. His whole case is this, that if only we understand the love of God to us, then we shall see the certainty and the finality of our salvation. He is not discussing our love, he is not interested in our attitude towards God. It is God's attitude towards us that matters. Get hold of that, he says, and you will have assurance. So that to import our subjective feeling of love towards God at this point is to contradict the whole purpose of the entire paragraph.

What the Apostle says in 2 Corinthians 5, will help us to see this still more clearly. In verse 18 he says, 'And all things are of God, who hath reconciled us to himself by Jesus Christ'. He has reconciled us, as we were, that is, as sinners, to Himself, by Jesus Christ – 'and hath given to us the ministry of reconciliation; to wit, that God was in Christ' – God, notice, is doing it all. 'God was in (and through) Christ reconciling the world unto himself'. How did He do that? 'Not imputing their trespasses unto them.' Strict law demands that God should impute our trespasses to us. We have sinned against God, we have broken the Law, and the Law demands in common justice that its verdict and its condemnation should be carried out. But Paul says that God has reconciled us to Himself by not imputing our trespasses to us. That is the first step. The next is that He has imputed our trespasses to the Lord Jesus Christ (verse 21). 'He hath made him to be sin for us, who knew no sin'. What then? He then imputes Christ's righteousness to us, 'that we might be made the righteousness of God in him'.

The great problem was, how can God treat us in love? The

answer is what God has done 'in Christ'. This matter of reconciliation must be regarded in an objective manner. We must realize that it starts in something that God has done, in order that He may not impute our trespasses to us, and in order that He may not treat us any longer as enemies. That is the first thing that was essential. So it is something on the Godward side, not on the manward side. The manward side follows. It is only after God has done this, that a man is brought to see it, and then his own attitude changes, and he rejoices in it. This happens when he comes to the knowledge of what God has done for us. That is the message of reconciliation. It is that which tells us that God has found a way of dealing with us, no longer as enemies, but as those whom He loves and whom He is ready to forgive. What happens to us is but a consequence of that.

In other words, what the Apostle means by reconciliation here, is that the wrath of God is no longer upon us, that He no longer looks upon us in wrath but in mercy. We are back again, so to speak, in verse 18 of the first chapter: 'For' – this is why he is so proud of the Gospel which 'is the power of God unto salvation to everyone that believeth, to the Jew first and also to the Greek. For therein is a righteousness from God revealed by faith'; 'for' – this is the reason why he so delights and glories in it – 'the wrath of God is revealed from heaven against all ungodliness and unrighteousness of men'. That was our condition. The wrath of God was upon us, and we were His enemies. The amazing and incredible thing is that God should have any dealings at all with us. And what makes the Christian message 'good news' is that it tells us that, though we were enemies and under the wrath of God, His love is so great that He devised a way of reconciling us unto Himself.

How important it is, therefore, to understand these terms – that both the term 'enemy' and 'reconciled' have an objective content primarily, and that the subjective is only secondary. As we proceed with the argument we shall see this still more clearly.

The next statement is that all this has been done to us 'by the death of his Son'. This is how God has brought about this reconciliation, this change in the relationship. Both words need to be emphasized, both 'by' and the 'death' of His Son. We have already done this in the previous verses, 6, 7 and 8, and again in verse 9 where we had the word 'blood'. We need not repeat that, therefore, but God forbid that anyone should fail to realize the crucial significance of that death! God has so loved us, though we were enemies, that He has even sent His only Son, His only begotten Son, His well beloved Son, to that death, even the death of the Cross – for us. From the Son's side it meant separation from God, it meant a break in the communion between Father and Son for the only time in all Eternity and so led to the cry of dereliction – 'My God, my God, why hast thou forsaken me?' Do you see the Apostle's argument? Again we speak with reverence and deliberately, but there is nothing more that even God could do. But He has done it. The argument is from the greater to the lesser, indeed I should have said, from the greatest to the lesser. Even God cannot do anything beyond this – He has given, He has sent, His only begotten Son to the death of the Cross. It is John 3:16 once more: 'God so loved the world that he gave his only begotten Son, that whosoever believeth in him should not perish but have everlasting life'. God has literally done this; we are 'reconciled to God by the death of his Son'.

But we must now put the emphasis on the 'death' in order to bring out the full force of the argument. God has reconciled us to Himself, not simply by sending His Son into the world, nor by the teaching of the Son. So many stop short at that. They think that we are saved by believing that the Lord Jesus Christ came into the world to tell us that God is love and that He loves us, and that when we believe that, we are reconciled. That is to be reconciled to God by the teaching of His Son. Others say that our Lord came into the world in order to tell us what we have to do to save ourselves, and to encourage us to do so by the life He lived. That means, again, that we are reconciled to God by the teaching of His Son, or by the example of His Son.

But that is not what the Apostle says, it is not what the Bible says. We are reconciled to God by the 'death' of His Son. The Apostle will not allow us to escape from this. That is why in verse 9 he has said, 'by his blood' – 'justified by the blood of

Christ'. So that no one might philosophize away even the meaning of death, he says 'blood' – blood, literal 'blood'. People hate what they call this 'theology of blood', but there is no theology worthy of the name apart from the shed blood of Christ. This is the ground of reconciliation, of justification, of salvation.

But I draw a second deduction. This was obviously the only way whereby God could reconcile us to Himself. Otherwise this would never have happened. Is it conceivable that God would have sent His only begotten beloved Son to the shame and the suffering and the ignominy of the Cross if it were not absolutely essential? If teaching could have saved us, the necessary teaching would have been given. Would God have allowed His Son to endure that agony in the garden, and still more on the Cross when He cried out, 'My God, my God, why hast thou forsaken me?', if it were not absolutely essential? It is unthinkable! This is not only God's way of reconciling us unto Himself, it was the only way. There was no other way. Why? That is the question. What is it that called for this? Why did this have to happen? Why was there no other way except that the Son of God should be crucified upon the Cross? There is only one answer to the question; it is the justice of God, as we have seen already in chapter 3, verse 26: 'That God might be just and the justifier of him that believeth in Jesus.'

There is no other explanation. Try to think of one if you can. Why had the Son of God to die on that Cross? There is only one answer: because God is just, because of the justice of God. 'Ah but', you say, 'God is also love.' I agree. But you see the danger of separating these attributes of God. God is one, and God is indivisible, and God always acts as Himself. You must not set the love of God against the justice of God. God always acts in the fullness of His being, He always acts in love; at the same time He always acts in justice, and you must never say that God's love acts apart from His justice or apart from His righteousness. Neither must you say that His justice and His righteousness act apart from His love. God acts as God and you must never drive a wedge between these attributes.

God is holy, and God is light, and in Him is no darkness at all.

That is why propitiation was essential, that is why an offering had to be presented to God, that is why Christ had to bear the punishment of our sins. The justice of God cannot be laid aside, and God cannot pretend that He has not seen sin. He has seen it, and He has said He will punish it. Because He is God He must punish it; and He has punished it. And by punishing it in the Person of His only begotten Son He can look at you and me and He can forgive us freely. His justice is vindicated. 'He is just and the justifier of him that believeth in Jesus.'

That is the whole point of the Apostle's argument here. Though we were in this state of enmity, God has found a way of forgiving us and of loving us freely, a way of reconciling us unto Himself, a way which at the same time vindicates His glorious character and essential Being. His justice shines out as gloriously as it has ever done, and so does His love. All the attributes are displayed in their divine perfection in that act which took place on Calvary. That is what Paul is saying. It is God's way of reconciling us, and it is the only way. There is no reconciliation for any persons unless they believe that Christ died for their sins. There is no entry into the presence of God 'except by the blood of Jesus'.

It is of no use your saying 'I have got a new view of God; I can see now that God is love and my old enmity has gone.' If you do not see that you are utterly dependent upon the death of His Son, the blood of Christ, what you imagine to be your view of God as a God of love is false, because you are denying His justice and His eternal righteousness. God remains eternally unchanged, 'the Father of lights in whom is no variableness, neither shadow cast by turning', and all He does is an expression of all His glorious attributes together. In the Cross on Calvary, the death of His Son, the blood of Jesus, I see the justice and the love shining out in all their glory together. That is the greater thing, the greatest thing of all, to which the Apostle is referring and which leads to the inevitable conclusion of the second great statement in this verse to which we now come.

In the light of that – what? 'Much more'. Having done the greatest thing of all, God will do the lesser; dare we not even say must do? 'Much more, being reconciled.' God does not look upon me now as an enemy, He looks upon me as a friend, and not only as a friend, but as a child. The relationship now is that between Father and child. Is it conceivable that God who has done that greatest thing of all for me when I was an enemy is suddenly going to abandon me or fail me now that I am His child? It is insulting to the very character of God to imagine such a thing. To talk about falling away from grace is, apart from anything else, nonsense, as we have seen earlier. Thank God, His love is a love that 'will not let you go'. That is the very basis of the Apostle's argument.

But take the word 'saved'. It means here, as we have seen, full and final salvation. Here, then, is the argument. The difficult part of our salvation was our justification; and if God has solved and dealt with that problem, the rest, if I may say it with reverence, is simple. The real problem was how to deal with that state of enmity. It was so great, that nothing less than the death of Christ on the Cross could deal with it. But as God has solved that biggest of all problems, how much easier is the rest! Once justification is established the rest will follow.

And then take the last expression, 'we shall be saved by his life'. Here there is a preliminary technical point. I have been quoting from the Authorized Version, 'we shall be saved by his life'. Other translations more correctly read, 'we shall be saved in his life'. The Apostle's statement is not that we shall be saved 'by' but 'in' His life. It is not the word for 'by', it is the word for 'in', and it means the state or condition in which anything is done, or the state or condition in which anyone exists or acts or suffers. So we are told that we are going to be saved in the state or condition of the life of Christ. You see the importance of this argument. Before, we were outside His life, outside His love, as it were – enemies. Now, we are in the life of Christ; and therefore our position is absolutely certain and secure. If God sent His Son to death for us while we were outside as enemies, how much more will He do for us now that we are inside as children! If a man does something for another man standing on his doorstep, who has vilified him and hated him and robbed him and been an enemy to him, if he shows kindness to him, how much more likely is he to show kindness to his children who come from his own body! That is the argument.

Let me put it in the form of another illustration. The difficult operation is the operation of grafting us into Christ. When you graft a new branch into a tree you take your knife and you strike that tree and then you take the branch and push it into the gash you have made. That is the difficult part of the process. Once you have put the graft in, the rest happens easily. The sap flows through the tree to the branch giving it life and strength; and so it grows. Once the actual act of grafting has been done you just wait for the results, and the fruit follows. 'How much more shall we be saved in his life!'.

But let us work it out in detail. 'If, when we were enemies, we were reconciled to God by the death of his Son'; surely nothing can fail from now on, because He is no longer dead and in the grave, He is alive! The author of the Epistle to the Hebrews puts this perfectly in chapter 7, verses 22–25. 'By so much was Jesus made a surety of a better testament. And they truly were many priests' (he is speaking of those under the Old Dispensation), 'because they were not suffered to continue by reason of death: But this man, because he continueth ever' – that is to say, because He is alive for evermore – 'hath an unchangeable priesthood. Wherefore he is able also to save them to the uttermost' (to the very end) 'that come unto God by Him, seeing he ever liveth to make intercession for them'. Have you realized the force of that? You may say, 'It is all very well to say my sins are forgiven and that I am saved. But what if I fall into sin again? Does not that cancel it all out, am I not back where I was?' Not at all, because 'He ever liveth to make intercession for us'.

John says the same thing in the first chapter of his First Epistle. The argument there is essentially the same argument. He says, 'If we say that we have fellowship with him and walk in darkness, we lie and do not the truth: but if we walk in the light, as he is in the light, we have fellowship one with another'. But what if I fall into sin, have I lost that fellowship? No! 'And the blood of Jesus Christ his Son cleanseth us from all sin'. We do fall into sin, but 'if we confess our sins, He is faithful and just to forgive us our sins and to cleanse us from all unrighteousness'.

Again in chapter 2 of his First Epistle: 'My little children, these things write I unto you that ye sin not. And if any man sin we have an advocate with the Father, Jesus Christ the righteous: and he is the propitiation for our sins; and not for ours only, but also for the sins of the whole world' (verses 1 and 2). There, and there alone, is the guarantee of our safety. Christ has died to reconcile you to God, and He is alive, and He is in Heaven as your Advocate interceding on your behalf. He will not let you go. That is the argument.

But not only does He deal with those sins of ours subsequent to salvation, He will also keep us from sin. 'Now', says Jude at the end of his Epistle – 'Now unto him that is able to keep you from falling'. He (Christ) is alive and He is able to 'keep us from falling and to present us faultless before the presence of his glory with exceeding joy'. 'How much more shall we be saved in his life!' He is ever there; He has gone on ahead of us; He will give us strength and life and power.

But even more, we are engrafted into Him, we share His life, we draw life from Him. 'Of his fullness have all we received, and grace for grace' [*John* 1:16]. We have to fight the world, the flesh and the devil, it is true. But can they destroy us? Never! If He has died for us He will not let us go, He will bring us through all this to the end, to the glory. If God could deal with the problems of justice and eternal righteousness, by the death of His Son, surely He is not going to be defeated by the lesser problem of the world and the flesh and the devil. No! Christ has already conquered them in His own death, He has 'put them to an open shame'. The devil has lost his power, 'the prince of this world has been cast out' [*John* 12:31]. Christ has triumphed, and He is alive in the glory and we are in Him. That is the argument – 'Much more shall we be saved in his life!' We are joined to Him, we are 'in Him', we are 'members of his body, of his flesh and of his bones'.

That is why we had to reject the translation of the Authorized Version – 'Much more shall we be saved by his life'. We are *in*

His life, we are engrafted into Christ. 'Ye are the body of Christ, and members in particular' [1 *Corinthians* 12:27]. The Apostle here, at the end of this verse 10, gives us a hint of what he is going to take up in verse 12. There he begins his treatment of the great doctrine of our being 'in Christ' and no longer 'in Adam'. Here he gives the first hint of that. We are now in the life of Christ, and because we are in the life of Christ we are eternally safe, we are eternally secure. We have been looking at the mightiest argument you have ever met in your life, and you will never meet a greater. 'For if, while (when) we were enemies, we were reconciled unto God by the death of his Son, how much more, having been reconciled, shall we be saved in his life!' He is in Heaven, says Paul to the Ephesians, and we have been quickened with Him. We have been raised with Him, and we are now seated with Him in the heavenly places [*Ephesians* 2:5–6]. 'Whom he hath justified, them he hath also glorified.' It is as certain as that. May God give us grace to work out this mighty argument in order that we may rejoice in our great salvation!

Twelve

*

For if, when we were enemies, we were reconciled to God by the death of his Son, much more, being reconciled, we shall be saved by his life.

And not only so, but we also joy in God through our Lord Jesus Christ, by whom we have now received the atonement.

Romans 5: 10, 11

You would have imagined that in the marvellous statements of verses 9 and 10 the Apostle had finished his argument; but such is not the case. He still feels that he has something to add to it; so we go on to verse 11, which ends the first half of this chapter. In verse 12, as we shall see, he takes up another theme which is not so much different as a continuation along another line. The end of this first argument, this first section, is found in verse 11. He introduces it by saying, 'And not only so', as if to say, All that I have just said is true, but it is not everything. 'Not only so'. That is true, but because of that, something else is also true. It is that 'we also joy in God through our Lord Jesus Christ, through whom we have now received the atonement'. Here is this further thing which the Apostle asks us to consider.

We start with the expression translated in the Authorized Version as 'joy in God'. It is exactly the same word as the Apostle used in the second verse and the third verse. In the second verse it is, 'rejoice in hope of the glory of God', and in the third verse, 'And not only so, but we glory in tribulation also'. As we have seen, the best translation of this word is 'glory'. 'We', he says, 'also glory in God through our Lord Jesus Christ, by whom we have now received the atonement.' The addition therefore is that, if we understand the teaching, we not only have safety, certainty, security, but in addition, and beyond it all, we glory in God.

What is the difference between this and what he said in verse 2, 'and rejoice (or glory) in hope of the glory of God?' Is that the same as to 'glory in God'? The answer is that there is a real difference between them. In verse 2 Paul says that we are looking forward to, and glorying in the fact that we shall share and enjoy the glory which God has prepared for us. There, we are looking forward to our enjoyment of the state of glory which we are going to enter into beyond this life and beyond death and the grave. But what he says here, in verse 11, is that we glory in God Himself; not only in the glory which we are going to share with Him, but in God Himself. That is the difference between the two statements. It is one thing to look forward with keen anticipation, and with rejoicing, to that ultimate state of glorification in which the very body will be glorified and entirely delivered from sin, when we shall dwell in a land where there is no sighing, nor sorrow nor sin nor shame; but it is something even greater to glory in God Himself here and now. That is glorying in what God is going to give us, and in what He gives us in anticipation now through the Holy Spirit, but this is glorying in the Giver Himself, in God Himself.

What does the Apostle mean by saying that we glory or rejoice or exult in God? The simplest and the most convenient answer that I can give is to remind you of the first question and its answer in the Shorter Catechism of the Westminster Assembly. The question is, 'What is the chief end of man?' And the answer is, 'Man's chief end is to glorify God, and to enjoy Him for ever'. That is the meaning here – to 'enjoy' Him. Glorying in God means to rejoice in God, to enjoy Him for ever. It means loving Him, praising Him, having God as our chiefest delight.

This idea is to be found frequently in the Psalms. Take, for instance, the opening of the thirty-third Psalm. 'Rejoice in the Lord, all ye righteous; for praise is comely for the upright.' Then, 'Sing unto him a new song; play skilfully with a loud noise'. Then take the thirty-fourth Psalm: 'I will bless the Lord at all times: his praise shall continually be in my mouth. My soul shall make her boast in the Lord; the humble shall hear thereof and be glad'. Then he invites everybody to join him:

'O magnify the Lord with me, and let us exalt his name together.' There is a man 'glorying in God', and he scarcely knows how to express himself adequately. 'Bless the Lord, O my soul, and all that is within me, bless his holy name', as says the one-hundred-and-third Psalm.

A beautiful expression of this glorying is found also in what is called the Magnificat, where Mary begins her exultation with the words, 'My soul doth magnify the Lord, and my spirit hath rejoiced in God my Saviour' [*Luke* 1:46–47]. That is what is meant by 'glorying in God'. The great question for us to ask ourselves is whether this is an accurate description of us? To the Apostle it is an inevitable deduction, a part of the mighty logic. 'Not only so', but 'also'!

Why should this follow inevitably? One reason is that God is the Source and Fount of every blessing that we have and enjoy. Many of our greatest hymns express this:

Ransomed, healed, restored, forgiven,
Who like thee His praise should sing?

And again:

Praise God, from whom all blessings flow.

All blessings come from Him.
And again:

Come, Thou Fount of every blessing,
Tune my heart to sing Thy grace.

'Every good gift and every perfect gift is from above and cometh down from the Father of lights . . .' It is all from Him. The Christian, the man who understands all the Apostle has been saying, of necessity must glory and rejoice in God. True Christian faith should always lead to this. I go further; a true Christian faith always does lead to this. That is why I asked the question, Are we glorying, rejoicing, exulting in God?

In the Epistle to the Philippians the Apostle puts this in the form of an exhortation, virtually in the form of a command. 'Finally, my brethren,' he says, 'rejoice in the Lord' [*Philippians*

3:1]. But he cannot leave it at that; in chapter 4 verse 4 he says, 'Rejoice in the Lord alway; and again I say, Rejoice.' This is the norm of the Christian life; this should be the chief characteristic of the Christian. It is the hallmark of a true Christian faith – 'Rejoice in the Lord alway'. There is something seriously wrong with the Christian of whom this is not true. It is sinful not to rejoice in Him always.

The Apostle, in order to help us, tells us here why we should rejoice in God, and how we can rejoice in God. As always, it is 'through our Lord Jesus Christ'. And then to make it still more plain and specific for us, 'By whom (through whom) we have now received the atonement'.

It is a pity that the Authorized Version translators should have used the word 'atonement' here, because it is exactly the same word that is translated in verse 10 as 'reconciled'. It means 'By whom we have now received the reconciliation'. Ultimately it does not matter; but I draw attention to the fact that it should have been translated 'reconciliation', for this reason. You may find yourself arguing with people who are heterodox and who really do not have a doctrine of the Atonement at all, and you say to them, 'But in verse 11 of chapter 5 of the Epistle to the Romans, we read, "By whom we have received the atonement". Immediately they will reply, to your discomfiture, by saying, 'That is a bad translation, it should have been "reconciliation"'. Technically they are right, it is 'reconciliation'.

This reminds us that we must not base our argument for the doctrine of the Atonement upon a single word. The argument for the Atonement, and the penal substitutionary view of the Atonement, does not depend upon the word 'atonement'; and we must be careful not to talk too much about at-one-ment, and so on. It is 'reconciliation', the word we have already interpreted, that which only happens 'by the blood of Christ' which is a propitiation for our sins. What the Apostle means is that we rejoice in God through the Lord Jesus Christ who has reconciled us unto God in the way that he has shown in verse 9 and 10 – by His blood, by His death. Surely, he argues, we cannot refrain from this, surely this needs no argument or demonstration. A man who knows that he has been reconciled to God, that his sins are forgiven, that he has been made a child of God through the Lord Jesus Christ, and especially through what He did on the Cross, surely such a man must of necessity glory and rejoice and exult in God.

That is the exposition. Let us now turn to the application, and let us begin by asking a question. Are we rejoicing and glorying in God? Do we realize that it is our duty to do so? It may help if we look at some of the causes of our failure to rejoice in God as we ought. Let me remind you again that not to rejoice and not to glory in God through Christ is to be guilty of sin. 'Not only so, but we also joy in God' – we do glory in Him says the Apostle; and we all should glory in God in this way.

What then accounts for failure to do so? First, a failure to grasp the truth of justification by faith only. That should be obvious because, as we have seen, the object and purpose of this section is to show the consequences of justification by faith only. If therefore we are not led eventually to glory in God, it means that somewhere or other we have failed to follow the argument, or perhaps are still not clear about justification itself. If we are still trusting to our own works and efforts, or our own goodness, it is not surprising that we are not glorying in God, because that means that we are glorying in ourselves. You cannot glory in God and in yourself at the same time. The man who glories in himself does not glory in God. Like the Pharisee in the Temple, depicted in our Lord's parable, he just thanks God for being what he is. 'Whose praise is in themselves and not in God.' As our Lord once put it to the Pharisees, 'How can ye believe which receive honour one of another, and seek not the honour (the glory) that cometh from God only?' [*John* 5:44]. No Pharisee ever rejoices in God; as far as they rejoice at all they rejoice in themselves; and there is always an element of misery even in that.

The second reason is, that there are many Christians who, while they do not fall into that first category, nevertheless still partly look to their own works. In a sense they have seen the uselessness of relying on their own righteousness only, and they have some idea of justification by faith, but still they feel that they have to supplement that. They still look partly to themselves and their own works for their salvation. They push self out of the front door, as it were, and before they know where they are, it has come creeping in at the back door. How difficult it is to keep out this reliance on works. We all know something about this. 'Having begun in the Spirit, are ye now made perfect by the flesh?' says Paul to the Galatians [*Galatians* 3:3]. We are all subject to this. In a most insidious way self and self-reliance, our works and goodness, will keep on coming back and creeping into our thinking. But they must not come in at all, and there can be no true glorying in God while any of this self-merit is left.

A third cause of failure to glory in God and to rejoice in Him is the result of looking too much at ourselves and at the plague and blackness of our own hearts. Some may be surprised at my saying that, because I constantly exhort people to examine themselves. I do that, of course, because of the popular evangelical teaching which says, 'Do not look at yourself, look away to the Lord'. Self-examination is vital and essential. A man who does not know something of the plague of his own heart is, to say the least, a very poor specimen of a Christian. But it is equally important that we should not press that to the point of morbidity and introspection, and spend the whole of our lives in looking into ourselves and at the blackness of our own hearts. For if we do, we shall certainly not know what it is to glory in God.

But let me say this. If I had to choose one or the other, I would prefer the man who may even be a little morbid, but who does know the plague of his own heart, to the glib, superficial, light-hearted kind of Christian who has never yet known and realized the foulness and the vileness of his own nature and the depth of sin within him. The joy of the second man is not a rejoicing in God; he does not realize the position, and therefore it is a false joy. But we must not allow ourselves to react so violently against the false, merely psychological joy, as to rob ourselves of the true joy which we are meant to have. I have known Christians who have done that very thing, with the result that they have gone through this world – to use the phrase of Milton – 'scorning delights and living laborious days'. They have never known what it is to rejoice in God in the way described by the Apostle here, and in the Epistle to the Philippians.

There, then, are some three reasons which explain this partial failure to understand justification by faith. The man who has examined himself and who finds sin and blackness should not stop at that. The discovery should drive him to Christ. So the explanation of this lack of joy in God is a failure somewhere to understand the work of the Lord Jesus Christ, what He has actually done and accomplished for us. It is a failure to realize the 'finished' character of His work and the 'sufficiency' of His work once and for ever.

There are many who fail at this point. They do not fully grasp all that the Apostle has been here expounding; they do not see the completeness, the wholeness, the fullness of the work that was done on the Cross and in the rising again of the Lord Jesus Christ. They do not fully grasp and realize the truth of the last verse in chapter 4: 'Who was delivered for our offences, and was raised again for our justification.' They have not grasped that as they should, and the result is that they are still somewhat confused about justification. They do not see its absolute character, and therefore they are not joying and rejoicing and glorying in God as they should. That is the first reason, some confusion still about justification by faith only.

A second cause of failure to glory in God as we ought is a failure to meditate as we ought, and a failure to spend sufficient time in studying and working out the doctrine and its implications. Our reading of the Scriptures is often far too superficial. We just read a few verses and a brief commentary on them, then offer a brief prayer and rush off to work or something else. But before we can know anything of joy in God we must spend time with these things, and meditate upon them. To use the word of Isaac Watts, you have to *survey* them: 'When I survey the wondrous Cross.' A mere hurried and cursory reading of the Scriptures profits but little and never leads to true joy. As we have 'to take time to be holy', so we need to take time in our reading and studying of the Scriptures.

This is, I suppose, the chief explanation of the difference between the modern type of Christian and the older type, of whom we read, who knew so much about this 'joy of the Lord'. We are all too busy and too active. Even rushing round from meeting to meeting is no substitute for meditation and that thorough study of Scripture which leads to a grasping of its doctrines. If you simply desire 'spiritual' entertainment you will not know the 'joy of the Lord'; you will only be listening to someone else telling you how wonderful it is. We must reflect upon these things ourselves. A butterfly type of Christian never knows much about glorying in God. *That* is always the result of facing the great doctrines, looking at them frequently and dwelling on them in your mind.

What does this mean exactly? It means that you reflect upon God Himself and His nature and His being and His character. You reflect upon what God has done – how He has shown and manifested His love and made it plain and clear. You look at it as He has expounded it Himself through His servants in the Word. You meditate upon the grace and the love and the kindness and the compassion of God. You do the same with the Lord Jesus Christ. We must look at Him, we must look to Him, we must think about Him and meditate about Him, and contemplate Him and His love.

Have you noticed, for instance, that in these eleven verses Christ is mentioned nine times? The Apostle started with Him in verse 1 – 'Therefore, being justified by faith we have peace with God'. Wonderful, so let us sing about peace! No: 'through our Lord Jesus Christ'. He makes sure at the beginning that you are not going to leave Him out. Then here he is winding up the argument in verse 11: 'And not only so, but we also joy in God'. Full stop? No! 'Through our Lord Jesus Christ, by whom we have received the reconciliation'. It is only those who know Him who truly know God. It is to the extent to which we realize that everything comes to us through the Lord Jesus Christ that we will praise God and honour Him and glory in Him and glorify His

Name and exult in Him. Let us meditate upon and contemplate these things; let us take time to read and re-read them and work out the argument.

That brings us to the third main theme or principle which is emphasized by the Apostle. We sometimes lack this glorying in God because we do not reason and argue sufficiently out of the Scriptures and draw deductions from them. This exercise is much misunderstood and neglected. If you have really followed the teaching of this section you will have come to the conclusion that there is nothing more important in the Christian life than to know how to reason and argue and deduce from the Scriptural teaching. It is an essential and vital part of faith. What is faith? Faith is an activity, especially an activity, in the first instance, of the mind. This is where we tend to go wrong. We are so concerned to contrast faith and reason that we fall into error. We say rightly that no man can ever reason himself into the Christian life, no man by his own understanding can ever make himself a Christian. 'Therefore,' we say, 'faith has nothing at all to do with reason.' At that point we are wrong. It is most important that we should be right about the relationship between faith and reason. Isaac Watts in a familiar couplet says,

Where reason fails with all her powers,
There faith prevails, and love adores.

And Isaac Watts is right, of course. He is thinking there of our entering into the Christian life, and of what is true sometimes even in the Christian life, when we are tried and fall back on natural reason with the result that we become miserable. What happens in such a case is that we have fallen back on 'natural' reason instead of the reason of faith. In 'the life of faith' reason and argument play a vital part. But it is not the old kind of reason and argument; it is reasoning in faith, reasoning from faith, reasoning to faith. 'Faith', we are told, 'is the substance of things hoped for, the evidence of things not seen' [*Hebrews* 11:1]. That means that we take certain statements and deduce other things from them. But that is reasoning. There is all the difference in the world between trusting only to reason at the expense of faith, and faith which reasons, faith which has her arguments – the kind of reasoning and argument that the Apostle has been deploying in this section.

But let me mention another danger, the danger of our resting too much upon feelings. Faith leads to feelings, and includes feelings, yet feelings do not come first. The first element in faith is intellectual, the emotional follows. As a phrase in a psalm puts it, 'Taste and see that the Lord is good' [*Psalm* 34:8]. You cannot see until you have tasted. We must be clear about the position of feelings. We must not rest too much on them, but neither must we exclude them. Faith is like walking on a knife-edge; if you go too far to one side or the other you will find yourself in trouble.

What then is faith? Faith really means believing God, believing all that He tells us about Himself, all that He tells us about what He has done for us, all that He tells us about what He is going to do, and trusting ourselves utterly and absolutely to that. What is faith? Faith means reasoning and arguing on the basis of revelation. Faith means, not that I try to reason myself to God, but that, believing the revelation given by God, I reason from it. Faith means drawing out the inevitable deductions from what God has said.

Now that is exactly what the Apostle has been doing in this section: 'If, while we were enemies, we were reconciled to God by the death of his Son, much more . . .'. He starts with a revelation and draws his deduction from it. That is what faith does. And we must do this concerning the love of God, and we must do it concerning the character of God, and the absolute certainty of His completing anything that He has ever started. I must argue like this – 'God is the Father of lights with whom is no variableness, neither shadow of turning'. God sees the end from the beginning. God proposes and it is done. So if God starts anything He cannot leave it in an incomplete or unfinished condition. His whole character insists upon His continuing, His eternal integrity demands it. I reason that. I know that God is absolute and unchangeable, 'from eternity to eternity', everlastingly the same, so I know that He will never change. Therefore, if He has set His heart upon me, He will never forsake me. He cannot begin a work in me and then drop it. No! what He begins He finishes. 'He which hath begun a good work in you will perform it until the day of Jesus Christ.' I deduce that; and that is faith.

I further deduce that He can never fail. Not only will sin within me not prevent the carrying out of His purpose, not only will sin without me not prevent it, the devil and Hell cannot prevent it, nothing can prevent it, because it is God who is carrying out His own purpose. That is deducing, that is arguing, that is reasoning; and that is faith.

Faith means doing all this very boldly. You remember how we were told in chapter 4 how Abraham did it – 'he staggered not in unbelief'. He believed God in spite of the fact that what God had said to him seemed utterly impossible. He reasoned boldly, and went on. And you and I must do this; we must not hesitate about these things. 'But', you say, 'is not this presumption? Are you not going too far?' Presumption! This is not presumption, this is the final proof of faith. To argue like this is not presumption, it is simply the exercising of faith. As Charles Wesley says:

Faith, precious faith, the promise sees,
And looks to that alone;
Laughs at impossibilities,
And cries, It shall be done!

Let me challenge you. If you and I do not reason and argue and deduce from this mighty revelation in such a way that it leads us to glorying in God, it means either that we have not understood the truth, or even, perhaps, that we have never really become aware of it; or else that, having seen it, we do not really believe God and trust Him. You may answer again that this sounds very wonderful, but that you have to go back to the streets of London and face the world, the flesh, and the devil, and that you are weak. By saying that, you reveal your lack of understanding! You do not believe that God is strong enough to overcome everybody and everything and to guarantee your final salvation. You either have not seen the truth or else you do not really trust God.

I must press this point. To be uncertain of these things is not a sign of humility or of unusual spirituality and piety; it is a sign of unbelief, which is dishonouring to God. It is an indication that you are listening to the 'accuser of the brethren', to the Adversary, rather than to God. I do not hesitate to make the assertion that the only bit of logic that you and I can be absolutely certain of in this world is the logic of verses 9, 10 and 11 in this chapter. There is no such watertight argument in any other realm, in science, or in mathematics or anywhere else. There are no 'assured results' anywhere else in spite of the arrogant claims. Some of the greatest scientists have been proved to be wrong. There is a fallacy somewhere, and in a century or two, and often much sooner, it will be discovered. I know that there is one argument that can never be refuted, and that will never fail in one iota. It is this: 'If, when we were enemies, we were reconciled to God by the death of his Son, much more, having been reconciled, we shall be saved (in him and) in his life'. That can never fail; it is absolutely certain. This is the only logic that can be guaranteed.

I say, therefore, that not to deduce what the Apostle deduces, not to argue, not to reason in this way, not to rejoice in God, which is the inevitable result of such reasoning, is a sign of unbelief – that horrible sin, the sin of sins! The miserable Christian is guilty of unbelief. The Christian who lacks joy and assurance is either not clear about the truth, or else he is guilty of something much worse, he does not trust God who has revealed that truth to him. Shame on us! We have no right to be uncertain or joyless. To be certain is not presumption and to be joyless is not being humble. The Apostle Paul is humble and yet he has the tremendous certainty of verses 9, 10 and 11. And as for the humility, here it is in verses 6, 7 and 8: 'While we were yet without strength'. You cannot be more humble than to say that about yourself. He has also said that we are 'ungodly'. You cannot think of anything worse than that, and he has added to it – 'while we were yet sinners'.

What fools we are! We regard humility and rejoicing as opposites. 'I am so afraid of false rejoicing', we moan, 'I am so afraid of presumption'. Such speech means that you have misunderstood it all. There is perfect balance here; humility and rejoicing go together and must never be thought of antithetically. Ultimately it is only the man who feels quite hopeless about himself who really trusts God. And he rejoices in his salvation because God has given it to him as a free gift. Many lack this balance in their thinking and experiences. They are so clear about the plague of their own hearts that they are not clear about anything else. They stop at that. They never glory in God, and they give the impression of being miserable. They are always analysing and dissecting themselves spiritually, but their real trouble is that they lack this balance in their thinking. True self-examination should drive us to Christ; and there we see the finished work which God sent Him to do, and we end by rejoicing. If your self-examination does not end in rejoicing it is wrong, it is false. There is a balance in these matters, and we must always have the two sides. Do not be so anxious to correct the false that you also deny the true.

I might illustrate this by relating an experience. I once listened to a man preaching on 'The rainbow in the cloud' after the Flood. He was a good and able man, and a pious man; but he so disliked the type of evangelical who is glib and superficial, and he was so afraid of false joy, that though his text spoke about 'the rainbow in the cloud' he sent us out of that service under a very black cloud! He was so afraid that we might go out with a carnal joy that he concealed the rainbow and magnified the cloud! That is not Scripture, that is not the balance of Scripture, that is not the proportion of faith. God's Word talks about Rainbow *and* Cloud, and we must not try to be wiser than the Scriptures. So let not the light-hearted modern evangelical say, 'There is nothing but a rainbow', for indeed, there are clouds and darkness – the judgment of God. But let not the other – and I say this with equal emphasis – let him not emphasize the cloud so much as to conceal the rainbow. 'Not only so, but we joy in God, through our Lord Jesus Christ.' As Johann Casper Lavater says:

That I am nothing, Thou art all,
I would be daily taught.

Yes, says Isaac Watts:

When I survey the wondrous Cross,
On which the Prince of glory died,
My richest gain I count but loss,
And pour contempt on all my pride.

But he does not spend the whole of his time in pouring contempt upon his pride. No! He goes on:

Forbid it, Lord, that I should boast
Save in the death of Christ my God;
All the vain things that charm me most,
I sacrifice them to His blood.

See from His head, His hands, His feet,
Sorrow and love flow mingled down;
Did e'er such love and sorrow meet,
Or thorns compose so rich a crown?

Were the whole realm of nature mine,
That were an offering far too small;
Love so amazing, so divine,
Demands my soul, my life, my all.

He is glorying in Christ and His wondrous Cross. 'God forbid that I should glory, save in the Cross of our Lord Jesus Christ', says the great Apostle to the Galatians. Do not stop at yourself, do not stay on the ground and in the mud of despair, in failure and in abject misery. Look unto Him; look to the skies, glory in Him and in His glorious Cross, His Resurrection, His Ascension, His heavenly Session, His Coming again, His glorious Kingdom! 'Finally, my brethren, rejoice in the Lord.' 'Rejoice in the Lord alway, and again I say, Rejoice.'

Have you followed the argument? Have you seen the security and the safety of your position? Have you looked rejoicingly at the glory that is awaiting you? If you have done so, if you have seen these things, if you have followed the apostolic argument, the powerful Pauline reasoning, you cannot help glorying and rejoicing in God with him who says:

Praise to the Holiest in the height,
And in the depth be praise;
In all His words most wonderful,
Most sure in all His ways.

O loving wisdom of our God!
When all was sin and shame,
A second Adam to the fight
And to the rescue came.

It was God the Father who planned it all and sent His Son into the world and even to the death of the Cross for us. The Son came and finished the work completely. And the Father and the Son have given the Holy Spirit to apply the salvation which was thus planned in eternity and wrought out in time.

Glory be to God the Father,
Glory be to God the Son,
Glory be to God the Spirit,
Great Jehovah! Three in One!
Glory, Glory, while Eternal Ages run.

Thirteen

*

Wherefore, as by one man sin entered into the world, and death by sin; and so death passed upon all men, for that all have sinned:

(For until the law sin was in the world; but sin is not imputed when there is no law.

Nevertheless death reigned from Adam to Moses, even over them that had not sinned after the similitude of Adam's transgression, who is the figure of him that was to come.

But not as the offence, so also is *the free gift. For if through the offence of one many be dead, much more the grace of God, and the gift by grace,* which is *by one man, Jesus Christ, hath abounded unto many.*

And not as it was *by one that sinned,* so is *the gift; for the judgment* was *by one to condemnation, but the free gift* is *of many offences unto justification.*

For if by one man's offence death reigned by one; much more they which receive abundance of grace and of the gift of righteousness shall reign in life by one, Jesus Christ.)

Therefore as by the offence of one judgment came *upon all men to condemnation; even so by the righteousness of one* the free gift came *upon all men unto justification of life.*

For as by one man's disobedience many were made sinners, so by the obedience of one shall many be made righteous.

Moreover the law entered, that the offence might abound. But where sin abounded, grace did much more abound:

That as sin hath reigned unto death, even so might grace reign through righteousness unto eternal life by Jesus Christ our Lord.

Romans 5: 12–21

This verse introduces a new section, or at any rate a new sub-section, of this Epistle. I have shown earlier that a new section began at the first verse of this chapter. The Apostle has rounded off the first theme at the end of verse 11. Now he takes up a fresh theme which he introduces with the word 'Wherefore'. This word suggests a connection with what has gone before; nevertheless,

I hope to show that we have here a very important point of transition. This means that we shall have to spend some time in considering this word 'Wherefore'. This will involve a good deal of thinking, and we shall have to obey Peter's exhortation, 'Gird up the loins of your mind', as we handle what may be called the mechanics of interpretation. We have to do that, otherwise we shall not be able to appreciate as we ought the real riches of this new section of the Epistle.

The section starts here at verse 12 and goes on to the end of the chapter. In working through the previous verses we have been revelling in the glorious statements concerning God's love to us and enjoying ourselves in contemplating that love in its various aspects. That kind of thing is sheer enjoyment. But we cannot always have that. It is right to have enjoyment, but you cannot live on enjoyment. You cannot have a living and functioning body without a skeleton; so you must start with the skeleton. You cannot put up a building without erecting a scaffolding. That is absolutely essential. In order to arrive at the great and moving doctrines we have first to struggle with the problem of correct exegesis. Failure to do that has often been the cause of heresy. It involves hard work, but it is essential, and always rewarding.

We are faced immediately by the question of the exact significance of the use of the word 'Wherefore' here. Why does the Apostle use it at this point when he is taking up a fresh theme? The word he used can also be translated by the word 'Therefore'. This problem has perplexed not only the ordinary readers of the Bible but also the commentators on this Epistle; and it has led to a good deal of disagreement and disputation. Some may be tempted to say, 'Does it matter? Why not get on with the interpretation? Why bother to notice the connection?' I trust I shall be able to show that the connection is really most important. You do not really understand the Pauline epistles unless you understand the way in which the mind of the Apostle works, and the reason why he says a thing where he says it, and when he says it, and not at some other point. In any case, it is surely unintelligent to pass a word like this 'Wherefore', and just to skip over it unthinkingly. When a man like the Apostle Paul says 'Wherefore' he has a reason for doing so, and it is insulting to the author whom we are reading if we do not ask questions in order to discover that reason.

In passing, may I give this bit of instruction with regard to the method of reading the Bible. If you really want to enjoy your reading and studying of the Bible, always ask it questions. So, when Paul says 'Wherefore', you ask, 'Why did he say "wherefore"? What was his purpose and object in doing so here?' You then try to work out the answer.

Some say that the Apostle from this twelfth verse to the end of the chapter is merely adding a kind of epilogue to what he has already been saying. They argue that he has been expounding the doctrine of 'justification by faith only' since the twenty-first verse of the third chapter, where he introduced it with the words 'But now', and that this has occupied him to the end of chapter 4. Then they say that in chapter 5, verses 1–11, he has been drawing deductions from the doctrine; and now in a kind of epilogue he sums it all up. It is nothing but a kind of epilogue to what has gone before. I hope to show, as we proceed, that this is a completely inadequate explanation of the Apostle's 'Wherefore'.

Others, disagreeing with the epilogue view, say that Paul introduces this question of Adam and our relationship to Adam, and the comparison between Adam and the Lord Jesus Christ, just because it was a matter of interest to him as a rabbinical Jew, and that it is but a kind of parenthesis between the doctrine of justification, which ends in chapter 5 verse 11, and the doctrine of sanctification, which he introduces in the first verse of chapter 6. To such, the word 'Wherefore' is just a word of transition, unimportant in and of itself, and verses 12–21 have no real connection with what has gone before or with what is going to follow.

Another view which I must mention by name because of its popularity is the view taken by the so-called Scofield Bible. The view taken there of this 'Wherefore' is that it refers back to the third chapter, verses 19–23, and is therefore to be regarded as a resumption of the discussion on the universality of sin there which – notice the word – was 'interrupted' by the passage on justification by faith and its results. So that here, Paul goes back again to that theme which had been 'interrupted' and takes it up and shows the universality of sin once more. In addition to that, says Scofield – and he has a big heading here – the Apostle starts his doctrine of sanctification at this point and goes on with it until chapter 8, verse 13. The heading is, 'Indwelling sin and the Gospel remedy'.

I must say that I thoroughly disagree with that analysis. To start with, it does not seem to realize the significance of Romans 3:21 – the 'But now'. What Scofield calls the 'interruption' about justification does not start at verse 24 but at verse 21; and far from being an interruption, everything that Paul had been saying had been leading up to it. The Apostle had shown the universality of sin in the second half of chapter 1 and in chapter 2, also in chapter 3 up to the end of verse 20. He had done so in order to introduce his glorious Gospel and to show its absolute necessity. The teaching about justification is no 'interruption'; it is indeed the great theme of the Epistle, the central theme of the Christian message. The view that the Apostle takes up here an interrupted theme seems to me to do grave injustice to the third chapter, the fourth chapter, and the first part of the fifth chapter, and completely misses the point in the verse we are now examining. Furthermore, the Apostle does not suddenly introduce the doctrine of sanctification here; he is, as I hope to show, doing something very different. The Scofield note shows the danger of becoming slaves to classifications, and of separating justification and sanctification. In other words that exposition does not really explain this 'Wherefore' at all; it leaves it in mid-air. It regards it as just an unimportant word of conjunction which has no real relevance or meaning.

The only other view I mention is that of the great Charles Hodge. He says that this passage, verses 12–21, is introduced here as an illustration of the doctrine of justification; and he seems to confine it to that. I agree that it has a connection with the doctrine of justification, and is in a sense an extension of it, but I reject the suggestion that it is nothing more than an illustration of that doctrine. It goes far beyond that to something yet more glorious. Charles Hodge in his Commentary, of course, brings in this other matter; but he does not seem to see the force of the word 'Wherefore', and the reason why the Apostle used it here. We must not confine it to justification since it goes well beyond that doctrine.

Rejecting such explanations of the use of the word 'Wherefore' in our text, let us face the matter positively. What was it that made the Apostle introduce at this point this whole section about Adam, and the comparison between Adam and the Lord Jesus Christ, and our relationship to the two? The questions that should be asked are these: Has this section any relevance to the whole argument of the Epistle to the Romans, and if so, what is it? Does this section follow naturally from what has just been said, or is it an entirely new departure? To these we add one final question: If this new section does follow on from what the Apostle has been saying before, does it follow on in a general way from the whole previous argument, or is it linked only with what he has just been saying in the immediate context? Both those explanations are possible. You can argue that the Apostle having finished his great exposition of justification by faith and its consequences goes on here to draw the greatest deduction of all from it; or you can say that the connection is a more local and immediate one with what he has said in verses 9–11. Which is it?

I suggest that both these views are correct – that these verses, from verse 12 to verse 21, have an immediate connection with verses 9–11, and at the same time can only be really and fully understood in the light of all the Apostle has been saying from the sixteenth verse in the first chapter. In other words, the 'Wherefore' must be given its due weight. The Apostle Paul, we must always remember, had a most logical mind. He generally moves from step to step and from stage to stage. There is always in his letters a skeleton, a definite structure. He did not write his letters in the way some of us tend to do. We think of something to say and we say it, and then we pause and ask ourselves, Is there anything else I can say or ought to say? If so, we put that in. Nothing is further removed from the Apostle's method. He thought clearly, and logically, and always planned what he wrote. He is always presenting a case, and he advances and develops it from step to step and stage to stage. Often, as we shall see here in this very section, he seems to fly off at a tangent because something draws him out, but he always comes back to his point and goes on steadily with his argument. He marshals his evidence and unfolds his case. He does not simply throw out thoughts at random without any connection between them.

In this respect Paul differs from certain modern preachers who are very good and helpful in their own way, but it is extremely difficult to discover a clear line in what they are saying. They make a number of remarks all of which are excellent and profitable, but it is difficult to see the connection between them, how they originated in the mind and why they introduced them at various points. This is particularly true of preachers who happen to be poets and who think in pictures. It is true also of the anecdotal type of preacher. They are difficult to follow because their sermons lack a scheme and order and arrangement. Other preachers are logical; they start with an introduction, then proceed to a first point, which leads in turn to a second point and that to a third point, and finally to a climax and conclusion. The Apostle Paul certainly belonged to the second class. His method generally was that which he employed in the synagogue at Thessalonica where we are told that he 'reasoned', 'opening and alleging' the facts of the Gospel [*Acts* 17: 1–3].

Let us see then exactly what he is doing here. 'Wherefore', he says. Why does he use that word? I suggest that the key is to be found in one little word at the end of verse 10. I directed attention to this when we were considering that verse which in the Authorized Version reads, 'For if, when we were enemies, we were reconciled to God by the death of his Son, much more, being reconciled, we shall be saved by his life'. But I emphasized that the final phrase should not have the word 'by' but rather 'in', so that it should read, '. . . much more, being reconciled, we shall be saved in his life'. 'In' was the word the Apostle actually used. In the margin of the Revised Version it is so translated – 'in' His life.

Arthur S. Way in his excellent translation of Paul's Epistles also has 'in' His life. J. N. Darby, in his translation of the Bible, actually puts it like this – 'in', and then in brackets ('the power of') 'his life'. That is right, that is exactly what it means. The word 'in' means 'in the sphere of', or 'in the realm of', or 'in connection with' His life. J. B. Phillips, whose translation is more a paraphrase, and often an interpretation, and with which I often find myself in disagreement, puts it like this: 'Surely now that we are reconciled we may be perfectly certain of our salvation through His *living in us*'. I do not agree with that as a whole but it certainly emphasizes the idea that there is an intimate connection between Christ and ourselves. We are not being saved 'by' His life, we are being saved 'in' His life.

But what bearing has this on the use of the word 'Wherefore' here? In the tenth verse the Apostle is asserting what he has already hinted at in the ninth verse, that we are not only forgiven in Christ, that the work of the Lord Jesus Christ on our behalf does not merely procure our pardon and our forgiveness. It goes beyond that. We are 'in Christ'. That is God's way of saving us. Our salvation is not only external and judicial and forensic. It is that, of course, primarily; it is His righteousness imputed to us; but it goes beyond that. The reconciliation in Christ Jesus not only leads to the forgiveness of sins and the declaration that God regards us as righteous, it puts us into Christ, and we shall be saved ultimately and finally 'in' His life. If by His death He has delivered us from the wrath of God and the punishment of our sins, it is by our being linked to Him and His life that we are going to be saved from everything that has separated us from the life of God. Was not that the argument of verse 10 – 'If when we were enemies we were reconciled to God by the death of his Son, much more, being reconciled, we shall be saved in his life'? The Apostle's purpose is to show us the absolute certainty and finality of our salvation, and the ultimate proof of that is that we are 'in Christ', in His life, and that nothing can ever sever that connection.

I suggest therefore that verses 12–21 come in in this way. We are now 'in' the life of Christ. But that at once suggests our previous position, and what caused it. The Apostle now proceeds to deal with that, and introduces it naturally by the word 'Wherefore'. He is going to show that we have the same relationship now to the Lord Jesus Christ as we had, before our salvation, to Adam. The connection expressed in the word 'Wherefore' thus becomes quite clear. Having used the expression about our being 'in Christ', Paul now goes on to emphasize that our salvation is not a matter of forgiveness only but a radical change in our whole position and standing before God. We are now 'in Christ', but formerly we were 'in Adam'. The apostle had emphasized our relationship to the Lord Jesus Christ in verse 10 in order to show the certainty and finality of our salvation, and he is still concerned about that. The certainty of our salvation depends ultimately upon our being in Christ, upon our status and standing in the sight of God. So the Apostle, in order to make this quite clear, deals with it in detail, showing how believers and all mankind were formerly in Adam but now as the result of their justification by faith, believers are 'in Christ'.

In doing so Paul shows us at one and the same time our need of salvation and the glory and perfection of the way of salvation in Christ Jesus. Indeed, verses 12–21 are a continuation of the 'much more' of verses 9 and 10, and in particular an exposition of the expression 'in his life' at the end of verse 10. But at the same time they provide an explanation of all that he has said about Jews and Gentiles in the section that runs from chapter 1 verse 8 to chapter 3 verse 20. The new section has both a local connection and a more general connection. It shows why we all need to be redeemed, and how justification by faith alone is the means of our salvation through Christ Jesus, but also how that makes possible new life in Christ Jesus.

I make bold to suggest, indeed to assert (and at this point I find myself in agreement with the Swedish Lutheran theologian Nygren) that in many ways this section from verse 12 to the end of the chapter is the very heart and centre of the Epistle to the Romans. First, it is a summary or summing up of all that has gone before. The apostle states it all here in a new way. But it is not only that, it is also the beginning of, and introduction to, all he is going to say right until the end of chapter 8. It is the most crucial section of the entire Epistle. Failure to realize this accounts for most of the vagaries in interpretation.

It is a summary, I say, of everything that has gone before. It takes us right back to the first chapter, verses 16, 17 and 18. There the Apostle announces what is going to be the theme of his letter. He has told them before how he longs to see them, how he longs to be with them because he has got a good deal to tell them. He has never met the greater part of them, so he writes them a letter. He is hoping to visit them, but until that happens he wants them to know more about the Gospel committed to his trust. Hence he writes, 'I am not ashamed of the gospel of Christ, for it is the power of God unto salvation to every one that believeth, to the Jew first, and also to the Greek. For therein is a righteousness of God revealed from faith to faith, as it is written, The just shall live by faith. For the wrath of God is revealed from heaven against all ungodliness and unrighteousness of men, who hold down the truth in unrighteousness.' That is the original statement which he then proceeds to work out. He had proved that the wrath of God is upon the Gentiles and upon the Jews; it is upon all mankind. But he thanks God that he has this new message, which is that God has done something in Jesus Christ which delivers us from that wrath and gives us His righteousness as a free gift. We can be justified by faith and be reconciled to God.

Having worked that out the Apostle now says in effect: 'I have been showing how the whole world was under the wrath of God.' But how is it that the whole world is under the wrath of God? What has happened to mankind that it should be in that terrible condition? Why should mankind be suffering under the wrath of God in the way that we have seen? His answer is that it is all because of what Adam did, and he tells us about that in this section. So he is taking one further step in the great theme of mankind fallen and under the wrath of God and Jesus Christ coming to save and to restore us to God. To understand our problem and our need we must understand what happened to Adam, and our relationship to Adam. In Adam we are all lost, but in Christ is redemption for all who believe. Now as this is the subject with which Paul is going to deal in this section he is surely justified in introducing it with the word 'Wherefore'.

That is the main idea; but there is also a subsidiary idea. The people to whom he was writing found it very difficult, as people still do, to believe in this doctrine of the imputing of the righteousness of Christ to us. People still stumble, as they did then, at this doctrine of justification by faith only. We tend to go on thinking that we have to save ourselves by living a good life, and that we can make ourselves Christians. There is always a difficulty about receiving salvation as a free gift through the righteousness of Jesus Christ. The Apostle deals with that in a new and fresh way here. He points out that there is nothing new in this idea of imputation because the story of the entire human race can only be understood in terms of our relationship to Adam and the imputation of his sin to us.

In other words God has always dealt with mankind through a head and representative. The whole story of the human race can be summed up in terms of what has happened because of Adam, and what has happened and will yet happen because of Christ. Consider the state of the world at the present time. Think of the armaments, the atomic bombs, the preparation for war, and the actual fighting taking place. What is going to happen? Will there be a third world war? Then think of all the misery and unhappiness, the moral breakdown, thieving, robbery, murders, divorce, separation, all these things. Why is it like that? And why has it always been like that? The history books tell us that this has always been the pattern of things. The world is no different today from what it has always been. But why is this so?

The Apostle Paul answers the question here. He says that it all results from Adam, that it is all tied up with what Adam did, and our relationship to him. But that is only one half of the story of mankind. There is the story of the Christian Church, and Christian people. There are people, and have been people, who are clearly different. Something has happened to them, they have undergone a great experience, they seem to be new creatures. They have found a new joy and happiness, they claim to know God as their Father, and they are being delivered from the tyranny of sin.

What has happened to them? It is all because of what Christ has done and their relationship to Him. That is the whole history of humanity, past, present and future. All depends upon our relationship to Adam and our relationship to Christ.

The Apostle puts it here in one great and momentous paragraph. He summarizes all he has been saying. He has taken us through it in great detail, but now he puts it in this new way. He had not mentioned Adam before, he had simply proved that all the Gentiles were in sin and under the wrath of God, and likewise the Jews. But he had not told us so far how we had become involved in this calamitous situation. Now he gives the explanation – it was the result of our relationship to Adam. Again, he has been describing positively the glorious salvation, and he has told us that it is through the blood of Christ, the death of Christ, the righteousness of Christ; but here he tells us that it is even more than that – our participation in the blessing is the result of our relationship to Christ. So we see that there is continuity, both in general and in particular, with what the Apostle has been saying before.

But, secondly, I have said that it is not merely a summary of the past, but that it goes far beyond that in thought and scope. Through this little word 'in' ('in the life of Christ', verse 10) the Apostle introduces us to this marvellous, amazing doctrine of our union with Christ. This is what he now desires to expound and to emphasize – all still, remember, in the interest of the absolute certainty of our full and ultimate deliverance – and he does so by showing that our old relationship to Adam provides us with a picture of our new relationship to Christ. He says that explicitly in verse 14: 'Nevertheless, death reigned from Adam to Moses, even over them that had not sinned after the similitude of Adam's transgression, who (Adam) is the figure of him that was to come'. Adam, he says, is a figure, a picture of Christ, in one sense a type of Christ. Understand Adam and in a sense you will begin to understand Christ. The relationship of mankind to Adam is a picture of the relationship of the redeemed to the Lord Jesus Christ. In his First Epistle to the Corinthians, chapter 15, he puts it still more plainly when he says that Christ is 'the last Adam'

[1 *Corinthians* 15: 45]. He calls Him 'the last Adam', and then in verse 47 he calls Him 'the second Man'. Adam was the first man, Christ is the second Man. Adam was the first Adam, Christ is the last Adam. There have only been two heads to the human race, Adam and Christ. There will never be another. And every one of us is either 'in Adam' or else 'in Christ'.

That is why and how the Apostle brings in this truth concerning Adam. The Lord Jesus Christ, he would have us understand, is the Head of a new humanity. There is a new race of men. As he says later in chapter 8, verse 29, 'Christ is the first-born of many brethren'. Indeed, the Lord Jesus Christ has introduced a new Age, a new Kingdom, a new Order altogether. What Paul wants us to see is that as Christians we are not only forgiven, we have become members of a new humanity, a new race. We are 'in Christ', and because we are in Christ we are in God, as it were, members of the household of God, and children of God. God is our Father in a new sense, and we are His children. Not only are we forgiven, we are delivered from the realm of sin and death and of wrath and of punishment. We are in a new realm of righteousness and joy and peace and life everlasting which can never be destroyed, and from which nothing can ever separate us. We are no longer under the reign of sin, we are destined to reign in life ourselves. That is what Paul wants us to see, and here he begins to introduce us to the glories of our state and position. He has already suggested it in verse 10 by that little word 'in'. He is now about to tell us something of what it means to be in the life of Christ. We were in the life of Adam before; we are in the life of Christ now. And if we are to rejoice in these things, if we are to 'joy in God', as he has been saying in verse 11, we must understand these truths. It is the man, the woman, who really knows what it means to be 'in Christ', who really rejoices. Not only forgiven, not merely forgiven, but 'in' this new realm, a part of this new humanity, an 'heir of God', and 'a joint-heir with Christ'!

I again assert that we are going to look at what is undoubtedly the most important section, in a sense, of the whole of this wonderful Epistle. It is the key to the understanding of the whole argument. If we do not understand this section it means that we have not yet got a clear understanding of what we have already been studying; and it certainly means that we shall not understand what we now proceed to consider.

What then are the subjects that are dealt with in this vital section? First, the doctrine of Original Sin. Have you realized that this is the classic passage in the Bible on the doctrine of original sin? This is the very hub of it, the centre, the *locus classicus*. It is the most important passage in the whole of Scripture on that doctrine. What a section it is!

Secondly, it is a most important passage with reference to the historicity of the first three chapters of the Book of Genesis. Alas, there are many Christian people today who say, 'Oh, it does not matter whether you accept the first three chapters of the Book of Genesis as history or not; it makes no difference to our salvation'. Quite apart from the attitude displayed to the authority of the Scriptures by such a statement, it is entirely wrong from the standpoint of the doctrine of salvation. This section insists upon our accepting the story in Genesis as literal actual fact and history. You do not really understand the need of salvation unless you believe that history, and understand what happened in Adam, and our relationship to Adam. So it is a most important section, and it is only those who have understood its teaching who have not allowed certain scientists to stampede them into accepting the theory of evolution.

Thirdly, it is a most important section in terms of what is known as the 'Covenant Theology' which teaches that God always deals with man through a covenant, through an agreement. This idea is prominent in the Epistle to the Hebrews. God always deals with man through a covenant, and He always has someone to represent man in the covenant. Adam was the first representative; the Lord Jesus Christ is the second.

For these reasons – the doctrine of original sin, the historicity of Genesis, covenant theology – it is plain that this section of the Epistle is absolutely vital to a true understanding of the doctrine of Redemption. Paul has already been explaining that in detail in terms of 'propitiation'. What we have here is the doctrine of Redemption stated in broad terms and especially its ultimate aspects. The scope and sweep of this paragraph is one of the greatest and widest to be found anywhere in the writings of this Apostle, or indeed anywhere in the whole of Scripture. Paul seems to stand back and take a grand view of the whole panorama of Redemption. There we were in Adam; here we are in Christ. And because we are in Christ we are in Him for ever and ever; we are safe, we are secure. As he will tell us at the end of chapter 8, 'Nothing can ever separate us from the love of God, which is in Christ Jesus our Lord.'

It is idle to jump into the details and the particular statements unless you have the background in your mind, unless you see exactly what the Apostle is doing, and why he does it at this particular point. I trust that that is now plain and clear. We can test ourselves in that respect by asking this question: Do you realize, have you realized, that you are 'in Christ'? Have you realized the meaning of that term? How often one meets it in the New Testament! Have you understood clearly why you are a sinner, why we are all sinners by nature? Are you clear about it? That is what is explained here.

But the positive aspect is still more important. Do you really understand what redemption, what salvation, really means? Do you see that the forgiveness of sins is but the first step, and that the really glorious thing is that we are in Christ, that 'old things are passed away, behold, all things are become new?' We are members of a new race of people, the people of God, men and women who shall be His people for ever and for ever. What grand security we have because we are 'in Christ'! The Christian is not one who is redeemed and saved today but who may fall from it tomorrow and be lost. There is no 'in and out' in salvation. You are either 'in Adam' or you are 'in Christ', and if you are 'in Christ' you have eternal security, you are in Him for ever.

Fourteen

*

Wherefore, as by one man sin entered into the world, and death by sin; and so death passed upon all men, for that all have sinned:

(For until the law sin was in the world; but sin is not imputed when there is no law.

Nevertheless death reigned from Adam to Moses, even over them that had not sinned after the similitude of Adam's transgression, who is the figure of him that was to come.

But not as the offence, so also is *the free gift. For if through the offence of one many be dead, much more the grace of God, and the gift by grace,* which is *by one man, Jesus Christ, hath abounded unto many.*

And not as it was *by one that sinned,* so is *the gift; for the judgment* was *by one to condemnation, but the free gift* is *of many offences unto justification.*

For if by one man's offence death reigned by one; much more they which receive abundance of grace and of the gift of righteousness shall reign in life by one, Jesus Christ.)

Therefore as by the offence of one judgment came *upon all men to condemnation; even so by the righteousness of one* the free gift came *upon all men unto justification of life.*

For as by one man's disobedience many were made sinners, so by the obedience of one shall many be made righteous.

Moreover the law entered, that the offence might abound. But where sin abounded, grace did much more abound:

That as sin hath reigned unto death, even so might grace reign through righteousness unto eternal life by Jesus Christ our Lord.

Romans 5: 12–21

We continue our study of this section which I have described as the turning-point or the centre of the Epistle, where the Apostle states in a few verses his great essential message, namely, salvation in Christ Jesus. It looks backwards and forwards and introduces us to central and fundamental biblical doctrines.

Having looked at it as a whole we now come to a general

analysis of the scope of the section. I say a 'general' analysis because with this section, as indeed with every other section of Scripture, if we know how to read our Scriptures properly, it is always wise to have a general analysis before we proceed to a particular analysis. If our minds understand the scheme, the drift and scope of the whole section, we shall be in a better position to deal with some of the intricacies and difficulties of the particular statements.

As we start with verse 12 we are arrested at once by the little word 'as'. 'Wherefore, as by one man sin entered into the world, and death by sin . . .' The word 'as' immediately suggests a comparison. The apostle is starting on a comparison, 'as' – 'so'; 'as' – 'even so'. We are familiar with this method in working out certain sums in arithmetic involving proportion – as this is to that, so is a third thing to a fourth. In verse 12, clearly enough, the Apostle is embarking upon a comparison. But we notice that in this verse he does not complete his comparison; he, as it were, leaves the word 'as' in mid-air and does not take us on to the 'even so'. This is important because some have argued that the 'and so' in the middle of the verse means 'even so', and would read the statement like this, 'Wherefore, as by one man sin entered into the world, and death by sin, even so death passed upon all men, for that all have sinned'. The simple answer to that is that the Apostle wrote 'and so', and 'and so' can never mean 'even so', for this good reason, that 'and so' does not suggest a contrast but rather a continuation. But it is clear that the Apostle is starting on a comparison and contrast. This is not a matter of opinion, for even those who would translate this as 'even so' have to admit that they are doing violence to the language that the Apostle actually used. The Apostle writes 'and so' and it is vital that we should bear that in mind.

For proof of this point look at verse 18 and observe the precise terms used by the Apostle: 'Therefore, as by the offence of one man judgment came upon all men to condemnation, even so . . .' There is an 'as' followed very rightly by an 'even so'. There, you have parallel, the comparison worked out, 'as' – 'even so'. But he does not speak in this way in verse 12. He continues with his statement in the words, 'Wherefore, as by one man sin entered into the world, and death by sin, and so death passed upon all men, for that all have sinned'. So we have this interesting point that a comparison is started here but not completed. Instead of completing his comparison he goes off on a parenthesis. In the Authorized Version there is a bracket at the beginning of verse 13 and it is not closed until the end of verse 17. The Revised Version really does the same thing by means of a dash, indicating again a parenthesis. This is clearly very important from the standpoint of our general analysis of the section. Instead of completing the comparison, instead of bringing in his 'even so' to correspond to the 'as', the Apostle obviously felt that it was essential that he should explain further, and elaborate his first statement.

I take it that what happened in his mind was something like this. First, he sets down this proposition, 'As by one man sin entered into the world, and death by sin, and so death passed upon all men, for that all sinned'; then he said to himself, 'I wonder whether the Christians in Rome are all clear about that? Before I complete the comparison I will make quite sure about the matter'. So it is that (in our English translation) we have bracket, dash, parenthesis.

He begins the parenthesis in verse 13. Let us follow it as far as the end of verse 14. This is an exposition of what Paul has just declared, 'death passed upon all men, for that all have sinned'. That is what needs to be explained, so he says, 'For until the law sin was in the world; but sin is not imputed when there is no law. Nevertheless death reigned from Adam to Moses, even over them that had not sinned after the similitude of Adam's transgression, who is the figure of him that was to come.' We shall not give a full exposition of these words until later. All I am asserting now is that verses 13 and 14 are an explanation of what he means by saying that 'sin passed upon all men, for that all have sinned'.

That brings us to verse 15, 'But not as the offence, so also is the free gift'. Here our translators differ in their punctuation. In the Revised Version the parenthesis seems to finish at the end of verse 14; but in the Authorized Version the parenthesis goes on to the end of verse 17. Which is correct? Actually it makes little difference, because the meaning is going to be very much the same; but on the grounds of intellectual neatness and understanding I personally agree with the Authorized Version for the following reason. I believe that what happened here was that the Apostle again felt that he had made a statement which needed explanation, amplification and qualification, and in particular his assertion that 'Adam is the figure of him that was to come'. There he gets near to using the 'even so' that is to correspond to the 'as' at the beginning of verse 12; but he again seems to feel that this statement needs to be explained, so in verses 15, 16 and 17 he explains in what respects Adam is really a figure of 'him that was to come', namely, Jesus Christ.

The figure is not an exact one and there are some tremendous differences. Adam's one transgression brought the condemnation upon many; but in the case of Christ, thank God, many transgressions were atoned for, and many people are delivered by the one act of one Man. There is a general comparison possible between Adam and Christ, but it must not be pressed too far, says the Apostle. There are differences and contrasts; and they are very glorious contrasts. So he follows them out, and glories in them, as we shall see when we come to work them out in detail. In other words, I am suggesting that verses 15, 16 and 17 are, so to speak, a parenthesis within the main parenthesis which begins at verse 13 and ends at verse 17.

Is this bad literary style? It is, but the Apostle frequently forgot all about style. Thank God that he did! Style has almost killed the Christian Church and her message, it seems to me. About a hundred years ago preachers began to get interested in style. They read Burke and Gibbon, and later began to read Macaulay, and to imitate their style. The great idea was to have a cultured ministry, so the preachers began to write pleasing essays and homilies rather than sermons. The manner became more important than the matter, the style mattered more than the substance. The important thing was not so much the truth which was being declared, but the way in which it was declared. Nothing is further removed from the manner of the Apostle Paul. Carried away by the great rush of his thought and by the majesty of the conceptions, and filled with anxiety to convey the truth to the Church at Rome, he does not hesitate to introduce a parenthesis, and then another parenthesis within the major parenthesis. Nothing is more fatal than to think of the Apostle in terms of a mere literary man. He was an evangelist, a preacher, teacher and pastor who had to write in the midst of a busy and often harassed life, indeed often in prison. Moreover his letters are but synopses of what he would have stated at great length had he been with the people to whom he wrote. However, by the end of verse 17 he has finished his parenthesis and so our translators close the brackets.

In verses 18 and 19 Paul completes at last and plainly the comparison which he began in verse 12 but which was interrupted by the parenthesis. 'Therefore as' is a return to the statement of verse 12. He takes it up again and repeats it. It is as if he says, 'Well now, I have put you right about the details of all this, so having grasped that, you will now be ready to follow me right through in what I have to say'. 'Therefore, as by the offence of one judgment came upon all men to condemnation; even so' – he completes the comparison now – 'by the righteousness of one the free gift came upon all men unto justification of life'. Then in verse 19, 'For as by one man's disobedience many were made sinners, so' – he has finished with digressions and parentheses, all is clear and he can state it quite plainly now – 'so by the obedience of one shall many be made righteous'. So he works it out after all! Actually the parentheses have greatly helped; because through them he is able to state the method of salvation more fully and explicitly than would have been possible had he completed his statement immediately in verse 12.

So we come to the further point introduced in verses 20 and 21, where we read, 'Moreover the law entered, that the offence might abound. But where sin abounded, grace did much more abound: that as sin hath reigned unto death, even so might grace reign through righteousness unto eternal life by Jesus Christ our Lord.' This is a kind of postscript, and a most important one. The Apostle was always most concerned to help and to deal with the difficulties of the Jews, and especially those Jews who were members of the early Christian Church. Even in the Gentile churches there were a number of Jews, and there were certainly Jews at Rome. In any case first-century Christians were always having to contend with the arguments brought forward by the Jews concerning the Law and its purpose.

As we have seen, the Apostle has been making a general statement which on the surface might have given the impression that the Law has no place or purpose at all, and does not matter. He has gone to Adam and seems to be inferring that nothing mattered after that until Christ came. The Jews would argue, 'Look at the place given to the Law in the Old Testament. Can you ignore and dismiss the Law like that?' These two verses are his answer to criticism. He is not ignoring or dismissing the Law but showing rather its true place and function. The Law was never introduced as a way of salvation. That was the cardinal error of the Jews. They made it a vital part of the way of salvation. But it was never meant to be that. Its function was to be a schoolmaster that should lead us to Christ and His salvation, as Paul puts it in Galatians 3: 24. 'The Law entered in.' What for? In order 'that the offence might abound', in other words, in order that we might see the real character of the offence – our sin. The Law makes it plain, magnifies it, in a sense, exaggerates it and draws it out.

But that is not all, thank God, for 'where sin abounded, grace did much more abound: that as sin hath reigned unto death, even so . . .' How fond the Apostle was of the 'as' and 'even so'! What a logical mind he had! 'As' – 'even so might grace reign through righteousness unto eternal life by Jesus Christ our Lord.' The Law, he says, came in, in order that this whole position of mankind in sin might be made perfectly plain and clear; in other words, in order that the whole world might be convinced and convicted and found guilty before God. But, over and above that, the Law came in so that the superiority of grace might be made to shine out yet more and more gloriously. The more we see and understand the nature of sin, and what it has done to the human race, and to every individual man without exception, the more we shall marvel at the wonder of God's exceeding and super-abounding grace.

Such, then, is our general analysis of the section. The main argument, the main statement, the main thrust of the whole paragraph is to tell us that, as we are all related by nature to Adam, so we who are Christians are related by grace to the Lord Jesus Christ. That is the great principle. We must get firm hold of it and keep it in the forefront of our minds, otherwise we shall go wrong in our detailed exposition. It is sometimes said that folk cannot see the wood for the trees. That is our danger at this point. When a difficult section of Scripture like this confronts us, it is always good to stand back, as it were, and look at it as a whole first. Do not get immersed in the details immediately or you will be confused. Stand back, get hold of the main principle, and having seen that, it will be easier for you to master the various particular statements.

In almost every walk of life this highly important principle holds good. Look at the whole before you look at the parts; inspect the whole before you begin to analyse. Take an over-all view, a broad view before you get immersed in the details. If the statesmen of the world were to bear that principle in mind, things would be much better today than they are. I am speaking internationally as well as nationally. The broad grasp, the over-all view is essential if you are to understand the particular difficulties. This is certainly vital in medical work and students are always urged to look at the patient as a whole before beginning a detailed examination. It is particularly important to apply this procedure as we grapple with this vital crucial section of our Epistle. The great truth taught here is that our relationship to Adam was the same in essence and principle as is our relationship now to our Lord and Saviour Jesus Christ.

We are now ready to look at the section in close detail. What an important verse is verse 12! It controls the interpretation of the entire passage, and yet at the same time I must point out that the meaning of the passage as a whole helps us to interpret this particular verse. When we tackle the real difficulty in this statement we shall have to use some of the other verses to help us, because they throw light upon it. They are extensions or conclusions drawn from it. This justifies our method of taking a general view of the entire statement first. The conclusions drawn from a statement help to clarify the meaning of the statement itself; the context often determines the exact meaning of a difficult text.

This twelfth verse is one of the most important verses in the whole Bible from the standpoint of theology. Let us approach it in this way. Anyone concerned about the problem of life, and the world as it is today, is confronted by two undeniable facts. First there is the universality of sin. Of course all do not call it sin, but even so they have to admit and to confess this, that there is something which is spoiling and ruining life. They have to admit further, that mankind at large seems to prefer to do that which is wrong rather than that which is right; that if you tell a child not to do a thing, he will want to do it immediately and will, as often as not, proceed to do it. The man of the world admits this frequently without your asking him and says gratuitously, 'Of course, I am not claiming that I am a perfect saint'. He is granting thereby the universality of sin. There is no such thing as a 'perfect saint'. It is a fact that sin is universal.

The second fact is the universality of death. 'Every man who lives is born to die', as the poet Dryden puts it. Think of a baby born five minutes ago. 'Ah,' you say, 'there is someone at any rate who is beginning to live.' But I have an equal right to say, 'There is someone who is beginning to die'. The moment you come into this world you are beginning to go out of it. The moment you breathe for the first time it is only one of a series that is going to lead to the last. 'It is appointed unto all men once to die,' says the author of the Epistle to the Hebrews.

But the two facts raise the question, How do you account for the universality of sin and the universality of death? Why are we all what we are by nature? Why this conduct, this mis-behaviour of which we are all guilty? And why do we all die? Why are these things universal? The answers to these questions fall into two main categories. There are sub-divisions and apparent contradictions but basically there are only two answers.

First, there is the non-biblical answer, found in a variety of forms. I mean by this all answers which are not based upon the biblical teaching but upon man's philosophies including science.

They represent man's statement of what he believes to be the explanation over against what the Bible gives as the explanation. The claim is essentially this; that man has never been perfect; that man was not made perfect but is a creature who has evolved and is still evolving out of the animal. The animal lives in response to its own lusts and passions and desires. But man has evolved somewhat beyond that; the convolutions of his brain have developed more; the cerebrum, the highest part of the brain, has developed over against the rest. That is the one thing that differentiates man from the animals. But still man has not entirely shed all his past, he still has the same basic animal nature, yet in addition he has his mind with its reason and understanding. Thus there is a conflict in man, the conflict between the higher and the lower parts. Such is their view of man. He has never been perfect, but he is evolving, and their hope is that in some millennia of years he will have so evolved as to shed and slough off all the things that cause trouble, thus becoming perfect.

According to that view there is really no such thing as sin, because man has always been like this. It is not that he was once created perfect, fell to temptation, and thereby became guilty of sin. But the proponents of the evolutionary view heartily dislike the term *sin*. What the Bible calls sin they regard as something negative in man's constitution. They say that the trouble with man is not that he is positively bad or positively evil; his trouble is that he has not yet developed sufficiently his good and his better qualities and propensities. They urge us to get rid of this biblical idea of sin and of guilt. We must take man as he is, and not expect him to be perfect at this stage. There is a day coming when he will have evolved these higher and better qualities so that he will be able to control the rest. But not yet. Man is still in the negative phase, he has not become sufficiently positive. Here, they say, is the source of man's troubles and problems and deficiencies. In other words, they would get rid of the notion of sin altogether, because sin, according to the biblical teaching, is positive and not negative. Man, they insist, is not really bad; what you should say about him is that he is not good. When you see a man who is guilty of drunkenness, and robbery with violence, and cruelty, and everything that is dastardly, you must not say that he is a bad man, what you should say is that he is lacking in good and ennobling and attractive qualities.

When you ask them to explain the universality of death, they reply that death is just a part of man's constitution, a necessary part of the whole mechanism of life. Life begins, develops and grows, matures and blossoms, and then having reached its peak and its zenith, it begins to wane and to decay until eventually it dies. This is the pattern of human existence; it is something that is inherent in life itself, that it should climb to its meridian height and then decline until it disappears. Death according to this view, is in reality but a part of the circle of life. Let me illustrate what I mean.

I remember some twenty-five years ago having a very long discussion with the principal of a certain theological college. In our discussion we came to this question of death and began to discuss the verse, 'Except a corn of wheat fall into the ground and die it abideth alone: but if it die, it bringeth forth much fruit' [*John* 12: 24]. 'Yes,' he said, 'that is quite simple.' I had introduced that verse in connection with the whole question of the Atonement, which, I maintained, was what our Lord was dealing with there. 'No, no,' he said, 'it isn't that. That is where you people with your legalistic minds keep imposing your own ideas on to the beautiful, simple view of life which was taken by Jesus. Don't you see,' he said, 'that He is just illustrating there this principle inherent in life? You put that seed into the ground; if it remains alive it is of no further value, but if that seed dies and degenerates and decomposes, then a chemical process takes place that leads to the renewal of life, and out of that one seed you will have many blades of grass or of corn. That is how it works. Nothing is lost. You say that when something dies that that is the end of it. But such is not the case. When trees and flowers and animals die the decomposed matter to which they give rise is most valuable. It produces nitrogen, which is after all the basis of life, and many other essential constituents. Death leads to life by liberating the nitrogen that is needed to form the molecules of new life. Death is just part of the cycle of life.' Such was the principal's contention. It amounted to this, that death is an essential part in the process and rhythm of life, and consequently there was never a time when there was no death. In essence, this is the non-biblical view.

What is the biblical view? It is found here in the twelfth verse of this chapter. Let us look at the words – 'Sin'. Do you notice how the Apostle personifies sin? 'Wherefore', he says, 'as by one man sin entered into the world . . .' Sin opened a door. Sin 'came in'. Sin is personified. Later he says that 'sin reigned'. What does he mean by this? It is his way of stating that sin is not merely a lack of certain qualities, not merely a negative phase, but that sin is active, sin is positive, sin is something that does things; it enters in, reigns, rules, governs and manifests a tremendous degree of activity. Clearly we have here a complete contradiction of the non-biblical view. This personification of sin is characteristic of the biblical teaching. That is not surprising, for sin entered in through the person of the devil. The other view of course does not believe in the devil. It ridicules the whole notion of the devil and laughs it to scorn. 'Fancy still believing in the devil!' they say. But here the Apostle shows that sin, as a thing most positive, must have a sufficient cause to account for it. So he personifies it to remind us that it entered in in that way.

What does the Apostle mean by sin? He means a number of things. He means an act of transgression and of disobedience which leads to guilt, an act which in turn leads to depravity, to a change in one's nature. Sin, to him, means also a falling away from righteousness and becoming unrighteous; it means a nature that is depraved and corrupt, and which leads in turn to a constant 'missing of the mark' and to further acts of disobedience and transgression and violation of God's holy Law. Sin is an attitude of rebellion and hatred to God and a refusal to obey His holy law. It has particular shades of meaning in various parts of Scripture; but the context will generally make the precise aspect quite plain. Sin means that a new reigning principle has come into the life of man. It means that we are in a fallen condition, that we are depraved and guilty, that our habits and our practices are governed by this reigning principle.

The second term is descriptive of what sin has done; sin 'entered into the world'. The verb really means – and it is a strong word – 'invaded'. The Apostle does not mean that 'it began to be'. It 'entered in', it 'invaded' the world. Sin broke in; it intruded into man's life. The implication of that statement is of the utmost importance and is an essential part of the entire biblical teaching concerning man and the world and the whole story of Redemption. There was a period in the history of the world when it was entirely free from sin. Sin is an invader. God made the world perfect and called it Paradise. He also made man perfect in His own image and likeness. He looked upon it all and saw that it was good. There was no sin. But sin entered in. How different this outlook, from the non-biblical view!

But to put the same truth in still stricter doctrinal, theological language, the Apostle in this tremendous phrase brings us face to face with the doctrine of the Fall. God made man in His own image. Man originally, at the beginning, was upright; he had an original righteousness and he lived a life of obedience to God and of communion with God. But he has fallen. Sin entered in and led to that act of rebellion and disobedience which produced guilt and that habit and corrupt course of life which we all know so well. The universality of sin is only truly explained by the doctrine of the Fall.

That leads us to the third statement: 'and death by sin'. Here we have the biblical explanation of the universality of death. By death, the Apostle means primarily physical death. He does not mean physical death alone, but that is what he emphasizes here. Sin also led inevitably to spiritual death for the reasons I have just been giving, but the main emphasis here is upon physical death. We have already seen that 'death', according to the biblical teaching, is not just the result of man's constitution, not merely one part of the cycle of life. That is not the truth concerning death. 'Wherefore, as by one man sin entered into the world, and death . . .' Where did death come from? Hear the Apostle's answer: 'by sin'. It is sin that has brought in death. Sin is the cause of the infliction of death. Death is penal; it came in as the punishment of sin; it was not there before. Death has been brought in by sin in demonstration of the fact that 'the wages of sin is death'.

All this shows the importance of believing, and being controlled by, the teaching of the early chapters of Genesis. Take Genesis 2 :17, the first statement of this truth. God said to the man, 'But of the tree of the knowledge of good and evil thou shalt not eat of it, for in the day that thou eatest thereof thou shalt surely die'. Eve repeated that statement to the serpent, as the account of the temptation in chapter 3 tells us, and it reappears in verse 19. God pronounces the judgment. 'In the sweat of thy face shalt thou eat bread till thou return unto the ground' – that is death – 'for out of it wast thou taken, for dust thou art and unto dust shalt thou return.' This teaching runs right through the Bible. Paul sums it up in 1 Corinthians 15: 56 by saying, 'The sting of death is sin'. In other words, were it not that he had sinned, Adam would not have died. That does not mean that Adam by creation was in a condition which was already immortal, and that he would continue as such to all eternity. He was perfect, but he was not glorified. Adam had still to achieve immortality, but there was no principle of death in him; and he would not have died if he had not sinned. To be glorified and to become immortal his body would have to be changed to make it correspond to that glorified body of the Lord Jesus Christ, but if he had not sinned he would not have died. Death has resulted directly from sin. It is the punishment of sin, it is penal. It is not just a part of man's constitution.

We come next to the fourth statement of the verse, which is that 'death passed upon all men'. 'Passed upon' means, 'made its way to' each individual member of the human race. So the fact of death has become universal, and we are all born to die. We shall learn more of this tragic truth later as the Apostle unfolds his message.

Finally, you notice the statement, 'by one man'. The universal death which has become the fate of all mankind, is the result of the action of one man. One man has produced all this, not humanity. Those who do not submit to the authority of the Scripture or accept it as the Word of God say, 'Adam stands for the race, he stands for humanity, he stands for man at large'. But Paul says 'one man', one individual. In verse 14 he refers to Adam specifically as an individual in the same way as he refers to Moses as an individual. Indeed the whole point of the entire section, as we have seen, is to compare and to contrast the one man Adam with the One Man Jesus Christ. If you say that Adam was not one man but the race, then you have to say that Christ was not One Man but presents a general idea of a new humanity. But then the whole point of the passage disappears. If you take the trouble to count you will find that Paul uses the term 'one' twelve times from the beginning of verse 12 to the end of verse 19, as if to anticipate the modern theories and to refute them before they were born. He keeps on saying 'One', 'By the one', 'the one man', 'the sin of one', 'the one transgression' – one, one, one!

The Apostle is not referring to humanity but to one person, one individual, whose name was Adam, the first man. Whether or not you agree with the Apostle's teaching is not the question at the moment; our concern is to discover and to understand what the Apostle says. To import and to implant these other ideas into his mind, and to suggest that the Apostle Paul, nineteen hundred years ago, held these modern, sceptical, scientific theories, is simply ridiculous. No one can read the writings of the Apostle honestly and with an open mind without granting that he believed that what we read in Genesis 1, 2 and 3 is literal history. Our Lord also believed the same. You remember how He said, 'From the beginning of the creation God made them male and female' [*Mark* 10: 6]. Our Lord believed the Old Testament, and received it as it stands. He quoted it freely, and there and elsewhere He clearly showed that He believed what is written in Genesis 2 and 3 to be history. He believed in 'the one man'.

To sum up, the teaching here – and it is the teaching of the whole Bible – is that both sin and death 'entered into' the life of man and into the story of the human race as the direct result of that one man Adam's act of disobedience. That is the teaching. We shall have to elaborate this later and to see how the Apostle states it still more clearly. But there, in general, is the statement of this twelfth verse.

Our study has substantiated our contention that it is not a matter of indifference as to what view you hold of Genesis 1, 2 and 3. If you do not believe that there was a literal Adam, and that what Paul says about him in this Epistle is true, why is there any need of forgiveness? Why is there any need of Atonement? Why did Christ have to take human nature upon Him? Reject a literal Adam and the whole of the Christian case and the Christian message, it seems to me, collapses. You cannot play fast and loose with the Bible. It is a consistent whole. Each part is intertwined with all the others, and they all depend upon one another in this amazing unity. The one great theme of the Bible from beginning to end is man and his world in relationship to God. It tells us how he went wrong and the consequence of that; but thank God it also tells us how he can be put right. Adam! Christ! 'As in Adam, so in Christ.'

Fifteen

*

Wherefore, as by one man sin entered into the world, and death by sin; and so death passed upon all men, for that all have sinned:

(For until the law sin was in the world; but sin is not imputed when there is no law.

Nevertheless death reigned from Adam to Moses, even over them that had not sinned after the similitude of Adam's transgression, who is the figure of him that was to come.

But not as the offence, so also is *the free gift. For if through the offence of one many be dead, much more the grace of God, and the gift by grace,* which is *by one man, Jesus Christ, hath abounded unto many.*

And not as it was *by one that sinned,* so is *the gift; for the judgment* was *by one to condemnation, but the free gift* is *of many offences unto justification.*

For if by one man's offence death reigned by one; much more they which receive abundance of grace and of the gift of righteousness shall reign in life by one, Jesus Christ.)

Therefore as by the offence of one judgment came *upon all men to condemnation; even so by the righteousness of one* the free gift came *upon all men unto justification of life.*

For as by one man's disobedience many were made sinners, so by the obedience of one shall many be made righteous.

Moreover the law entered, that the offence might abound. But where sin abounded, grace did much more abound:

That as sin hath reigned unto death, even so might grace reign through righteousness unto eternal life by Jesus Christ our Lord.

Romans 5: 12–21

In our exposition of this crucial verse (5:12) we come now to the last statement which is the most difficult of all. As found in the Authorized Version it is: 'for that all have sinned'. It is connected, as you notice, with the previous statement, 'and so death passed upon all men, for that all have sinned'. Now this statement, it is generally agreed, is the most difficult single statement in the entire

Epistle. But though difficult, it is at the same time highly important.

The first thing to determine is the correct translation; and, unfortunately, the Authorized Version is not good here. A better translation would be to replace the 'for' by 'because', and 'have sinned' by 'sinned', so that we have, 'because all sinned'. But, you may ask, What is the difference? This is a crucial point. If you say that 'all have sinned' you are making a general statement which is of course true. It means that all men actually and in fact have committed sin. But that is not what the Apostle was concerned to say. What he actually says is that 'all sinned'.

I am not alone in holding this opinion. You will find that the translators and the expositors are all agreed about this matter apart from the Authorized Version. The Apostle used here the aorist tense, which conveys the idea of an act completed once and for ever, in history, an historical event or fact, not a description of a general state. It is because the Apostle deliberately used that tense that the right translation is 'because all sinned'. He is referring to a specific action which took place at a particular point of time. If you say 'all have sinned' you mean that they might have sinned yesterday or last week or any other time; but the Apostle's term has a specific reference to one definite completed action. 'All sinned.'

Here then is our problem: What does the Apostle actually mean? He says that 'so death passed upon all men because all sinned'. As we approach this problem let us lay down two principles which will help us. The first is this (and incidentally this is a good way in which to approach any difficult passage), do not rush at it, do not approach it too directly. The second principle of interpretation is: try to find certain related positions of which you are quite sure, and start from them, and then move towards your problem. Applying that method we can proceed as follows. We must remember that the chief point of the entire section is to hold before us the comparison between Adam and the Lord Jesus Christ. Adam was 'the figure of him that was to come'. The object of that comparison is to emphasize the fact that our relationship to the one is exactly parallel with our relationship to the Other. What is true of us in Adam is true of us in Christ. It is vital that we should hold on to that, because if our exposition or interpretation of any particular statement, this one or any other, cuts across that controlling principle we have to reject it at once. The second thing which helps us is, as we have seen, that verses 13 and 14 are expressly designed to expound this phrase at which we are now looking.

Let me repeat the Apostle's affirmation: 'death passed upon, entered into the life of the whole of humanity, because all sinned'. The universality of death is the result of the fact that all sinned. That is what Paul is saying; there is no room for two opinions about it. But what is his precise meaning? Let us look again at verses 13 and 14. 'For', he says (he is explaining, he is expounding) 'For until the law sin was in the world; but sin is not imputed when there is no law. Nevertheless death reigned from Adam to Moses, even over them that had not sinned after the similitude of Adam's transgression.' We need go no further because the remainder is clear – 'who is the figure of him that was to come'.

What does Paul mean when he says 'until the law'? That is obviously a reference to something which was true before the Law was given by God to Moses for the children of Israel. He is referring to that period of history, of which we read in the Book of Genesis and the early part of Exodus, which elapsed between the fall of Adam and the giving of the Law through Moses. What establishes this meaning beyond any doubt is his reference in verse 14 to death reigning 'from Adam to Moses'. The Law is the Law that was given to Moses when he was with God on the Holy Mount, and which he gave to the people later. So the statement is that during that period of history 'sin was in the world'.

Why does the Apostle speak in this way? One of his reasons for doing so (we have already met it in earlier chapters) was that the Jew found it difficult to think about sin at all apart from the Law. He had become so accustomed to thinking of sin and Law together that he could not separate them. The Apostle therefore is simply establishing the fact that there was sin in the world before the giving of the Law through Moses. He is asserting that everyone, obviously, was born in a state of sin, and that all men proceeded to show this by committing acts of sin. But he says more than this. Not only was the fact of sin evident and plain in history, the consequences of sin were equally evident. God punished sin in a very striking way at the Flood when the whole world was drowned. That is conclusive proof that sin was in the world. But both before and after the Flood the striking fact is that, apart from the unique case of Enoch, everybody died during that period. That, the Apostle says, was a direct result of sin. So sin and its vast consequences were evident in the world before the giving of the Law through Moses. This means, he argues, that men were obviously regarded as sinners during that time; that they were dealt with as sinners, and that they died because they were sinners. That was true before the Law was given through Moses.

We now move on to the second statement of verse 13, and this too is really difficult. 'But sin', Paul says, 'is not imputed when there is no law.' The word 'imputed' is not the same word as he used in chapter 4, where it meant 'reckoned' or 'counted' for righteousness. There, the Apostle was dealing with the theme of justification, and he says that 'Abraham believed God and it was counted unto him for righteousness'. But he does not use the same word here but one which means that a person's sin is not recorded in the ledger, as it were; it is not taken account of.

But what does the Apostle mean by saying that 'sin is not taken account of when there is no law'? There is great disagreement about this; but it seems to me that we must adopt the same exposition here as we did when we were expounding chapter 4, verse 15, where we read, 'Because the law worketh wrath; for where no law is there is no transgression'. In other words, Paul does not say that 'when there is no law there is no sin', for he has already been saying that sin was in the world, and he has already been telling us (in chapter 2) that the Gentiles who had never known the Law of Moses nevertheless were a law unto themselves because they had the Law written in their hearts (verses 14–15). So it does not mean that there was no sin and that God did not regard sin as sin before the giving of the Law. The Flood proves that God regarded sin as sin at that time. He drowned the ancient world for that very reason; and yet the Law had not been given. What then does the Law do? The Law proves that sin is transgression, it establishes and defines it as such. Paul will tell us this much more plainly when we come to verses 20 and 21 at the end of the chapter. So what he is saying here, in verse 13, is that sin can exist, and that God regards it as sin, and deals with it as sin, apart from its being defined as transgression by the Law given through Moses. Sin is still sin, but it is not regarded or counted as transgression, as it were, in the books, until the Law has been clearly given.

The Apostle makes this still clearer at the beginning of verse 14 where he says, that though 'sin is not imputed when there is no law, nevertheless death reigned from Adam to Moses'. He says it is obvious that, though the Law as such had not been given, and though sin was not pin-pointed as transgression, yet it is clear that God was dealing with sin as sin because death reigned during the period from Adam to Moses. There was a law obviously working whereby God regarded all the people of the Adam–Moses era as sinners, and He dealt with them as such; and that is why they all died with the one exception noted. The Apostle's argument is that as 'death comes by sin' and it is a fact that death came upon all those people, it is obvious that their death must have been because of sin.

Then, and to make it still more plain, Paul says, 'even over them that had not sinned after the similitude of Adam's transgression'. There are two possible explanations of these words and I am not at all sure but that I accept both of them. Some expositors say that 'even', as used here, is an explanation of what the Apostle has just been saying, and that it refers to everybody who died between Adam and Moses. There are others who reject this interpretation, and assert that Paul is referring to a particular section of people who 'had not sinned after the similitude of Adam's transgression'. Who are these? 'Oh,' they say, 'this is a reference to infants who die before they are capable of taking any action at all.' As I say, it is almost impossible to decide which interpretation is correct. At this point Charles Hodge and Robert Haldane are not in agreement; and yet ultimately, of course, they are in agreement because, as I am suggesting, the acceptance of both explanations covers the situation perfectly.

Expositors who say that Paul means 'everybody' put it like this. They say that because there was no Law in words prohibiting particular actions, as there was in the case of Adam, people from Adam to Moses did not sin in exactly the same way as Adam had sinned. We must be clear about this. Although Adam had the as yet unwritten Law in his being and in his nature, God said to him specifically, 'You are not to eat of a particular fruit; and if you do eat of that particular fruit then you shall die'. There we have a law stated openly, plainly and in words. So Adam sinned against a known stated law. The Adam to Moses people, say the expositors we have mentioned, did not do that because the Law of Moses had not yet been given; they only had the law in their hearts. They were in the position that Paul says the Gentiles were always in, they did not have a particular prohibition in words. So when they sinned they did not sin in exactly the same way as Adam, because Adam was sinning against a specific law and these people were not. Thus they did not sin 'after the similitude of Adam's transgression'.

I am prepared to accept that. But I also feel that we must emphasize the other point, that obviously this does also refer to infants. Amongst all the people who died between Adam and Moses there were undoubtedly large numbers of infants. Some of them may have died very soon after their birth, before they were capable of any moral decision or of taking any action for themselves and as the result of their own volition; and yet they died. The meaning then would appear to be that the persons described as those who had 'not sinned after the similitude of Adam's transgression' had not committed any act of sin whatsoever. And yet, says Paul, the fact remains that death reigned even over them. Death had been universal during this period, including even infants.

The big question now confronting us is: Why did these children die? Why was it that death 'passed upon' these children? To find the answer, let us go back to verse 12. There, Paul tells us that death is always introduced as a punishment for sin, and he argues, and we must argue in the same fashion, that the death of children, including infants, is therefore due to sin. But infants have not committed acts of sin; and yet they die. That proves that they are guilty of sin. How can this be explained?

The answer the Apostle himself gives is found in the phrase at the end of verse 12 – 'all sinned'. It is because all sinned that all die, even infants. What does 'all sinned' mean? There are those who would say that it means just what the Authorized (King James') translation suggests that it means, namely, 'all have sinned'; and the Apostle is simply saying that it is a fact that everyone born into this world has sinned. Why have they sinned? Some have said that we have all sinned because we see others sinning before us; and that the earliest generations of all saw Adam sin and imitated him. This process of imitation, they say, has gone on from generation to generation.

Others say that all have sinned because all born into this world have a sinful nature. The Psalmist tells us in Psalm 51 that we are 'shapen in iniquity'; hence, being born with sinful natures, we all sin, and therefore you can say that 'all have sinned'.

But we cannot possibly accept this as an exposition. The case of infants makes it quite impossible. It is not true to say of the infant that he has sinned in that sense. The infant dying soon after birth has not sinned, and yet he dies. He has not sinned in the sense that he has committed acts of wilful disobedience. He was not capable of doing that; and yet he has died. It is important therefore for us to keep our eye on verses 13 and 14. People 'who have not sinned after the similitude of Adam's transgression' nevertheless die; and if we look at the infants in particular the meaning here cannot be that all have actually sinned in practice, because infants have not done so.

But I have a second reason for rejecting that exposition, namely, that if we accept it, the great parallel drawn by the Apostle throughout this entire section between Adam and the Lord Jesus Christ, and our relationship to the two, disappears entirely. If the 'all have sinned' of verse 12 means that all have actually sinned you would have to say that all die because all have actually sinned. But if you say that, the parallel on the other side would be that those who are saved are saved because they have done good; and so the doctrine of justification by faith would be thrown out. If you argue that the Apostle is saying that death passed upon all men because they have all committed sin, then you have to say on the other side that life comes to the Christian because he has done good acts, and has obeyed the Law. But then, I repeat, there is no longer justification by faith, and there is no longer any parallel between Adam and the Lord Jesus Christ. So, for two reasons, the case of the infant, and the importance of the parallel, I reject that suggested explanation.

But let us look at a second explanation which is put forward, and which can claim the support of the great name of John Calvin. He says that 'all sinned' means that all have sinned in the sense that all are sinful. He says that we all inherit from Adam a polluted, depraved and sinful nature. Now all are agreed about this, apart from a very small section which is hardly worth mentioning, namely, those who are guilty of what is called the Pelagian heresy. The argument is, that we all inherit a sinful, depraved and polluted nature from Adam, and that God regards that as sinful. He regards that nature in us as sin, and punishes it as such by visiting death upon us; so that we are guilty for having this sinful nature.

What about this explanation? I am afraid that we have to say that we cannot accept it, in spite of John Calvin! We must not turn him into a pope! He was as liable to error as anybody else. If we can prove that his exposition is not true to the plain teaching of Scripture we must say so; and we have to say so on this occasion. And for this reason, that what the Apostle says is not that we have all 'become sinful' but that 'we all sinned', which is a different thing. He does not say that we all have a sinful nature; what he says is 'all sinned'. This is a very important point.

But in addition to that, we can show that if we accept this exposition the Apostle's parallel between Adam and Christ disappears again, and in this way. If we are regarded as guilty and condemned in the sight of God, and death comes upon us, because we have a sinful nature, then on the other side, we shall have to say that we are justified by God through Jesus Christ because we have a holy nature. But that is precisely what we must never say, because, as we have seen so many times, Paul goes out of his way to say that God 'justifies the ungodly'. He justifies the sinner. Time and time again we have had to emphasize that we are not justified because we are regenerate, not justified because we have a new nature, not justified because we have become sanctified. That is the Roman Catholic error and heresy: but Paul's teaching is that we are justified by God, and in His sight, as we are, while 'ungodly', while sinful, without any change in our nature. Justification and regeneration, of course, generally go together, but we must never say that we are justified because we are regenerate. In our thinking the order and sequence in our minds must always be to put justification before regeneration. Obviously when God determines to justify a man He has already also purposed to regenerate him; but He justifies him as 'ungodly', as 'sinful', as an 'enemy'. This has been emphasized repeatedly in chapter 4 and the first part of this chapter 5. So the parallel excludes that explanation completely and we must therefore reject it.

If, then, we reject both these possible explanations (the one which says that all die because all have actually sinned, and the other that says that we all die because we all have sinful natures) what then is our exposition of this statement? It is that all sinned 'in Adam'. I contend that that is precisely what the Apostle is saying. The reign of death ('death passing upon all men') according to the Apostle proves that; and it does so in this way. Death is always part of the punishment of sin; death therefore always presupposes guilt and condemnation. Death is universal, even in the case of infants who have not committed any actual sin; but because death comes upon them they must therefore be guilty of some particular sin. They have not sinned by their own personal acts; but they would never have died if they had not been guilty of some sin.

This, to my thinking, is the basic argument. So going back again to verse 12 we have, 'Wherefore, as by one man sin entered into the world, and death by sin, and so death passed upon all men because all sinned', and we see that it is a perfect sequence, that it is perfectly logical. Each step leads on inevitably to the next.

Death means that we are guilty of sin; even infants die, therefore infants must be guilty of sin. But as they have not committed an act of sin we ask what sin are they then guilty of? Paul asserts that they are guilty of the act that brought sin into the world, the act of that one man Adam. In other words, the teaching here is that Adam's sin is imputed to the whole of mankind. That is my contention, and it is not mine alone; it is the commonly accepted interpretation, apart from details, in all Reformed teaching, indeed the teaching of all who have not become liberals or modernists in their theological outlook. The latter, of course, believe none of this. But it has been the universally accepted exposition in the Church, apart from certain details. Let me repeat it therefore. The Apostle's contention is, that the fact that death has come upon all is proof of the fact that all sinned. Death is the result of sin, and therefore he says, 'all sinned', that is, all sinned in the original sin of Adam.

Let me give further proof of this. I can do so by going on a little further into the section. This exposition is not dependent on verses 12, 13 and 14 alone; the Apostle keeps on repeating it; from verse 15 to verse 19 he five times over repeats his statement about this 'one offence', 'the one offence of Adam', or 'the offence of one man'. Let us follow it through. Look at verse 15. 'But not as the offence, so also is the free gift.' 'For if through the offence of one many be dead . . .' You see what he says – 'through the offence of one', namely, Adam. He says that because of this one offence of Adam many are dead. But how can this one act lead to the death of many except in this way, that the many are guilty of that one act? But that is what Paul has already said in verse 12 in the words 'all sinned'. 'Through the offence of one.' He does not say that indirectly through our fallen nature many are dead. He says that many are dead because of (or through) the offence of this one person Adam.

We can prove this further by working out the parallel between Adam and Christ. 'Much more', says Paul, 'the grace of God, and the gift by grace, which is by one man, Jesus Christ, hath abounded unto many.' One man's (Adam's) sin has brought death upon us all. Christ's one action, this one Man's (Christ's) action brings life to us. The parallel thus proves that it is 'through the offence of one' that 'many are dead'.

Going on to verse 16 we find that the Apostle says a similar thing. 'And not as it was by one that sinned, so is the gift.' There it is again – 'one that sinned' – 'for the judgment was by one to condemnation'. He repeats it. The judgment, the condemnation has come upon us all as the result of the sin of this one man Adam. Then he completes it, works out the parallel and goes on to say, 'but the free gift is of many offences unto justification'. He is contrasting here the many offences with the one offence. The one offence of Adam brought death upon all, and condemnation. But, he says, on the other side the many offences that men have since committed are all dealt with and put aside by the one action of the Lord Jesus Christ. That is still saying the same thing. It is that one act of Adam that matters. It is that one sin of Adam's that has brought death upon all men, and there is only one explanation as to how it did so – we were all in it, we all sinned there in Adam our head and representative.

Look next at verse 17: 'For if by one man's offence death reigned by one . . .' There it is, quite plainly and clearly; and, completing the parallel, 'much more they which receive abundance of grace and of the gift of righteousness shall reign in life by one, Jesus Christ'. He continues to put his emphasis upon the one man and this one action.

In verses 18 and 19 it is still plainer. Look at verse 18: 'Therefore' (he is summing up) – 'Therefore as by the offence of one judgment came upon all men to condemnation.' But how can judgment come on all men to condemnation as the result of that one action? There is only one way in which that can be just and righteous and fair, and that is that we sinned in Adam – all sinned – which is precisely what he says at the end of verse 12. But Paul is anxious to emphasize that it is as the result of the offence of one that 'judgment came upon all men to condemnation'. And again the parallel proves it – 'even so by the righteousness of one the free gift came upon all men unto justification of life'.

But for a clinching and a closing argument you have but to turn to the next verse, verse 19: 'For as by one man's disobedience many were made sinners.' There are two very important words here. Consider the word 'made' and its meaning. It is agreed by almost all the commentators that the better translation here would be 'constituted' – 'by one man's disobedience many were constituted sinners', 'put down' as sinners, 'regarded' as sinners. Once more the parallel comes to our aid – 'by the obedience of one shall many be made (the same word meaning 'constituted') righteous! We have emphasized repeatedly that that is what is meant by justification by faith only, that God regards us as righteous, constitutes us a righteous people. Not by regenerating us; He 'constitutes' us, 'regards' us, 'pronounces' us to be such. It is a forensic matter. Now what is true on the one side of the parallel must be equally true on the other. By one man's disobedience we were put into the category of sinners, we were constituted sinners.

I must emphasize again that Paul does not say that we were constituted 'sinful', which is the exposition of Calvin and certain others. He says we were constituted 'sinners' – not just that we have a sinful nature – that we are regarded by God as sinners, which is simply another way of saying that we all sinned. Here, then, is a very clear statement to the effect that it was Adam's disobedience and sin that has put us all into the position of, and leads God to regard us as, sinners. The argument is that the reign of death proves that we are all regarded by God judicially as sinners; and that that is so because of Adam's sin. That is the Apostle's statement.

This particular piece of exposition is the most difficult that confronts us in the entire Epistle; but it is essential and vital that we should follow and grasp it, if we are to reap the glorious benefit of what the Apostle will go on to say. The parallel is with our Lord and His work. The whole paragraph is concerned about justification and the finality of justification, so I can put what Paul is saying briefly like this. As Adam's one act of disobedience has constituted us all sinners, so the obedience of the Lord Jesus Christ constitutes all who believe in Him righteous, and justifies them by faith. Here is the parallel. On the one hand Adam's sin is imputed to us; on the other, Christ's righteousness is imputed to us. But you must maintain the parallel. It is foolish and wrong just to say, 'Ah, I like to hear that second statement, that Christ's righteousness is imputed to me'. If you take that, you have to take the other side also, says Paul.

Again, let us never forget, that, as 'Adam is the figure of him that was to come,' so Adam's sin is imputed to us in exactly the same way that Christ's righteousness is imputed to us. We inherit, of course, a sinful nature from Adam; there is no dispute about that. But that is not what condemns us. What condemns us, and makes us subject to death, is the fact that we have all sinned in Adam, and that we are all held guilty of sin. Such is the Apostle's teaching. Death is always the punishment for the guilt of sin, actual sin; and therefore its universality, even in children, can only be explained by the fact that we all sinned in Adam, and became sinners when Adam sinned. The opposite is that those who are in Christ have all the benefits of His life and what He has done.

Let me put it in this way. In 1 Corinthians 15:56 we read, 'The sting of death is sin, and the strength of sin is the law'. The thing that puts the sting into death is sin. That is how death comes, it is sin that produces it. But, everybody dies, even infants. What is the sting? It must be sin. But infants have not personally committed any sin. What sin is involved then? It is the sin of Adam. When Adam sinned we all sinned – 'all sinned'. Back we come to the end of verse 12. That is the only way in which we can see how the sting of death comes in, in the case of the whole of humanity. It is our union with Adam that accounts for all our trouble. It is our corresponding union with Christ that accounts for our salvation. When Adam sinned all sinned, and death and punishment came upon all. And as Paul explains in 1 Corinthians 15, in Christ all can, and shall be, made alive who are united to Him. The parallel runs right through the section from the beginning to the end. The Apostle is affirming that it is that one act, that one disobedience, that one sin, of the one man, that has brought death upon us all, has 'constituted' us all sinners. It is not merely that Adam has given us a sinful nature, God has 'constituted' us sinners because of our relationship to Adam; and the penalty for sin has come upon the whole race in the form of death.

That being the exposition and the meaning of the statement, we are left with this question: How exactly is it that we are, by nature, united to Adam? That in turn will lead us later to ask, How is it that, correspondingly, we who are Christians are united to Christ?

I have been outlining and explaining what has always been known as the doctrine of Original Sin, and that doctrine includes this principle, that we are all guilty and held guilty in God's sight for the sin of Adam. 'Ah, but,' you say, 'I do not understand that sort of thing.' I am not surprised; I do not understand it myself. I, and all other preachers, are not called to say things that we fully understand, we are to expound the Scriptures. If you begin to say, 'Ah, but I do not understand this, or I do not see that' what will you have to say to the man of the world outside who says that he cannot see how One can die for all, and so rejects your doctrine of the atonement and salvation through the blood of Christ? That is the argument of the unbeliever, 'I don't understand'. The moment you bring in that argument and say that you do not understand, and that you do not see, you lack faith, and you have become a rationalist. Your understanding becomes the authority, and it is no longer the Word of God that regulates your thought.

Who can understand such a doctrine as this? My business is to put as clearly as I can what the Apostle taught. I am well aware that liberal theologians say, 'Ah yes, but Paul was governed by Jewish ideas'. If you adopt that line, what is your reply to the liberal when he takes the miracles out of the Bible, the Virgin Birth, and everything else of that character? You either accept this as it is or else you do not. When you accept this you will often find that you have to say, 'I do not understand'. Who can understand the doctrine of the Trinity? Who can understand the doctrine of two natures in the Person of the Lord Jesus Christ, and yet say that there is only one Person? Understand! The root of all trouble is this desire to understand, and to say, 'I cannot accept and believe unless I understand'. You will never understand this. But God, in His own infinite wisdom, has made it plain and clear to us through His servant, that when Adam sinned all sinned, and it is because of sin that death has come upon all, and we are in this predicament. But, thank God, there is this other side, which, again, I do not fully understand; but I am told it, and I believe it, that 'He hath laid on him the iniquity of us all'. 'Ah, but that's immoral,' says your liberal; 'how can one die for another, and for his sin?' Let him ask his questions. I thank God for that truth. It is my only hope and it is enough. And so here I do not fully understand either side, but I can see the perfect balance, that as I was in Adam I am now in Christ.

We shall proceed to try to understand the teaching of the Bible with regard to this relationship of ours – our union originally with Adam, and our union now in Christ. That is essential if we are to derive the full benefit from the teaching of this paragraph. And still more when we go on to chapter 6, where we shall be told that we have 'died with Christ', that we have been 'buried with him' and 'raised with him'. How can any man understand such glorious truths? I do not; but I glory in them. They are facts, and they are true; and we are given the privilege of looking into them, and marvelling at them, and being amazed at them. And do not forget that what we have been considering is a vital part of the entire biblical message – the world is as it is today because when Adam sinned all sinned, and ever since, sin and death have been universal and have come upon the whole of mankind. It is a mystery, it is an astounding fact; but 'Who hath known the mind of the Lord, that he may instruct him? O! the depth of the riches both of the wisdom and knowledge of God! His ways are beyond searching, and beyond finding out!' But 'He knows the way He taketh', and faith means that we believe where we cannot understand and cannot prove. We accept this Word as the Word of God through His inspired servants. We believe this Word is infallible; and as we find in it this marvellous parallelism we see and can follow the argument. We do not understand it in an ultimate sense, but we can follow the reasoning. Believing it, we rejoice that the righteousness of Christ is imputed to us while we were yet sinners, while we were without strength, while we were ungodly, while we were enemies! Thank God for imputation!

Sixteen

*

Wherefore, as by one man sin entered into the world, and death by sin; and so death passed upon all men, for that all have sinned.
Romans 5 : 12

In the light of our exposition of the phrase 'all sinned', a question immediately presents itself. If we say that we have all sinned in Adam, how exactly did we do so? What is our relationship to Adam? This question arises because, as we have seen already, the Apostle is arguing that on the one hand we had a relationship to Adam, and now have a relationship to the Lord Jesus Christ. So the question suggests itself, What is the relationship of the natural man to Adam? How can it be said that all people born into the world sinned in Adam, for Paul asserts that 'all sinned' and that sin is the cause of death passing upon all?

This paragraph that we are studying actually does not deal explicitly with this question that I am posing; nevertheless, it is important that we should look at it, because, though it does not do so explicitly, it does so in a sense implicitly.

There are two main answers to this question as to the exact relationship of the whole of mankind to Adam. The first is what is called the 'realistic view', which tells us that Adam was the totality of human nature. In that one man Adam was the whole of human nature. He was the father of all mankind. In him, therefore, according to this view, resided the whole of human nature, and the human nature in every person who has been born ever since is said to be a division, a part of this totality of human nature that was in Adam. But because the whole was in Adam, when he acted the whole of human nature acted, and therefore all these sub-divisions which were in him were acting at the same time. So the realistic view explains the statement as meaning that when

Adam sinned we all sinned in that way; we were there in him, parts of him. What the whole does the parts do of necessity, because the whole includes all the sub-divisions, the various parts. Men who hold this view argue, therefore, that every part in this whole is guilty with Adam of that transgression which he committed when he rebelled against God.

This is a view which has been held by many notable men in the Christian Church, and it seems to me that there is a great deal to be said for it, at least in part. As I have just stated it I believe it goes a little too far. I cannot accept the suggestion that there is a kind of mathematical division of human nature, and that the human nature of every individual person is merely some kind of fraction of that original totality which was in Adam. That, to me, is philosophy, and speculation, and I believe it goes too far. But while I believe that it goes too far, it seems to me that we have got to consider it because of the statement found in the first ten verses of the seventh chapter of the Epistle to the Hebrews. Incidentally it is interesting to observe that in his famous Commentary on this Epistle to the Romans Dr. Charles Hodge, who is a very strong opponent of this realistic view, in refuting it does not mention the statement in Hebrews 7 at all. That seems to me to be very significant. He should surely have considered it, and said something about it. But he does not do so.

The crucial statement in Hebrews 7 is that found in verses 9 and 10, 'And as I may so say, Levi also, who receiveth tithes, paid tithes in Abraham. For he was yet in the loins of his father when Melchisedec met him.' The reference there is to the story recorded in the fourteenth chapter of the Book of Genesis, where we are told how Abraham, when he had gained a notable victory over certain kings, paid a tenth of the spoils that he had gained from them and, indeed, even more than that, to a King Melchisedec. We are not concerned about the history as such, but about the argument of the author of the Epistle to the Hebrews, which runs thus. He argues that the fact that Abraham paid tithes to Melchisedec is proof positive that Melchisedec was greater than Abraham. Then he goes on to say that Levi, one of the children of Jacob, who was himself a grandson of Abraham, was in the loins of Abraham when Abraham paid those tithes, and we can say, therefore, that Levi also paid those tithes. He is assuming that his readers knew that the Aaronic priesthood consisted of those who belonged to the tribe of Levi, and that all the Children of Israel had to pay their tithes to the Levites because the latter were members of the Aaronic priesthood. But there, he says, we see that Levi, the father of these Aaronic priests to whom tithes are customarily paid, himself paid tithes. He did so in Abraham, 'for he was in the loins of his father when Melchisedec met him'. There is no need to stumble at the word father, which really means great-grandfather. That is a common practice in the Scriptures; very often they do not distinguish between father, grandfather and great-grandfather, but simply say; 'father'. Abraham was the father, in a sense, of Levi as he is 'the father of all who believe' now.

The interesting point in the statement is that the writer says that Levi was in the loins of Abraham when Abraham paid the tithe; and that therefore Levi paid the tithe himself because he was in the loins of his father Abraham at the time. That is a very interesting expression. The term actually used is in the passive sense. It does not mean so much that Levi paid tithes, as that Levi was tithed in Abraham, which ultimately comes to the same thing, except that, of course, it does not say that Levi actively, voluntarily and consciously was paying the tithes. What it does say is that because Levi was in the loins of Abraham, the latter was virtually paying tithes for himself and all his progeny, including Levi, at one and the same time. This must surely be brought into this discussion concerning our relationship to Adam in this fifth chapter of the Epistle to the Romans. As it is true to say that Levi was already in the loins of his father Abraham when Abraham paid his tithe to Melchisedec, in exactly the same way it is true to say that the whole of humanity was in the loins of Adam when Adam sinned and transgressed and so came under the condemnation of the law and its penalty. Thus death came upon Adam, and also therefore upon all who have come out of his loins, namely, the whole of mankind.

We must be careful here because that is all the Scripture tells us. We must not speculate or press these statements beyond what is legitimate, but at the same time we must certainly pay full attention to them. So, though we may reject the view that human nature in all its aspects has come out of that original mass of human nature that was in Adam, as being pure speculation and too mechanical, there is a sense in which we were all 'in the loins' of Adam and therefore were acting in Adam. Or, at least, we can say that passively we were involved in and committed by Adam's action; and therefore in that sense it is true that when Adam sinned 'all sinned'.

The two things (relationship to Adam and relationship to Christ) must surely be taken together; they are parallels. If, in thinking of Adam, we refuse to pay sufficient attention to this parallelism, it seems to me that we weaken somewhat, and detract from, the other side of the comparison – which is our relationship to the Lord Jesus Christ. However, let us leave it at that. This is what is called the 'realistic' view of our relationship to Adam.

The second view is what is called the 'representative' view, or the representational view. This means that not only is it true to say that Adam was actually the head of the human race – that the whole human race came out of him – but that beyond that, and above that, he was our representative. This view says that Adam was not only the 'natural' head of the race but that, in addition, God constituted him the federal head or representative of the entire race. This, say the advocates of this 'representative' view, was an action taken by God Himself. He made Adam, and having made him, He said to him in effect: 'Adam, I regard you as not only the first of a series, not merely the head in a natural sense of all who are going to come out of you, I constitute you the representative head, the federal head of all humanity; I am going to make a covenant with you, and I am going to deal with you as the representative of the entire human race of which you will be the progenitor. I intend to make a covenant with you to this effect, that every benefit you enjoy will pass to your progeny; and also any punishment that may come to you will likewise pass upon your progeny. When you act you will not simply be acting for yourself, I am constituting you the federal head and representative of the human race and therefore what you do will involve all of them.' That is the sense, they say, in which we must construe this statement that 'all sinned' in Adam.

This is an idea, of course, with which we are all familiar in many walks of life. For instance, an ambassador belonging to this country and representing us in another country acts on our behalf. When he makes a statement he does so on behalf of every one of us; when he signs a document he commits every one of us. He is our federal representative. We delegate powers like this quite frequently to certain people. That is the idea here, but with this difference, that it is God who has appointed Adam as our federal head and representative. He has a perfect right to do so. If God chose so to act, there is no reason why He should not do so; and there is no force in the argument which says, 'How can Adam represent us when we have not asked him to do so?' That question does not arise, and for this reason, that if the Lord God Almighty, the Creator of all persons and things, the Creator of man, chose then to say to Adam, 'I intend to make you the federal head of all that are coming out of you', there was no reason at all why He should not do so, because He is who He is. Adam acted as the responsible head and representative of the whole race. He was told quite plainly that if he obeyed, not only would he personally have great benefits, but that all his progeny would also enjoy them. He was told equally plainly that if he sinned, all who came out of him would be involved in the catastrophe and in the calamity that would come upon him.

Hence Adam is our federal head and representative. That is the 'representation' or 'representational' point of view. It emphasizes the principle of solidarity in a federal sense, and is found frequently in the Scriptures. Take, for instance, the statement in the Ten Commandments where God says that He will 'visit the iniquity of the fathers upon the children, to the third and fourth generation of them that hate me'. That is another statement of the same principle. There, God says that He will impute the action of an individual to his successors, to his progeny, even to his great-great-grandchildren.

As I said previously, it seems to me that both of the ideas I have now explained are surely taught here. The first is that Adam is our representative as Christ is our representative. But not only that; Adam was also the head of the race as Christ is the head of a race. Furthermore, there is this union, this mystical union which we have been considering, the teaching concerning our being in the loins of Adam, and then as believers our mystical union with the Lord Jesus Christ. Incidentally the teaching about our being in the loins of Adam, as Levi was in the loins of Abraham, is known as the theory of 'Seminal Identity'. In the loins means as it were in the semen. We were identified with Adam because we were in his seminal, germinal principle of life. We come out of that and have been produced by that means.

We cannot go any further than that. What I am anxious to emphasize at this point is that there are two principles which we always have to observe when we are studying the Scripture. The first is, never to go beyond the Scripture. It is a temptation to which theologians are particularly subject. They tend to go too far, and to press their own logic. Natural ability and reason begin to insinuate themselves and they speculate beyond the teaching of the Word. We have no right to do that, and we must not do that. On the other hand, it is equally important that we should always go as far as the Scriptures go. So if someone should say to me, 'I cannot be bothered with this Seminal Identity theory of yours', I say to him, 'My dear sir, you have got to be concerned about it, because when you read the Epistle to the Hebrews and come to chapter 7, verses 9 and 10, if you are reading intelligently you will have to ask, What does the author mean when he says that Levi paid tithes to Melchisedec because at the time of payment he was in the loins of Abraham? You have no right to skip over that; you must stop and face it.' What I have been attempting is to explain it, and to understand it, and to show its bearing upon our whole position. It will become tremendously and increasingly important as we go on with this Epistle, and especially as we come to the amazing doctrine of our unity and our identification with the Lord Jesus Christ.

What is clear then is this, that Paul is saying here quite plainly that all sinned in Adam, and that all are guilty before God on account of that one sin of Adam when he deliberately transgressed God's commandment. God has imputed to the whole of the human race, including ourselves, that one sin of Adam. Adam sinned and we all sinned. This is an essential part of the doctrine of Original Sin.

Once more I must repeat what I said previously, that we must not begin to question our relationship to the world's first man, Adam, because every time you put the question I will make you ask the same question about our relationship to the Lord Jesus Christ. If you say to me, 'Is it fair that the sin of Adam should be imputed to me?' I will reply by asking, 'Is it fair that the righteousness of Christ should be imputed to you?' If you say, further, 'I cannot understand that sort of thing', I will ask, 'Can you understand the other?' The result is that you will be left without a Gospel, without a hope, and without a salvation. This is high doctrine. It is beyond our understanding, but, as I say, it is our business to take the Scriptures as they are.

I am well aware that most modern commentators entirely disagree with what I am saying; and I can give you the reason for this. They say, 'In Romans 5 : 12 and to the end of that chapter Paul is simply showing that he was once a Pharisee. He is giving the typical Rabbinical teaching, which was taught commonly at that time'. 'Of course,' they add, 'nobody believes anything like that now. Science and anthropology have shown and proved that the whole theory is impossible, and that there never was a first man Adam. Adam is a generic term standing for the whole of humanity. There never was such an individual as Adam at all; and what you read in the first three chapters of Genesis is not actual history. But Paul – no blame to him! – did not know that, as we now know it, and therefore he repeated this Rabbinical teaching.' They have solved the problem, apparently, quite simply. The Apostle Paul was making a big mistake, a grievous error, and it was due to sheer ignorance.

For myself, if I accepted such a position, I would then feel bound logically to go further and ask something like this: 'What about this idea that Christ died for my sins, that He was set forth to be a propitiation for me? Is not that typical Rabbinical teaching also? Is not that just Paul, the old Pharisee, coming back into operation again? It is but another example of Paul foisting his ideas, his erroneous ideas upon us.'

'But if that is so', asks someone, 'have you any Gospel left at all?' 'Oh yes,' reply the modern critics, 'we have a Gospel; our Gospel is this, that "God is love". That is the whole of the Gospel; everything is going to be all right at the end for everybody. There is no such thing as sin – that was but a legalistic Jewish idea; that and all ideas with regard to justice and wrath and punishment are all wrong.'

To this I reply: if you begin to say that the Apostle was in error with regard to any one matter, and that he was simply governed by the ignorance of his time, how do you decide what to believe and what not to believe? That is your ultimate position and problem. In other words, we are driven to this question: What exactly is the authority of the Scripture? What is the authority of the Apostles? That is the basic question. Therefore, before you begin to argue with people about this particular section of the Epistle, and the particular question of the imputation of Adam's sin, get that clear with them. What is their view of these Apostolic writings? Are they, or are they not, divinely inspired? Were the writers just able men putting forward their ideas (some of which were current teaching) or is it right to say, what the Scripture itself says, that these men were 'moved by the Holy Ghost?' [2 *Peter* 1: 21]. The Apostle Peter refers to the writings of Paul and talks about 'the teaching of our beloved brother Paul', which, he says, certain people 'wrest to their own destruction, as they do also the other Scriptures' [2 *Peter* 3: 13, 16]. He puts the writings of Paul into the same category as the Old Testament of which he has earlier said that it is not 'of any private interpretation' but produced by the Holy Ghost.

The early Church accorded to these Apostles a unique authority. The Apostle Paul himself claims that what he taught was not his own teaching, neither had he received it from men, but that it was given him by revelation [*Galatians* 1: 11, 12]. He says, also, in the third chapter of Ephesians, that the whole of his teaching was something that had been revealed to him and to the other

Apostles. In direct consequence of this we are back to that fundamental question. If, therefore, I regard this man Paul as an inspired and infallible writer, I cannot say as I expound this section that it is just Rabbinical teaching, because that means that I have to agree with those who say he was wrong at this point. So I am driven to this position, that I have to accept it as it is; and accepting it as it is, I find that it is wholly consistent with apostolic teaching everywhere – indeed with the message and the teaching of the Bible everywhere. I have a complete whole, and there are no contradictions at all. But if I take out this section and reject it, I do not know where I am; I have an equal right to take out other sections.

In the end it would come to this, that the Gospel is what I think it ought to be; and I am the ultimate authority. I take out this section, and I eliminate another. Of another section I may say, That is correct and I accept it. This attitude obviously means that I set myself up as the authority; but, as I know myself, I am not fit to be an authority. I am not big enough to be an authority; I am too fallible to be an authority. No man is capable of being such an authority. I either submit to the authority of the Scriptures or else I am in a morass where there is no standing. I may try to satisfy myself by saying that this is what modern scholarship teaches. I have quoted earlier from the Commentary on this Epistle to the Romans by Dr. C. H. Dodd. He does not hesitate to adopt the attitude I have mentioned. He does not shrink from saying that the teaching of the Church until modern times has been wrong on some of these crucial matters. He says, 'The new light that has come to us on the Greek and the Hebrew languages enables us to understand'. The Protestant Reformers did not understand, the great Fathers of the Church before that did not understand; there was no true understanding of the Scriptures until this present century! If you are content to believe that, I have no more to say. But in that case I ask you to explain the history of the Church, I ask you to explain the revivals, I ask you to explain a man like Jonathan Edwards and the things that God did through him. According to this modern teaching, what Jonathan Edwards taught on original sin and the wrath of God was wrong; but the Holy Spirit of God honoured it to the salvation of countless hundreds. The same was true also of Whitefield, and the same applies to the preaching of the Puritans and, before them, to the Protestant Fathers themselves, and still further back to Augustine.

Like the Apostle Paul before me I have digressed, but it is an essential digression, made for this reason, that the moment you begin to base your position upon your inability to understand, you are putting yourself into the position of those present-day critics and liberals who ultimately have no Gospel at all, and whose ministry is in consequence utterly ineffective. They talk about learning and scholarship, but one never hears of a soul being saved under their ministry. Such teaching has all but emptied the churches. It is time that these things should be said plainly and clearly in order that we may realize the consequences that follow when we begin to set up our understanding and our reason as the ultimate sanction and the final authority.

So much, then, for the exposition of the last clause in verse 12; with this understanding of the relationship of all men to Adam, we must now proceed to follow Paul when he says that Adam is 'the figure of him that was to come'. This is what the Apostle is ultimately concerned to show. His statement is that over and above the historicity of Adam and our fall in him, Adam is a type of Christ. He is a figure or a pre-figuring of the Lord Jesus Christ who was to come. So what is seen in our relationship to Adam, should also be seen in our relationship to Christ.

Here, then, he introduces this wonderful comparison. He begins to outline it but he interrupts himself at the beginning of verse 15. In verse 14 he says, 'even over them that had not sinned after the similitude of Adam's transgression, who is the figure of him that was to come', which at once suggests that the parallel between Adam and Christ is identical in every single respect. But that is not so. 'I must safeguard this' he seems to say. There is the great central similarity, but there are also contrasts, and striking differences. 'Do not run away with the idea,' he seems to say, 'that I am going to say that everything that is true of our relationship to

Adam is exactly and in the minutest detail true also of our relationship to the Lord Jesus Christ. It is not so. There are differences as well as similarities.'

What, I ask, are the similarities? In what senses is it true to say that Adam was a type of Christ? Adam – Christ! Here are the two pivotal personages of the whole of human history. Here are the similarities. Both were appointed by God. As I have been showing God appointed Adam as our head and representative, and in the same way the Lord Jesus Christ, as we are told in many places in the New Testament, was sent and appointed and set apart and sealed by God for His work and to be our representative.

Secondly, it is true to say of each of them that he is the head of a race, of a humanity. This same point is made in a particularly clear and extended manner by the Apostle in the fifteenth chapter of the First Epistle to the Corinthians. He says it not only here, he says it there in those glowing words with which we are so familiar at funeral services, and which so few understand: 'The first man is of the earth, earthy; the second man is the Lord from heaven' (verse 47). He puts it in another way, saying, 'The first man Adam was made a living soul; the last Adam was made a quickening spirit' (verse 45). Adam was the 'first Adam' and the 'first man'. The Lord Jesus Christ is the 'second Man' and the 'last Adam'. That is a most important distinction. John Henry Newman's famous hymn, beginning with the words 'Praise to the Holiest in the height', describes Him as the 'second Adam', but that is not strictly correct. He is the 'second' Man, but He is the 'last' Adam. Why does Paul draw this distinction? For this reason; there will never be another. There are only two heads of a race; the first was Adam, the second and the last is the Lord Jesus Christ. He is the last Adam. There will never be a successor to Him, there will never be another appointed to head a race of men.

Thirdly, each had a covenant made with him and is therefore a covenant-head. God, as we saw, made a covenant with Adam. He said to him in effect, 'You can stay and enjoy this life of communion with Me as long as you obey certain conditions. You can eat the fruit of the trees, but you must not eat of the fruit of the tree of the knowledge of good and evil – that is prohibited, that is forbidden. If you eat of that, then dying you shall die', and so on. That was a covenant. In exactly the same way God made a covenant with His own Son. Having appointed Him as the Head and the Representative of His people, He makes a covenant with Him, and the covenant is that if He bears their sins He will deliver them and they shall be His people. If He is obedient to the Law and gives God satisfaction, and takes the sins of these people upon Him and suffers their penalty, then they shall be set free and pronounced to be just in God's sight. Such is the Covenant of Redemption which God made with His own Son. So each of them – Adam and the Lord Jesus Christ – is the Head of the Covenant made with him.

The next point of similarity is that each represented all his seed. Listen to this in 1 Corinthians 15 again, verses 21, 22: 'For since by man came death, by man came also the resurrection of the dead. For as in Adam all die, even so in Christ shall all be made alive.' Each represents all his seed.

And the last point of similarity is that each has passed on to his seed the effects and the fruits of his work. Adam's sin and its consequences was passed on to us all without exception: Christ's obedience and righteousness is passed on to all who believe in Him.

Those are the similarities, the points shared in common by Adam and the Lord Jesus Christ. It is in these ways that Adam is a figure or a type of Him that was to come.

We leave it at that for the moment. A number of most interesting points will emerge. The Apostle goes on also to show the contrasts, the dissimilarities, the differences between the headships of Adam and Christ. He does that, as we shall see, in order to bring out his characteristic and resounding 'Much more' with respect to the grace of God, the free gift of God's grace, in our salvation. And as we work that out we shall have to face another problem which perplexes many.

People often put that problem in the form of a question: 'You are talking about these similarities – "as in Adam, so in Christ"

– and there are these many statements such as "Not as the offence, so also is the free gift. For if through the offence of one many be dead, much more the grace of God, and the gift by grace, which is by one man, Jesus Christ, hath abounded unto many." If you are going to say', they continue, 'that this is a perfect parallel, and you have already told us that, because of the one sin of Adam, everybody is guilty before God, and all die, are you therefore going to say, on the other side, that Jesus Christ saves everybody? Are you therefore a universalist? Do you believe that salvation reaches to all? Is the "many" in the one place identical with the "many" in the other? Does "all" always mean the same thing? How do you interpret these "manys" and these "alls"?' We shall face these questions honestly and then go on to show the 'much more' of the grace of God in which Paul delights so much.

Seventeen

*

But not as the offence, so also is *the free gift. For if through the offence of one many be dead, much more the grace of God, and the gift by grace,* which is *by one man, Jesus Christ, hath abounded unto many.* Romans 5 : 15

We are now ready to work out the comparison which the Apostle makes here between our relationship to Adam and our relationship to the Lord Jesus Christ. He introduces it at the end of the fourteenth verse where he says, speaking of Adam, 'Who is the figure (the type) of him that was to come'. We have seen already that there are certain striking resemblances and similarities between Adam and the Lord Jesus Christ. Both were appointed by God; each was the head of a race; each was the head of a covenant; each represented his seed; each passed on to his seed the effects and the fruits of his own work. In those respects there is this obvious parallel between our relationship to Adam and our relationship to the Lord Jesus Christ; and that is what the Apostle is anxious to show. But we have also seen that the Apostle immediately interrupts himself to point out that, while there is this obvious parallel, there is also a most obvious difference and contrast. Let us be clear, however, as we go on, that the differences do not do away with the parallel; the parallel is the fundamental thing. The Apostle's main concern is to unfold the glory of grace, and he does so by showing that while the fundamental parallel is true, the moment you come to look at it in detail what impresses and strikes you most of all is the series of contrasts all reflecting the glory and the wonder of grace.

He proceeds to do this in the three verses, 15, 16 and 17. In our preliminary analysis of this section we pointed out that at the end of verse 12 there is a bracket indicating a parenthesis.

We also indicated that there is a further parenthesis – a parenthesis within the parenthesis – and that after he has finished with these at the end of verse 17 he comes back again in verse 18 to his fundamental statement which he began in verse 12. We shall now work out in particular the contrasts, the differences between our relationship to Adam and our relationship to the Lord Jesus Christ.

The most convenient way of classifying these contrasts is to consider them under the headings of general and particular. The main general difference is one which the Apostle does not state explicitly in words, but it is implicit right through. We must extract it and emphasize it. The one basic general contrast follows from the fact that our relationship to Adam is a natural one, a physical one. As we have seen previously, we were all 'in the loins' of Adam – he is the father of us all, the beginning of the human race; the entire race comes out of him. So our relationship to Adam is based on physical connection and physical descent. We can even go beyond that and say that we were all created in Adam, and essentially so in this physical respect. But when we come to speak of our relationship to the Lord Jesus Christ at once we see the contrast. The relationship is no longer physical, but spiritual. That, of course, is obvious on the surface; and yet people sometimes seem to miss it when they try to press the parallel in every detail, as I shall show. They forget that there is this essential difference. We all come out of Adam physically, but our connection with the Lord Jesus Christ is a spiritual one and not a physical one. We must bear that in mind constantly.

Let me illustrate this point by reference to an obvious contrast between the Old Testament and the New. In the one case everything tends to be material and materialistic. A man was blessed in the Old Testament, and seen to be blessed, by the number of oxen and sheep and camels he possessed. You do not find that in the New Testament; indeed you find almost the exact opposite. In the Old the truth is conveyed in an external, physical, material manner; in the New it is spiritual. In the same way one belonged to the nation of Israel by physical descent; you but do not belong to the Kingdom of God by physical descent but as the result of a spiritual rebirth. That is the kind of thing which we must have in our minds here. Our relationship to the Lord is not physical, it is spiritual. That is the big general point of contrast in this parallel drawn by the Apostle.

But now, turning from the general, let us look at the particular differences. The Apostle draws a bold picture of these particular differences in the fifteenth verse: 'But not as the offence, so also is the free gift.' That means that what is true of the offence is not true of the free gift in every respect; there is a contrast here as well, and it is a glorious contrast. The very terms, 'the offence' and 'the free gift', immediately suggest a contrast to our minds; but the Apostle is not content with stating it generally, he divides it up for us into details. However, the fundamental thing is that on the one side you have an offence, and on the other you have this great and glorious free gift.

Let us look at these terms. First, 'the offence'. When we think of Adam, and our relationship to Adam, what comes to our minds immediately is his offence, the sin which he committed, the transgression into which he fell, the disobedience of which he was guilty. The Apostle has been emphasizing that: 'By one man's offence sin entered into the world, and death by sin, and so death passed upon all men.' The very mention of Adam's name reminds us of the offence. He disobeyed the commandment of God, he broke the law and so he was guilty of a transgression. To what did such conduct lead? The answer is found in the Authorized Version in the words, 'through the offence of one, many be dead'. That means that 'many died', and as we have seen so many times, the expression means that we were involved in the guilt. Offence and guilt always lead to death. We have seen how the Apostle has kept on emphasizing this truth from verse 12: 'Sin came into the world', and then because sin came, 'death came by sin'. Death is always a part of the punishment of the guilt of sin. Hence, because of this one offence many died. But as death is something that follows as the result of guilt it is necessarily true that death is the just desert of all of us. If we are punished for sin it is obvious that we deserve it. An offence is always deserving of punishment because it involves guilt. And that is what happens to us all because of our relationship to Adam. When Adam sinned we all sinned – 'for that all sinned', as we are told at the end of the twelfth verse. So our relationship to Adam has rendered us all offenders and sinners, and that has meant that we all die; and we deserve that death because we are involved in the guilt of the sin.

Let me summarize this by putting it as the Apostle himself puts it at the end of chapter 6: 'The wages of sin is death, but the gift of God is eternal life, through Jesus Christ our Lord.' Death is a kind of 'wages' which we have earned. God made a covenant with Adam. He told him what he must not do, and that if he offended he would be punished, and that the punishment would be death and banishment out of His sight, and out of the Garden of Eden. And that included death physical as well as death spiritual. Adam did what was prohibited and he received the wages due to what he had done. So the punishment meted out to us as the result of sin can be thought of in terms of something earned, wages received. 'The wages of sin is death.' We get our deserts, we die, and we deserve it because of our involvement in the guilt of Adam's sin. The covenant was made with Adam as our head and representative. We were also in the loins of Adam. He was not merely acting for himself, he was acting for us all. And what that action deserves is, 'The wages of sin is death'.

'BUT not as the offence so also is the free gift'; and the very terminology at once stresses the complete contrast – 'Free gift'. We are now out of the realm of 'wages'; it is no longer a question of deserts. And here Paul has stated his great and glorious contrast – on the one hand 'offence', and all that that leads to, and on the other hand, the 'free gift'.

But he is not content with the bare use of the term 'free gift'. He expounds it, and allows us to follow him as he does so. 'For', he says, 'if through the offence of one many died, much more the grace of God, and the gift by grace, which is by one man, Jesus Christ, hath abounded unto many.' Here we have one of those glorious statements of the Gospel and of salvation which the Apostle has been scattering so freely in this particular chapter of our Epistle, and none is more glorious, surely, than this one,

Every term is important, every word counts, and therefore we must look at them and examine them carefully.

We must start with the expression 'much more', because, in a sense, it says it all. But though he says it all there when first used, he keeps on repeating it. 'If through the offence of one many died, much more . . .' – and the whole Gospel is in this 'much more'.

What does it mean here? Quite a number of things! First, it means that if our connection with Adam, who was only a man, led certainly and inevitably to the result that we all die, 'much more' will our connection with the Lord Jesus Christ, who is God as well as Man, certainly lead to the result promised. I put that first because I am quite sure that that was the thing that was uppermost in the Apostle's mind, and for the following reason. We have seen from the very beginning of this chapter that what was gripping the mind of the Apostle and thrilling him so much that he scarcely knew how to express himself, was the absolute certainty of salvation. 'If', he says, 'a man is in Christ Jesus and is justified by faith, he has peace with God. Moreover, he has access into this grace wherein we stand, and rejoices in hope of the glory of God.' And he repeated that time and again. We saw him arguing it out very strongly in verses 9, 10 and 11: 'Much more then, being now justified by his blood, we shall be saved from wrath through him. For if, when we were enemies, we were reconciled to God by the death of his Son, much more, being reconciled, we shall be saved by his life. And not only so, but we also joy in God through our Lord Jesus Christ, by whom we have now received the atonement.' But that is not all, he comes back again here to this 'much more'. The argument is, in a sense, that which we have found in verses 9 and 10. Adam was only a man, but even in his case the result of his one act was certain and sure. But now, as the Lord Jesus Christ is the God-Man, the result of *His* one act is infinitely more certain, it is bound to ensue. The certainty of it all is brought out by the 'much more'.

But there is another element here. I believe that in the 'much more' the Apostle has in his mind the contrast between death and life. Death is inescapable, death is a certainty; there is a finality about death. But, after all, death is not as powerful as life;

and this is the contrast. He is contrasting death and life. 'Because of the offence of one, many died.' Ah! but here is One who has life, everlasting life, eternal life, the life of God. This is 'much more' than death. If death was certain, how much more must life be certain. We are no longer under the power of death; but in the realm, and experiencing the power of life, so we say, 'Much more'.

But there is yet another meaning, surely, in this. If God's justice and His righteousness led to punishment, 'much more' will His love and grace and mercy and compassion lead to salvation. The more we know about God, the more we realize that everything He does is absolute. That is why, when God had made the covenant with Adam, and had laid down the conditions, it was inevitable that death should follow. But (and surely we are entitled to say this) God delights in His love even more than He delights in His justice. Love is His very nature; His nature and being are love. So we are entitled to bring in the 'much more' in this way. If we can say (as we can) that God's essential and eternal justice led to man's punishment and death, oh how infinitely more certain and sure can we be – and especially having seen it all displayed in a living manner in Christ – that His love is really going to do for us that which He has said He would do, namely, give us life. So here we have a contrast between justice and righteousness on the one hand, and love on the other. There is no division or contradiction, because all these attributes are present together in God. It is just a matter of a mental contrast in our minds, as it were, emphasizing that God delights in His love and in His graciousness.

But I venture to believe that there is one other element in this contrast; and this is a very important one for us from the practical standpoint, indeed from every standpoint. What the Lord Jesus Christ has done for us who believe in Him is not merely, and not only, to restore us to where we were in Adam. He has done more. Look at it in this way. There we were in Adam. Adam sinned, he committed that offence; and we all fell with him, we all died. What does the Lord Jesus Christ do for us? I assert that He does not stop at putting us back where we were in Adam. Isaac Watts' well-known hymn beginning with the words, 'Jesus shall reign where'er the sun', brings out this idea very well. In the original there is a verse which for some completely inexplicable reason is left out of many of our hymn-books. I believe I am right in saying that you will only find this particular verse in the Baptist Church Hymnary and in the Methodist Hymn-book. In that missing verse you will find these two lines:

In Him the tribes of Adam boast
More blessings than their father lost.

I believe that Isaac Watts is right when he says that the blessings of salvation exceed the losses consequent on Adam's fall. Our Lord does not put us back just where we were before the Fall; He takes us beyond that. 'Much more'; 'More blessings than their father lost'! But we shall take up this point again, in more detail, shortly.

So much for the first term then, the 'much more'. That leads us inevitably to 'the grace of God'. It is the grace of God that produces this 'much more'. We have defined the word 'grace' many times already in previous studies, but it is to me, as it was to Philip Doddridge, such 'a charming sound, harmonious to the ear', that I must remind you again of what it means. Grace is that quality in God, that attribute of God which leads Him to be gracious towards and to bless the utterly undeserving. Grace is favour shown to people who do not deserve any favour at all, who, indeed, deserve the exact opposite. We cannot be reminded too frequently of this; that is why the New Testament repeats it so frequently. It was 'while we were without strength'; it was 'while we were ungodly'; it was 'while we were sinners'; it was 'while we were yet enemies' that God sent His only-begotten dearly-beloved Son into the world, and even to die for us. That is grace! It is favour shown to people who deserve anything but favour, who deserve wrath and hatred and punishment and perdition. The grace of God! 'Much more', says Paul, 'the grace of God.'

To what then does the grace lead? 'Grace', says the Apostle, leads to 'a gift'. 'Much more the grace of God, and the gift by grace', or 'the gift that comes through grace'. The contrast is seen everywhere, in every term used. No longer is he talking about 'wages', he is talking about a 'gift'. Salvation is something that is given to us, and which we receive absolutely freely as the gift of God. If you in any way feel that you are saved and forgiven because of anything in you, I doubt whether you are forgiven. The Apostle has already told us this very plainly in the twenty-fourth verse of the third chapter: 'Being justified freely by his grace, through the redemption that is in Christ Jesus.' If we do not see that it is all the gift of God, something which we have done nothing whatsoever to deserve, or to earn or to merit in any shape or form, we just have not seen 'the truth as it is in Jesus'. It is all to the glory of grace. That is the essence of salvation. God 'justifies the ungodly'. It is a free gift. There is nothing in us that merits it. If you are even relying upon the fact that you believe you are spoiling it. There is nothing in us at all. It is entirely the free gift of God's grace. It is altogether 'given'. The Apostle does not actually define the gift here; he does that later in verses 17, 18 and 21. The 'gift' is 'eternal life'; again, the contrast with the death – 'because of the offence all died'. The free gift of God's grace is eternal life, through Jesus Christ our Lord.

That brings us to the next term. 'Much more', says the Apostle, 'the grace of God, and the gift by grace, which is by one man, Jesus Christ, hath abounded unto many'. Here we have the term – the most charming of them all, I think – a term that Paul so delights in that he repeats it again in verses 17 and 20. 'For if by one man's offence death reigned by one; much more they which receive abundance of grace and of the gift of righteousness shall reign in life by one, Jesus Christ.' Again in verse 20: 'Moreover the law entered, that the offence might abound. But where sin abounded, grace did much more abound.' Clearly, what is gripping the Apostle and moving him deeply and producing this terrific eloquence is – the 'abounding' character of grace.

Again, what a wonderful contrast! Death is non-productive; death is the end; death is final; death does not produce fruit. Death by definition is something which is completely unfruitful.

So when you say 'death entered and all died', if no other factor operates you can say no more about them except that they go on in that condition to all eternity. There is no development. But that is not the case with God's grace. The 'much more' leads to life, and so it leads to something which abounds. It is of the very nature of life to develop and to multiply itself and to go on increasing. Look at it in the realm of nature. Think of the one seed you sow, and then look at the abundance of fruit that comes up out of it. It divides by a process of fission and that goes on and multiplies. That seed is full of life, and life multiplies and reproduces itself by some kind of geometric progression. 'The abundance hath abounded', says the Apostle. If we have not seen this element in grace we have missed one of its most glorious aspects. John Bunyan had seen it, and that is why he gives one of his most famous books the title of 'Grace abounding to the chief of sinners'.

Grace always abounds. Grace must never be thought of in static, mechanical, mercenary terms. No, no! There is no measure to grace, no limit – it is illimitable. Look at the terms that are used in connection with it in the Scriptures. John in the first chapter of his Gospel in verse 16 says, 'And of his fulness have all we received, and grace upon grace' – grace for grace; grace after grace. You think you have it all, and then there is more, and then there is more, and on and on to all eternity. There is no end to it, to His 'fulness'; it is eternal, it is illimitable, it is immeasurable. This same Apostle Paul in writing to the Ephesians speaks in the second chapter of 'the exceeding riches of his grace'. In the third chapter of the same Epistle he says that he has been called to, and has, the great privilege of preaching among the Gentiles 'the unsearchable riches of Christ'. 'Unsearchable', inestimable, can never be computed, can never be added up, there is no end to it. As this is the realm into which we have been brought, is it surprising that the Apostle says 'much more'? Is it surprising that he is so fond of the expression 'hath abounded', or that he talks about an 'abundance?'

What does grace, abounding grace, mean? Oh! how important this is for us! Will I offend anyone, I wonder, if I say this? As the preacher I have a great advantage over people who listen to me expounding these great terms. You come from your offices, from your professions, or whatever you do; and you have been busy during the day. You have no choice, it is your duty to attend to your various callings; but I have spent my day with these great terms and thoughts which I am expounding to you. The privileges of the preacher are very great and his responsibility is correspondingly great. He of all people should be ready to extol God's matchless grace. But all Christians who believe these things should meditate upon them and consider them carefully and so be ready to sing with the whole of their being –

Blessings abound where'er He reigns;
The prisoner leaps to lose his chains.

Remember these things the next time you sing that hymn. It reminds us of that 'grace abounding', and that there is no limit to it.

Let us look at this grace and analyse it a little. It does not mean that we are simply forgiven. We *are* forgiven, thank God. The first thing we need is forgiveness; we are undone without it, we are lost. We need forgiveness, we need to be washed clean from the guilt of sin. But the grace of God does not stop at forgiveness. The Lord Jesus Christ did not come from heaven, and live and die and rise again, just to procure forgiveness for us and to ensure that we should not go to hell. Salvation does not stop there; it includes much more than putting us back to where Adam was before he fell.

Consider the situation. Adam was made in the image and likeness of God. He was in a state of innocence. He had not sinned and his nature was without sin. And yet there was something negative even about that state; innocence suggests the absence of something. But that is not the position to which God's abounding grace introduces us. We are put into a position in which, as Isaac Watts says so rightly, we have a better status than that of Adam. We have something that Adam lacked; for we are 'in Christ'. Adam was not in Christ. Adam was made in God's image but he was, as it were, outside the life of God. But we are 'in Christ'. God the Son came down to earth; He took human nature unto

Himself; and we are 'in Him'. Adam was never in that position. We are incorporated into Christ. We are members of the household of God. Not so, Adam. He was perfect man, he was innocent, he had not sinned; but he was not a member of the household of God.

I will go further. Are you ready to follow? We are no longer in a state of probation and liable to fall; but that was Adam's position. He was made in the image of God, he was innocent, he was perfect, he was without sin, but he was on probation, there was the possibility of his falling, and he fell.

In Him the tribes of Adam boast
More blessings than their father lost.

I say that in Christ we are not in a state of probation, and that there is no possibility of our falling from grace. We are beyond that. Our glorification is guaranteed as we saw in verses 1 and 2 of this fifth chapter, and as we shall see again and again as we proceed.

'What is your authority for saying such things'? asks someone. There is no difficulty about answering. My authority is the whole argument of the following chapter (chapter 6) and still more of chapter 8. But if you want it in particularly specific statements you will find it in chapter 2 of the Epistle to the Ephesians. This is how it reads from verse 4: 'But God, who is rich in mercy, for his great love wherewith he loved us, even when we were dead in sins, hath quickened us together with Christ, (by grace are ye saved); and hath raised us up together and made us sit together in heavenly places in Christ Jesus.' That, says Paul, has happened to us already. It is not a prospect; it has happened. If we are in Christ we are 'seated with him in the heavenly places'; we are not on probation and we cannot fall. That was not true of Adam; but it is true of us as Christians.

Again, look at it as it is stated in the eighth chapter of this Epistle to the Romans, 'Moreover whom he did predestinate, them he also called; and whom he called, them he also justified; and whom he justified, them he also glorified' (verse 30). We 'rejoice in hope of the glory of God', we exult in it, we are sure of it. We know that we are going there. 'No man shall be able to pluck them out of my Father's hand', says our Lord [*John* 8: 28, 29], nor out of His hand. The final perseverance of the saints is guaranteed by this 'much more' of the grace of God which has abounded toward us. If you are in Christ you are going to glory, and neither sin, nor hell, nor the devil can stand between you and getting there. 'I am persuaded (I am certain) that neither death, nor life, nor angels, nor principalities, nor powers, nor things present, nor things to come, nor height, nor depth, nor any other creature, shall be able to separate us from the love of God which is in Christ Jesus our Lord' (chapter 8: 38, 39). Are you afraid of this doctrine? Not one of Christ's people will be missing, not one will be lost. We are not merely restored to Adam's condition, we are taken beyond that. The Son of God guarantees it, and the end is as certain as the beginning.

The next term we have to consider is one which the Apostle never leaves out. You notice the phrase I have not mentioned yet. 'Much more', he says, 'the grace of God, and the gift by grace, which is *by one man, Jesus Christ*'. The Apostle, I say, never leaves this out; and this is the most glorious contrast of all. In Adam we were united to a man, a created human being. But Jesus Christ was not created. He is the only-begotten Son of the Father – 'begotten, not created'. He was born as a man, but not created; He was begotten of the Virgin Mary, but not created. He is not a created being. It is heresy to say that He is. The angels are created beings, but He is not. He is the eternal Son of God. He was from the beginning; He is everlastingly in the bosom of the Father; He is one with the Father. 'In the beginning was the Word' – 'begotten, not created'. He is the eternal Son; and we are united to Him.

As united to Adam we were concerned with the question of disobedience; but in Christ it is a matter of glorying in His perfect obedience. The blessing has come to us through Him and through His obedience. If you have never realized this before, realize it now. There is no blessing that ever comes to man from God without coming through the Lord Jesus Christ. There is no salvation apart from Him. I say it with reverence, but even God could not forgive us apart from what happened in Jesus Christ. The Incarnation is not a show. The death on the Cross is not a tableau. No, no! They were essential, they had to happen, it was the only way. God's justice demands this; the integrity of the divine and eternal Being insists upon it. The grace of God comes to us exclusively and only in and through the Lord Jesus Christ. If He had not come, if it could not be said of Him that, though He 'counted it not robbery to be equal with God', He had humbled Himself and made Himself of no reputation, and taken upon Himself the form of a man, and even the form of a servant; if He had not further humbled Himself and become obedient unto death, even the death of the Cross, and submitted passively to having the sins of men laid upon Him and punished in Him – I say, if He had not done all that, if His blood had not been shed, and if He had not risen again, there would be no abounding grace, there would be no talk of the 'abundance of the grace of God' with respect to us. It all comes to us through that one Person – truly Man, truly God, the two natures in the one Person, the God-Man, Christ Jesus. 'Much more the grace of God, and the gift by grace, through the one man Christ Jesus, hath abounded unto many.'

The vital question, the all-important question, is this: Do you know this abounding grace? Are you rejoicing in it? Are you thrilled at the contemplation of it? Are you experiencing it? Can you say with Charles Wesley,

Thou, O Christ, art all I want,
More than all in Thee I find.

Is Christ this to you? Is your salvation merely a matter of saying 'I believe my sins are forgiven', or are you rejoicing in it? Are you 'receiving of His fulness'? Are you aware of His meeting your every need? Are you looking forward to the glory and rejoicing in anticipation of it? Are you certain of it – 'the abundance of the grace'?

I am more and more convinced that it is only when you and I, and others who are members of the Christian Church, are rejoicing in this abounding grace as we ought to be, that we shall begin to attract the people who are outside the Church. That is my understanding of evangelism. If you and I and all other Christians walked through this world as men and women who are experiencing the 'abundance of grace' and this 'much more', we should find that people would stop us at work, and in the business or the profession, and on the street, and they would say, 'Tell me, what is this? I want to know about it, I want it for myself'. But as it is, far too often, they look at us and say, 'If that is Christianity, then I do not want it'. It is a sin not to be living in the enjoyment of 'the abundance of grace'. It is a sin to live as a pauper when you are meant to be enjoying the life of a prince. We were never meant to walk about in penury; we are 'children of the Heavenly King'. Hold up your heads. Walk through the world showing the abundance of the riches of God's grace in your life and in your experience; and, thereby, tell forth His grace and show forth His praise.

Eighteen

*

But not as the offence, so also is *the free gift. For if through the offence of one many be dead, much more the grace of God, and the gift by grace,* which is *by one man, Jesus Christ, hath abounded unto many.* Romans 5: 15

We have already looked at the contrast between Adam and the Lord Jesus Christ in general and have also given some attention to the Apostle's more particular treatment of the subject. But before we enter into further details, it is perhaps best for us at this point to consider a question that seems to arise in many people's minds as to the use of the terms 'many' and 'all'. Actually the term used by the Apostle which in the Authorized version appears as 'many' should be translated 'the many'. Not that that makes the slightest difference, but it should read: 'Not as the offence, so also is the free gift. For if through the offence of one the many died, much more the grace of God, and the gift by grace, which is by one man, Jesus Christ, hath abounded unto the many.' Then you find that later Paul uses the term 'all'. Take verse 18: 'Therefore as by the offence of one judgment came upon all men to condemnation, even so by the righteousness of one the free gift came upon all men unto justification of life.' Then in verse 19 he goes back again to 'the many'. 'For as by one man's disobedience the many were made sinners, so by the obedience of one shall the many be made righteous'.

We are compelled to consider these terms in order to discover to what extent the parallel applies numerically. There are people who would say, 'Obviously the terms "the many" and "all" mean exactly the same in the one case as they do in the other'. They say, 'After all, the word "all" means "all", and "the many" means "the many", and if "the many" means "all" in one place it must also mean "all" in another place'. So they deduce that clearly the Apostle is teaching that all are going to be saved. And if you press the words literally that is the only conclusion to which you can come. The teaching is quite plain and clear that 'all died in Adam' – everybody. We have been emphasizing that from the very beginning – infants, everybody. All those who lived between Adam and Moses died, all men die in Adam. Therefore, they argue, as you have the same term on the other side, it must mean that all will be saved in Jesus Christ.

This view is called universalism. There are people who believe it and teach it. There are many such at the present time who believe that all without exception are going to be saved. This is one of their chief arguments, that you have 'the many' and 'the many', and the 'all' and the 'all'; and they say, ' "All" means "all", and there you are!'

Is it really as simple as that? Is that really the way to handle and apply Scripture? I suggest very strongly that it is not; and for the following good reasons. This, to begin: To use Scripture in that way is to be guilty of sheer literalism, which, it seems to me, is unintelligent. It is wrong to take every single word in the Scripture in that literal manner, for the Scripture often uses pictures and symbols. 'How do you know when it is doing that?' asks someone. The answer is that the context will generally make it quite plain and clear. Certainly we must not in an unintelligent manner just pick out a word here and a word there, we must take every statement in its context.

If you do that you will discover that terms like 'all' and 'the world' and 'many', and so on, as used in Scripture, quite frequently do not mean every individual person. They seem to be all-inclusive terms – 'all', 'the world', and so on – but there are many instances in Scripture where quite clearly they do not mean every single member of the human family. Take for instance, what we are told at the beginning of the second chapter of Luke's Gospel, at the time of the birth of our Lord, 'that all the world should be taxed'. That does not mean that every individual in the entire world had to submit to the taxation. You will find a similar use of the term 'all men' in the twenty-sixth verse of the third chapter of John's Gospel. A question had arisen between some of John the Baptist's disciples and the Jews about purifying, and we read: 'They came to John and said unto him, Rabbi, he that was with thee beyond Jordan, to whom thou bearest witness, behold, the same baptiseth, and all men come to him.' If you choose to say that that means that everybody in the world, every single person, was going at that time to the Lord Jesus Christ, of course no one can stop your doing so; but surely it is nonsensical to do so. The Jews were speaking hyperbolically; it was their way of saying that large numbers of people were going to Christ. It looked as if all were doing so. We sometimes say 'The whole world has gone after him' in the case of a popular man; by no stretch of imagination does it mean that every single person in the world has literally gone after him. It means that a very great crowd has found him a centre of attraction.

These are two instances of the imprecise use of expressions belonging to this category. But they are not the only ones. Take again what the Apostle Peter quotes from the prophet Joel on the day of Pentecost in his sermon at Jerusalem. Peter says, 'These men are not drunken . . . this is that which was spoken by the prophet Joel: And it shall come to pass in the last days, saith God, I will pour out of my Spirit upon all flesh.' That was the amazing promise of the coming of the Holy Spirit, 'the promise of the Father'. 'I will pour out of my Spirit upon all flesh.' Do you really believe that that means that every single person who is alive in the 'last days' – and Peter applies the promise to the Gospel age – is to be baptized by the Holy Ghost? Joel's statement, if you take it literally, seems to imply that and can mean nothing else – 'all flesh'. The universalist should say here, 'all flesh' means 'all flesh', and that means 'everybody'. So on that argument you have to say that a man who has lived an evil and a foul life all his days, and has died blaspheming the name of God, has received the baptism of the Holy Spirit: God has poured out His Spirit upon him. But how patently ridiculous that is! So we cannot just say that 'all' means 'all', and 'the many' means 'the many', and that is all there is to it. This is, I repeat, an extremely foolish form of literalism which no one should ever be guilty of who attempts to understand the teaching of the Scripture.

But there is a second reason for the rejection of a foolish literalism. This word 'all', as it is often used in the Scripture, is limited by conditions which Scripture itself makes clear; this is true of the very words we are looking at here – the 'all' and 'the many'. The limit here is perfectly clear in verse 17: 'For if by one man's offence death reigned by one' – and Paul has just been saying that it reigned over all, and he has kept on repeating his statement – 'much more they which receive abundance of grace and of the gift of righteousness shall reign in life by one, Jesus Christ'. He does not say that 'all' have received abundance of grace and of the gift of righteousness. What he says is that they, and they alone who have received that grace, are the people who are going to 'reign in life by one, Jesus Christ'. There, we notice, a limit is introduced. All died in Adam, but not all are going to reign in life. Who are going to reign in life? Only those 'who receive the abundance of grace, and of the gift of righteousness'! So the context itself at once puts a limit upon 'the many' on the Christ side. They and they alone are going to reign in life who receive this abundance of grace and of the gift of righteousness. So that without going outside our immediate context we find that there is a limit upon this second 'the many', and upon the second 'all'. This is not a limit introduced by me; it is a limit that the Apostle himself has deliberately introduced.

But there are other places where a condition is introduced. In the third chapter of this Epistle to the Romans, the Apostle, as we saw, says in verses 21 and 22, 'But now the righteousness of God without the law is manifested, being witnessed by the law and the prophets: even the righteousness of God which is by faith of Jesus Christ unto all and upon all them that believe.' 'Them that believe'! It is not all, meaning every single individual, but 'all them that believe'. There is the condition. So the 'all' there is immediately qualified by this condition of believing, as in this fifth chapter it is conditioned by the 'receiving of this abundance'. Then you find exactly the same thing in chapter 4, verse 16: 'Therefore', Paul says, 'it is of faith that it might be by grace; to the end the promise might be sure to all the seed; not to that only which is of the law, but to that also which is of the faith of Abraham, who is the father of us all.' Abraham is the father of all who believe, as he has been saying before in the immediate context. Abraham is the spiritual father of all who have this faith, and of nobody else. 'For they are not all Israel, that are of Israel' [*Romans* 9: 6]. They are the children of Abraham who are the children of faith. So, at once, the 'all' is again limited by this particular condition.

We must realize how important this is, so let me give another illustration out of the Book of the Acts of the Apostles. Paul, preaching at Antioch in Pisidia, says in Acts 13: 39, 'By him (Christ) all that believe are justified from all things'. All that believe are justified; not everybody, not the whole world; 'All that believe are justified'. Now the Apostle does not say one thing in Antioch of Pisidia and another when he writes to Christian people in Rome. His teaching is consistent everywhere. So that invariably there are conditions brought in to qualify the use of these apparently all-inclusive and all-comprehensive terms.

But I need not have said all that. I have done so simply in order to show that on grounds of language alone universalism cannot stand for a moment. But there is something which is much more obvious. Surely, if there is one thing that stands out prominently in the whole of Scripture from beginning to end, it is the fundamental division of mankind into two great final groups, the saved, and the lost. You have it clearly in the Old Testament. God Himself separates the people of Israel from all others, and the distinction is preserved throughout in a most detailed manner. Coming to the New Testament you find John the Baptist, the forerunner, making this final distinction quite clear. When he is talking about our Lord he says, 'Whose fan is in his hand, and he will throughly purge his floor, and gather his wheat into the garner; but he will burn up the chaff with fire unquenchable' [*Matthew* 3: 12]. There it is as plain as it could be.

You find the same distinction in our Lord's own teaching. 'God so loved the world, that he gave his only-begotten Son, that whosoever believeth in him should not perish but have everlasting life' [*John* 3 : 16]. What about those who do not believe? He says that they are 'condemned already, because they have not believed in the name of the only begotten Son of God' (verse 18). And at the end of that third chapter of John's Gospel is found the tremendous statement, 'He that believeth on the Son hath everlasting life, and he that believeth not the Son shall not see life, but the wrath of God abideth on him'. What could be plainer? This final division is found everywhere. Our Lord says again in John's Gospel chapter 5 that He has been sent in order to judge. He puts it like this: 'And hath also given him authority to execute judgment, because he is the Son of man. Marvel not at this, for the hour is coming, in the which all that are in the graves shall hear his voice, and shall come forth; they that have done good, unto the resurrection of life, and they that have done evil, unto the resurrection of damnation' (verses 27–29). There again is the division into two classes of men, as it is found indeed throughout the whole of the Scriptures.

The Apostle has already said the same thing in chapter 2 of this Epistle to the Romans. Look at verses 7 and 8: 'who will render to every man according to his deeds. To them who by patient continuance in well doing seek for glory and honour and immortality, eternal life; but unto them that are contentious, and do not obey the truth, but obey unrighteousness, indignation and wrath, tribulation and anguish, upon every soul of man that doeth evil, of the Jew first, and also of the Gentile.' However, if we had nothing but the Book of Revelation it would be enough; everywhere we have this same separation. But nowhere is it put more plainly than in Matthew 25 out of the mouth of our Lord Himself where He speaks about the sheep and the goats, and the division into those on His right hand and those on the left. And it is an absolute and eternal division.

Despite all this, people foolishly say, 'Ah but, it says here "the many", and "the many", and it says "all" and "all"; and 'all' must mean all . . .' They do not realize that, if they argue in that way, they are making sheer nonsense of the plain teaching of Scripture. In any case it is clearly and obviously an unintelligent procedure. Let us be careful as we handle the Word of God, and realize that every single statement in Scripture must be taken in the context of the whole. We are to compare Scripture with Scripture. We are to 'rightly divide' the Word of truth. We must not found a doctrine on one particular statement and we must always remember that Scripture never contradicts itself. It is all from God; it is a complete whole; and it is everywhere consistent with itself. For these compelling reasons it should be quite clear that the passage we are considering does not teach universalism. The Bible nowhere teaches us that all are going to be saved.

'Very well,' says someone, 'if it does not mean universal salvation, does it mean that what the Apostle is teaching here is that the opportunity or the possibility of justification is to be offered to all? Is he saying that in Jesus Christ there is the chance or the opportunity for all to justify themselves if they believe and accept the message? Is it the possibility for all, if it is not a fact concerning all?' Once more it seems to me that we have no difficulty as to the answer. We must reject that for this good reason, that what Paul is emphasizing in this chapter is not possibility but certainty. When we began the exposition of this chapter we said (and we have been able to demonstrate it time and time again) that what the Apostle is concerned with throughout is the finality, the absolute certainty of salvation, and how nothing can prevent it. And we have followed him as he works it out in terms of the expression 'much more' which he uses in verses 9 and 10, and again in this later section. What he is emphasizing is not what may happen but the certainty of what does and will happen. He is not talking about possibilities, he is talking about actualities.

Furthermore, the analogy would break down completely if it were merely denoting a possibility. It was not the mere possibility of falling that arose for us when Adam fell, it was the certainty of it; it did happen. And what Paul is asserting, on the other hand, is that the salvation of those who are in Christ is an absolute certainty also and not a mere possibility. It cannot be less than the other, indeed he says that it is 'much more', that it is 'abounding'. Therefore it must be still more certain, and so we are not dealing with the mere possibility of grace, or the mere possibility of salvation.

But there is another reason for rejecting this second suggested interpretation; it is based on the word 'constituted' in verse 19. 'For as by one man's disobedience many were constituted sinners, so by the obedience of one shall many be constituted righteous.' In these words it is God's action in justification that Paul is emphasizing and explaining, not our action. He is not stating what we may possibly do, but what God does, and because God does it, it is a certainty.

Since, then, we reject both ideas as erroneous, you are entitled to ask, 'How do *you* interpret these terms, "the many" and "all" '? I suggest that if we allow the Scripture to speak for itself the answer is really quite simple. The perplexity arises from the fact that we all are natural philosophers, and we begin to say, 'If you reject those possible explanations and emphasize certainty, then how can the love of God be reconciled with that position?' But that is to introduce philosophy. If we allow the Scripture to speak then the position is quite simple. Let me explain. It is surely abundantly clear that what the Apostle is contrasting is 'all' who are connected with Adam and 'all' who are connected with the Lord Jesus Christ. He is not really interested in numbers as such; what he is interested in is the fundamental principle. He says, in effect, that those who are connected with Adam fell with Adam, and those who are connected with Christ are saved with Christ. Incidentally, all without exception were involved on the one side, but that is not the point with which he is concerned; what he is concerned about is the nature of the relationship linked with Adam, and the nature of the relationship linked with Christ. He will deal with numbers later, in chapter 9. There, the Apostle really does deal with numbers; but here he is not concerned to deal with numbers. He has a weighty comparison and contrast in his mind, and it is, as I have been trying to show (and I shall have to continue to show it) that whereas certain things were true of those who were connected with Adam, there are other things that are true of those who are connected with the Lord Jesus Christ. These latter things, he says, are much more marvellous; the 'gift by grace' always leads to superabundance.

Let me adduce one further illustration of this same point. Notice the way in which the Apostle speaks in 1 Corinthians 15 from verse 20 onwards. His theme is the Resurrection and he begins by saying: 'But now is Christ risen from the dead, and become the first-fruits of them that slept.' Then he goes on, 'For since by man came death, by man came also the resurrection of the dead. For as in Adam all die, even so in Christ shall all be made alive. But every man in his own order: Christ the first-fruits, afterward they that are Christ's at his coming.' Here, again, we come across the word 'all': 'as in Adam *all* die, even so in Christ shall *all* be made alive'. At first glance he seems to be saying that the whole world, all men and women who have ever lived, are going to be made alive in this way in Christ. But if you take the entire statement you find that he makes it quite plain that he is only talking about those who belong to Christ. Actually in this fifteenth chapter of First Corinthians the Apostle is not concerned at all with those who are lost. The chapter is devoted solely to the destiny of those who are in Christ, as he makes perfectly plain in verse 23. 'But every man in his own order; Christ the first-fruits, afterward they that are Christ's at his coming.' The only people in whom he is interested in that chapter are Christ's people. He speaks of the 'all', but he makes it absolutely plain that he means by 'all', all who are Christ's, all who are 'in Christ'.

That is precisely the same as we have here in this fifth chapter of the Epistle to the Romans. The Apostle's great concern, I say, is to describe the certainty and the glory of that which is to happen to those who are in Christ. It is the certainty of the fulfilment of the promise, as he says in chapter 4: 16 – 'to all the seed'. Adam has a seed, Christ has a seed. All men are not 'born of the Spirit', all are not 'born again', all are not 'born from above', but there are those who are. Adam has his seed, Christ has His seed. That is what the Apostle is concerned about here. He is anxious to show the 'superabundance' that is given to the seed of Christ, to the 'all', 'the many', that are in Christ; and he is not concerned to do anything but that.

One thing we must be clear about; we must never proceed to draw deductions beyond what is stated in the Scripture. For instance, certain people hearing the exposition I have given may think that I have been teaching, and that the Apostle Paul teaches, that all infants who die go to hell. I have never said that, nor do I believe it. The Apostle Paul does not say so either. Why should anyone make such a deduction? What the Apostle does say is that when Adam sinned all sinned – the whole of humanity sinned. He says that 'all died in Adam', infants included, and that those infants died because they sinned in Adam. Death is *always* the punishment of sin, as we have seen. That is why death comes to anybody and everybody. That has been proved abundantly by the Apostle. So when an infant dies it dies because of the guilt connected with the sin of Adam. That is all the Apostle says. But to say that, does not mean that all those children go to hell, any more than it means that all of us will go to hell.

The Apostle is not concerned at this point to deal with who is saved and who is not saved. God has His own wonderful way of doing things. I do not know the fate of every infant that is born. There are those who hold the Reformed Faith who say that every child that dies in infancy has the salvation of Christ applied to it. Is that so? I do not know. It may be so. I do not know because I cannot find a specific statement in Scripture to that effect. But neither do I find a specific statement in Scripture that all dying in infancy are condemned to everlasting perdition. All I know is this, that all die in Adam, every one of woman born; but as to the salvation, that is something that belongs to the inscrutable wisdom of God. It is as easy and as simple for God to apply Christ's redemption and salvation to a new-born infant as it is to a hardened sinner at the end of his life. But the point I am making is that the Apostle does not raise the question here; and so nobody else need raise it. What he tells us is that we were all involved in Adam and his action, and that in consequence certain things happen. Then he proceeds to say on the other side that there are certain things that are true of those who are involved in Christ, who are 'in Christ', who have received this gift of eternal life from Christ.

At this point the Apostle really is not concerned to say anything else. So that as you read this chapter you must not draw false deductions from what the Apostle says. That would be to misuse Scripture, to 'wrest the Scriptures'. We must not do that in any respect. The Apostle does not consider here that other question which a certain man one day put to the Lord Jesus Christ Himself: 'Lord, are there few that be saved?' Our Lord's answer is most striking: 'Strive to enter in at the strait gate' – by which I understand Him to mean, 'Do not trouble your head about those theoretical questions; make sure you are in' [*Luke* 13: 23, 24].

We are face to face here with the greatest mystery in the universe. People have said to me many a time, 'I cannot quite understand it. If all were lost in Adam, why then are not all saved?' It is very easy to say things like that, very easy to make sweeping statements, and to ask what sound like 'catch' questions. But 'who hath known the mind of the Lord? or who hath been His counsellor?' All we can do is to read the Scriptures and observe what they teach, and submit ourselves entirely to that. It is a solemn and a terrifying matter. All will not be saved finally. The Son of God Himself has said that, in the parable recorded at the end of Matthew 25 where He says that the people on the left will be sent to everlasting destruction, and where He speaks of sheep and goats and the final division. But next you say, 'But then I do not understand how a God of love . . .' No, I know you do not, neither do I. But I will say this much; I have given up trying to understand. As I understand the meaning of the word 'faith', it means that I am content not to understand certain things in this life and in this world. Deuteronomy 29: 29 has the essence of wisdom for us all in this matter – 'The secret things belong unto the Lord our God, but those things which are revealed belong unto us and to our children for ever, that we may do all the words of this law.' That is as far as we can go, and are meant to go.

The real trouble with man in sin is that he always wants to understand. The ultimate sin of man is pride of intellect. That is why it is always true to say that 'not many wise men after the flesh, not many mighty, not many noble are called'. The wise man after the flesh wants to understand. He pits his brain against God's wisdom, and he says, 'I don't see'. Of course he doesn't. And Christ says to him, 'Except ye be converted, and become as little children, ye shall not enter into the kingdom of heaven' [*Matthew* 18: 3]. If you think that with your mind, which is so small when you compare it with the mind of God, and which is not only small but also sinful, and perverted, and polluted, and twisted – if you think that with the mind you have you can comprehend the working of God's eternal mind and wisdom, obviously you do not know God, you are outside the life of God, and you are lost. The first thing that must happen to you before you can ever become a Christian is that you must surrender that little mind of yours, and begin to say, 'Of course I cannot understand it; my whole nature is against it. I can see that there is only one thing to do; I submit myself to the revelation that God has been pleased to give. I submit myself to the One who was once in this world and who said He had come from God, and that His mind was one with the mind of God. I see that He talks about this division between the saved and the lost; I do not understand it, but I will trust Him. I know that whatever God does is right and just and good and holy and loving. I cannot understand.'

More and more I see that many of us who are Christians are quite unconsciously guilty of terrible sin in complaining of our inability to understand the ways of the Lord. That is the position of the man who is not a Christian at all; he cannot see this, he cannot understand that; and because he cannot, he rejects the whole Gospel. The moment you come to see that that attitude is wrong, you should see that it is wrong everywhere in the spiritual realm. So if you find a passage that you cannot quite understand, do not be troubled by that; go as far as you can, but do not try to go beyond that. Stop at the revelation; humble yourself before it. Say, 'I know that the Judge of all the earth will always do right; I know that he is righteous in all His ways, and holy in all His works.' [*Genesis* 18: 25; *Psalm* 145: 17].

Eventually, I believe, in glory we shall be given an understanding of some of these things that baffle us now. But it seems to me to be tragic that certain Christian people, when they come to difficult points in the teaching of the Scripture, suddenly go right back to the world's ways and ask the foolish questions that philosophy has always been asking. It is very sad that, having come under grace, and into the realm of revelation, they should suddenly go back again to the realm of reason and of human understanding. True understanding at this point teaches us and indicates that we must be content to 'believe where we cannot prove', to accept where we cannot understand, and to realize that the final synthesis is to be found in God's holy Being and character.

I have given time to this matter because I know that some people are troubled by these questions. I trust that the Apostle's teaching is now clear. There is no universalism taught in the Scripture; the exact opposite is taught there. People find themselves unconsciously saying things which are universalistic simply because they do not understand the Scriptures, or fail to interpret them correctly, or because in their folly and ignorance they revert again to the old philosophical way of thinking. May God keep us to 'the simplicity that is in Christ'. May we be men of the Word, men of the Book, content not to know certain things, not to understand certain things, but to know that 'God doeth all things well'.

Nineteen

*

And not as it was *by one that sinned,* so is *the gift; for the judgment* was *by one to condemnation, but the free gift* is *of many offences unto justification. For if by one man's offence death reigned by one, much more they which receive abundance of grace and of the gift of righteousness shall reign in life by one, Jesus Christ.*

Romans 5 : 16, 17

We continue our study of the striking contrast which the Apostle draws between what has happened to us all in Adam and what happens to those who believe in the Lord Jesus Christ. Having dealt with the question of the exact meaning of 'the many' and 'all' we can now return to what is after all the Apostle's main object in this section, and the main purpose which he had in his mind in bringing out the contrast. At one and the same time he is concerned to show that there are similarities and dissimilarities in our relationship to Adam and our relationship to the Lord Jesus Christ – Adam is 'the figure of him that was to come'.

In verse 15, as we have seen, the Apostle states the big difference in a general manner, but in verses 16 and 17 he works out in detail what he had there stated in general. This is a method he frequently adopts. He states the proposition as a whole, and then, in order to help us, he divides it up into its component parts, his purpose being to show the glorious superiority of that which the Lord Jesus Christ has done for His people over what Adam did. We shall see what Adam did for all whom he represented but the object is to show the 'much more' of what the Lord Jesus Christ has done for those whom He represents, those who belong to Him. Verse 15 has told us that through the offence of the one 'many died'. There Paul states the truth in general, but now in verses 16 and 17 he proceeds to give us the intermediate steps.

Notice that in verse 16 he once more starts with a contrast.

'Not as it was by one that sinned, so is . . .' 'Not as – so is'. Here he tells us that we are not going to find in the case of the Lord Jesus Christ, exactly what we found in the case of Adam. It is true to say that we were all in Adam; and it is true to say that all His people are in Christ. So far there is a parallel and a similarity, but the thing to notice is the great and striking contrast – 'Not as', 'so is'. Clearly Paul is about to compare and to contrast Adam's disobedience, Adam's sin, Adam's offence, with the perfect work that the Lord Jesus Christ has done on our behalf.

What were the consequences of sin? The Apostle tells us quite plainly, 'Not as it was by one that sinned, so is the gift'. To what did the sin lead? The answer is, 'for the judgment was by one to condemnation'. Here he is giving us the steps and the details. Adam offended, Adam sinned, and that sin led to judgment. What is judgment? Judgment means a sentence, or a decision on the part of a judge. The very term 'judgment' conjures up the picture of a law court and a judge sitting on a bench. He has heard the case. The evidence has been produced, the prosecution has presented it and called for a conviction, what defence there is has been put forward, and now, having listened to it all, the judge pronounces his judgment, delivers his sentence. So sin led to a judgment.

God had warned Adam beforehand that if he sinned and disobeyed this judgment would follow, and, says Paul, this is precisely what happened. But notice that he says, 'for the judgment was by one to condemnation'. One what? There are those who say that it means 'by one man'. Certainly it means 'by one man', but I believe that it means something much more particular than that. Rather we must interpret this 'one' as referring to 'one sin', for has not the Apostle already been emphasizing that very point? He did so in the first clause of verse 12 – 'by one man sin entered into the world and death by sin'. That refers to his one first sin. But there is a further reason. We must say that this 'one' refers to 'one sin' because of the contrast which the Apostle will draw in the second half of the sentence. He says that the judgment was by 'one' sin to condemnation, but the free gift is of many offences – many sins – unto justification. The only possible contrast with the many offences is the 'one offence'. That is why it is so important to bear in mind that Paul is anxious to emphasize the contrast, the 'much more'. On the one side, the one sin of Adam led to that judgment, and on the other side 'the many' offences are covered by the 'one' act of the Lord Jesus Christ.

The judgment was the result of the one sin, and this, says the Apostle, led to condemnation. We have already considered this doctrine but the Apostle is so concerned that these Roman Christians should understand it that he repeats it. It means, in other words, that a sentence of condemnation was passed on all men on account of, and as the result of, that one sin of Adam. We have already gone into the doctrine exhaustively, but we must at least observe the way in which the Apostle goes on repeating it. We are not left with merely the one statement in verse 12. We find it repeated in almost every one of these verses. Yet people still stumble at it, and dislike it, and object to it, and reject it. But here it is plainly and clearly. That one sin of Adam led to the judgment of condemnation.

We must be clear about this. Paul does not say that that one sin of Adam has had the effect of leading us to follow Adam's example, and sin ourselves, and thereby bring ourselves under condemnation. He says that the judgment of condemnation has come as the result of that *one sin* committed by Adam – and that is his whole case throughout. Neither does he say that as the result of that one sin of Adam we have all inherited from Adam a sinful nature, and that because of this God condemns us. He says that the judgment to condemnation came on the 'one sin'. He does not say that because we have that sinful nature we all in turn fall into sin, and thereby come under condemnation. It is emphatically the 'one sin' that has produced the judgment to condemnation, and brought in its trail all those evil and terrible consequences. So we sum it up once more by saying that the Apostle's assertion is that as the result of Adam's 'one sin' the sentence of condemnation has been passed upon the whole world of men.

But, thank God, we can turn to the other side. 'Not as it was by the one that sinned, so is the gift.' Thank God, I say, that we can turn to this, 'for whereas the judgment was by one to condemnation, the free gift is of many offences unto justification'. Notice these contrasts; they are most important. The contrast is complete, and it is the contrast between what Adam's disobedience has produced for us on the one hand, and what Christ's obedience has procured for us on the other. Then there is reference to 'the free gift'. To what is this opposed? It is to the judgment. 'Not as it was by one that sinned, is the free gift.' Note the expression 'free gift' again, and how Paul delights to repeat these terms. He glories in free grace and in the free gift of salvation. It is all so free, it is always a gift. He will never allow us to forget that for a moment. Though he said it so plainly in verse 15, it is here again, 'not as the offence, so also is the free gift'.

It is a very good test of our Christian profession to ask ourselves, and to discover, how we react to these terms. Are we as fond of them as the Apostle was? Do we delight to talk about 'free grace' and 'free gift?' Pharisees never do so because they realize that these terms make them out to be paupers as all others. They like to feel that they have earned salvation or at least that they have made a contribution towards it. They do not like to emphasize the 'freeness' of salvation. If a man delights in free grace, and in the 'free gift', you can be sure he is a man who has seen his utter sinfulness and hopelessness and helplessness. The free gift is the opposite to the judgment.

Then notice this second contrast. The Apostle says that what we have in Christ is that those guilty of 'many offences' have been justified, that is, declared righteous in spite of that. As I have shown, the 'many offences' are in contrast to the 'one offence' of Adam, and therefore it is most important for us to notice that the 'many offences' include not only the one original sin of Adam, but also all the sins that have ever been committed, or ever will be committed, by any and all of Christ's people. We were condemned because of the one sin of Adam; but when we come to be justified, we are not only justified in respect of that one sin, but also in respect of all the sins that we have committed ourselves – the 'many offences'. By the work of Christ on our behalf we are not only delivered from what we have inherited from Adam, we are also delivered and cleared from all the sins and offences of which we ourselves have ever been guilty. What a large, what a free, what a glorious salvation this is! All our sins, all the sins of all His people, were laid upon Him; all the sins even of those yet unborn who will yet become His people were laid upon Him; in Him all who believe are justified from all sins, past, present and future! That is what Paul is saying; he brings it out in this contrast between the one offence and the many offences.

The final contrast is introduced by the word 'justification' which, you notice, he uses as the antithesis of 'condemnation'. That is a most important point. Justification must never be thought of in terms of our state and condition; certainly never in terms of our sanctification. As I have emphasized repeatedly, justification is a legal or a forensic term; it refers to a judgment delivered by a judge upon a bench. Justification is always the opposite of condemnation; and here is the verse which perhaps says that more plainly than any other single verse. In other words, as condemnation is a forensic term, the contrast, which is the result of the free gift, is a forensic, that is, a legal pronouncement of justification. God as Judge pronounces us to be righteous in Christ. In spite of what we have inherited from Adam, in spite of all the sins of which we ourselves have been guilty, God pronounces us to be clear; and that He regards us as righteous in Christ. All our sins are blotted out, and God declares us to be acceptable and righteous in His most holy sight. It is the complete and exact opposite and antithesis of that condemnation that came upon us as the result of Adam's sin and the judgment that was pronounced upon it. Nothing could be more full, nothing could be more free, nothing could present such a glorious and such a striking contrast.

So the Apostle has brought us to this point. He said in verse 15 that this one offence of Adam had led to this result – that many died. Now, in verse 16, he has taken us as far as this; the one offence, the one sin led to judgment, and the judgment was condemnation; but 'the free gift is of many offences unto justification'. In verse 17 he takes us a step further. Sin leads to judgment, and the judgment is one of condemnation, but now he tells us that the condemnation that is passed and pronounced is 'death' – 'For if by one man's offence death reigned by one'. There he has completed the general statement of verse 15, and he has shown us the various steps that bring us to this point of death. Then, on the other hand, he tells us that salvation does not stop at justification but leads on to what he calls 'our reigning in life by one, Jesus Christ'. So he has now worked out the full statement of verse 15 in all its details and component parts.

Let us follow him again as he leads us step by step. Notice that he does not hesitate to repeat, 'For if by one man's offence'. It really is astonishing that anyone should fail to see that truth or try to argue against it. Indeed, it is not a matter of argument at all. You either accept this as it is, or you have to say, as many modern expositors do say, that the Apostle Paul was wrong at this point, that he was making a mistake, and that he was merely following the rabbinical teaching of his age. There is no question as to what Paul says; and they grant as much. They are therefore driven into the position of saying that he was wrong, and that they just do not agree with him. He was a child of his age, they say, and fell into error at this point. We must grant that that is a clear and a logical position, but no Christian who believes this to be the Word of God has any right to be muddled or confused, for the Apostle in every verse in this section keeps on repeating his words concerning 'one man's offence'. That one man was Adam, and it is by his one offence that death has reigned over all.

We must now examine the phrase, 'death reigned by one'. Again the stress falls upon the one man. The Apostle's continuing repetition of this is proof of the fact that he regards this as a crucial and essential matter. The one man, Adam, and the one offence of that one man! In the one sentence (verse 16) he says 'by one' twice over. One man Adam and his one offence brought in death. But you notice that the Apostle puts this in a most extraordinary phrase – 'If by one man's offence death reigned'. 'Death reigned'! What a graphic statement that is! Can you think of, or imagine, any statement which more perfectly sums up life in this world apart from Christ than that particular phrase? 'Death reigned'! Death came in as a conqueror; death triumphed over all; death held sway over 'all flesh'. And so the whole of mankind, as the result of this one sin of Adam, has been subject to death and to the tyranny of death.

The Apostle has already said this in verse 12, 'Wherefore, as by one man sin entered into the world, and death by sin; and so *death passed* upon all men'. In verse 14 still more definitely: 'Nevertheless *death reigned* from Adam to Moses.' What a terrible, horrible phrase that is, but nevertheless true! He says it again in verse 15, 'many be dead'. But now he puts it still more plainly. It is not merely that death has passed upon, or come upon, all men; death, he says, has been reigning. A very good commentary on this statement is to be found in the second chapter of the Epistle to the Hebrews in verses 14 and 15: 'Forasmuch then as the children are partakers of flesh and blood, he also himself likewise took part of the same; that through death he might destroy him that had the power of death, that is, the devil, and deliver them who through fear of death were all their lifetime subject to bondage' – that is, mankind in bondage to sin. This truth is illustrated frequently in the Old Testament. A psalmist, for instance, sees death coming and says in effect, 'I want to praise God here and now, for can the dead praise Thee?' Then you find the wise man in Proverbs saying, 'Better a live dog than a dead lion'. Death is so devastating apart from Christ; it seems to be the end of everything. That is why in the Old Testament, before the glorious doctrine of the Resurrection is fully expounded and brought clearly to light, as it is by the resurrection of the Lord Jesus Christ, you feel that there is a kind of gloom and sense of doom. The Patriarchs and others were given sufficient faith to see beyond death. But apart from that, apart from the preview they were given, there is gloom, and death seems to be the end. The poets and literary men of the world have always acknowledged this and confessed it. Listen to John Dryden's lament:

Since every man who lives is born to die
And none can boast sincere felicity;
With equal mind, what happens, let us bear,
Nor joy nor grieve too much for things beyond our care.
Like pilgrims to the appointed place we tend;
The world's an inn, and death the journey's end.

Or listen to Thomas Gray as he meditates and ruminates in that churchyard in Stoke Poges. This is what you will find him saying:

The boast of heraldry, the pomp of power,
And all that beauty, all that wealth e'er gave
Awaits alike the inevitable hour;
The paths of glory lead but to the grave.

'Were all their lifetime subject to bondage'! And the world today is as terrified of death as it has ever been. Much of the excitement concerning the hydrogen bomb has this as its cause. Men of the world have no hope beyond this world, and beyond death and the grave, so they are protesting; and that is the reason for it. They know nothing about the life in the Glory; this life is everything to them, so the most horrible thing conceivable is death. They are confessing that unconsciously. That is quite apart from one's own personal views about the use of hydrogen bombs, which on any showing is sheer madness. But it is interesting to note the type of person who gets most excited about it. Unwittingly these offspring of Adam are just acknowledging that death is reigning over them, and they are horrified and terrified. Again, the modern cult of trying to keep young and to look young instead of ageing gracefully is all a part of the same thing; it is occasioned by the horror and terror and dread of death; it arises from the awful spectre that amazes them and haunts them and which they see coming nearer and nearer to them. Let me quote another bit of poetry, this time, Walter Savage Landor:

I strove with none, for none was worth my strife;
Nature I loved, and next to Nature, Art.
I warmed both hands before the fire of life;
It sinks; and I am ready to depart.

What utter hopelessness! Such people have nothing to fall back upon – 'death reigned'.

Let me quote also the words of the President of an Oxford college from his Autobiography written during the last war. He said, 'But for me the war brought to an end the long summer of my life. Henceforth I have nothing to look forward to except chill autumn, and still chillier winter. Yet I must somehow try not to lose hope!' I know of nothing more hopeless than that.

'Death reigned' – and so it has done! Ever since Adam fell death has reigned over all mankind, world-wide. The world is a place of cemeteries; it is a place of death and gloom and end. 'Death reigned.' How true it is, and how thankful we should be that we can turn to the contrast, and that we have something else to consider! Listen: 'For if by one man's offence death reigned by one, much more' – 'much more' – 'they which receive abundance of grace, and the gift of righteousness, shall reign in life by one, Jesus Christ'. Let us look at the terms. What is the contrast? 'Much more', he says, 'they which receive.' The contrast is that while on this Christian side we actively and voluntarily receive and believe, we are unconsciously involved in the sin of Adam. This is not a point of contrast that occurred to me personally; it is a part of John Calvin's exposition. Calvin says that one of the contrasts here is brought out in the phrase 'they that receive', denoting the activity of faith. The Apostle is not concerned for the moment with the question of how a man gets faith; that he deals with elsewhere. He is simply saying here that Christians receive an abundance of grace. We were unconsciously involved in Adam; here we consciously embrace the gift of salvation – and every man who is a Christian does just that.

Here, then, is the first contrast. 'They that receive' is contrasted with what happened to us away back in the Garden of Eden so many centuries before we were born. We were involved in it; we sinned there unconsciously. But here we receive; 'they that receive'. Then there is this great phrase with which we need not stay because we dealt with it in verse 15; but let us give ourselves the pleasure of repeating it again: 'They which receive abundance of grace and of the gift of' – what? 'The gift of righteousness.' Here we must pause because Paul has taken a step further in doctrine. At the end of verse 16 he left us with justification. Here he says that justification is not the end, it is only the beginning; it is only a part of what we receive, namely, the 'gift of righteousness'. Let me explain this.

Justification means that we are pronounced to be righteous. It includes forgiveness of sins, and the pronouncement that we are righteous, that God smiles upon us, and that we are reconciled to God. But Paul here informs us that there is even something further. It is not only that we are forgiven, but over and above being forgiven, the righteousness of Jesus Christ is put to our account, is put upon us. We are clothed with the righteousness of Jesus Christ: 'Much more they which receive abundance of grace and of the gift of righteousness.' We are not merely told that our sins are forgiven while we are still left as we were. Not at all! The righteousness of Christ is imputed to us, it is put upon us. So Zinzendorf could write his hymn and John Wesley translate it, saying,

Jesus, Thy blood and righteousness
My beauty are, my glorious dress.

We are robed in the righteousness of Jesus Christ.

I must remind you once more that Isaac Watts was right when he said,

In Him the tribes of Adam boast
More blessings than their father lost.

Unfallen Adam was righteous, but it was his own righteousness as a created being, it was the righteousness of a man. Adam never had the righteousness of Jesus Christ upon him. What he lost was his own righteousness. But you and I are not merely given back a human righteousness, the righteousness that Adam had before he fell – we are given the righteousness of Jesus Christ. 'Much more' – abundance, superabundance – give full weight to it! We receive this abundance of grace and of the gift of righteousness.

How important this is! and at no time is it more important than when we pray to God. For what is prayer? Prayer is going to have an audience with the King; and there is nothing more important as you enter into the audience chamber than to know you are suitably clad, that you are sufficiently respectable, if you like, to go in. That is the thing that would engage our attention if we were going to have an audience with the Queen of England;

we would want everything to be right and perfect. How infinitely more important this is when we go to have an audience with the Maker and Creator of the universe, with God! Let us never forget that our only right of entry, the only way in which we can enter at all with any kind of confidence, is to know that we have received 'the gift of righteousness', that we are clothed with the righteousness of Jesus Christ, and that therefore in a sense we have a right to stand there. 'Having therefore, brethren' (says the author of the Epistle to the Hebrews) 'boldness to enter into the holiest by the blood of Jesus' – confidence, assurance [*Hebrews* 10: 19]. It is all because we have received the righteousness of Jesus Christ. It is not only forgiveness; it is not only absolution; it is being given, and being clothed upon with, the righteousness of Jesus Christ.

What else? The final antithesis is that between being dominated by death on the one hand, and being identified with the living Christ on the other. Death reigned over every man. 'If by one man's offence death reigned.' What is the opposite to that? Clearly the opposite of 'death reigning' is 'life reigning'. But the Apostle says that there is much more than that, because the contrast to death reigning is that 'we shall reign in life by one, Jesus Christ'. What a tremendous distinction! In other words he is not only saying that, as the result of our Lord's work and because death no longer reigns over us, we are going to receive the gift of eternal life, and that therefore life is going to reign over us. That is gloriously true, but he goes beyond that and says that we ourselves shall reign in life. 'Much more' – it is not merely the exact opposite, it is 'much more' than that.

What, then, does he mean by 'our reigning in life by one, Jesus Christ'? He partly means that we reign in life by Jesus Christ even here and now in this present world. You will find that in his Epistle to the Ephesians in the second chapter he says, 'Even when we were dead in sins, (God) hath quickened us together with Christ; and hath raised us up together and made us sit together in heavenly places in Christ Jesus' (2: 4). That has happened to us; it is a part of the reigning in life even here and now. Another statement of this truth is found in Hebrews 2: 15, where we are told that Christ's work brings deliverance to 'them who through fear of death were all their lifetime subject to bondage'. Through Christ the Christian is delivered from the fear of death. Far from being any longer under the vile bondage of such a fear, he is 'reigning in life' over conquered death. He has had a victory over death already before he has met it.

But not only that, sin does not reign over the Christian either; for sin, you remember, leads to judgment, and judgment to death. Hence if we are to reign in life we must be free from the dominion of sin. In the next chapter the Apostle will tell us in verse 14, 'For sin shall not have dominion over you, for you are not under the law but under grace'. And not only do we have a victory over sin, we even get a victory over the devil. 'Resist the devil', says James, and he will flee from you' (4: 7). And Peter says much the same thing: 'Your adversary the devil, as a roaring lion, walketh about, seeking whom he may devour: whom resist steadfast in the faith' [1 *Peter* 5:9].

That is what Paul means by 'reigning in life'. We have lost the fear of death, we are no longer under the dominion of sin, we are no longer under the dominion of the devil, we can resist him and make him flee. Indeed, we are no longer under the tyranny of life itself. In the eighth chapter the Apostle will say, having given a list of the things that are set against us: 'For thy sake we are killed all the day long; we are accounted as sheep for the slaughter; nay, in all these things we are more than conquerors through him that loved us.' We are 'more than conquerors', are 'reigning in life'. And he says the same thing in a glorious statement in the fourth chapter of the Epistle to the Philippians: 'Not that I speak in respect of want, for I have learned, in whatsoever state I am, therewith to be content. I know both how to be abased and I know how to abound; everywhere and in all things I am instructed both to be full and to be hungry, both to abound and to suffer need. I can do all things through Christ which strengtheneth me' (4: 11–13). Paul is reigning in life. He has mastered sin, Satan, life, death, everything; he is more than conqueror. That is true of us already in the present.

But tremendous and glorious things are coming. Our present

reigning is but a 'first-fruits', a 'foretaste' of it all. Not until the Lord returns, when we shall be with Him, shall we really know what it means to 'reign in life' fully. And how can our future reigning be described? The Apostle has already hinted at it in chapter 2 verses 7 and 10, where he says that we are looking for 'glory, and honour, and immortality, and peace'. Our Lord Himself has told us about it. He will one day say to His people, 'Come ye blessed of my Father, inherit the kingdom prepared for you from the foundation of the world' [*Matthew* 25: 34]. Says the Apostle Paul, at the end of his long and arduous and suffering life, 'Henceforth there is laid up for me a crown of righteousness' [2 *Timothy* 4: 8]. And again, we find the author of the Epistle to the Hebrews saying in chapter 2, verse 5, 'Not unto the angels hath He put in subjection the world to come, whereof we speak'. And if not to angels, to whom will it be subject? To the 'heirs of salvation'. John, in the Book of Revelation, chapter 1 verse 6, says much the same thing: 'He hath made us kings and priests unto God'; better, 'a kingdom of kings and priests unto God'; and in chapter 3 verse 21, we find Christ Himself saying, 'To him that overcometh will I grant to sit with me in my throne, even as I also overcame and am set down with my Father in his throne'. 'The crowning day is coming.' Again in chapter 5 verse 10 we read: 'And hath made us unto our God kings and priests; and we shall reign on the earth'. And to conclude this point, the Apostle Paul writing to the Corinthians in his First Epistle chapter 6, verse 2, writes, 'Do you not know that the saints shall judge the world?' And then in verse 3, 'Know ye not that we shall judge angels?' Such is something of the rich content of the teaching that we 'shall reign in life by one, Jesus Christ'.

Jesus Christ is described as the 'King of kings'. Who are the 'kings' of whom He is the King? You and myself! It does not mean earthly kings. All that will have gone by then. He is 'King of kings'. His people are the kings. Every one of us is made a king. We shall reign with Him, we shall judge the world, we shall judge angels. It is not surprising that the Apostle therefore puts it as he does in the seventeenth verse of this chapter: 'For if by one man's offence death reigned by one, much more they which receive abundance of grace and of the gift of righteousness shall reign in life by one, Jesus Christ.' Adam was made lord of creation, but he lost that position. We shall not only have that back, we shall have infinitely more. We shall share a throne with the Son who shares the throne of thrones with His Father. That is the prospect awaiting us! Is it surprising that he keeps on using expressions such as, 'Much more', and 'Abundance', and that he stresses the freeness and the fullness of it all?

Realizing these things, this is what we can and must say about ourselves –

Changed from glory into glory,
Till in heaven we take our place;
Till we cast our crowns before Thee,
Lost in wonder, love and praise.

Do we realize at this very moment that He has already made us 'kings and priests', that we are seated with Him in the heavenly places now, and that therefore we should be reigning in life here and now, no matter what may be set against us? And should we not regard ourselves always as those who are destined to judge the world with Him, and even judge angels?

Twenty

*

> *Therefore as by the offence of one* judgment came *upon all men to condemnation; even so by the righteousness of one* the free gift came *upon all men unto justification of life.*
> *For as by one man's disobedience many were made sinners, so by the obedience of one shall many be made righteous.*
> Romans 5: 18, 19

These two verses are designed to do two main things. The first is to sum up and summarize what the Apostle has been saying in the previous verses. He has been working out an argument in detail in verses 13 to 17 which are placed in brackets in the Authorized Version. And now, having done so, he puts it all before us in a concluding summary; he states again the great principle he was concerned to enunciate.

But these two verses subserve a second function, or, if you prefer it, they are to be regarded in another way. You remember that when we began the study of this great paragraph – beginning at verse 12 and going on to the end of the chapter – we gave an analysis of its contents in order that we might understand its main thrust. It can be a very confusing passage if we fail to realize clearly how it is divided up, and the relationship of the various clauses to one another and to the whole. He begins in verse 12 with the statement, 'Wherefore, as by one man'. You then expect him to go on to say, 'even so. . . .' But he did not do that, thus completing his statement there and then, but instead went on to say: 'Wherefore, as by one man sin entered into the world, and death by sin, and so death passed upon all men, for that all have sinned.' Then you expect the other half of the statement, but it does not come there; and instead you get the statement which is in parenthetical brackets in the Authorized Version. Indeed in verses 13 to 17 there are two parentheses.

The first is in verses 13 and 14, where he explains and expounds the last statement in verse 12, namely that 'all sinned'. He wants to establish that. It is such an important matter that he cannot just leave it like that, so he sets out to prove it and to demonstrate it by pointing out that until the Law sin was in the world, and that death had passed on all – even between Adam and Moses when there was no Law – thereby not only proving the universality of death, but also the universality of sin, because death is the punishment of sin. That is the meaning of the first parenthesis.

You will remember, too, the Apostle's assertion that people who had never sinned 'after the similitude of Adam's transgression' had nevertheless died. This we interpreted as referring in an especial way to infants who die before they have committed any voluntary act at all. All are involved in Adam's trangression. The mention of Adam leads Paul next to say that Adam after all was the type, or the shadow, or the figure, of Him that was to come. Having said that, he has to qualify it immediately, so you have the second parenthesis. Adam is the figure of Christ, and in a very interesting way. There is one conspicuous common feature, but in the main it is a question of contrast rather than of comparison. He is the figure of Christ, but as you work it out in detail what strikes you is the extraordinary contrast, the 'much more' of what God has done for us in Christ over against what had happened to us in Adam. In other words, verses 15, 16 and 17 are designed to show the exact nature of the comparison between our position in Adam and our position in the Lord Jesus Christ.

Now, having said all that, he says 'Therefore', as if telling us that he is going to resume what he was setting out to say in verse 12. But having the thoughts of verses 13–17 still in his mind, in verses 18 and 19 he gives a summary of all the intervening argument and at the same time completes the original statement which he intended to make. Now notice the interesting fact that he says it in two different ways, doubtless because he wants to give particular emphasis to what he says in verse 19. Verse 19 begins with the word 'For', indicating that it is an explanation of verse 18. And we shall only be able to get a firm grip of its content if we remind ourselves time and again that the purpose of the paragraph (as indeed of the entire chapter) is to show us the completeness and the fullness of justification by faith.

Justification by faith leads to certain inevitable results. This the Apostle makes perfectly clear. He began in verse 1 by saying, 'Therefore, being justified by faith we have peace with God through our Lord Jesus Christ'; and he has been elaborating that same statement in virtually every verse of the chapter, proving to a demonstration the absolute certainty of it all. Justification by faith is one of the profoundest truths that we can ever grasp. But the Apostle is also eager for us to see that, if we are justified, our final salvation is sure and certain, and that nothing can ever rob us of it, or stand between us and it. And he will keep on saying this, and arguing it out, until he comes to the magnificent climax at the end of chapter 8 where he says, 'I am persuaded that neither death, nor life, nor angels, nor principalities, nor powers, nor things present, not things to come, nor height, nor death, nor any other creature, shall be able to separate us from the love of God which is in Christ Jesus our Lord.' Who are the 'us'? I answer: Those who are justified in Christ Jesus. The great theme of chapters 5, 6 and 7 is assurance of salvation. We must never forget that, and must not allow ourselves to be misled by other suggested sub-divisions which say that Paul takes up sanctification in chapter 5, verse 12, and so on. It is not so: his theme is assurance of salvation, the certainty and the finality of it all in the case of those who are justified, and how this is brought about.

In particular in this section the Apostle's argument is that our salvation is certain and sure because we are 'in Christ'. We are 'in his life', as he puts it in verses 9 and 10; if so much has happened to us as the result of His death, how much more will be achieved by His life? We are 'in his life', we are 'in Christ'.

Such is the background to the Apostolic argument, and I am stressing it again because Paul himself does so. He has made it perfectly plain, we would have thought, but still he says it once more, and particularly clearly in verses 18 and 19. Surely the reason is, that from the experimental standpoint, and for the sake of our happiness and joy while we are still in this world, it is of vital importance that we should grasp this particular truth. This is the way to enjoy assurance of salvation; and it was because the Apostle was so anxious that these Roman Christians should have it that he thus works it out in detail with them, and then repeats it, and as it were underlines it.

One principle we must carry in our minds is this, that while it is of course true to say that God deals with us individually in this matter of salvation, it is also the case that God deals with us federally and as parts of a whole. The Lord Jesus Christ died for His people, the people God had given Him; and we are made members of this people. What Adam did led to certain results for his people, and what Christ has done leads likewise to certain results for His people. We must get hold of the idea that we belong to a people, and that as Adam was our federal head so the Lord Jesus Christ is the Federal Head and Representative of His people. Paul's argument here is that God has always dealt with mankind in this federal manner, that is, through a head and through a representative – through the first Adam, through the last Adam. So what he is going to put before us again is the difference between our being in Adam and our being in Christ. Let us look at this difference.

First of all we look at what has happened to us in Adam. He puts it like this in verse 18: 'Therefore, as by the offence of one judgment came upon all men to condemnation.' In most Bibles certain words are in italics because they are not found in the original. They have been supplied by the translators in order to make the meaning plain and clear; and they are of great value, and undoubtedly right. But what Paul actually wrote was, 'Therefore, as by the offence of one upon all men to condemnation.' And in the same way in the second half the translators have supplied the words 'the free gift came'. What Paul there wrote was, 'even so by the righteousness of one upon all men unto justification of life.' That is a mere technical point. What the Apostle is saying is, that because of that one sin of Adam the whole of mankind are treated as sinners. That is what he said originally in verse 12, 'By one man sin entered into the world, and death by sin, and so death passed upon all men, for that all sinned'. Here he says it again, 'As by the offence of one judgment came upon all men to condemnation'. Because of that one sin of Adam we are all under judgment, and it is a judgment of condemnation. We are all treated as sinners, and the judgment and the punishment that comes upon sinners has been pronounced upon all.

Now that is the first statement in verse 18. But let us take with it the first part of verse 19. 'For', he says, 'as by one man's disobedience many were made sinners.' This statement goes further than the statement in verse 18. Verse 18 says that because of this one offence of Adam all were treated as sinners. This goes further and it says that, not only were all treated as sinners, but all were regarded as sinners, indeed Paul's expression is, 'made sinners'. 'Made' is an important word. I referred to it earlier but I must remind you of it because it is a vital part of this argument. The word translated here as 'made' is much stronger than our English word suggests. It means 'to set down in the rank of', or 'to place in the category of', or 'to appoint to a particular class'. Let me explain it by an illustration. In the twelfth chapter of Luke's Gospel we are told that when our Lord was preaching on one occasion He seemed to stop for a moment, and a man shouted out saying, 'Master, speak to my brother that he divide the inheritance with me'. We are told that our Lord looked upon this man and said, 'Man, who made me a judge or a divider over you?' [*Luke* 12: 13, 14]. The word there translated as 'made' means 'Who has appointed me?' or 'Who has designated or constituted me as a judge or a divider over you? Who has put me into the category or into the class of a judge?' The same word for 'made' is used by the Apostle in the verse before us, and with the same meaning. It is imperative that we should understand it – namely, that 'by one man's disobedience many were constituted sinners'.

Furthermore I must emphasize the word 'sinners'. Paul does not say that many were constituted 'sinful,' suggestive of possibility, but that 'many were constituted sinners'. He does not use an adjective, but a noun. He does not say that because of Adam's disobedience the whole of mankind was made sinful, and therefore liable to sin; and because they were liable to sin they sinned, and because they sinned they were then punished. That is not what the Apostle says. He asserts that because of this one disobedience of Adam all were constituted sinners, made sinners, regarded by God as sinners.

You will appreciate the importance of my emphasis at this point, for the second half of this nineteenth verse says that on the other hand in Christ we have been 'made' or 'constituted' righteous – and you have to give the word the same force and the same meaning on the two sides. If we do not give it its full force here how can we give it its full force there? The apostle maintains that because of Adam's one act of disobedience the whole of the human race has been constituted legally as sinners, all men have been put into the category of sinners, we are all regarded personally and individually as sinners in the sight of God. That is our judicial standing before God. Because of that one sin of Adam we were all put into the category of sinners.

I have often used an illustration in order to make this plain. If one member of this country should be guilty of a misdemeanour in another country, that other country may well declare war against this country: and though you and I have not committed the misdemeanour we nevertheless suffer the consequences. The other country declares war, and we, therefore, legally in international law, have been constituted enemies of that country though we have done nothing at all in our own persons. It is a judicial procedure. According to the Apostle that is what has happened to us – our position before God judicially has become that of sinners. And, notice, we became sinners, not by any personal act on our part at all, but entirely and solely by that one disobedience of the first Adam. The Apostle has repeated this in almost every single verse from verse 12 up until this point. He has done so because it is clearly the controlling thought in his mind.

It will be recalled that in verses 13 and 14, the Apostle clinches his statement about the Fall and its consequence by taking up the case of infants. Why should infants die? His answer is that death is always the punishment of sin; therefore if an infant dies it has died because it is guilty of sin. But the infant has done nothing personally; why, therefore, should it die? For what is it being punished? The explanation is that all sinned in Adam. I have already made it plain that it does not mean that every infant who dies, of necessity goes to hell, but it does mean that every infant from the moment of birth has been constituted a sinner. That, God may apply His redeeming grace is another matter. What we must grasp is that all of woman born since Adam, including infants, have been constituted and put into the category of sinners. Christ Jesus is the sole exception. We are not sinners because we have a sinful nature and because we commit acts of sin. It is the other way round. It is because we are sinners that we have this sinful nature and commit acts of sin. What Paul asserts is that by the one disobedience of Adam the whole of mankind has been constituted, put into the category of, sinners. The sinful nature, the depravity, the pollution, and the resulting acts of sin are simply part of the punishment that has followed, the form that the punishment has taken. What is really vital is that we should see that because of Adam's one act of disobedience we are all 'made sinners'.

Now this is God's judicial act. God made man, and He appointed Adam as the representative of the entire human race. He had a perfect right to do so. He decreed that the whole of humanity should be represented by the first man, and should suffer the consequences of that man's action. And that is what happened. When Adam sinned, God therefore did what He said He would do, and He constituted all the progeny of Adam as sinners. We all sinned in Adam and with him, because he was our federal head and representative; and therefore God pronounced us all to be sinners. The Apostle proclaims that this is a fact; and it cannot be rightly disputed, because you are confronted by the twin facts of the universality of sin and the universality of death. How can you explain the universality of sin and of death except in terms of this great and tremendous background fact that we all sinned in Adam and were pronounced to be sinners by God?

There then is the one side, but, thank God, we can turn to the other side. That is what happened to us in Adam; what happens to us in Christ? This is what the Apostle wants next to bring out, and to emphasize; this is the assurance he desires to give them. What he is saying in effect is this: As all that has happened to you in Adam is a fact, realize that all that has happened to you in Christ is also a fact. If the one was certain, realize that the other is equally certain, and more so, because here it is God's grace that comes in and not His wrath and His judgment. That is the Apostle's argument. The great truth is that all we are and have comes out of the obedience of this second One. All the benefits of salvation come to us solely and entirely because of the obedience of the Lord Jesus Christ. Our salvation is entirely of Him, and from Him, and in Him. As my being a sinner came entirely from Adam, all my righteousness and my being a Christian comes entirely from the Lord Jesus Christ.

The corollary of all this is, that if you want to have assurance of salvation, the place to start is not with your feelings, but with your understanding; then the feelings will follow. The way to get assurance is not to try to feel something, but it is to grasp this objective truth. Look at yourself in Adam; though you had done nothing you were declared a sinner. Look at yourself in Christ; and see that, though you have done nothing, you are declared to be righteous. That is the parallel. We must get rid of all thoughts of our actions. There is no boasting. We do nothing; all we are and have results from the obedience of the One – our Lord.

There is no more glorious theme than that of our Lord's obedience. Consider first His active obedience. He was 'made of a woman'; He was 'made under the law' – He came under it. He who as Son of God had made the Law with His Father put Himself under it in order to redeem us. The Law of God must be satisfied; it must be honoured, it must be vindicated; and so having come on earth to redeem men and to rescue them from 'the curse of the Law', He gave an active obedience to the Law.

Think also of what happened at His baptism. 'Why do you come to seek baptism of me?' said John the Baptist to Him; 'I ought to be baptized of you.' 'Suffer it to be so now', said our Lord, 'for thus it becometh us to fulfil all righteousness.' He put

Himself 'under the Law'. He put Himself in our position. He is our Head and Representative. The Law is there and demands to be kept; so He kept it, and never failed in any jot or tittle. He rendered a perfect and a full obedience to God's holy Law.

Then look at His passive obedience upon the Cross, and, before that, the struggle in the Garden of Gethsemane. 'Father,' He said, 'if it be possible let this cup pass from me; nevertheless not my will but thine be done.' What does that mean? There He was face to face with the terrible decision of submitting passively to having the sins of men put upon Him and of bearing their awful punishment. That would mean separation from His Father for a terrible moment. He asks, 'Is there no other way? If not, I am going on.' That was a part of His passive obedience. He went 'as a lamb to the slaughter'. He did not resist, He did not object. Our sins were laid upon Him and He bore them. He bore the pain and the suffering of our punishment. He made the atonement. He endured the wrath of God against sin. That is His passive obedience! He was perfectly obedient – His obedience was active, His obedience was passive. It is this obedience of His, says the Apostle, that has produced this entire change in us and our position, and has led to the extraordinary results listed in the verses we are now studying.

The Apostle mentions the first result in verse 18 – 'Justification of life'. This is what he has been expounding ever since the seventeenth verse of the first chapter – 'Justification by faith'. 'The just shall live by faith'. 'The just by faith shall live'. This, as we have seen, is God forgiving us, blotting out our transgressions entirely. But more: it is God pronouncing us righteous. And still more: it is our being delivered from the whole realm of death in which we were held. We worked that out in studying verse 17: 'For if by one man's offence death reigned by one, much more they which receive abundance of grace and of the gift of righteousness shall reign in life by one.' Justification is not only the forgiveness of sins; it means also that we have finished with the realm of death; we are 'in life', we are 'reigning in life'. We belong now to the realm and territory of life, everlasting life, and we look forward to an eternal hope. Verse 19 states it still more strongly: 'For as by one man's disobedience many were made sinners, so by the obedience of one shall many be made righteous'. Yes, the people who belong to Christ are made righteous. Give to the word 'made' its full content – 'constituted', 'put into the category of', 'judicially regarded as'. That is what it means here, as it meant the same thing on the other side in our relationship to Adam.

This, says Paul, is what has happened to all of us who are in Christ; and it happens to us because of, and on the ground of, His obedience alone. This was the great theme of the Apostle. Look at it in 2 Corinthians 5: 21: 'For he (God) hath made him to be sin for us who knew no sin.' Why so? 'In order that we might be made the righteousness of God in him.' That is precisely what he is saying in these two verses. As we were constituted sinners because of Adam's one sin, and apart from any action on our part, so we are constituted righteous persons entirely apart from anything that we do. It is entirely and only because of Christ's obedience. That is the great principle emphasized repeatedly in this paragraph. 'You were once there in Adam,' he says, 'you are now in Christ.' All that was true of you formerly was the result of that one act of Adam. All this is true of you now as a result of the obedience of Christ.

I have emphasized that Paul did not say that in Adam we were constituted sinful, but that we were constituted sinners. Here, on the other hand, we must realize that in Christ we are regarded as righteous persons. God puts us into the category, into the class, of righteous people. He looks at us as if we had never sinned at all. We have finished with that old position; we are no longer sinners. We have been taken out of that class, we have been put into this new class. We are constituted righteous persons. We are taken right out of the realm of death. Death has no more dominion over us in that sense, it has become sleep to us. We belong to the realm of life. That is what the Apostle wants us to understand. That is the assurance we are to enjoy. And it is all true because we are not only forgiven and regarded as righteous, but what makes it still more certain is that we are 'in Christ', we belong to Him. Our relationship to Him is the same as our relationship was to Adam at the beginning. It is as definite a fact, and it is as certain. We are 'in Christ'.

Let me put it again in this form. We must not think of our salvation in too individualistic a manner. We must get hold of the idea that our salvation is entirely in Christ, and that what saves us is that we are put 'into' Him. We must not think of God dealing with us one by one in this connection, and that a separate act of salvation is necessary for each one of us. Not at all! It was all done once and for ever in Christ – in His life, death and resurrection. If I am put into Christ then I was crucified with Him, I died with Him, I am risen with Him, I am in the heavenly places with Him. I am 'in Christ'. That is the way to look at it, and as long as we do this our certainty and our assurance can never be shaken.

Paul states the same truth in the First Epistle to the Corinthians: 'But of him are ye in Christ Jesus, who of God is made unto us wisdom, righteousness, sanctification and redemption' [1 *Corinthians* 1: 30]. It is all in Him, and if I am in Him it all becomes mine. As that sin of Adam led to so much in my case, so that obedience of Christ leads to much more in my case. If I am in Christ at all, He is not only my justification, not only my righteousness, but also my sanctification, and also my final redemption. I cannot take parts of Christ. He is a whole Christ, and if I am in Him all His benefits come to me. That is the argument. I am regarded by God as a righteous person because I am in Christ. I am constituted righteous, and as it is God who has done all this, as it is God who has constituted me a righteous person – even as He formerly had constituted me a sinner – as it is God's own judicial act, obviously my salvation must be certain and secure, and nothing can ever change it. If God has made a judicial pronouncement with respect to me, to the effect that because I am in Christ He regards me as a righteous person, then certainly I am a righteous person. But I will go further; I shall always be a righteous person.

'Ah,' says someone, 'but what if you sin tomorrow?' I reply that I am still a righteous person. The fact that I may sin tomorrow does not mean that my standing before God is changed and that I go back and am 'in Adam' once more, as I was before. You cannot go back and fore like that as to your position – such a suggestion is monstrous. We are either 'in Adam' or else we are 'in Christ'. And as Paul will go on to show us in the next two verses, and then still more in chapters 6 and 7, though I as a man 'in Christ' may sin, I do not go back under the Law. I have finished with that for ever, 'old things have passed away, behold all things are become new'. That is one of the most important of the 'old things'. The Christian in that sense has finished with law, he is no longer 'under' the Law.

This does not mean that the Christian should not keep the Law; but he is not 'under' it. We must be clear about this. I am constituted a righteous person – that is how God regards me. I am now in His family, I am now His child, and when I sin now I am not sinning against Law, I am sinning against Love. It is no longer the action of a criminal, it is the action of a child. It is in the relationship of love that we now fail. The whole situation is different. I do not cease to be a righteous person when I sin; though I am an unworthy one, I am still a righteous person. God has declared it. He has established me there, He has put me into the category, and you cannot pass in and out of the category. Cannot you see how monstrous it is to suggest that at one moment you are amongst the righteous, and the next moment you are 'in Adam'? The very idea is ridiculous, and, of course, it is totally untrue. When God makes this pronouncement, this declaration, when God constitutes us righteous in this way, we are righteous, we are in Christ. That is our new position, and 'no man shall ever be able to pluck us out of his hands'. Nothing shall ever be able 'to separate us from the love of God which is in Christ Jesus our Lord'.

Such is the great statement which the Apostle makes in these two momentous verses. It is the summing up of his argument. 'As,' and because, when you were in Adam his act of disobedience led to all evils and woes, 'so' – 'even so' because you are in Christ, His obedience, and His obedience alone, leads to unspeakable blessednesses. The Apostle tells the Corinthians that every Christian man's work is going to be judged at the end, and that if a man has been building with wood, and hay, and stubble, it will all be burnt up, yet he himself shall be saved 'yet so as by fire'. In other words he is saved because he is a righteous person. Though all his building has been useless and does not stand, he himself stands – 'saved, yet so as by fire'.

That is the assurance that you and I as Christians should possess. The Apostle wrote all this, and repeated the same point many times in order to promote that in us. Why does he keep on telling us that it was the one sin of Adam that made us sinners? Why does he put it in this explicit manner in the nineteenth verse, where he says we were 'constituted' sinners? Why is he so concerned to press that upon us? There is only one adequate explanation; namely, that we may see clearly the other side. The consequences of Christ's obedience are as certain and sure as were those which ensued on Adam's disobedience, indeed much more so. What are these consequences? We are put into the category of the righteous; we are 'in Christ', in the very life of Christ, joined to Him, the living Head of His people, and our eternal future is safe and secure. Nothing can ever rob us of it.

It follows from this that the way to test whether you really grasp the argument or not is this: Are you certain and sure of your salvation? Or do you still go on saying, 'I would not like to say that I am sure, because I cannot trust myself. I may sin tomorrow or next year.' To speak in this fashion is tantamount to confessing that you have not followed the argument. Your salvation and mine depends only and entirely and exclusively upon the obedience of Christ. 'Ah,' says someone, 'does not that amount to an invitation to us to go and commit sin?' But that is precisely what people were saying about Paul and his teaching. That is what he says in the first verse of the sixth chapter: 'Shall we continue in sin that grace may abound?' In other words, if you do not sound as if you were preaching antinomianism you are not preaching the Gospel! The Gospel sounds dangerous to the merely moral man, but of course it is not dangerous, because the man who is in Christ will not argue like that. The man who is in Christ will see this wondrous truth and will be so amazed and will so rejoice in it that he will spare no effort to be worthy of it. 'Every man that hath this hope in him, purifieth himself even as he is pure' [1 *John* 3: 3]. The argument works the other way round.

I leave the question with you: Have you followed the argument? Have you really seen yourself 'in Christ'? Do not simply look at yourself; look at yourself 'in Him', because that is where you are. You have been put there, you have been engrafted, you are in Him, and therefore you are constituted a righteous person. That is how God looks at you. God no longer looks at you as a sinner and as you were in Adam. That is the whole point of the Gospel, and you must never look at yourself as a sinner again. You are not a sinner, you are a child of God. You are a child who fails, and who falls, but you are not a sinner any longer; you are not a 'miserable sinner'. For a Christian to call himself a 'miserable sinner' is to deny this entire argument. He was a 'miserable sinner', but he is now a righteous person; and when he fails and falls he does so in the realm of the family, in the realm of love. But, thank God, he does not change his position; his standing is not changed, the relationship to God is not changed. Look at yourself always exclusively and entirely in Christ, even as, before, it was all entirely and exclusively in Adam.

Do you feel as I feel? I thank God that He ever by the Spirit led the Apostle Paul to emphasize this point about Adam and Christ, and also the point that we all were sinners because of Adam's sin. It drives and enables me to look on the other side and say, 'I am righteous, in spite of all I know to be true of myself, because I am "in Christ". I am no longer a sinner, I have been constituted a righteous person.'

Twenty-one

*

Moreover the law entered, that the offence might abound. But where sin abounded, grace did much more abound;
That as sin hath reigned unto death, even so might grace reign through righteousness unto eternal life by Jesus Christ our Lord.
Romans 5: 20, 21

These two verses come at the end of that most important and interesting paragraph we have been considering, the paragraph which starts at verse 12. The very word 'Moreover' at the beginning of verse 20 arrests our attention at once. Here is obviously something additional to what has gone before.

Why does the Apostle say 'Moreover'? Let me put it like this. You remember that we demonstrated that verses 18 and 19 sum up the argument which the Apostle was concerned to put before us: 'Therefore as by the offence of one judgment came upon all men to condemnation; even so by the righteousness of one the free gift came upon all men unto justification of life. For as by one man's disobedience many were constituted sinners, so by the obedience of one shall many be constituted righteous.' That was the great truth he was anxious to convey, and in a sense he has really finished his statement and his argument at the end of verse 19. But he goes on, 'Moreover . . .' He still has something further to say. What is it, and why does he say it?

This style of speech is very typical and characteristic of our Apostle. Obviously, he has a feeling that he has left a kind of loose end, and that he cannot just leave it at that. He has made a reference in the thirteenth and the fourteenth verses to the Law. 'For until the Law sin was in the world; but sin is not imputed when there is no law. Nevertheless death reigned from Adam to Moses, even over them that had not sinned after the similitude of Adam's transgression.' Having mentioned the Law there, he now comes back to it and shows its exact relationship to what he has been saying in the course of the argument. It is not essential to the argument but he knew that it would help Christian Jews especially if he resolved the matter.

The Jews, as we have already seen from time to time, were in great trouble concerning this question. When I say the Jews, I do not mean only the unbelieving Jews, I mean also many Jews who had actually become Christian. It took them a long time to understand the exact place of the Law in the economy of God, in His great plan and purpose of salvation. When the Apostle wrote his letters he did so primarily not to produce theological treatises, but as moved by a pastor's heart and desire to help simple people to understand their faith. He takes great trouble to explain things to them, in order that they might be happy in their minds.

Paul knew that, because of what he had been writing, certain people would raise questions and say, 'In the light of what you preach, what was the object and purpose of God in giving the Law at all? As far as we understand your argument the Law has no value and never did have any. You have taken all this time to tell us, and you repeat it constantly, that the Law is not the means of our justification. We are clear about that. We thought formerly that we could justify ourselves by keeping the Law, but now you have established and emphasized clearly that "no man can be justified by the deeds of the Law". To this extent we accept that the Law was not given in order that we might be justified through it; but now you have gone further. In this paragraph, beginning at verse 12, you are now saying that the Law does not even condemn us. If so, what was the object and purpose of the Law? You have convinced us that it was not given to justify us, but now you are telling us that it was not given even to condemn us because, as you have been at pains to say, we are all condemned by "the one sin of Adam". It is by the one man's disobedience that many were constituted sinners; it is because of the offence of this one man that judgment came upon all. The Law does not justify, the Law does not even condemn us; what then does the Law effect? Does it do anything at all? Was there any purpose in the giving of the Law?'

It is easy to imagine what an acute question this must have been to the Jew, because to him the Law that had been given through Moses was the greatest thing in his life. To him nothing had been more momentous than what happened at Sinai. That had really marked the Israelites out from all the other nations who had not received the Law in that way. And here comes a teaching which seems, at any rate on the surface, to say that the Law is of no value at all, that it neither justifies nor condemns. They were fully entitled therefore to ask what was the purpose and the function of the Law. The question arises because Paul has really been pressing this point in verses 13 and 14. He says, 'Until the Law' – that is to say, until the Law was promulgated through Moses – 'sin was in the world'; and 'death reigned from Adam to Moses'. It is clear therefore that the human race was not condemned in the first instance by the Law that was given through Moses, because the condemnation was already present before the Law was given. That is proved by the universality of sin and death from Adam to Moses. So the question as to the Law's function arises in a very pertinent manner; and the Scripture lets us know the answer to it.

Thank God, the Apostle does deal with it. He adds this postscript: 'Moreover', he says, as if to indicate that he had not forgotten about the problem of the Law. But he seems to have a certain amount of interest in style after all. He has already introduced a parenthesis, as we have seen, in verses 13 and 14, and even a second one in verses 15, 16 and 17; and so he seems to remind himself that there is a limit to the number of parentheses a writer can introduce. So avoiding the introduction of yet another, he finishes his argument, and then takes up the question of the Law in the postscript that we find in verses 20 and 21.

I must confess that I am charmed by this man and everything he does. I admire his method, I like his style, I am drawn to his way of doing things. But particularly, and above all else, I admire his great pastoral heart. He was not the kind of teacher who avoids difficulties; he does not leave out difficult subjects and problems and confine himself to easy and simple matters. His burning desire was to help the churches; as a teacher he must give them an explanation of this matter. And he does so here in his customary and characteristic manner. The question he poses and answers is: What is the function of the Law given through Moses? The Law – let us be quite clear about this – in verse 20 means the Law that was given through Moses on Mount Sinai, not the Moral Law only but the Ceremonial Law also, in fact the whole of the Law.

Perhaps some are inclined to ask why we cannot skip over verses 20 and 21 and go on at once to the interesting chapters 6, 7 and 8? Need we trouble about these two verses? I suggest that we must for this reason, that you cannot understand the New Testament truly unless you understand this teaching concerning the Law. This is because it is introduced so frequently in the Apostle's letters. Take the third chapter of the Epistle to the Galatians, for instance, and all places where the position of the Jews is considered, or the Apostle is answering the wrong teaching of the Judaizers. One cannot possibly understand the teaching of the Apostle unless one knows exactly what he is saying in these verses in the Epistle to the Romans.

'Moreover', Paul says, 'the Law entered . . .' The word 'entered' is an interesting word. Every word the Apostle uses has to be observed. We came across this same word 'entered' in our study of verse 12: 'Wherefore, as by one man sin entered into the world, and death by sin'. But the Apostle did not write exactly the same word in the two places, for in verse 20 he adds a prefix, 'para', to the word which he used in verse 12, and this carries the meaning, 'alongside of', 'by the side of'. This addition produces a more comprehensive and telling word, than that used in verse 12. In verse 12 he says that 'sin entered into the world'; here he says that 'the Law entered in by the side of'. By the side of what? By the side of the sin that had already entered. There was a state of affairs already existing; but now into that situation something else comes. It is not so much that it creates a new situation; it comes in alongside of the other situation. If we understand this principle we are at once more than half way to an understanding of the function of the Law. The very word 'added alongside', that Paul uses here, tells us that the Law, in and of itself, is not something that is of fundamental importance to us. It is something additional, it is something that has come in for the time being, for a particular function. It is not fundamental in the sense that sin and salvation are fundamental; it is something that enters, an addition, something that 'comes in alongside of'.

The Apostle sometimes uses this word in another sense. In the Epistle to the Galatians he talks of some people who have crept in privily' or 'stolen in'. 'And that because of false brethren unawares brought in, who came in privily' [*Galatians* 2: 4]. The idea of 'privily' does not apply in Romans 5: 20; but the word has the same general meaning. It indicates that the Law is not something fundamental, not something that is essential. It has a function, but it is not vital in the matter of salvation. That is the key to the understanding of this statement.

It came in alongside, says Paul, 'in order that the offence might abound'. The word 'offence' refers to Adam's offence, but not only so; it means everything that has come out of Adam's offence. And that, as we have already seen, includes our offences also, for the Apostle has already told us in verse 16 that 'the free gift is of many offences unto justification'. So when he says, 'that the offence might abound', he is referring to the sin of Adam and to all the sins of men ever since. The Law has come in alongside in order that this sin, these actual sins and offences, might abound – that is to say, 'might increase' or 'be augmented'. What then is the function of the Law according to the Apostle? It has been brought in alongside in order that the offence, the sins, might abound.

We are now in a position to discuss the real business and object of the Law. The Law, obviously, was never intended as a way of salvation. There is no need to linger over this because the Apostle has made that abundantly clear in the first four chapters, as, for example, in the words: 'By the deeds of the law shall no flesh be justified in his sight; for by the law is the knowledge of sin' (chapter 3: 20). As I have said in the general analysis of this whole section concerning justification by faith and its results, this is the end of a great section, so once more he sums up the position concerning the Law. We find the same thing explicitly in the third chapter of Galatians, verse 21: 'Is the law then against the promises of God? God forbid: for if there had been a law given which could have given life, verily righteousness should have been by the law', which obviously means that that is impossible. No law is capable of giving life.

So let us get rid once and for ever of the idea that God gave the Law to the Children of Israel in order to give them the opportunity to save themselves by obeying it. It was never intended for that; it was not added as a possible means of salvation. Preachers and evangelists sometimes say that God gave them the opportunity to save themselves by the Law. But that is not true. The Law entered that the offence might abound, and was never intended as a way of salvation.

'But', someone may ask, 'does this mean that the Law was deliberately 'brought in alongside' by God in order to make us sin the more, that the offence might abound? We reply at once that that is utterly impossible. 'God cannot be tempted with evil, neither tempteth he any man', says James (1: 13). God will never do anything to incite us to sin; such a thing is utterly impossible, indeed the suggestion is blasphemous.

What then is the Apostle teaching? He is asserting that the Law has actually increased, and was meant to increase sin in three main ways. The first is that the Law increases our knowledge of sin. Go back again to chapter 3, verse 20: 'By the law is the knowledge of sin.' The same truth appears again in the seventh verse of the seventh chapter: 'What shall we say then? Is the law sin? God forbid. Nay, I had not known sin, but by the law: for I had not known lust, except the law had said, Thou shalt not covet.'

The first business of the Law, then, is to increase my knowledge of sin; and it does that in four main ways. One is that the Law increases my knowledge of sin because it defines sin for me. In a certain sense we are all ignorant concerning sin; people commit sin without knowing that they are committing sin. So we need to be educated concerning sin. A man may have done a thing for years and have seen no harm in it; or he may have seen a certain amount of harm in it in a vague kind of way; but still he does not realize exactly what he has been doing.

The business of the Law is to codify, is to define sin. That, of course, is what has obviously happened in the laws of most countries. In primitive societies they virtually had no laws at all, but then as time went on they found it was necessary to put certain things down in writing in order that they might know what was right and what was wrong, what they could do and what they could not do. It is necessary to codify these matters and to define them, because two people may not agree about certain practices. So laws come to be written, or case-law begins to operate – we need not pursue the matter further – and in the outcome communities have a number of principles and a complex of rules and regulations to guide them. Now that is one of the functions of law; it is to define sin, to pinpoint it.

The Apostle has already said this twice. First of all in chapter 4 verse 15, where he says, 'Because the law worketh wrath; for where no law is, there is no transgression'. There is sin, but there is no transgression. Here we note the difference between sin and transgression. Transgression is sin, defined as such, by the Law. It is no longer merely a wrong act, it now involves breaking a law as well. Because the Law has defined it, it has become what it was not before, transgression. We have also found this teaching in verse 13 of this section, 'For until the law sin was in the world; but sin is not imputed when there is no law'. I interpreted that as meaning that though sin was in the world before the Law was given, it was not 'entered into the ledgers', as it were, until the Law was promulgated. It was sin, people committed sin, but in the absence of a code of written Law, it was not put into the account. The difference made by the Law is that it pinpoints and defines sin.

But, above and beyond that, the Law helps us to an understanding and a knowledge of the real nature of sin in its depths. We all know something about sin and have within us a sense of right and wrong. We all, by nature, as Paul argues in chapter 2 – and he includes in his survey even the pagans who have never had the Law – have a conscience within us by which our thoughts 'accuse or excuse one another' (2: 15). We all know when we have done something wrong; but the fact that we have this knowledge does not mean that we know much about the nature of sin. It is only the Law that really gives us a true understanding of the nature of sin. We shall find Paul saying this very clearly in chapter 7, verse 13: 'Was then that which is good made death unto me? God forbid. But sin, that it might appear sin, working death in me by that which is good; that sin by the commandment might become exceeding sinful.' The Law teaches me about the depth of sin, the foulness of sin, the real nature of sin, the exceeding sinfulness of sin. I could not know this without the Law. A man does not really understand the nature of desire, and of lust, and of coveting, and what Paul calls 'concupiscence', apart from the Law. But the Law teaches us.

Consider some of the Apostle's other terms such as that in chapter 7, verse 5, where he talks about 'the motions of sin' that are at work 'in our members to bring forth fruit unto death'. It is the Law that stimulates this activity, he says, makes us more fully aware of its significance. We did not know it before, but the entering in of the Law gives us a knowledge of the character of sin, and thereby it increases sin, and makes it greater.

In that same seventh chapter the Apostle teaches us about the terrible power of sin. Until the Law comes and teaches us we do not really see sin in and of itself and as it exists apart from ourselves. We know that we do wrong, but we merely pass it off as regrettable and as some negative defect. But when the Law has taught us and enlightened us, we are amazed at this horrible thing, this terrible power, that has entered into the world and tyrannizes over us all. It is the Law that opens our eyes to this tragedy. People who are not taught and instructed in the Law know nothing about this; that is the measure of their ignorance and their darkness.

This aspect of the Law as conferring enlightenment leads us, in turn, to the third point. It is the Law alone that reveals to us the terrible grip which sin has taken on the human heart. It is the Law alone that teaches us that sin is not simply a matter of doing things that are wrong, but that it has twisted our entire nature. The Law alone shows me that I am a fallen creature, and that, as the result of Adam's transgression, every man born into the world is morally diseased, his whole nature being marred and warped. In the seventh chapter the Apostle will tell us again what sin has done within the human heart.

Finally, the fourth point, the Law brings out the awful deceitfulness of sin: 'For sin, taking occasion by the commandment, deceived me, and by it slew me' [*Romans* 7: 11]. No man knows that until he understands the teaching of the Law. By nature, he knows nothing of the deceitfulness of sin. It is the Law alone that teaches him that sin has so adversely affected him that the very Law which was meant to help him makes him sin all the more. That is what sin has done.

So then, to sum up on this first point, we see that 'by the law is the knowledge of sin'. This should make those of us who are ministers see the importance of preaching the Law. One of the greatest troubles in the Church today, as well as in the world, is that men do not have a knowledge of sin as they should have. Sin is regarded very lightly and very loosely. We are regarded as being morbid if we preach the message of the seventh chapter of Romans, and if we hold before people their own sinfulness. Men are prepared to admit that they need a little help, and that they are weak in this or that respect; but the Scripture teaches the depth and the foulness, and the exceeding sinfulness of sin. Our fathers, our grandfathers, and especially those who preceded them, knew all about this, and it was in such times that great spiritual revivals occurred. It is when men and women realize the depth of iniquity and sin that is in them that they begin to cry out to God. But if men have no real understanding of sin, if they are lacking in the knowledge of sin which is given only by the Law, then they will be content with a superficial evangelism. This is surely one of our main troubles today; hence the importance of going carefully, and in detail, into this postscript to this fifth chapter. The first thing the Law does is to increase our knowledge of sin.

Secondly, and because of this first factor, the Law increases our conviction of sin. This is not merely a matter of head knowledge or of intellectual information. If we really have the knowledge it will convict us. I suggest that it does so in two main ways. First, it makes our sin the greater because, with the knowledge that the Law has now given us, we not only do wrong but we know that we are doing wrong. We did not know that before; we were like children. A little child does something wrong but he does not really understand what he is doing. It is only as he learns and gets greater knowledge that he will have an understanding of the wrongfulness of the wrong that he commits.

The Law convicts us more deeply of our sin. With this knowledge we realize that when we do wrong we are not only committing a wrong action, but are also defying the majesty of God, we are pitting ourselves against God's holiness and righteousness, against His Law. This is one of the most terrible aspects of sin. It is not merely that we have done something that makes us feel sorry afterwards, and that we have hurt ourselves or hurt somebody else; it is above all an action against God. David saw something of this when he said in the fifty-first Psalm, 'Against thee, thee only have I sinned'. He says that, though he was actually an adulterer and a murderer. But at the same time he had seen the real and the ultimate meaning of sin. The most terrible aspect of what he had done was not that he had committed adultery with Bathsheba and that he had murdered her husband, but – 'Against thee, thee only have I sinned and done this evil in thy sight.' David has learned his lesson. That is what humbles him to the dust and makes him feel that he cannot forgive himself.

The same becomes true of all of us once we know something about the Law. It is not only that we do wrong things; we are flouting God's holy will, we are spurning the voice divine, we are deliberately pitting our wills against the will of God. Adam did that; and we, in turn, once we know the Law, become conscious of a similar transgression. Those who lived between Adam and Moses, as we are told in verses 13 and 14, did not realize it fully; they sinned, but they did not know what they were doing – they did not sin 'after the similitude of Adam's transgression'. But once the Law comes in, it gives us this knowledge, and so it makes our sin much worse. By the Law our sin becomes a much greater and a more heinous offence.

Why am I so concerned about this? and why am I giving it such strong emphasis? Because of my conviction that this is the way to convince your 'good moral man' that he is a sinner. There are so many people in the modern world, educated people, good moral people who resent the suggestion that they are and have been sinners. Of course they are not drunkards or adulterers or murderers! They are the most respectable people in the land, and they can sit and listen to preaching that denounces such sins, and hippies and drug addicts, without being touched. They have never done or been any of these things, and they do a lot of good; they are idealists, they are philanthropists, they do good with both hands. There is only one way to convict such people of sin; it is to ask them these questions: What place does God take in their lives? Do they ever think about Him? Do they live their 'good' lives because of Him and for His glory?

The plain fact is that God is entirely ignored by such persons and thereby insulted by them. I would say that the greatest sinners in the world are the self-satisfied, self-contained, good moral people, who believe that, as they are, they are fit to stand in the presence of God. Moreover, they are in reality telling God that He need never have sent His Son into the world as far as they are concerned, and that the Son need never have died upon the Cross. There is no greater insult to God than that; but it is precisely what they are guilty of. There is no greater sinner in the universe than the man who has never seen his need of the blood of Christ. There is no sin greater than that – murder and adultery and fornication are nothing in comparison with it.

It is most important therefore that we should realize this truth concerning the Law; it determines the character of our preaching and our evangelism. If we preach and evangelize merely in terms of, 'Are you in trouble, are you unhappy?' the good moral man will say, 'Of course, this has nothing to do with me, I am perfectly happy, and I am not in trouble at all.' If we then go on to preach about those who are victims of drink and of sex and so on, he says, 'He is not preaching to me, these things do not worry me at all. I am a happily married man, with good children, and all is well.' This good moral man sits as the Pharisees sat listening to the Lord Jesus Christ. We are told that they were 'sitting by', looking on as spectators. Preaching that omits the teaching of the

Law's relationship to sin is seriously defective. We must not start with men's needs, with their weaknesses, their fears, their phobias and so on. Our preaching must not be subjective only. What then must we preach? We must preach GOD, the LORD of the universe, the Creator, the Lord God Almighty, the Everlasting God. We must tell all men that they were made by Him, that they are responsible to Him, and that they are before Him. Your 'good moral man' comes in there; everybody comes in there.

It is not surprising that so many people are outside the Church. We have been guilty of preaching the Gospel in a manner that seems to many of them to be irrelevant. We must hold mankind face to face with God, and the moment we do so it is not difficult to prove that there is 'none righteous, no, not one', and that 'the whole world lieth guilty before God'. That includes the self-contained man with his self-satisfaction and his self-contained everything, who never thinks of God, never worships Him, and never comes on Sunday to join with others in singing His praises; he is the greatest sinner of them all. He thinks he can live without God, he is not interested in God, and the Son of God was never necessary as far as he is concerned. It is the Law that teaches us this and convicts us of sin, because the Law always brings us face to face with God.

Let me give the final proof of what I am saying. You remember the man who came one day to our Lord with his clever question. He asked, 'Which is the first and the greatest commandment in the law?' He knew, for he came from the circles in which they were always arguing about these things. Some said that adultery was the greatest sin, others said that it was murder, and others said various other things. But it was always something that a man did. Our Lord's answer was devastating; they never expected it. He said, 'Thou shalt love the Lord thy God with all thy heart and soul and mind and strength'. That is the first commandment – our attitude towards God. It is only then that our attitude to our neighbour comes in. That is the second commandment; it is 'like unto' the first. Actions do not come first; the first thing is our relationship to God and our attitude towards Him.

It is the Law alone that teaches us this lesson; and so it convicts us of our basic failure, and therefore of the extent of our sinfulness. As Paul will say in chapter 7: 'I was alive without the law once; but when the commandment came, sin revived and I died.' Why should he write about himself as he does in chapter 7, where he calls himself a 'wretched man' and tells of his utter helplessness to do anything to save himself? It is because of what the Law has taught him. The Law has convicted him of the depth of his sinfulness, his inability, his total inability to contribute anything at all to his own spiritual health, and has compelled him to say, 'In me (that is, in my flesh) dwelleth no good thing' (7: 18).

That brings us to my third main heading. The Law not only increases our knowledge of sin, and not only strengthens our conviction of sin, but, because of what sin has done to us, it actually makes us sin, and incites us to sin. Listen to the evidence in chapter 7, verses 5, 8, and 11: 'For when we were in the flesh, the motions of sin, which were by the law, did work in our members to bring forth fruit unto death.' That is the first statement of it. Then take verse 8: 'But sin, taking occasion by the commandment, wrought in me all manner of concupiscence. For without the law sin was dead.' And then the ninth verse follows: 'For I was alive without the law once; but when the commandment came, sin revived, and I died.' Then in verse 11: 'For sin, taking occasion by the commandment, deceived me, and by it slew me.' Because of what sin has done to us, because it has perverted our nature, and because it has such a grip on our hearts, the very Law that tells us not to do things creates within us a desire to do them all the more. 'Unto the pure', says Paul to Titus, 'all things are pure: but unto them that are defiled and unbelieving is nothing pure; but even their mind and conscience is defiled' [*Titus* 1: 15].

I have never believed in what is called morality teaching – I mean the teaching about sex which in some quarters is now being introduced into the schools, and for this reason, that, as the result of sin, the minds of the children are not pure, and what such teaching is likely to do is to create in them a greater desire to know about these things and to do them. They already find out about these matters surreptitiously; and the teaching will simply intensify that interest and so stimulate them to sin. Knowledge of sin has never prevented anybody from sinning. Indeed, the more one knows about it the more one is subject to the temptation to do it. So Paul says that the Law has increased sin even in that sense, that it has made us sin even more. It was never meant to do so. The Law 'is just and holy and good'; the trouble is in us. We must not say that there is anything wrong with the Law. The Apostle says: 'Was then that which is good made death unto me? God forbid. But sin, that it might appear sin, working death in me by that which is good; that sin by the commandment might become exceeding sinful.' What a terrible thing sin is! It is the Law alone that shows us this.

My fourth and last point is not actually stated here, but as the Apostle puts it so plainly in the parallel statement in Galatians 3 it seems well to introduce it here. The ultimate object of the Law (and this leads to the second half of the twentieth verse) is to bring us to Christ. In Galatians 3: 22–24 it is put thus: 'But the Scripture hath concluded all under sin, that the promise by faith of Jesus Christ might be given to them that believe. But before faith came we were kept under the law, shut up unto the faith which should afterwards be revealed' – that was the Law's purpose – 'Wherefore the law was our schoolmaster' – our pedagogue, the one who takes us by the hand and takes us to the school where we can learn our much-needed lesson – 'the law is our schoolmaster to bring us unto Christ, that we might be justified by faith.' That is what the Law was meant to do. Far from being designed to save us, it was given in order to show us that nothing and nobody can save us but the Son of God, our blessed Lord and Saviour Jesus Christ. Here it is then: 'Moreover the law entered, that (in order that) the offence might abound', in order that we might so see ourselves as we are in sin as to know and feel our utter and complete hopelessness.

I have explained the question of the Law and its function at some length because I feel that somehow or another we have forgotten this law-work in connection with our preaching. The great preachers of two and three hundred years ago would spend a long time over what they called a 'law-work'. We do not hear much about that today; and my feeling is that the Church is as she is partly for that reason. Our preaching is too superficial; to appreciate the glory of salvation we must know something of the depths of sin. For this express reason 'The law entered, that the offence might abound; but where sin abounded there grace did much more abound.' You cannot appreciate the second half of this verse if you do not appreciate the first half.

The man who really knows most about the grace of God is the man who knows most about his own sinfulness. The man who thinks that there is very little wrong with him believes also that it can easily be put right, and so has little if any understanding of grace. But Samuel Davies who lived about two hundred years ago in the United States of America, and was one of the successors of Jonathan Edwards as Principal of Princeton University expresses the true Christian understanding. He was a towering genius, worthy of comparison with Jonathan Edwards himself, and, like Edwards, he was a mighty preacher greatly used of God. He speaks of grace in this way in his famous hymn:

Great God of wonders, all Thy ways
Are matchless, godlike, and divine;

(He works in creation, in nature, everywhere)

But the fair glories of Thy grace
More godlike and unrivalled shine.

(That is the amazing thing!)

Who is a pardoning God like Thee?
Or who has grace so rich and free?

It is only as we realize the depths of sin that we can really sing these words. 'Where sin abounded, grace did much more abound.'

We shall resume this theme of 'grace' later. Meanwhile, let us meditate upon the knowledge that the Law has given us. Let us see ourselves as we really are in the light of the Law. Let us not be like the false prophets of Israel against whom the charge is brought, 'They have healed the hurt of the daughter of my people slightly, saying, Peace, peace, when there is no peace' [*Jeremiah*

6. 14; 8. 11]. It is not enough merely to say to a sinner, 'Come to Jesus'. Rather, let him know what he is doing, let him see himself. If you want him to admire the matchless grace of Christ, see to it that he first realizes what he is face to face with God's holy Law. He cannot realize the nature and the power of grace fully apart from the ministry of the Law. He must first see that sin has abounded; and the Law makes it abound in the way that the Apostle explains. Then he can go on to look at the other side, and begin to enjoy 'the wonders of His grace' even in this world, and prepare himself to go on to enjoy it more and more throughout the countless ages of eternity.

Twenty-two

*

Moreover the law entered, that the offence might abound. But where sin abounded, grace did much more abound;
That as sin hath reigned unto death, even so might grace reign through righteousness unto eternal life by Jesus Christ our Lord.
Romans 5: 20, 21

We have seen that the Apostle takes up the question of the function and the purpose of the Law in these two verses because this was such a vital and urgent question to the Jews. The preaching of salvation in Jesus Christ gave the impression to some of the Jews that the Apostles were saying that the Law had never had any value at all; at any rate it seemed on the surface to be suggesting that. So the Apostle, in order to disabuse their minds of that error, tells them here why the Law was introduced, and what its function really was. That is the main purpose served by these two verses; but in doing that they also do something else, for in them the Apostle incidentally gives us one of his amazing summaries of the whole of the Gospel. I make bold to assert that these two verses can be regarded as a summary of everything the Apostle has been saying right up to this point – from the sixteenth verse of the first chapter of the Epistle. That is always his method. He states his proposition; he next establishes it by working it out in detail; and then, having done that, he always gathers the various points together again into a mighty statement.

That is what he does here. These two verses are a wonderful summary of the way of salvation that has come to men in Jesus Christ. But at the same time – and again it is a characteristic of the Apostle's method – they also provide us with an introduction to what is to come. You cannot really understand chapters 6 and 7 of this Epistle if you do not understand these two verses. I shall show that these two following chapters are virtually nothing but an extended commentary on what he says in chapter 5, verses 20 and 21.

We have looked at the first statement in these verses, 'The law entered that the offence might abound', and have seen something of its meaning. But, thank God, the Apostle does not stop there; he would never have written at all if that was all he had to say. 'But', he says, 'where sin abounded, grace did much more abound.' Always watch this Apostle's 'buts', because you will almost invariably find that he introduces the Gospel with the word. He delights in doing it in that way. He paints the dark side, stops, and says, 'But', and with that word he introduces his wondrous Gospel.

We must give our closest attention to this statement, and as we do so it is important that we should pay careful attention to the actual words that the Apostle used. Unfortunately our Authorized (King James's) version does not bring out the meaning as well as it should; the words it uses are too weak. Take, for instance, the word 'abound'. 'Moreover the law entered that the offence might abound. But where sin abounded, grace did much more abound.' You might well assume that the Apostle had used the same word each time it is translated here as 'abound'. But actually the Apostle did not do so; he took the trouble to use two different words. Where we read, 'grace did much more abound' the word for 'abound' is not the same word as had been used previously; the Apostle deliberately uses a stronger word. But he does not stop at that; he adds a prefix to it; and the prefix is a superlative which means 'super'. This is a term which we also commonly use. When we want to bring out the idea that something is superlative, we say 'That was super'. The Apostle added that to the word that stands for 'abound' in order to emphasize the point he is making, which is that whatever sin may have done, grace has done much more, altogether more.

Let me emphasize this. The Apostle does not use a comparative, he uses a superlative. He could not possibly have said more; he said as much as he could say. So we should translate the expression 'much more abound' as 'superabounded', or, if you like, 'abounded beyond measure'; or still better, 'overflowed'. The idea is that of an overflowing, as if a mighty flood were let loose, sweeping everything before it. Indeed, we might well use the term 'engulfed'; such an abundance, such a superabundance that it drowns and engulfs everything.

Let me use an illustration. The idea is the same as the Apostle employs in 1 Corinthians 15 : 54, where he says that 'Death is swallowed up in victory'. That is the idea. It is not merely that it is balanced or barely cancelled; it is much more than that. Death has been 'swallowed up' in victory – it has gone, it has been gobbled up, if you like, and it is out of sight. That is the idea the Apostle is conveying here; that of a tremendous superlative, an overflowing. The Revised Standard Version in this particular instance comes nearer the right translation; it has 'Where sin increased, grace abounded all the more'. That is quite good, because it brings out the difference between 'increasing' and 'abounding'. The first word should be translated 'increased'. 'Moreover the law entered, that the offence might increase (might be augmented); but where sin increased, grace abounded all the more.' It is a pity that the A.V. translators used the term 'abound' on the negative side, because it prevents them from bringing out the contrast sufficiently even though they add 'much more abound'. It is better to think of it in terms of 'increasing', and, 'abounding all the more'.

The principle taught, then, is that what grace has done is not merely to counteract exactly what sin has done. If grace had done just that, and that alone, it would still be something wonderful. If the effect of grace had merely been to wipe out, and to cancel, all that had happened on the other side, we should have had a theme for praising God sufficient to last us through all eternity. But, says the Apostle, it is not an exact counterbalance; what I have on the right side does not exactly tally with what I have on the left. In fact there is no comparison; it is a superfluity, an abounding, an engulfing, it is an overflowing on the side of grace.

We must hold on to this truth at all costs and get it clear in our minds. The point is that grace does not merely exactly balance, it does not just undo what sin has done; it does much more. Look at it in another way; consider the two words 'death' and 'life' in verse 21. Suppose that I said of a person who is alive, simply that he is not dead? That would be a perfectly true and accurate statement. If a man is alive, he is not dead. But who would ever dream of saying, 'Well, that man is not dead'? You would feel that such a man needed a little dynamite or tonic to waken him up and to infuse energy into him. Well, says Paul in effect, that is exactly it; grace does not merely cancel death – it gives us life. It is not merely a balancing; it abounds, it overflows. Life is positive; it is not merely the negation of death. It is that, but it does not stop at that.

Thus we are back again to one of Paul's 'much more' statements. We have already met them, but they are so wonderful that I must repeat them. The first is found in verse 9: 'Much more then, being now justified by his blood, we shall be saved from wrath through him'; the second in verse 10: 'For if, when we were enemies, we were reconciled to God by the death of his Son, much more, being reconciled' – there it is! It is the difference between life and death – 'we shall be saved in his life'. Then in verse 15: 'But not as the offence, so also is the free gift. For if through the offence of one many be dead, much more the grace of God, and the gift by grace, which is by one man, Jesus Christ, hath abounded unto many.' Then in verse 17: 'For if by one man's offence death reigned by one; much more they which receive abundance of grace and of the gift of righteousness shall reign in life by one, Jesus Christ.' And so we reach the climax: 'Moreover the law entered, that the offence might abound. But where sin increased, grace abounded much more', and overflowed and overwhelmed in its greatness and in its glory.

The Apostle keeps on repeating this 'much more' because although he is virtually saying the same thing each time, he is also bringing out different aspects of truth. He does so, I say, because to him this is, above all else, the truth we must grasp and understand with regard to the Gospel. For this same reason he declares in the very introduction in chapter 1, verse 16: 'I am not ashamed of the Gospel of Christ, for it is the power of God unto salvation to every one that believeth.' He is exulting in it, he is rejoicing in it. Why? Because of its greatness and glorious overwhelming character. He goes on to bring out that aspect of greatness by multiplying these 'much more' expressions. He is thrilled with the thought of this victory. He sees what the Lord Jesus Christ has done, and he wants his readers to rejoice in it also.

In other words I am suggesting that if we do not get hold of this 'much more' principle as we should, we have not got a true view of the way of salvation. The Apostle is deeply concerned about this 'righteousness from God' that has come in, this justification by faith. He wants us to see all that is comprehended in these terms. Justification is not a mere formality, it is the source and fount of salvation; all blessings flow out of it. In the same way, and to the same extent, we must grasp the principle of the 'much more', of the superfluity, in order that we may have a true assurance of salvation.

The Apostle wants us to see the absolute certainty of our salvation; to see that if we really have learned to look to the Lord Jesus Christ by faith, and have seen ourselves justified by faith, we should have an assurance that nothing can shake. We have a hope, he says, which enables us to 'glory in tribulations also; knowing that tribulation worketh patience; and patience, experience; and experience, hope. And hope maketh not ashamed.' All this results from justification by faith. It is the ground of our assurance. I would put it also in this way, that it is only to the extent that we have some conception of this 'much more' element in grace that we shall rejoice in our salvation as we are meant to and should.

Let us be very practical, for, after all, one should never expound Scripture without being practical. I am not a lecturer, I am a preacher. I do not believe that one should lecture on the Bible. The Bible should be preached, and its message should be applied. What I mean is this. It is one thing for us to look at these repetitions of the 'much more'; but the question is, how are we reacting to them? Are we rejoicing in salvation? Are we thrilled by the very thought of it? Do we realize in experience the truth of all that I have been stressing? The Epistle is not just a piece of literature. It is wonderful literature, glorious and masterly; it is eloquent, it is moving. But are we moved, not by the language only, but by the thought and by the concept? Are we rejoicing in the victory of grace over sin?

Such is the Apostle's concern and desire. The great saints of all the centuries have always taken hold of this. Martin Luther was a very miserable man until he saw the truth about justification by faith. But then, having seen it, he began to sing. The rediscovery of justification by faith at the time of the Protestant Reformation changed many things; it even changed the singing of the Church. Have you heard the kind of music they used to sing before the Reformation? Some regard it as great music, and it may be so; but it is dull, and it is negative. To me it is pagan, because it has a wail in it. There is no triumph, no victory in that 'plain song', as it is called – indeed that is exactly what it is. It lacks fullness and a sense of glory, and triumph, and victory. That element is entirely absent. As you hear it you can see the monks marching with their heads down. They are wailing. Why? Because they are in bondage. But when the Protestant Reformation came as the result of Luther's eyes being opened to this wonderful doctrine of justification by faith, he himself began to sing, and all others who saw the truth began to sing in the same way. Oh, the glory of what God has done in Christ! It dwarfs and engulfs everything else – even God's own mighty act of creation.

All the saints have gloried and delighted in it. Look at John Bunyan. When John Bunyan comes to write his Autobiography he calls it, 'Grace Abounding to the chief of sinners'. He did not just sneak, as it were, into the Kingdom of God. He had what Peter calls 'an abundant entrance'. And that is the way we should all enter the Kingdom. The Apostle has already emphasized this in the second verse of this great chapter, 'By whom also', he says, 'we have access by faith into this grace in which we stand.' We are not to lie down in grace; we are meant to stand in it, and to be erect. Why? Because we have understood this 'much more'. We have the sense of victory, and we go 'with boldness' into the presence of God. So John Bunyan talks and writes about grace, about grace abounding, about grace abounding to himself as the chief of sinners.

Charles Wesley likewise is not content with barely saying that he has found grace in Christ. This is how he puts it:

Plenteous grace with Thee is found,
Grace to cover all my sin;
Let the healing streams abound,
Make and keep me pure within.
Thou of life the fountain art,
Freely let me take of Thee;
Spring Thou up within my heart,
Rise to all eternity.

Plenteous! Abounding! Not merely just enough! Springing up! Rising to all eternity! It is all in Christ, and there is no end to it!

All these books and hymns are interpretations of the teaching of this portion of Scripture. You notice the Apostle using the same superlatives in the second chapter of Ephesians: 'The exceeding riches of his grace.' Later he talks about the 'unsearchable riches of Christ'. These are his characteristic terms. I tarry with this point for this reason, that I suggest that this is the way in which we can discover where we ourselves stand. Once we have a glimpse of this superabundance, this abounding grace, it of necessity puts us on our feet and makes us sing. We have assurance, and we have joy. We must have! 'Ah, but' you say, 'what of the blackness and the darkness of my own heart?' I know! But my argument is this, that the more you know the blackness and the darkness of your own heart, if you are a Christian, the more it should eventually make you sing. If you only look at the blackness and the darkness of your own heart, and stay there, you are not behaving in a Christian manner. You must start there, but you do not stop there. That sight should make you fly to Christ; and then when you see the superabundance of grace that is in Him you begin to sing.

So even your sin makes you sing, because you see how it has been dealt with so gloriously and so superabundantly. Indeed, as

I have been trying to show, and as these verses make us see, it is when you put these two sides together that you have a real concept of salvation – the depth of iniquity, and the heights of grace and of mercy and of compassion. When you have the two, the down and the up, you really begin to measure the immeasurable, and you join Paul and all the saints in trying to assess and to discover 'the breadth, and the length, and the depth, and the height, and to know the love of Christ which passeth knowledge'.

There, in verse 20, Paul has stated it all. But in order to help these people, and in order to help us, he does not leave it just as a general statement; he goes on in verse 21 to give us an exposition of it: 'That (so that) as sin hath reigned unto death, even so might grace reign through righteousness unto eternal life by Jesus Christ our Lord.' Are we aware of how grace has superabounded over sin? That is what he wants to know, and he is ready to help us. Look at it again, he says in effect. He has been dwelling on the comparisons and contrasts between what happened to us in Adam, and what has happened to us in Christ. We have worked it out in detail. Here he says it once more and sums it up.

Look at what sin did, the Apostle says. You must start there. Every man in the world is in one of two positions – he is either 'under sin' or else he is 'under grace'. He is either being ruled over and governed by sin, or else he is under the reign of, and is being ruled over by grace. Those, I repeat, are the only two possible positions. As Paul has kept on saying, you are either 'in Adam' or else you are 'in Christ'; you are either 'under sin' or 'under grace'. He will say that frequently in the sixth chapter, but his point here is to bring out the contrast, the 'much more'. That is done, he says, by first of all looking at what sin has done to us.

I must again stress this point. No man can ever have a true appreciation of the greatness and the glory of grace unless he has a clear understanding of what sin has done to him and to everybody else since Adam. Need I repeat it, need I emphasize it again? We start as it were at ground level; but if you want to be able to measure the greatness of grace you have to go down as well as up. You have got to see what we have been delivered from, as well as what we are delivered to. That is why I emphasized that if there is not an adequate preaching of the Law there will never be a true conception of grace and of salvation. It is because of serious defect at this point that it is true to say that the note that is most lacking in the Church today – and, alas, I include even evangelical circles – is the note of true praise and of glory. We have neglected the law-work, we have been too anxious to hurry people into some kind of 'decision'. It is when you have suffered a great deal of pain that you most appreciate the relief. It is the man who has been healed at the very door of death who is most grateful for his cure. It is the sinner who has had a glimpse into hell who is most appreciative of the glories of heaven.

This is a principle that runs throughout the Bible. Our Lord makes it plain in His parable given in Luke's Gospel at the end of chapter 7, and spoken in connection with the woman who washed His feet with her tears and wiped them with her hair. She loved Him much more than did Simon the Pharisee. And our Lord supplies the explanation. Because much had been forgiven her, He says. Actually she was a greater sinner than Simon as moralists reckon sin, but the point Christ is making is that her sense of sin was much greater than his and therefore her appreciation of forgiveness was the greater. She knew she was a sinner. A Pharisee never truly sings the praises of God; he is never really joyful. He does not know the 'abundance' of grace, because he has not seen his sinfulness. In our verse 20, therefore, the Apostle stresses that we must understand this truth, that 'sin reigned unto death'. That expression we must proceed to analyse.

The state of the whole of unregenerate mankind, as the result of Adam's sin, is just that. Mankind apart from Christ is 'under the reign of sin'. The trouble with all of us since the fall of Adam – with everyone born into this world – is not simply that we sin, but that we are born under the dominion of sin. This is what the unregenerate do not understand. At the same time it is the key – so it seems to me – to a concern for the souls of men and women; as it is also the real key to evangelism. The world that is not 'in Christ' is under the 'dominion' of sin. The Apostle will use that very term in the next chapter. That is why I say that these verses are the introduction to the next chapter. Sin is a tyranny. The Apostle here seems to personify sin, he says that it acts as a tyrant over us as the result of Adam's sin. When Adam rebelled and sinned against God he and all his progeny fell under the dominion of sin, they became slaves under the government and the tyranny of sin. Freedom vanished.

The Apostle says the same thing in the second chapter of the Epistle to the Ephesians. 'You hath he quickened, who were dead in trespasses and sins; wherein in time past ye walked according to the course of this world, according to the prince of the power of the air, the spirit that now ruleth (governs) in the children of disobedience' [*Ephesians* 2: 1, 2].

Such is the biblical teaching with regard to sin everywhere. Sin is a tyranny. We must cease to think of the sinner as a man who occasionally does something that is wrong. That is true of him, but it is the least part of his trouble. The real trouble with the sinner is that he is a slave under the dominion of sin. From the moment man fell there was no such thing as freedom. There has been no such thing as freedom since Adam fell. Adam was free. Not a single child of Adam has ever been free. Adam lost our freedom for us, and we are born 'shapen in iniquity'. 'In sin did my mother conceive me' [*Psalm* 51: 5]. We are born under the dominion of sin.

Let me put it like this. Man in sin is not free to sin. He is governed and ruled and controlled by sin. Sin 'reigns'. This is the key to the understanding of the modern world. Have you listened to the clever people on the television and radio trying to face the moral problem of today? It is very pathetic. As they are not Christian, they do not understand it, and they admit that they do not understand. They do not see that the one explanation of the situation that troubles us all is that it is all due to the reign of sin. No Christian should be surprised at the state of the world today; he should expect it. What is surprising is that the world should ever have periods when it is a little better. You will always find that such periods follow in the wake of some great religious revival that has even influenced people who have not actually become Christian; sometimes, too, Acts of Parliament have been passed to improve conditions. Take the question of the laws governing national observance of the Lord's Day. When were those Acts passed? Either in the Puritan period, or as the result of the Evangelical awakening of two hundred years ago.

But apart from such happenings man is governed by sin, and sin is slavery. Hear the Lord Jesus Christ telling us so in John chapter 8, verse 34. The incident that provoked that statement brings out its significance exactly. Our Lord was preaching and telling the people about the relationship between His Father and Himself. Obviously it was a notable occasion, because we are told that as He said these things 'many believed on him'. And our Lord looked at them and said in effect: This is very good. 'If ye continue in my word, then shall ye be my disciples indeed; and ye shall know the truth, and the truth shall make you free' (verses 31 and 32).

You would have expected them to shout, 'Hallelujah! Praise the Lord!' But they did not. Instead they said, 'We be Abraham's seed, and were never in bondage to any man; how sayest thou, Ye shall be made free?' A part of our Lord's answer to them is in the thirty-fourth verse: 'Verily, verily, I say unto you, whosoever committeth sin is the servant of sin.' In other words, He says that the trouble with a man that commits an act of sin is not merely that he has committed an act of sin, but that he is the servant of sin. And 'the servant', He continues, 'abideth not in the house for ever'. But then He goes on to say that, 'If the Son shall set you free, you shall be free indeed'. However, the operative phrase is that 'whosoever committeth sin is the servant of sin'.

Now man by nature does not like that. He likes to think that he is morally neutral, and that when he is tempted and falls to the temptation he has but committed an act of sin, and that after expressing his sorrow he is free again. The fact is that he has never been free at all. Why did he commit the sin? Because he is 'the servant of sin', he is the slave of sin. Man is always a slave. We are either slaves of sin, or else, with Paul, we are 'the bond-slaves of Jesus Christ'. Thc point I am emphasizing is that sin is always a form of slavery. The tragedy of the men and women in the world is that they are ignorant of this fact. They are sorry for those of us who meet together to study the Scriptures, when we might be in a cinema or in a theatre or in a dance-hall or in a public-house, or doing one of the other things that they do. They think they are free, and that we are the poor slaves of religion who are not intelligent enough to have seen through it all, and to have shaken it off. But they are free men! The tragedy, I say, is that they are slaves without knowing it; they have been so blinded by sin that they do not know the truth. But they are under the thraldom of sin.

The Apostle works it out in Ephesians chapter 2 where he says that they are slaves of the way of the world, 'the course of this world'. They all do the same thing. Why is that so? Because everybody else does it. It is not because they are free. Their whole outlook, their whole life, is determined by 'the course of this world'. They do what they read of in the newspapers and what they see other people doing. They do it simply because they are slaves to the common pattern. They are like sheep; they all go together, they crowd through the same gate. They do not know why. It is sheer slavery. How true is the message of Scripture!

But we must work it out still further. The way of the world, as dictated by the mind and the outlook of the world, is the cause of the major problems in life today. The moralists are troubled about this. They are faced by the problem of juvenile delinquency, by the growth of violence, by the innumerable evils in the pattern of life, but they cannot see that as long as the people are controlled by the standard of the cinema, the newspaper, the television and the radio you inevitably get the conditions prevailing today. Is it surprising that little boys want to shoot when they constantly see people shooting one another on the television screen, and think it is exciting and wonderful and entertaining? If you keep on telling people that the most glamorous people in the world are those who are constantly passing through the divorce court, are you surprised that others want to follow their example? But there it is! The principle that sin is slavery is not understood by the men and women of the world around us.

The mind and spirit of the world, energized by the devil himself – 'the prince of the power of the air', 'the spirit that now worketh in the children of disobedience' – governs all non-Christians. And, alas, it works and tyrannizes over the whole life of man. It controls man's mind. Sin controls and governs the mind of the unregenerate. It controls and turns it positively in the direction of evil. The regenerate, too, know something of the power of sin, though it does not reign over them. When you may be trying to read a good book, or to pray, your thought may suddenly be switched on to something evil. What did that? Sin! the awful power that can even enter into your mind and turn it like that in a moment! It turns it in the direction of evil and it turns it against truth.

Again, take the statement in 1 Corinthians 2: 14, 'The natural man receiveth not the things of the Spirit of God, for they are foolishness unto him; neither can he know them, because they are spiritually discerned'. Why cannot he know them, why cannot he receive these things? Because sin is controlling and governing his mind against them. As the Apostle puts it again in the second Epistle to the Corinthians, chapter 4, verses 3 and 4: 'If our Gospel be hid, it is hid to them that are lost, in whom the god of this world hath blinded the minds of them that believe not', lest they be enlightened. They cannot believe because they are being governed in their minds by the devil. Their hearts are equally governed by sin. The natural mind, the natural heart, is enmity against God. The natural man hates God. The natural man, of course, has made a god of his own, which he thinks is God, but he hates the true God and shows it the moment God reveals His holiness. He does not like that, and immediately God brings in the Law and shows him his true condition as the helpless slave of sin he detests Him. 'The carnal mind is enmity against God.' That is sin shown in control of the heart.

Sin controls the will in the same way. There is no such thing as free will. 'The Bondage of the Will' was Luther's title for the famous book he wrote in his disputation with Erasmus – and how right he is! Man's will has been bound ever since the fall of Adam. By nature man is not free to choose God. The 'god of this world' makes it impossible for him to do so. We are 'dead' in trespasses and sins. It is a bondage, sin reigns. And it does so, as the Apostle explains in Ephesians 2, in a twofold manner – there are the 'desires of the flesh' and there are 'the desires of the mind'. That is to say, there are lustings of the animal, bodily part, and there are lustings of the intellectual part, the mind. Sin reigns by inflaming men's lusts and making them the creatures of desires and of lusts. Are not the Apostle's words a masterly analysis of modern society? Sin is reigning in the world, and the world does not know it, so it talks foolishly about its freedom and its permissiveness.

But the Apostle tells us that sin exercises this reign in the realm of death – 'sin reigned unto death'. A better translation is, 'sin reigned in death'. This means that sin leads to death in every shape and form. When Paul says 'sin reigned in death' he is summing up all the evil consequences of that first sin of Adam of which he has been speaking so much since the twelfth verse in this chapter. The death of which he speaks is both a spiritual death and a physical death. Of the latter I have spoken previously. But what is spiritual death? What does Paul mean when he tells the Ephesians 'You hath he (God) quickened, who were dead in trespasses and sins'? It means the loss of fellowship with God. What is life? Life eternal? 'This is life eternal, that they might know thee, the only true God, and Jesus Christ, whom thou hast sent' [*John* 17: 3]. If you do not know God you are dead spiritually; you are merely existing. Life means to know God and to have fellowship with Him. Life also means spiritual understanding. So death means the loss of spiritual understanding, a lack of a spiritual awareness. Such was your condition, says Paul to the Ephesians. You had no spiritual awareness at all; you were living your animal life, you were unaware of the great spiritual realities. You did not think about your souls, or your eternal destiny. You were merely thinking about eating and drinking and gambling and dancing, and engaging in that sort of activity. You were spiritually dead, you had no spiritual awareness.

Is not that the state of the world today? and does not this prove that sin is reigning? Sin reigns by blunting and mortifying the spiritual faculty. Then another terrible thing enters, namely, the element of degeneration and pollution. When sin reigns a coarsening process always follows, and increases as the grip of sin over men tightens. Have you not seen and observed this coarsening process? Men's taste changes, their sensibility changes, their discrimination changes; indeed their very appearance changes. No man can go on drinking to excess and still have the same face, and the same eye. Sin coarsens everything; the very body becomes coarsened. It is one of the most tragic things to observe in life. Sin coarsens everything because it causes this element of death to come in. It introduces degeneration and pollution, even in a physical sense; and it always brings misery and trouble, wretchedness, unhappiness and sorrow. These are always associated with death. 'Sin reigned in death', the death of everything that is pure and clean and noble. But above all, it is the death of the spiritual faculty which links a man with God, and enables him to enjoy the fellowship of God.

Finally, sin leads to physical death. We have already expounded that in the seventeenth verse, where we saw that 'if by one man's offence death reigned by one; much more they which receive abundance of grace and of the gift of righteousness shall reign in life by one, Jesus Christ'. Where sin reigns death reigns. And it is reigning today; that is why the world is in a hopeless plight. A clever non-Christian woman recently admitted that on the Brains Trust in a television programme. She admitted frankly that she had no hope, she had no comfort. She was taking part in a discussion about people in need of comfort. The question as to whether the philosophers could give comfort to people was also raised. Her answer was 'No, because being non-religious there is no comfort. There are just facts, but there is no comfort.' She thus gave a demonstration of what it means to be without God – 'without hope, without God in the world'. She admitted the dilemma frankly; she was honest to that extent. Tragedy inevitably results when a life is governed by sin; it is in truth no longer life, it is death. There is no hope, there is nothing, it is the end. As far as *they* are concerned it is the end – 'without hope and without God in the world.' But it is not the end, as the Christian very well knows.

Oh, the hopelessness of the world under the dominion of sin! What men and women regard as life is mere existence; it is not even that, it is a living death. And as Christians we should realize that about them. Our hearts should be filled with compassion as we think of people who are not Christians. God forbid that we should be impatient with them; God forbid that we should despise them. Our business as Christians is to see them as the dupes and the victims and the slaves of sin. They are not free; they cannot help themselves. They cannot please God, they cannot believe, because they are dead. 'The natural man receiveth not . . . neither can he.' 'The carnal mind is enmity against God; it is not subject to the law of God; neither indeed can be', says the Apostle again in Romans 8: 7. It is impossible, for it is being 'reigned over' by sin. The 'strong man armed' whom Christ spoke about – it is the same idea exactly – 'keeps his goods at peace' – his peace – tyrannizes over them.

Our minds need to be crystal-clear on this matter. Let us see that the world is as it is because it is being governed by sin, and that it cannot extricate itself; that nothing but the other side of this picture can give any hope. It is only as grace begins to reign in men and women individually, or as grace begins to reign in a great revival, or as grace will finally reign when Christ returns to this world, that there will be full emancipation and liberty and deliverance – of course only for those who have believed in Him.

I close the exposition of the chapter with this question: Have we Christians realized, as we should realize, how sin once reigned in us? The trouble with us by nature is not simply that we do things that we should not do, but that we are under the dominion of sin and of Satan. What God in His wondrous grace has done is not only to enable us to live a better life, but to set us free. We are no longer 'under sin', we are no longer 'under the dominion of sin' or of Satan. Are we singing with joy as we realize this superlative quality of the grace of God that has 'much more abounded' and has set us free?

Twenty-three

*

That as sin hath reigned unto death, even so might grace reign through righteousness unto eternal life by Jesus Christ our Lord.
Romans 5 : 21

It is important that we take this twenty-first verse with the twentieth, because, as we have seen, it is an exposition of that verse. It explains how it is true to say that 'where sin abounded, grace did much more abound'. But at the same time it is a striking summary of all that the Apostle has been saying up to this point in this Epistle. It is one of those comprehensive statements in which this Apostle in particular seems to delight, in which he puts the whole of the Gospel in one big, thrilling statement. His object is to show that as sin increased, grace has abounded, overwhelmed, swallowed it up in an altogether greater manner. Whatever may be true about sin, and what sin has done to mankind in the past, what God has done by His grace through Jesus Christ is infinitely greater. To expound this has been the Apostle's object throughout the entire chapter, brought out by the 'much more' which he keeps on repeating.

The particular method he adopts here is to personify sin and to personify grace. It is a very good way of bringing out an emphasis. Sin he says, 'reigned' – as if sin were a person. Only a person can reign. In order to show the power of sin, and the effects of sin, he employs that figure; and he does exactly the same with grace. His argument is that what obtained on the one side obtains on the other, the only difference being that it is much greater on the side of grace than it was on the other side. But as in the case of his comparison between Adam and the Lord Jesus Christ, we took note both of differences and similarities, so too in this case, we must be careful to keep the two distinct elements in the forefront of our mind. We saw that certain things were true about our relationship to Adam in exactly the same way as they are true of our relationship to the Lord Jesus Christ, and these we must not lose sight of in emphasizing the 'much more' which belongs to the realm of grace.

The Apostle uses his own familiar and, in a sense, favourite formula. We have met it before: 'As sin hath reigned unto death, . . . even so . . .' – and should always pay great attention to it. He began this important paragraph in verse 12 with the formula. He used the word 'As' there, but he did not complete it with the 'even so' because of the parenthesis. But he came back to it in verse 18, 'Therefore as by the offence of one judgment came upon all men to condemnation; even so by the righteousness of one the free gift came upon all men unto justification of life'. Observe the logical way in which the Apostle conveys the truth to his readers. As we have seen, it is the sure way of obtaining assurance of salvation. Assurance is a matter of deduction in the first instance. Apart from the ultimate assurance that is given immediately by the Spirit, the highest assurance can be obtained by deducing, by using the logic of this 'as' . . . 'even so' principle of the Apostle.

We have already considered the reign of sin – 'As sin hath reigned unto death'. Thank God we do not have to stop there. Here Paul turns to the other side – 'Even so . . .' Here, the Gospel comes in. But for grace there would be no Gospel to preach. We would still be 'under sin', and in a hopeless case. We would be dead, because sin reigns in death, death in every shape and form, spiritual and physical. But that is not the end of the story, there is this other side, 'the reign of grace'. The Apostle wants these Romans to realize the characteristics of the reign of grace, the glory of the reign, the 'much more' element in this reign of grace. Why does he do this? Because his ultimate object is to give these people strong assurance of salvation. People say, 'These things sound wonderful, but how am I to have assurance?' The only way, initially, to have it is to follow the argument, to see the truth objectively. The Apostle has outlined his doctrine of justification, and he wants to show that if a man is justified he is finally secure, certain, and safe. It is all in justification because of God's peculiar and particular way of salvation. So he shows us at one and the same time the glory of grace, and the triumph of grace. We shall have to keep those two points in our mind as we go along.

This is one of the most glorious statements in the whole of Scripture – 'That as sin hath reigned unto death, even so might grace reign through righteousness unto eternal life by Jesus Christ our Lord'. What a tremendous statement! I am told that I repeat my texts! Of course I do! It is the best thing I do in the pulpit. I cannot go beyond the Apostle Paul. If only I could utter these texts properly I believe nothing else would be necessary. So I go on repeating them.

What does it say exactly? There are those, and among them the famous Charles Hodge in his Commentary, who say that the 'That' at the beginning of the verse means that God 'permitted' and 'allowed sin' to enter into the world in order 'to bring good out of evil'. Notice the words 'permitted' and 'allowed'. God did not send it. God is never the author of sin or of evil, but He permitted and allowed sin to enter into the order of creation and of man's life in order to reveal and display the glory and the wonder of His grace.

What of that interpretation? For my part, I must confess that I cannot regard it as more than speculation. I do not really believe that the Apostle is concerned to say that. What Hodge says may be true; we do not know. That, surely, is one of those ultimate mysteries which we cannot at present solve, but which we shall hope to understand in the glory. I mention it in passing, but it seems to me to be unnecessary to give the impression that the Apostle is at all concerned here to deal with the question of the origin of sin and evil.

What the Apostle is surely concerned to put before us here is the glory and the triumph of the reign of grace. We remind ourselves that grace means undeserved favour, kindness shown to undeserving people, something given freely. It means that though there is no merit in us – indeed the reverse is true of us, for we were 'without strength', 'ungodly', 'sinners', even enemies of God and deserving of nothing but His wrath – God nevertheless has shown favour toward us; favour toward the utterly undeserving.

The Apostle's affirmation is that grace is the alternative to sin, and the only alternative to sin. Or to put it in another way, grace is the only antagonist of sin, the only antithesis of sin. The Law was never an alternative to sin, and was never meant to be. Paul has already dealt with that – 'the law came in alongside'. So the Law must never be put over against sin as an alternative. It was never meant to save, and it cannot save, because of our weakness in the flesh. Nothing but grace can be set over against sin. So we can make this statement; everybody in this world at this moment is either 'under sin' or 'under grace'. There is no other position possible. We are either being governed, and tyrannized over by sin, or else we are under the power and the rule and the reign of grace. They are the only two possibilities.

Let me put this in yet another way. What is the history of redemption? It is the history of the struggle between sin and grace, leading to the triumph of grace. That is what the whole Bible is about; it is essentially the history of the struggle between these two powers. From the moment man fell the story begins. The enemy came into God's Paradise, into God's perfect world, tempted man, and got him down. From that moment sin begins to reign. But immediately God gives the promise and grace enters into the conflict: 'The seed of the woman shall bruise the serpent's head.' The remainder of the Bible records the great conflict between these two mighty forces which Paul personifies here – sin . . . grace. Grace is the only power that is big enough to take the field against sin. As you read through your Bible next time from beginning to end keep that in your mind and watch the breathless struggle. You almost feel at times that sin is going to triumph, and that grace will be defeated. But never! Grace always revives and reasserts itself. See it in the story of the Children of Israel; watch it everywhere, the fight between grace and sin, leading finally to the triumph of grace.

The Apostle says that 'grace reigns'. The moment a man becomes a Christian, what has happened to him is that grace begins to reign in him. What, then, does this term suggest to us?

Grace is the exact opposite of what we were emphasizing about sin. We saw that the trouble with the sinner is not simply that he sins and does things he should not do; the tragedy of his position is that he is under the dominion of sin. The real trouble with the vast majority of people in the world is not merely that they are drinking, gambling, dancing and doing things which are worse – that is not the trouble. The real tragedy of mankind is that it is the slave of sin, and cannot free itself. Once we see that, we have a heart of compassion for them. We, like our Lord, will look at them and see them 'as sheep without a shepherd', and will be sorry for them. It is only as we see the reign and the tyranny of sin that we can possibly have that compassion.

But now, says Paul, the same thing is true of grace – 'grace reigns'. What does this mean? Let me put it negatively first. He is not saying that there is a possibility of grace intervening; he does not merely say that God in His kindness is offering grace. Neither does he say that grace just comes in as it were alongside to help us, and to supplement our efforts and our strivings and activities. I have got to use these negatives because many think of grace in that way. There are those who preach that grace is just a possibility held before the whole of mankind, and that then it is for a man to decide whether he takes it up or not. Grace, they say, is something that is offered. Again, there is the teaching, found more particularly in the Roman Catholic Church, that grace supplements human reason, and endeavour and activity. But that is not the teaching of the Apostle; and thank God it is not! For if that were the truth about grace, assurance would be a complete impossibility. If the problem of salvation is left ultimately to man, even partially, then there will be nothing but failure. But that is not the position. 'Grace reigns.'

Go back again to the parallel, the 'as' in connection with sin. What we saw was that mankind has no choice about sinning. That was the whole point of the Apostle's argument about our being in Adam, and of our sinning with him, and of our inheriting pollution, and so on. We are all sinners and we all sin, because we are under the dominion of sin, and cannot help ourselves. We are not born neutral. There is no such thing as a Peter Pan who is born in complete innocence and then decides which way to go. The entire doctrine taught by the Apostle is against that. Sin reigns and it compels us to sin; that is why we sin. But, thank God, 'as' sin reigned . . . 'even so' grace also reigns. Grace is no mere possibility; grace produces a certainty.

In other words, the Apostle teaches that grace is not simply offered to us; grace acts. As sin was a power in our lives, so grace becomes a power in our lives. If it were not so, not a single person would ever be saved. Grace acts, and acts as a king. It reigns as a king. It reigns in the Christian in exactly the same way as sin reigns in the unregenerate. It is the power of grace, therefore, that matters; and the Apostle's whole purpose is to show that grace is supreme. The King who reigns controls everything. He does not need any assistance, his is the power. The very term 'reigns' suggests this power.

The term also suggests the conquering of enemies. If grace is going to reign 'much more', it has to conquer sin and many other hostile forces; and the Apostle's point here is that it does so. He is out to shew the triumph of grace. Grace reigns, it exercises this governmental power; it controls us and keeps us under control. I shall develop this aspect later; I mention it now only in principle. It is grace that preserves us and causes us to persevere. If it did not do so we should all fail. The power of grace is an almighty power, and the Apostle is particularly concerned to emphasize this, that grace in its reign is going to complete what it has started. If it is not going to do so then I have no guarantee of final salvation, I have no assurance at all. But the Apostle has been emphasizing certainty and assurance throughout the chapter. So here he emphasizes that grace does not just start a process and then leave it to us to carry on. Far from it! Grace not only initiates salvation; having started it, grace completes it. Salvation is of grace from beginning to end. If it were not so the plan of salvation would fail. When God initiated and set going the power of grace, He determined the beginning, the middle, the end – every item, every step and every detail. Grace reigns, grace controls from beginning to end. Every single step of our salvation is governed and controlled by grace.

The Apostle Paul is very fond of stressing this truth. He says it again in Ephesians chapter 2: 'By grace are ye saved, through faith, and that not of yourselves, it is the gift of God.' No man is to boast, or can boast of his own works at any point. Salvation is all of grace, every bit of it; it is entirely and only by grace. Grace reigns, and it does not share the Throne with anybody or anything else. You must not put your good works there, or the Church, or priests, or saints or the Virgin Mary or anything else. Grace occupies the Throne alone; and if you try to put anything alongside it, it means that you have not understood 'the reign of grace'.

I am concerned to emphasize that it is because this is true that we can have assurance. I repeat the matter – if grace merely started the process of salvation in me and said, 'There now, I have given you a good start, it is up to you to carry on', how would I feel? My assurance, my confidence rests on this, that

The work which His goodness began,
The arm of His strength will complete.

If it were left to me I would fail. And such is the case with all of us. We are dull, we are slow, we are apathetic, we are ignorant, we are tempted, we are tried, we fall. If this work of salvation were left at any point to us the end would be certain ruin. When we consider the strength and the power and the might of sin and its reign, who are we to face such an antagonist? My only hope is this, that grace reigns, that it controls the whole situation from beginning to end in detail, in every respect. It is all of grace. We now proceed to show that. That is the theme, the glorious 'reign of grace'.

Where do we start on such a theme? Let us go back to the beginning – the establishment of the reign of grace. That is the method of the history books in which we read of great dynasties rising and falling. A certain king reigns and rules over a wide area, but suddenly you begin to read about someone arising in another country who founds a dynasty and conquers the first king, and begins to reign. And on and on the process goes. Paul uses that picture in order to help us to understand the truth. He talks about this dynasty of grace, this reign of grace, that has come into being.

How did it come into being? What is the story of the establishment of the reign of grace, and the inauguration of the kingdom of grace? The answer is given in many places in the Bible. For instance, in the First Epistle of Peter, chapter 1, verse 20, we read of One 'Who verily was foreordained before the foundation of the world'. That is when the kingdom was established and inaugurated, 'before the foundation of the world'. Grace was set upon its throne in the eternal Council, held before time began, between the Father, the Son, and the Holy Spirit. The problem of sin arose, and the question was how to deal with it. Was man to be destroyed because of sin? The divine decision was that grace was to be introduced, and in due time grace was established and set upon the Throne. As the old theologians used to put it, a covenant was entered into between the Father and the Son, the 'Covenant of Redemption'. That was the setting up of the kingdom of grace. The moment the decision was taken that all men were not to be destroyed, grace was set upon the Throne. Such was the great inauguration – the Covenant of Redemption. And that involved the division of offices as between the three blessed Persons in the Most Holy Trinity – the gracious purpose and plan of the Father, the willing subordination of the Son to carry it out, and the work of the Holy Spirit in applying it to the needs of sinners.

Thus did salvation originate 'before the foundation of the world'. The Son as it were said, 'Here am I; send Me'. He took it upon Himself to come down to earth and to divest Himself of the outward signs of His eternal glory. We shall consider the details later, but at this point I am merely describing the inauguration of the reign of grace. The Son said, 'I will go down and take their nature upon Me, and I will submit Myself'. The Holy Spirit likewise subordinated Himself for the purpose of our redemption; He subordinated Himself to the Father and to the Son. The reign of grace! Do you like to meditate on this theme? That is what we are told in the Scripture. Away there in eternity grace was set upon the Throne.

Let us now venture to look at the Throne from which grace reigns. What is its character? What kind of reign is this reign of grace? Every dynasty has its own special characteristics, ferocity in one case, generosity in another; firmness and legality in one, ease and laxity in another. We are left in no doubt as to the outstanding characteristic of this great dynasty, this great Throne, this rule and reign of grace. It is, says the Apostle, righteousness – 'that grace might reign through righteousness'. This is central and basic, and we have already considered what it means. He is summarizing here, as I have previously explained. He began dealing with this theme in the first chapter, verses 16 and 17, where he tells us that he is proud of the Gospel, and ready to preach it at Rome because, as he says, 'therein is a righteousness from God revealed from faith to faith: as it is written, The just shall live by faith'. From there on, this great truth has come in repeatedly.

What exactly does Paul mean when he says that the characteristic of this Throne and reign of grace is righteousness? It is important to give emphasis to this, for the grace is the grace of God, and therefore it must always be righteous. We emphasize it also because there are many who seem to think that grace is weak and flabby. Some seem to think that grace means that God ignores sin, or forgets sins, or pretends that he has not seen it, or that it has never happened at all. But God does not act in that way, and cannot do so. He is eternally just and holy and righteous.

Others are of the opinion that grace means the putting aside of the Law. God, they say, until the advent of Christ looked upon mankind through the Law, but now He puts the Law on one side. 'God no longer deals with us in righteousness', they say, 'He acts in grace now.' They put Law and grace over against one another. But that is entirely unscriptural. Indeed, it is not the Gospel, but an insult to the name of God. Yet many hold the view that God's grace means that God, as it were, now tells us that all is well, that sin does not matter, that He is going to forgive it all, indeed has already done so. That is not God's way of salvation, but a complete misunderstanding of grace.

'Grace reigns through righteousness.' How? We can best answer by asking another question: How can God, who is holy and eternally just and righteous and pure, how can He reconcile the sinner unto Himself? God cannot set aside His own Law. He has given it, and cannot and will not detract anything from it. That would be to imply a defect in it. God cannot violate His own nature. God does not and cannot change. 'He cannot deny himself', says this Apostle in 2 Timothy 2: 13. The question is, how can God at one and the same time remain what He eternally is, and yet forgive the sinner, and have any dealings with him? How can this grace, this kindness, this undeserved favour, come to man? Salvation must always be righteous, says Paul, because God's character requires it. So what grace, the grace of God, has contrived is the reconciliation of those two things.

It all happened in Jesus Christ and on the Cross. That was the great message that we found in chapter 3, verses 24–26: 'Being justified freely by his grace through the redemption that is in Christ Jesus; whom God hath set forth to be a propitiation through faith in his blood' [listen!] 'to declare his (God's) righteousness for the remission of sins that are past, through the forbearance of God; to declare, I say, at this time his righteousness; that he might be just, and (at the same time) the justifier of him which believeth in Jesus'. Grace has found the way, and that was the way.

'Grace reigns through righteousness' – the righteousness of Jesus Christ. He came, 'made of a woman, made under the law'; taking on Him human nature. He was under the Law. He obeyed the Law, He kept it, He honoured it, He carried it out to its last iota. Then on the Cross He bore the punishment the Law pronounces on sin. 'God hath set him forth as a propitiation.' God poured forth His wrath against sin upon Him. Christ has taken it upon Himself: 'By his stripes we are healed.' The Law is not set aside. The Law is vindicated, the Law is honoured. Justice does not turn away, it looks upon Him, and pours out upon Him the vials of God's justice and wrath. Because that has happened you and I can be forgiven; and God remains just and righteous in forgiving us. More, He puts on us, puts to our account, imputes to us, the righteousness of Jesus Christ. That is how grace reigns; it always reigns 'in righteousness'. It does not set aside justice and Law. It honours them, it satisfies them, it fulfils them. Christ says, 'Think not that I am come to destroy the law or the prophets; I am not come to destroy, but to fulfil' [*Matthew* 5 : 17].

It is vitally important that grace and righteousness should never be separated; the moment you do so havoc results. Let me illustrate the matter from the fascinating phrase that is used by the author of the Epistle to the Hebrews in the fourth chapter and the last verse: 'Let us therefore come boldly unto the throne of grace.' Note the term – 'throne of grace'. Grace reigns. When we pray, what we do is to come to the Throne of Grace. The term has two sides, and at first hearing they sound quite contradictory. A throne! A throne is a place where law is dispensed, where justice is administered, where power is exercised. A throne is an august and majestic place. How can I go to, and stand before a Throne? Ah, but the Throne to which I go is the Throne of Grace, and that makes all the difference. Grace is the new element that is added to the Throne. This only happens because God is God, and because God is the King, and because it is God who is reigning through grace by this righteous method.

We must always remember the two sides. Whenever we pray we must remember that we are approaching a throne, that we are drawing near to God who is holy and righteous. Some people, when they talk about grace, forget the Throne, and so they are glib and familiar and talk about 'Dear God!' They think that thereby they are showing that they are under grace; that the more familiar they make themselves with God, the more they show that they are under grace and not under Law. But what they forget is, that their approach is to a Throne – that grace reigns. It is a Throne of grace.

We must not forget this aspect for it not only affects our praying, but the whole of our lives. Some people say happily and glibly, 'Ah, I am not under Law, I am under grace; now I can do what I like'. So they go headlong into Antinomianism, the terrible condition to which such frequent references are made in the New Testament. The man who says Because I am under grace, it does not matter what I do, I can sin as much as I like', has forgotten the Throne.

But, then, on the other hand, there are people who forget the grace. They react so violently against that first type of person that their method of prayer is equally wrong. They go in a fearful, timorous, doubtful, hesitant spirit; they are solemn and uncertain, and in their lives they are legal. They are essentially wrong because we are told to 'come boldly unto the throne of grace'. But boldness does not mean glibness; it is not an easy familiarity, it is not lawlessness.

On the surface the Bible seems full of contradictions. But that is not so, and you realize that only on condition that you remember that 'grace reigns', that grace is on the throne. In other words, as the author of the Epistle to the Hebrews emphasizes, I have to come with boldness and assurance and confidence into the presence of God, but, at the same time, I must come 'with reverence and godly fear, for our God is a consuming fire' [*Hebrews* 12: 28, 29]. There is no contradiction at all in these words, because the throne is the Throne of Grace. These two aspects must never be separated. To put emphasis on one only without the other is to deny the Gospel, and to open the door to grievous heresy and to ultimate terrible failure in life and in experience.

Let us ever remember this aspect of the matter, that the great characteristic of the reign, and the throne from which grace reigns, is righteousness. Grace does not contradict the righteousness of God. Grace is the way that God has devised, by means of which He can be righteous and yet forgiving, remain what He is and yet justify the ungodly – 'That he might be just and (at the same time) the justifier of him that believeth in Jesus' [*Romans* 3: 26].

This is but the beginning of the matter. I trust that having looked at it in this particular manner, and up to the point at which we have arrived, we realize how much we miss if we fail to pay attention in detail to what the Scripture tells us, and if we do not meditate upon it, and work it out. Think of the inauguration of this 'reign of grace'. If you want to know God's love to you, that is where you must begin. Before the foundation of the world God knew you, and He contrived this way that you might be saved and reconciled to Him. It is the most wonderful and amazing conception in the whole universe. There is nothing more sublime than this way that God has devised to reconcile sinful men unto Himself, and yet without in any way detracting or derogating or subtracting from His own everlasting righteousness and holiness and justice and truth. And remember, there was only One who could give effect to God's plan; the Apostle never forgets that: 'Through (by) Jesus Christ our Lord'.

Believing these things we can go to the throne of grace 'to obtain mercy and find grace to help in time of need' [*Hebrews* 4: 16]. So go 'with reverence and godly fear', but go also with 'a holy boldness', confident and assured. Because you know it is a way of righteousness you need have no question or doubt. The devil will say to you, 'Are you a fit person to pray? Look at what you have done, look at what you have been' – and you feel that you cannot answer him because this accusation is true. There is only one answer to give him, there is only one way to be confident and to be bold; it is to say to him, 'I know I have a right to go to the Throne'. And the devil will say, 'How do you know you can go there? How do you know that God has forgiven your sin? Is it righteous in God to forgive you your sin?' And you can say, 'It is, for God has dealt with my sin in such a way that I know that His forgiveness is righteous.' If I did not know that to be true I would not dare to go to God and to ask even for forgiveness. I would fear that somehow I was but persuading myself that it is really true. But God, in this way, has dealt with my sin in such a manner that I can be certain that the Gospel is true. I know that He is righteous and just and holy, but that, at the same time, He can forgive me. It is 'the throne of grace', and also a 'throne of righteousness', because of what He has done in the Person of His dear Son when He 'delivered him up for us all', and laid our sins on Him and punished them in Him to the uttermost.

God grant that we all, in the light of this, may have this blessed assurance as we think, and as we pray, and as we live.

Twenty-four

*

Moreover the law entered, that the offence might abound. But where sin abounded, grace did much more abound;

That as sin hath reigned unto death, even so might grace reign through righteousness unto eternal life by Jesus Christ our Lord.

Romans 5: 20, 21

In looking at this tremendous theme of the glory and the triumph of the reign of grace, we have already considered the inauguration of the reign, and we have also found that its supreme characteristic is righteousness. That is the glory and wonder of this way of salvation. It does not set up the love of God against His justice; there is a perfect agreement between the two. The attributes of God all shine out with the same glory in man's salvation. Everything that God does is just and holy and righteous; His love is a holy love, a righteous love.

We must next consider other aspects of this glory and triumph of the reign of grace, the first of them being what we may call the 'programme', or the 'method', of the reign of grace. Every kingdom, every form of government, has its programme and policy. In keeping with its authority, it outlines what it proposes to carry out. The same is exactly the case with the reign of grace. Not only is it true that the reign of grace was set up in eternity, the entire reign was planned in eternity; and every step, every portion and every detail was determined in what we customarily term the eternal Council between Father, Son, and Holy Spirit. The policy was decided upon and determined then. Grasp this truth firmly, for it is a very material part of the biblical doctrine of assurance of salvation. According to the declaration made by the Apostle Peter in his sermon on the day of Pentecost at Jerusalem, everything is 'according to the predeterminate counsel and foreknowledge of God' [*Acts* 2: 23].

That is true of the reign of grace. Grace is never haphazard in its method. Grace is in no sense contingent upon or dependent upon what man does. It is essential that we should emphasize that. There are notes in a certain famous 'Bible' which teach the exact opposite, and say that God had to modify and change His plan because of the failure of the Jews to believe in His Son. They say that the Son came to set up the Kingdom, but the Jews rejected Him and it; so then God had to suspend the programme for a while and introduce the Church, which, they say, is a kind of parenthesis. The 'prophetic clock' stopped at that time and it will only start going again when our Lord returns. All this had to be done, we are told, because the Jews failed to recognize the Lord Jesus Christ and to believe in Him. In other words the whole programme had to be readjusted because of something that men did or failed to do.

That, surely, is a denial of this concept of the reign of grace, and especially that aspect of it which reminds us that everything was determined in eternity before the foundation of the world. The carrying out of the programme is in no way dependent upon the decisions of men either for or against. It is the 'reign' of grace. That in turn reminds us also that it is a strong, a powerful reign. We often tend to think of grace in a somewhat sentimental manner. We persist in setting it in contrast with Law in a manner that is not true. Grace, as we have seen, is not weak; because it is righteous it is strong. Grace neither breaks the Law nor abrogates it. It must not be thought of in terms of sentiment or feeling. That is an entirely wrong way of thinking of grace. The very term that Paul uses here, 'the reign of grace', should rid us at once and for ever of all sentimental notions with respect to grace, and should enable us to see its strength and its power.

All this becomes clear as we consider the programme of grace. Grace, when it was set upon the throne, had from the beginning a particular end in view. It started by stating and defining that end. He is a poor statesman who acts in a contingent manner, and keeps on saying, 'Well now, what is going to be my next move?' The right approach, at the very beginning, is to say, 'What am I aiming at? What is my ultimate objective? What goal am I really going to make for?' That is what happened with respect to grace. Grace set up the ultimate, final, objective and goal; and having done that, it then planned every step that was essential to the attaining of that goal. That is the marvel and the wonder of the programme, or the method, of grace. There is nothing else that I know of that is so strengthening to faith, nothing else that gives such a large measure of assurance.

We can look at the programme of grace in two chief ways. It can be looked at historically and in general on the one hand, and in a more experimental and particular manner on the other.

Look first at the programme of the reign of grace historically. This, again, is something that we can view from two different angles. We can see it in the actual history; but in the Old Testament particularly (and also to a lesser degree in the New) the history is always linked with the element of prophecy. We shall consider the two together – the actual history, and the earlier prophetic anticipation. As you look at these two, and trace them right through the Bible, you can come to one conclusion only, that grace had decided upon it all, and upon every step of it, away back in that eternal Council before time. Let us examine it and watch it.

The programme of grace was first announced in Genesis 3: 15. Man has fallen. There he is in his shame and fear in the Garden, and God comes to him and addresses him. He tells man that He is going to cause enmity between the seed of the serpent and the seed of the woman. There, immediately, is the prophetic declaration that God will bring in and set going one type of history. But the historical aspect of grace comes in also, for God at the same time as He announces that conflict makes the statement that 'the seed of the woman shall bruise the serpent's head'. Now that is the first announcement of the reign of grace and also there is this prophetic anticipation. Some people call that the 'Proto-evangel', and that is right in a sense; but it is indeed the Gospel itself, it is the first announcement of the Gospel – that 'the seed of the woman shall bruise the serpent's head'. That is the ultimate end and object of the reign and it is made as an announcement at the beginning. That is the beginning of salvation history.

But let us watch the unfolding of this history as the book of Genesis proceeds. We read about the children of Adam and Eve. We have to concentrate upon Seth, the son that was born to them after the death of Abel. Here is a new line with which the history of the Old Testament is mainly concerned. We see at once that there was a separation and a division in accordance with the out-working of this programme of grace. Seth is selected. Next we find that the world got into a terrible sinful state, and God announced that He was going to judge it and to punish it; but He selected out of this line of Seth a man called Noah and his family. There were only eight altogether, but God selects them, spares them, and saves them. This is a continuation of the reign of grace. Judgment comes in, but grace comes in at the same time. Grace still has its eye on that ultimate objective, so it saves Noah and his wife and family – eight souls out of a world of unbelievers (1 Peter 3: 20). It is most rewarding to go through these facts of history step by step and stage by stage. It is a very good thing to take a frequent bird's-eye view of the Scriptures and their teaching and history lest you become lost in the details. Keep your eye on the line of Seth!

That brings us, next, to Abraham. Here God does an amazing thing. He looks upon this man Abram in Ur of the Chaldees and He takes him out, separates him, and brings him to another country. It is still a part of this reign of grace. God is going to form a nation out of this man, a people for Himself. Then there is the story of Isaac – 'In Isaac shall thy seed be called', and 'In (Isaac) shall all the nations of the world be blessed' [*Genesis* 21. 12; 22. 18]. The line and the plan are not to be continued through the other son that Abraham had through the bond-woman; it is to be through Isaac.

Then Isaac, in his turn, had two sons, Esau and Jacob. But the history of grace is not to continue through Esau; Jacob's is the line of promise. All this is not haphazard; all this was planned, all this was determined before the world was ever made. It is surprising to us in many ways, but such is the plan. God's action goes steadily on, and out of this man comes the chosen people. Jacob's name is changed from Jacob to Israel, and there you see coming into being this family, this people, this special nation. Then Jacob or Israel, as we are told, had twelve sons, and of them the one that is chosen is Judah. That is not accidental, it is a deliberate choice.

Then comes an amazing fact – the next in the line is a man called Phares. In the genealogical table at the beginning of the Gospel according to St. Matthew we find all this summarized. The object of that table is to bring out this very idea we are now dealing with – the plan and the power of the reign of grace. We read, 'And Judas begat Phares and Zara'. Judah had many other children, but we are told that he 'begat Phares and Zara of Thamar'. If I may so put it, he should never have begotten them from Thamar. It involved sin, it involved incest; but there it is, and it is a part of the line of salvation. It is Phares that is chosen. Follow his descendants and you will find that you come eventually to the father of David, and then to David himself, in this line of Judah. David was not the eldest of his family, and everything seemed to be against him; but he is the one that is chosen. David had a large number of children but the one that was chosen was Solomon.

We need not go further; but I am trying to give some impression of this extraordinary programme of grace which, without any oversight or mistake, always picks the right person at the right point. It frequently seems quite contrary to all our ideas, and yet it is done, and done by God, and on and on it goes.

Follow on from Solomon and come down the years until eventually Jesus of Nazareth is born of the Virgin Mary, and of 'the house and lineage of David'. There it is! We have rushed through it; but you cannot read this history without seeing this definite purpose and programme being brought surely to pass. Think of the time element. How frequently it is emphasized! We are told that God allows certain things to continue because 'the iniquity of the Amorites is not yet full' [*Genesis* 15 : 16]. Why does He not strike and punish at once? Because that is not His time; He has another time in mind. The exact length of time that the Children of Israel were to spend in captivity was known, and stated to Abraham beforehand, long before it came to pass, indeed four hundred years [*Genesis* 15: 13]. Nothing is accidental. These are God's people, so everything about them is determined.

Again, in the prophecy of Daniel (chapter 9) we are told the exact time when the Son of God, the Messiah, would be born. The time is so exact. And Paul sums it all up in his well-known phrase, 'When the fullness of the time was come, God sent forth His son, made of a woman, made under the law' [*Galatians* 4: 4]. It was the exact time. There is nothing accidental, nothing haphazard about it. That moment was determined 'before the foundation of the world', and then it had come. We can go on. Our Lord Himself makes a certain statement in Mark 13: 32. He is talking about the time of His second advent and He says that 'of that day and that hour knoweth no man, no, not the angels which are in heaven, neither the Son, but the Father'. In other words, the time of the end of the 'day of grace' is known to God and has been known to Him before the foundation of the world, even before the initiation of the time process. Then think of all the details that are given by the prophets concerning our Lord – details about His coming, the place of His birth, the mode of His death, His resurrection, His kingdom, and the characteristics of the kingdom. The Old Testament foretells all these happenings, and in the New Testament we find the fulfilment of the prophecies. And there are still further prophecies with respect to what is to take place in the ages yet to come.

What is the point of all this? It is to show us that grace is reigning, as the Apostle tells us here. It suggests a definite plan, and what is more important, an absolute control. If I may put it like this – 'the reign' suggests 'the holding of the reins'. Everything is in the hands of grace and so everything comes to pass according to the dictates of grace, according to the government of grace. All these details imply inevitably a reign and a purpose which is progressively – step by step, bit by bit, portion by portion – being brought to pass, leading up to the final end and completion of the plan and the purpose.

But not only does all this history point very definitely to the '*reign* of grace', it also points to the fact that it is the 'reign of *grace*'. Have you noticed it in some of the details I have already mentioned? It is clear that grace reigns in spite of the unworthiness of the people it uses. All the men I have mentioned were guilty of sin and failed at some point, some of them grievously; and yet grace covered it all, and the 'reign' and the 'grace' together take the whole process forward. That genealogical table in the first chapter of Matthew is one of the most astounding things in the Bible. There we find reference to the incest of Judah, and are shown how even that is a part of the process, and that God overruled the sin – 'grace did much more abound' – to bring His grand design to pass.

We find the same gracious hand at work in the case of David. The line goes on from David to Solomon, but that involves Bathsheba; and Bathsheba became the wife of David because David committed adultery and then murder. But grace was involved – 'grace to cover all my sin' – the reign and the grace worked together. Because grace was reigning, in this odd and strange way, and in spite of the failure and the unworthiness, and even the gross and grievous sin of the very agents used, the plan goes steadily forward and leads eventually to that ultimate objective which was originally planned in the eternal Council.

But if this is seen in individuals, it is also seen in a very striking manner with regard to the whole nation of Israel. God, in the call of Abraham, clearly decided that His purpose was to be carried out through this particular nation. The Messiah when He comes will be of the seed of Abraham and of the seed of David; He will come as a member of the nation of Israel. God has made this people for Himself in order to bring that to pass. But look at them, look at that nation! Look at their failure, their miserable failure constantly! How can this purpose possibly be brought to pass through them? There is only one answer; it is the 'reign' of grace. If it were not for the element of the reigning, and the power of the reigning, the entire purpose would have collapsed. It was in spite of the children of Israel that it all eventually came right. Nothing but the grace of God to that people, that nation, could ever have kept it in being at all; so the two elements are constantly merging together in the wonderful history that unfolds itself to us.

But – and this is important – the historical aspect of the reign of grace does not end with the biblical history. It has continued beyond that, and it is seen clearly in the long history and record of the Christian Church. The setting up of the Church was a vital point in the story of the reign of grace, but the New Testament seems to leave us with the Church weak, with heresies coming in and enemies arising. You begin to wonder how it can possibly go on; it looks so small, so miserable, and so unworthy. But here we are, still meeting under the auspices of the Christian Church in this twentieth century. There is only one explanation – it is the reign of grace. Grace is carrying out its purpose and its reign even through the Christian Church. It is seen in the regular work of the ministry, and the preaching of the Gospel. Men and women are being called out from the world into the Kingdom – one here, one there – that is all part of the reign.

But you see the 'reign' still more strikingly in the great revivals of the Church. The history of the Church has been one of 'ups and downs'. She starts in a great revival at Pentecost, but after a while that begins to wane and the Church seems to be about to die; then God sends revival. That story has been repeated many times, and it proves abundantly that grace continues to reign. If the Church had been left to us, and to people like us, the story would have ended long ago. It is in spite of us and our failures, it is in spite of the world and the flesh and the devil, it is in spite of all these set-backs and fallings and failures that she goes on. There is only one explanation – grace is reigning. Man would have ended the story of the Church at the very beginning were it not for the 'reign of grace'.

We have now looked at the matter historically and in general. Let us now look at it experimentally and by a consideration of the work of grace in the salvation of the individual. Have you ever considered the process involved in the salvation of the individual? 'Ah but,' you say, 'there is nothing in that; the individual is saved in this way – he is taken to a meeting by a friend and he listens to the preaching of the Gospel. He says, "Yes, I will accept it, I will believe," and so he is saved. That is it, that is the process of salvation.' What a poor conception of salvation! Do you not know that the programme for the salvation of every individual was all determined and decided upon before the foundation of the world?

Have you ever pondered and contemplated the steps and the stages in the salvation of an individual? Have you ever looked into what is called the order of salvation, the 'ordo salutis' as the old theologians used to call it? Let me tell you something about it. We must be careful here, for we must not become too dogmatic, as if the one mode is the same in detail in all cases. At one or two points it is a little difficult to ascertain the exact order of divine operation; but there is a definite order. The Apostle Paul gives us a hint as to it all in the eighth chapter of this Epistle. 'We know', says the Apostle, 'that all things work together for good to them that love God, to them that are the called according to his purpose' (verse 28). Then, 'For whom he did foreknow, he also did predestinate to be conformed to the image of his Son, that he might be the first-born among many brethren. Moreover whom he did predestinate, them he also called; and whom he called, them he also justified; and whom he justified, them he also glorified' (verses 29, 30). The Apostle was not concerned there to give us the whole programme in detail, but he was concerned to show that grace always works methodically. Grace never works haphazardly; it always works on a system. Indeed, if I may so put it with reverence, it is to the glory of God that He always works systematically.

Have you not marvelled frequently at the way in which He always follows the same pattern in Nature – for instance Spring, Summer, Autumn, Winter? The same is seen indeed in detail in the whole of creation; there is a definite pattern and order. There is never any suspicion of muddle in God's work. It is man in sin who is muddled. God always plans everything; the great eternal God with His illimitable power always works according to a pattern. You would think that He would vary the way in which He operates. Never! God always works in the same way. That is why men are able to discover what they call 'the laws of Nature'. They are not the laws of Nature; they are the laws that God has put in Nature. That is why men can work at their inventions, because these laws are so exact and dependable. It is because of this that the scientists are able to talk about 'cause and effect' and to argue that any given cause will always produce the same effect. God always works like that.

The same truth holds good in the Kingdom of God. God, in grace, is as exact and methodical in working salvation as He is elsewhere in all the work of His great universe. Let us therefore look at these steps and stages as they are mentioned in the Scriptures. We start with foreknowledge. God knows beforehand what is going to happen, but 'foreknowledge', as the term is used in the Scripture, means something much more precise and exact than that. It means that God knows individuals beforehand, takes a special interest in them. It is not merely that He knows about them, for He knows about all men without exception. 'Knowledge' in the Scripture generally means the taking of a particular interest. The classic illustration of this is the second verse in the third chapter of Amos. God, addressing the Children of Israel says: 'You only have I known of all the families of the earth'. Of course, He knew about all the nations; but He says, 'You only have I known'. That is foreknowledge. He takes a special interest in them. What He was saying there to those Israelites was, 'I have taken a special interest in you only of all the nations of the earth, and this is how you have behaved!' Foreknowledge! I know nothing that is at once more humbling and exalting than the fact that God knew me before the foundation of the world.

The next thing that follows in the Apostle's list in Romans, chapter 8 – and we have it in the first chapter of Ephesians, and everywhere in his writings – is predestination. That is a part of the reign of grace in the individual. No man is saved unless He is predestinated and elected. This is not my statement; it is Paul who says it. There is nothing accidental about salvation. All this was known before the foundation of the world, says the Apostle. And he is not the only New Testament writer who says it. The Apostle Peter says exactly the same thing: 'Elect according to the foreknowledge of God the Father, through sanctification of the Spirit unto obedience. . . .' [1 *Peter* 1: 2]. All this, says Peter, was determined before the foundation of the world, but it has been brought to pass 'in these last times'. The same truth is found in the Gospel of John in a particularly clear manner in chapters 6, 10 and 17. Foreknowledge, Predestination, Election – what next?

The next step is 'effectual calling'. These people who have been predestinated and elected must be called; and they are called generally through the preaching of the Gospel. There is a preaching to all in general, but there is this effectual, special call to those who have been predestinated and elected, to those whom God has foreknown. He calls them in an effectual manner. I am not concerned now to work out this scheme; I am simply giving it briefly from the Scripture: 'Whom he did predestinate, them he also called', but I must add that, if He has predestinated us, He is not going to leave it at that. If He has predestinated us to salvation, then He will *call* us unto it and brings us into it – 'out of the darkness into his marvellous light'. Thus the Word speaks of effectual calling. The Gospel is preached to all; that is the general call. Here, however, is the effectual call – 'whom he did predestinate, them he also called.'

Regeneration follows. It is at this point that the order becomes a little difficult, and we must not be too dogmatic. The effectual call and regeneration seem to be almost synchronous. But we have to separate them in thought, so we put next – regeneration. Grace has decided to put this new principle of life into this man who is predestinated, and who is called; so he is regenerated. At the same point you have – adoption: 'predestinated unto the adoption of children' [*Ephesians* 1: 5]. God has adopted us into His family. He has made us one with Christ, He has put us into Christ, we have union with Christ. It is a part of the outworking of the programme of grace.

Then justification! You and I become aware of justification because we exercise faith, and we exercise faith because we have a new nature within us, because we are regenerate. As we have seen, we are not justified because we are regenerate, but it is the first sign we ever give of life, that whereas we once hated all this, we now desire it. Then sanctification – and, eventually, glorification!

Is not this amazing and glorious? It is not only a question of believing. God has planned all these steps and stages. There is a certainty about it all, each step leads inevitably to the next. As God has arranged that the farmer should plough up the earth, and break it up, and then put in his seed and roll it, and the seed later germinates and sprouts and appears above the ground, and then develops and finally matures – so He does in the matter of our salvation. This is a part of 'the reign of grace'. And again I emphasize that grace is in control at every step and stage; for if grace ceased to be in control the entire process would collapse. It is grace that starts it, it is grace that keeps it going. 'By grace are ye saved through faith, and that not of yourselves, it is the gift of God.' It is grace from beginning to end, from first to last.

How wonderful is this programme of the reign of grace! We have seen how, before time, the triune God determined that all this should happen to us in detail. What a programme! We have looked at it in general as it has been brought about historically, and, in particular, as it is applied to us in detail.

But at this point, having considered the method of grace, we must look at the power of the reign of grace. With such a programme it is obvious that there must be unusual power to carry it through. The analogy with an earthly government applies throughout. If the government of any country lacks power it cannot operate its programme. Likewise, the reign of grace must have power. How is this tremendous programme to be carried out both historically and in the case of the individual? The Bible has a very clear answer to these questions. The position would be completely hopeless were it not that the reign of grace is a very powerful reign.

Let us first look at the matter in general. Its unfolding is to be seen very clearly in the history set out in the Old Testament. We remind ourselves that grace is enthroned; the programme to save men in the way I have just been describing is settled and determined. But how can that programme be carried out, for at the very outset it meets with the opposition of the devil, the Adversary. He, because of man's folly in listening to him, has literally become 'the god of this world', 'the spirit that now worketh in the children of disobedience [2 *Corinthians* 4: 4;

Ephesians 2 : 2]. He has become 'the strong man armed, that keepeth his goods in peace' [*Luke* 11 : 21]. It is one thing to draw up a great programme, a plan and purpose; but how is it to be carried out in a world of men who are dominated by Satan and by the principles of sin and hell? The answer is given in the history that I have outlined.

You see the devil exercising his power in the history as given in the Book of Genesis. In its sixth chapter you find that the whole world was under his power: 'Every imagination of the thoughts of man's heart was only evil continually'. The world has become a sink of iniquity. The purpose of grace seems to have been defeated once and for ever. But I have explained already that it was not so, that while the whole world was drowned by the Flood the eight souls were saved. Later, in the story of the Tower of Babel you may feel that man, under the power of the devil, has surely overthrown God's programme. But no! God confounded man's pride and ambition, and grace continued to manifest its power. You see grace at work repeatedly in the story of Abraham. From time to time he is seen in the hands of some mighty king, quite helpless and defenceless; but always he is delivered. What is the explanation? It is the power of the reign of grace.

Call to mind the story of the Children of Israel. God has brought them into being as a family. But they had to go down into Egypt because of a famine, and a Pharaoh arose 'that knew not Joseph'. He disliked the Israelites because they were becoming too strong and too numerous; so he decided to exterminate them or at least to thin them out. They were literally helpless in his hands. But then came the miracle of the Exodus! What is the Exodus? It is but a part of the story of the powerful reign of grace, the carrying out of a purpose that nothing can frustrate. The power of grace brought them out in a supernatural manner. Think of the ten plagues, the dividing of the Red Sea and the destruction of Pharaoh's hosts. Nothing 'can make Him His purpose forego'. Call to mind the whole sorry story of the Children of Israel, their repeated disobedience and their defeats. Eventually they were carried away into the captivity of Babylon, and their situation seemed utterly hopeless once more; but again a remnant is brought back to Jerusalem and to Canaan. How can we explain it? Only by the power of the reign of grace; nothing can stop it.

In the same way we have seen the reign of grace in the case of the individual men to whom I have made reference. It was in spite of their frailties and weaknesses and sins and disobedience that God was still able to use them. There is nothing that can withstand the power of the reign of grace. It masters all enemies and brings its purposes to pass at the stated moment in spite of everything – men, 'principalities and powers, the rulers of the darkness of this world and spiritual wickedness in high places'.

Thus we have seen the power of this reign of grace in outline and in general, and on a broad canvas. The Bible goes on to tell us, as we shall see later, that its march will continue, and that, from generation to generation. There have been times in the story when some terrible power has arisen and Christianity has seemed finally doomed to extinction, but God has arisen and scattered His enemies as the sun dispels the morning mist; kings and armies and empires and infernal powers have melted into nothing before Him. Oh the power of the reign of grace! That is why there is no need for a Christian to be alarmed or excited at the present time. Christianity is at a very low ebb today, but it has been at a very low ebb many a time before; and there is no power, no philosophy, nothing that can ever raise its fiendish head that can ever frustrate this purpose or stand between the reign of grace and the final accomplishment of its originally designated and determined objective.

Once more I am constrained to ask a question. Do you know of anything that is so comforting as 'the reign of grace?' Do you know of anything that gives such assurance as the reign of grace? Recall once again the Apostle's words: 'As sin hath reigned unto death' even so shall 'grace reign through righteousness unto eternal life, by Jesus Christ our Lord.' Have you realized that you are in this great plan, this great scheme? Cease to think of yourself and your salvation in too individualistic a manner; think of it as a part of the great whole. We are brought into the whole purpose, we are made members of His body. The marvel is that this great purpose, which can never fail, has in His infinite grace included us. But do not look at yourself; look at Him, look at the purpose, look at the plan, look at the reign of grace. As you do so you will know that you have your feet firmly planted on the Rock of Ages, and that nothing can ever shake you off it, nothing 'can sever your soul from His love'. Blessed be the reign of grace!

Twenty-five

*

Moreover the law entered, that the offence might abound. But where sin abounded, grace did much more abound;
That as sin hath reigned unto death, even so might grace reign through righteousness unto eternal life by Jesus Christ our Lord.
Romans 5: 20, 21

We remind ourselves that in these two verses the Apostle sets out to show that the power of the reign of grace is altogether greater than the power of sin. He is concerned to bring out the 'much more', the 'abounding', the 'superabundance' of grace; he is therefore very much concerned to give prominence to the overwhelming power that characterizes the reign of grace. We have already looked at this in general by reviewing the carrying out of the programme of the reign of grace as seen in the Old Testament history. We saw the same principle also in the case of individuals whom God has taken up and used in spite of their frailty and ignorance and sin.

We now turn to consider the power of the reign of grace in a more experimental and particular and personal manner, a subject which is frequently dealt with in the Scriptures. Let me put it in the form of a question. There is the whole of mankind under the reign and dominion of sin and the power of the devil. The great question therefore is – How can a single human being ever be saved? How can anyone ever be redeemed and rescued out of the terrible power and tyranny and thraldom and reign of sin? The answer is that nothing can do this but the power of grace which is altogether greater even than the power of sin and of the devil. We must look at this in detail and analyse it, because this power of grace in our individual salvation and deliverance is the most amazing of all God's mighty deeds. It is the great theme of the whole of Scripture; and we can never know too much about it. It is particularly important from the standpoint of assurance of salvation which is the theme of this entire chapter. The Apostle wants Christians to be certain of their salvation, and to know that nothing can ever rob them of it; and he does that by showing them the power of grace.

Let us then study the power of grace as it manifests itself in the deliverance and salvation of a lost soul that is under the reign and dominion of sin. What is it that the power of grace has to overcome? Beyond any question the first thing is our spiritual deadness. We have already quoted the first verse of the second chapter of the Epistle to the Ephesians, 'And you hath he quickened, who were dead in trespasses and sins.' By nature we are all spiritually dead. That is the position of the whole of mankind apart from the grace of God in Jesus Christ. We have all died – as we have seen repeatedly – in Adam. We are born into this world spiritually dead. There is nothing stronger than death. Death is the end. 'While there is life there is hope', but when death comes it is the end, and you give up the contest. Death is the last enemy. Nothing is stronger than death.

The first thing, therefore, that grace has to deal with is this condition of spiritual deadness in which we are all found by nature. I mean by that, that we are dead to the interests of our souls, we are dead to the life of God, we are dead to spiritual things. They do not interest us at all. That is the condition of the vast majority of people in the world today. They give no thought to the things of God, and they dismiss them when they are mentioned to them. That is because they are spiritually dead. They have no spiritual awareness, no spiritual understanding, no conception of these things at all. So grace has to overcome this state of death; and nothing but the power of grace can do it. But grace has done it. That is the whole point of the Apostle's statement: 'You hath he quickened, who were dead in trespasses and sins.' Those Ephesians, as all other Christians, had been quickened, that is, made alive.

We must immediately add, however, that there is a second element in the problem. At first sight it appears to contradict the first element; but that is not so, because both things are true. We are not only spiritually dead, but also in a state of antagonism to the Truth, and of antagonism to God. That is the tragedy of the situation of the natural man. Not only does he fail to respond to spiritual truth, he hates it, he spurns it, he opposes it. The Apostle makes many statements to this effect. Later we shall find him telling us in the eighth chapter of this Epistle, in the seventh verse, that 'the carnal mind is enmity against God'. It is not simply that man by nature is dead and does not respond to the Truth; he is at enmity against God, his mind and heart are not subject to the law of God, neither indeed can be. And again, in a passage which is most important in this connection [1 *Corinthians* 2 and especially verse 14], we are told that 'the natural man receiveth not the things of the Spirit of God'. And why not? 'Because', says Paul, 'they are foolishness unto him; neither can he know them, for they are spiritually discerned.' He laughs at these things of the Spirit of God. They are nonsense, they are folly to him; they are utter rubbish. That is why he does not receive them. It is not only that he cannot receive them, but that he is actively, bitterly opposed to them; he rejects them altogether.

The Bible says that that is the position of all men by nature. Let me quote just one particular case by way of illustration, that of the very man who wrote this Epistle which we are studying. Look at Saul of Tarsus. 'I verily thought with myself that I ought to do many things contrary to the name of Jesus of Nazareth', he tells us [*Acts* 26: 9]. He blasphemed His name, he persecuted His followers, He hated Him with all the intensity of his powerful nature. He did his utmost to exterminate Christianity. That was the result of a positive antagonism to the Christian truth and the Christian message. That was the position of Paul himself while he was yet Saul of Tarsus. Here then is the question – How can a man like that ever become a Christian? How did it ever come to pass that Saul of Tarsus, the persecutor, the blasphemer, the injurious person, becomes the greatest Apostle and the greatest preacher that the Christian Faith has ever known? There is only one answer to that question: it is the power of grace. It is because the power of the reign of God's grace is altogether greater than the power of the reign of sin. Satan does not want to lose his citizens, his slaves. He is 'the strong man armed that keepeth his goods at peace'. He guards them, and surrounds them; he is clothed with armour, and has his mighty fortifications around them. How can anyone ever be redeemed? Oh, nothing other than the power of grace can do it; but the power of grace can do it, and has done it.

In order that you and I may be saved and delivered, our spiritual deadness and our antagonism to God and Truth have to be overcome; and it is grace that overcomes them. That is why the great theologians of the Church have spoken and written about what they call 'irresistible grace'. There should be no trouble or difficulty about this; not only is grace irresistible, it must be irresistible. For if grace were not irresistible no one would ever have been saved. That follows of necessity from the fact that we were dead spiritually, and were at enmity to God, hating His Truth. How can we be saved therefore? There is only one answer – the power of grace is irresistible. We explained this previously in terms of the 'effectual call'; and if the call were not effectual it would never succeed in bringing anyone from death to life. The Gospel may be preached to all and sundry, but that alone does not save; it needs this power behind it, the power of the Spirit. Then it becomes irresistible, effectual grace, and the call becomes effectual. Our antagonism is removed, our deadness is overcome by the mighty action of grace which 'quickens' us, and puts new life into us.

This is a vitally important point. Grace does not merely help us, grace does not merely assist us. The idea that grace presents itself to us, but that the final choice remains with us as to whether we are going to take advantage of it or not, is not only a contradiction of the verse we are considering, it is a contradiction of the entire biblical teaching concerning the way of salvation. If that idea were true then no one would ever be saved. If man is dead; if he regards spiritual truth as utter folly; and if he is at enmity against God, how can he suddenly decide to make use of grace and to thank God for it, and to take it. He cannot do so as he is by nature; he must be changed. It is only the grace of

God which is irresistible in its power that can accomplish such a work. And it is because it is irresistible that it is saving and efficacious.

There are many statements of this truth in the Scriptures. Take, for instance, the way the Apostle puts it in that bit of autobiography he gives us in 1 Corinthians 15. He is talking about the people to whom the risen Lord had appeared; and he says, 'And last of all he was seen of me also, as of one born out of due time. For I am the least of the Apostles, that am not meet to be called an apostle, because I persecuted the church of God'. How did Paul ever become an apostle? Here is the answer – 'But by the grace of God I am what I am; and his grace which was bestowed upon me, was not in vain' [1 *Corinthians* 15 : 9–10]. It was because of the grace that was 'bestowed' upon him, and because of its power; and for no other reason. The result was that he 'laboured more abundantly than they all', and that was because the grace of God 'was not in vain'. The power that took hold of him was so great that it lifted him up out of that condition of being a persecutor and a blasphemer. If grace were not irresistible there would be no salvation; not a single soul would ever have been saved; and the great purpose of God would never be carried out.

Grace, then, manifests its power in our salvation through the Holy Spirit; and it starts by seeking us. Take that phrase the Apostle uses in the eleventh chapter of this Epistle where he says, 'There is a remnant according to the election of grace' [*Romans* 11 : 5]. Grace does the electing. Grace first of all seeks us. Then it convicts us of our sin. What a power is needed to do that – to convince the natural man of his sin! You may say that it is an easy thing to convict and convince a drunkard or some open profligate sinner of his sin. But is it? Well, try it; and you will find that he defends himself and rationalizes his sin and explains it away in a most astonishing manner. It is extremely difficult to convince such a person of his sin. But when you come to a proud Pharisee, such as Saul of Tarsus was, what can possibly convince and convict such a man of his sin? I repeat that there is only one power that can do so. It is this power of grace that can strike him on his forehead and cast him on his back to the ground. Nothing else can do it. Nothing could ever have made the proud Pharisee from Tarsus say of himself, 'In me (that is, in my flesh), dwelleth no good thing'. But the overwhelming power of grace can do it, and has done it. Grace convinces us and convicts us of our sin.

Then grace goes on to persuade us of the Truth. It displays the Truth before us in magnificent colours, and at the same time it acts upon our mind and our understanding. This is part of the quickening process. The result is that we look at a truth we used to ridicule, and suddenly we see it to be the Truth of God. We love it and desire to embrace it, and we are enabled to do so. Oh! if it were not that grace is so powerful, not one of us would ever have believed the Gospel. 'By grace are ye saved through faith, and that not of yourselves, it is the gift of God.' What I am emphasizing now is the power, and that nothing but this irresistible power of grace could ever have produced a single believer.

We can but glance at the twin truths described as 'quickening' and 'regeneration'. We have already referred to them. Both of them illustrate the irresistible power of grace. What is regeneration? It is most certainly the work of the Creator, the One who made everything out of nothing at the beginning, the One who said 'Let there be light: and there was light'. The Apostle Paul, again in the Epistle to the Ephesians, reminds us of this at the end of the first chapter. He prays that the Ephesian Christians might know three things: (1) the hope which belonged to their calling, (2) the riches of the glory of God's inheritance in the saints, and (3) the exceeding greatness of God's power (that is, the measure of the power of grace): 'the exceeding greatness of his power to us-ward who believe, according to the working of his mighty power' (or, as the Revised Version reads, 'that working of the strength of his might').

What is the measure of this mighty power? Paul goes on to tell us. It is 'the power that he wrought in Christ, when he raised him from the dead, and set him at his own right hand in the heavenly places, far above all principality and power, and might and dominion, and every name that is named, not only in this world, but also in that which is to come' [*Ephesians* 1 : 19–23]. Had you realized that the power that was necessary to make believers out of you and me is the same power that God used in bringing up His Son from the dead and in raising Him and seating Him at His right hand in the glory? Many people seem to think that to believe the Gospel is easy and simple; that a man sits as a kind of judge of truth. Someone comes and preaches the Gospel to him, and then after some consideration he decides whether he is going to believe or not. He has the power to do either, they believe; and he just exercises this power. But, says Paul, it takes the power that brought the Lord Jesus Christ from the grave to deal with that man and change him. Nothing less than that power must be exercised in a soul to enable it to believe and to be saved. Nothing less! The natural man is totally incapable of this, as Paul says in 1 Corinthians 2 : 14, '. . . neither can he know (the things of the Spirit of God) for they are spiritually discerned'. Were it not, I say again, that grace is irresistible, not one of us would ever have believed the Gospel.

But let us go on, for the power of grace does not end with the seeking, the quickening, and the regenerating. The next heading, number four, is the 'restraining' power of grace. Thank God for that! The restraining power of grace is manifested in God's people even before their conversion. They are not allowed to sin to such a degree that they put themselves outside the scope of salvation. They are never allowed to blaspheme against the Holy Ghost. They may say many things they should not say against Him; but they are never allowed to blaspheme. But the power of restraining grace is necessary even in the Christian, surrounded as he is by temptations, and often tempted from within. True Christians can say with Lawrence Tuttiett –

How oft to sure destruction
Our feet had gone astray,
Wert Thou not, patient Shepherd,
The Guardian of our way.

Oh thank God for the power of restraining grace, the grace that holds us back, the grace that prevents us from doing things that would harm and damage our immortal souls.

The fifth aspect of the power of grace is sanctifying grace, or the power of grace in our sanctification. Here we see the power of grace manifesting itself against indwelling sin, sin in the flesh, sin in the body. Paul's argument is that we are all by nature under this dominion, this power of sin, and that nothing but the tremendous power of the reign of grace could ever deliver us from any aspect of its tyranny. This is particularly true of indwelling sin. At the end of the seventh chapter of this Epistle the Apostle puts this in the well-known words: 'O wretched man that I am! who shall deliver me from the body of this death?' I cannot deliver myself. My knowledge of the Law cannot, for that makes it even worse because of the reign of sin within me. What, then, can I do? Who can deliver me? There is only one answer – 'I thank God through Jesus Christ our Lord'. And then: 'For the law of the Spirit of life in Christ Jesus hath made me free from the law of sin and death.' This is the power that does the work; it is the power of grace sanctifying me, delivering me from sin dwelling within me.

The Apostle makes exactly the same point in Philippians 2: 12, 13: 'Work out your own salvation with fear and trembling, for (because) it is God that worketh in you both to will and to do.' If He did not 'work' in that way we would not have the power, and we could do nothing. We have the power to work it out because He has already been working it in. 'Work it out because it is God that works in you.' He gives us the power, and He works in us in this way 'both to will, and to do'. Was not Isaac Watts right when he wrote in a hymn –

His power subdues our sins;
And His forgiving love,
Far as the east is from the west
Doth all our guilt remove.

Thank God for this – 'His power subdues our sins'. Otherwise our case would be hopeless. All this is a part of the power of the reign of grace as seen in the matter of our sanctification.

The next, the sixth heading, is 'supporting' grace, of which we are all constantly in need. I have been describing the power of indwelling sin, and we have seen that only the power of grace is great enough to overcome it, and subdue it; but what of 'the world and the flesh and the devil' that are against us, and are for ever attacking us and threatening us? Let us turn this time to James for a statement about the problem. It is in the fourth chapter of his Epistle, in verses 4 to 6. 'Ye adulterers and adulteresses, know ye not that the friendship of the world is enmity with God? Whosoever therefore will be a friend of the world is the enemy of God. Do ye think that the Scripture saith in vain, The Spirit that dwelleth in us lusteth to envy?' This passage means that the Spirit that God has put in us as Christians is jealous on our behalf, and is fighting for us, over against that spirit of the world that is attacking us. The Spirit that God has put within us is 'lusting' for us and for our salvation. 'Do ye think that the Scripture saith in vain, The Spirit that dwelleth in us lusteth to envy? But he giveth more grace. Wherefore he saith, God resisteth the proud, but giveth grace unto the humble. Submit yourselves therefore to God. Resist the devil, and he will flee from you.'

What a statement! We all know something about the power of the devil. His power is second only to that of God Himself. That is how the devil became 'the god of this world', 'the prince of the power of the air, the spirit that now worketh in the children of disobedience'. What a power! His power was so great that he really believed he could have overthrown the Son of God when he tempted Him. We are told that the archangel Michael, when he was contending with the devil about the body of Moses, 'durst not bring a railing accusation against him, but said, The Lord rebuke thee' [*Jude* 9]. The angels, the holy angels, do not joke about the devil; and no Christian should ever joke about the devil. The power of the devil is terrifying; he is 'the god of this world'. And yet James says, 'Resist the devil, and he will flee from you'. But notice that he only says that after saying that He (God) 'giveth more grace'. It is only because the power of the reign of grace is in us, and we realize it and depend upon it, that we can defy the devil. Peter says the same thing in his own way: 'Your adversary the devil, as a roaring lion, roameth about seeking whom he may devour.' What hope can there be for us? Here it is: 'Whom resist steadfast in the faith' [1 *Peter* 5: 8, 9]. That is the power that grace gives us in order to help us, and to strengthen us, against the terrible power of the world and of the devil. And that is why, as Christians, we sing words like these –

O Lamb of God, still keep me
Close to Thy piercèd side.
'Tis only there in safety
And peace I can abide.
What foes and snares surround me
What lusts and fears within!
The grace that sought and found me
Alone can keep me clean.

Thank God, the grace of God can keep us clean. The power 'that sought and found' us, and delivered us from death and antagonism, alone can, and will, keep us clean.

But what about the trials and tribulations that come to meet us? Though we are children of God we are not promised an easy time in this world. The Bible does not tell us, as the Cults tell us, that we shall walk in some Elysium and never have any more troubles or problems as long as we live; that we shall just go on singing, 'And now I am happy all the day'. Not at all! That is not true. On the contrary, we find Paul and Barnabas telling the early Christians that 'we must through much tribulation enter into the Kingdom of God' [*Acts* 14: 22]. That means entering into it finally beyond this world. 'In the world', said Christ, 'you shall have tribulation, but be of good cheer, I have overcome the world' – and that is still where our hope lies.

But perhaps the best example of all in respect of the power of grace is found in Paul's Second Epistle to the Corinthians, chapter 12. Here he tells us that he was troubled with 'the thorn in the flesh' (undoubtedly some physical ailment) and he 'besought the Lord three times', that it might be removed. But it was not removed. How, then, can he go on doing his work? How can he maintain his witness? How can he stand up to this trial, this 'thorn in the flesh' as he describes it? The answer was remarkable. The thorn was not removed, but what the Lord said to him was, 'My grace is sufficient for thee'. So 'I have come to learn', says Paul, 'that when I am weak, then am I strong'. It is when I am brought to the end of my own power, and realize that it is the power of His reigning grace that matters, that I am strong. He goes so far as to say that he can now 'glory in infirmities', in the trials and the tribulations, because their effect is to remind him of this power that will never let him go, but will carry him right through, whatever may come to meet him or assail him.

This glorious truth is constantly celebrated in the hymn-books. Edward Mote puts it like this:

When darkness seems to veil His face –

In other words, when you feel that you are spiritually dry, and that you have lost the face of God, and are surrounded by problems and trials and tribulations –

When darkness seems to veil His face,
I rest on His unchanging grace;
In every high and stormy gale,
My anchor holds within the veil.

His oath, His covenant, and blood
Support me in the 'whelming flood;
When all around my soul gives way
He then is all my hope and stay.

On Christ, the solid Rock, I stand
All other ground is sinking sand.

Many other hymns say precisely the same thing. God will never forsake the soul that He has chosen. Though you may be called upon to go through trials and troubles, through stormy waters, and be surrounded by everything that is black and threatening –

The soul that on Jesus has leaned for repose,
He will not, He cannot desert to its foes;
That soul, though all hell should endeavour to shake,
He'll never, no never, no never forsake.

He has promised – 'I will never leave thee, nor forsake thee'? [*Hebrews* 13: 5]. Thank God for the power of 'supporting grace'. 'Underneath are the everlasting arms' [*Deuteronomy* 33: 27] – that is the power of grace.

That brings us to the last, the seventh heading, namely, 'enabling and persevering' grace. Here again is something we constantly need. We have seen how we are brought out of the bondage, and the death, and the antagonism. We see how we are restored and how we are sanctified and supported. But how are we to continue on the rest of the journey? How are we to hold out in the Christian warfare and the fight of faith? The answer is still the same. It is the power of reigning grace alone that makes possible and that guarantees the final perseverance of the saints. This was very much in the Apostle's mind at this point; and we shall see later how he develops it in chapters 6, 7 and 8. Meanwhile let us note how he expresses it in a phrase that is found in Philippians 1: 6 – 'He who hath begun a good work in you will perform it until the day of Jesus Christ'. There can be no possible answer to that. It means that if, because of this great plan and purpose and programme that we have considered, and because of all this power, God has started a work, He will not give it up; He will carry it on to completion. 'He which hath begun a good work in you will continue performing it until the final end, the day of Jesus Christ.'

The prophet Zechariah had proclaimed the same truth. In his day a remnant had been brought back from captivity in Babylon and great problems were facing them; but, by grace, they are enabled to say this; 'Who art thou, O great mountain? before Zerubbabel thou shalt become a plain: and he shall bring forth the headstone thereof with shoutings, crying, Grace, grace unto it' [4: 7]. Of course! The headstone will certainly be brought forth because grace will enable the Lord's people to persevere right until the end.

There is no teaching that is so contradictory of the whole argument of the Apostle Paul in his letters as the foolish notion that you can fall away from grace. There is no falling from grace. 'What about Galatians chapter 5, verse 4?' you may ask. I answer – all the Apostle is saying there is that if those foolish Galatians persisted in saying that circumcision was essential they would be denying grace, they would be 'falling away from the grace position', and returning to talk about 'justification by works'. That is all he means there, and that is all he says. He says in effect, You are then talking about justification by works and not justification by grace. He does not say there that anyone can fall away from grace as a state or condition. If that were a possibility we could not talk about 'the reign of grace'. If it were possible for us to fall away, we should all certainly fall away, every one of us. But we are under the 'reign of grace'; and it is a powerful reign. 'No man', says Christ, 'shall be able to pluck them out of my hand' [*John* 10: 28]. Of course not! If it were possible, it would happen. But the reign of grace is infinitely more powerful than that of sin and the devil. Nothing and no one can ever snatch us from Him or separate us from His love. That is what the Apostle asserts in the great climax at the end of chapter 8: 'I am persuaded that neither death, nor life, nor angels, nor principalities, nor powers, nor things present, nor things to come, nor height, nor depth, nor any other creature' – anything you can think of! – 'shall be able to separate us from the love of God, which is in Christ Jesus our Lord' [verses 38, 39]. And again, 'Whom he did foreknow he also did predestinate. . . . Moreover whom he did predestinate, them he also called; and whom he called, them he also justified; and whom he justified, them he also glorified' [verses 29, 30]. We are seated now, at this moment, 'in Christ', 'in the heavenly places', says Paul in Ephesians 2: 6. It is as certain as that! Persevering grace, enabling grace, keeping grace! If this were not true the whole system would collapse. 'O yes', says Augustus Toplady –

The work which His goodness began,
The arm of His strength will complete;
His promise is Yea and Amen,
And never was forfeited yet.
Things future, nor things that are now,
Nor all things below or above,
Can make Him His purpose forgo,
Or sever my soul from His love.

And we can say with Toplady –

My name from the palms of His hands
Eternity will not erase;
Impressed on His heart it remains
In marks of indelible grace.
Yes, I to the end shall endure,
As sure as the earnest is given;
More happy, but not more secure,
The glorified spirits in heaven.

'Indelible grace!' Let the devil, let hell, let the universe try to erase it. They cannot. My name has been printed on the 'palms of His hands' by a power that nothing can remove. It is 'indelible grace'. That is the term – 'In marks of indelible grace'. And because of that I can go on and say, 'Yes, I to the end shall endure'. Is that boasting? No! I cannot endure if left to myself, but because my name is impressed on His heart, I know that I shall reach my destined end. The power of grace will take me on, and hold and guide me, and will never let me go.

Yes! I to the end shall endure,
As sure as the earnest is given;
More happy, but not more secure,
The glorified spirits in heaven.

Thank God for the power of the reign of grace. This is the ground of assurance. It is because of this that we can be certain He will never let us go. Our frail grasp often lets go of Him, but He will never let us go. Hudson Taylor used to translate the statement in Mark 11 : 22 which in most Bibles reads, 'Have faith in God'. He said it should be, 'Hold on to the faithfulness of God'. That means this: Hold on to the fact that He is holding on to you, and that He will never let you go. So when you feel spiritually dry, and that you scarcely have any faith at all; when you feel that you can do nothing, and are nothing, rest in this, that He will never let you go. It is not my frail hold on Him that matters, it is His strong grasp of me. 'I have been apprehended by Him', says Paul, 'and I am trying to apprehend that for which I have been apprehended' [*Philippians* 3 : 12]. What matters is that He has apprehended us, that He has taken hold of us, and that He will never let us go, come what may. He has said, 'I will never leave thee, nor forsake thee', and because His power is an infinite, eternal, everlasting power, nothing can ever take us out of His grasp. Oh, the blessed, the powerful reign of grace! Do you feel it around and about you? Are you aware of its clutches and of its hold? Do you know your security? It is all in the power of grace. Thank God for it!

Twenty-six

*

That as sin hath reigned unto death, even so might grace reign, through righteousness, unto eternal life, by Jesus Christ our Lord.
Romans 5 : 21

I am loth to leave this great and exalted theme, and indeed we cannot do so until we come to what I regard as the climax. Thus far we have been looking at the reign of grace, the triumph and the glory of grace; and we have done so under various headings. We now come to a further aspect of the subject, to what I would call the bounty or the bountiful character of the reign of grace. This word 'reign', as we have seen, means to 'reign as king'. We always associate with Monarchy or the name of a King or a Queen the idea of munificence, of bounty and of largesse; and certainly that is very characteristic of the reign of grace. There is no point, therefore, at which we see its contrast with sin in a more striking manner than just here. Grace always gives, whereas sin always takes away.

The Scripture gives us a perfect illustration of this contrast. If you want to see how sin always takes away from, and robs a man, look at the Prodigal Son who found himself in the position that 'no man gave unto him'. He had lost everything, he had squandered his fortune, and 'no man gave unto him'. Sin always deserts, it always takes from us; and it leaves us exhausted, with nothing but empty husks. That is the terrible thing about sin, and nothing shows so clearly the blindness of mankind as the fact that it is fooled by it. Sin seems to give so much; but actually it does not give anything. Sin always robs. It tires a man, and exhausts him. It stimulates him in a false and artificial manner, and leaves him helpless at the end. Talk tomorrow morning to the man who was so excited under the influence of drink tonight, and see his exhaustion. He was not being stimulated at all; he was being exhausted, for alcohol is classified pharmacologically as a depressant. That is the characteristic of sin always; that is the effect of the reign of sin.

But the characteristic of grace is that it gives. It not only gives, it gives regally, it gives in a royal manner. There is nothing parsimonious about grace, there is nothing partial or puny about it. It gives and gives freely; it gives abundantly. 'Grace abounding', says John Bunyan, 'to the chief of sinners.' That is the essential characteristic of grace. The Apostle has already been reminding us of this. He has told us in chapter 3, verse 24, 'Being justified freely by his grace, through the redemption that is in Christ Jesus'. We have also seen in this very chapter, and in the paragraph we are looking at, how he keeps on talking about this 'much more' and this 'abundance' and 'superabundance', this 'excess' of grace. It is the point he has been emphasizing right through, and in doing so the Apostle is only doing what the Scriptures do everywhere. To demonstrate that I have but to quote the Scripture.

Here are some other statements about the munificence, the largesse, the superabundance of grace: 'Of his fullness', says John in the first chapter of his Gospel, verse 16 – 'Of his fullness have all we received, and grace upon grace.' Listen to our Lord saying in the same Gospel to the woman of Samaria: 'Whosoever drinketh of this water shall thirst again, but whosoever drinketh of the water that I shall give him shall never thirst, but the water that I shall give him shall be in him a well of water springing up into everlasting life' [4: 13–14]. 'He that cometh unto me', He says in chapter 6, verse 35, 'shall never hunger, and he that believeth on me shall never thirst.' There you have this typical biblical emphasis upon the munificence, the bounty of grace. Then look at the statement in Acts 4: 33, 'Great grace was upon them all'. Then observe Paul comforting the Corinthians who were passing through a difficult time; says he, 'God is able to make all grace abound toward you' [2 *Corinthians* 9: 8]. What more can you need than that? Nowhere perhaps does this truth receive greater emphasis than in the Epistle to the Ephesians where it is a recurring theme – 'according to the riches of his grace' [1: 7]; 'the exceeding riches of his grace' [2: 7]; 'the unsearchable riches of Christ' [3: 8]. These are but examples chosen at random in order that we may have some conception of the fullness and the abundance, the superabundance, of this reign of grace. We were introduced to it at the beginning of this very chapter in the second verse, where the Apostle said, 'By whom also we have had our access by faith into this grace wherein we stand'.

If you and I, as Christian people, give the impression that we are very poor and needy, and that we are having a difficult and a miserable time, what unworthy representatives we are of 'the God of all grace'. Grace gives with a superabounding munificence; and if we are not receiving it and enjoying it – shame on us! It is entirely due to our lack of understanding. We must be listening to the devil who would always have us believe that to be a Christian means that we have to give up so much and then proceed to trudge along a hard and difficult road. The world, he would have us believe, has so much and is full of enjoyment, whereas we have so little. Shame on us! To come to Christ means to receive, and to receive of 'His fullness, and grace upon grace'.

Then there are other terms. Consider the way the Apostle Peter puts it in his First Epistle: 'But', he says, 'the God of all grace, who hath called us unto his eternal glory by Christ Jesus, after that ye have suffered awhile, . . . establish, strengthen, settle you' [1 *Peter* 5: 10]. 'The God of all grace'! There is nothing beyond that. But there is another very interesting term used by the Apostle Peter about grace. He says in his First Epistle, chapter 4 verse 10: 'As every man hath received the gift, even so minister the same one to another, as good stewards of the manifold grace of God.' 'The manifold grace!' What a wonderful term! What he means is that grace not only looks after every one of us, and in every part of our experience, but that this wonderful reign of grace is to be seen among God's people in the division of offices in the Church. 'Now', he says, 'as every man hath received the gift, even so minister the same.' We are not all called to do the same work but we are all called to do something, and we are enabled by this many-sided, many-faceted grace of God to carry out the functions which He has allotted to us.

Here Peter is just saying what we shall find Paul saying in the twelfth chapter of this Epistle to the Romans in the sixth verse. 'Having then gifts differing according to the grace that is given to us, whether prophecy, let us prophesy according to the proportion of faith; or ministry, let us wait on our ministering; or he that teacheth, on teaching; or he that exhorteth, on exhortation'; and so on. That is a description of 'the manifold grace of God' at work in the Church of God. The Apostle says exactly the same thing in the fourth chapter of the Epistle to the Ephesians and the seventh verse, 'But unto every one of us is given grace according to the measure of the gift of Christ'.

How wonderful is this reign of grace! It expresses itself in a manifold manner; and grace is given to us to play any particular part that God has appointed us to in the Church. If you are a doorkeeper you need grace; if you are giving out hymn-books you are to do it with grace. Whatever you do, whatever your part, if you are simply saying a word to someone sitting next to you, or if you are visiting the sick, do it with grace. In the twelfth chapter of this Epistle Paul mentions all these things – love, friendliness, cheerfulness, fervency, joy, honesty, and so on – 'Grace is given to everyone of us according to the measure of the gift of Christ'. In every single instance we are enabled by grace to do the particular thing He calls upon us to do. Thus grace reigns in the ministration of the Church and her members. Not only the preacher, but everyone of us is given a gift 'differing according to the grace that is given to us', in order that the Church may be built up and the Kingdom of God extended amongst men in this world of time. That, very briefly, gives us some idea of the bountiful character of grace and its reign.

We come now to the sixth matter, the ultimate victory of grace. We have seen that our salvation was planned before the foundation of the world, and that the end is planned – 'That as sin hath reigned unto death, even so might grace reign through righteousness unto eternal life by Jesus Christ our Lord'. That is the goal. This, again, can be considered from two different aspects: first, as regards ourselves, the believers, God's children, the citizens of the Kingdom; and secondly, in a more general manner.'

In the working out of the programme we looked at the various steps and stages, and when considering the power of the reign of grace we saw that it was manifested in our regeneration and calling, in our justification, and in our sanctification. But to what does it lead? What is the ultimate goal? Where shall we arrive at the end? There is no doubt as to the answer. Listen to it as we find it in Ephesians 5: 27: 'That he might present it to himself a glorious church, not having spot, or wrinkle, or any such thing; but that it should be holy and without blemish.' That is the goal, that is what Paul means here by the term 'eternal life'. We are given eternal life here and now; but in its full completeness it lies ahead of us, and the Apostle's words here describe our condition when we shall have that life in all its plenitude.

Jude puts it in the twenty-fourth verse of his little Epistle thus: 'Now unto him that is able to keep you from falling' (while we are here God has the power and the ability to keep us from falling, but He does not stop at that) 'and to present you faultless before the presence of his glory with exceeding joy.' That is the end, that is the final triumph. Yes, He is able to keep us from falling while we are still here in this life on earth (you remember that we referred to 'sustaining grace'), but that is consummated in the glorious perfection we shall know when He 'presents us faultless before the presence of his glory with exceeding joy'.

Again, consider the way the Apostle Paul puts it in his letter to the Philippians. He says that 'Our conversation (citizenship) is in heaven; from whence also we look for the Saviour, the Lord Jesus Christ, who shall change [this] our vile body, that it may be fashioned like unto his glorious body, according to the working whereby he is able even to subdue all things unto himself' [*Philippians* 3: 20, 21]. That again describes this ultimate goal and objective, the final triumph of the reign of grace. We are conceived, born under sin, and under the reign of sin; and we have seen what that means and to what it leads. To what is the reign of grace bringing us? It will bring us to that final perfection when we shall be 'without spot or wrinkle or any such thing'. We shall be 'holy and without blemish', we shall be 'faultless' in every respect – body, soul and spirit. There will not be a trace or a vestige left of sin or any of its consequences. That is the goal to which the reign of grace is bringing us. So much then for the particular aspect of the matter.

Let us now look at it in general; for, alas, when sin and the devil gained control they not only gained control of human beings, they also gained control of the whole world. The devil is 'the god of this world'. The very ground was cursed; briars and thorns came up, diseases entered in. That is a part of the reign of sin; let us never forget that. What, then, is the triumph, the final triumph of the reign of grace? It will be seen in that great time that is coming which the Apostle Peter writes about in his Second Epistle, in the third chapter. 'The Lord is not slack concerning his promise, as some men count slackness, but is long-suffering to us-ward, not willing that any should perish, but that all should come to repentance. But the day of the Lord will come as a thief in the night, in the which the heavens shall pass away with a great noise, and the elements shall melt with fervent heat, the earth also and the works that are therein shall be burned up.' And it is going to end, he says, thus, 'Nevertheless we, according to his promise, look for new heavens and a new earth, wherein dwelleth righteousness'. I say again, every trace and vestige of the evil effects of sin upon the cosmos itself will be entirely burned up, incinerated, and there shall be 'new heavens and a new earth wherein dwelleth righteousness.' 'The wolf also shall dwell with the lamb, and the leopard shall lie down with the kid; and the calf and the young lion and the fatling together; and a little child shall lead them. And the cow and the bear shall feed; their young ones shall lie down together: and the lion shall eat straw like the ox. And the sucking child shall play on the hole of the asp, and the weaned child shall put his hand on the cockatrice' den. They shall not hurt nor destroy in all my holy mountain: for the earth shall be full of the knowledge of the Lord, as the waters cover the sea.' It has all been foretold in those words in the eleventh chapter of Isaiah's prophecy.

That is what is coming! Its glory is indescribable; it baffles the imagination. But it is coming! We shall be brought, you and I who are Christians, to that final state, the eternal state of men under the reign of grace. We shall be perfect, we shall be glorified and the whole world will be glorified, and we shall spend our eternity in the glorious presence of God. That is what the reign of grace is leading to; that will be the final triumph of grace; that is the everlasting state of all who are in Christ and who belong to Him. As by one man sin came, by this second man, Christ Jesus, all this is going to come, so that 'as sin hath reigned unto death, even so might grace reign through righteousness unto eternal life'. Thus we have had a glance at the final consummation of the programme that was planned and arranged before the foundation of the world, before the very process of time had been brought into being.

That brings us to the last, and the most glorious thing of all – the One through whom all this happens, the One who alone makes the reign of grace possible, the One in whom grace shines out most gloriously of all. 'That as sin hath reigned unto death, even so might grace reign through righteousness unto eternal life by Jesus Christ our Lord.' We have noticed several times previously how the Apostle finishes all these sections by mentioning this blessed Name. He will do so again at the end of the sixth chapter: 'For the wages of sin is death, but the gift of God is eternal life through Jesus Christ our Lord.' Then at the end of the eighth chapter he ends that mighty passage with the words, 'Nor height, nor depth, nor any other creature shall be able to separate us from the love of God which is in Christ Jesus our Lord'.

So Paul compels us to look at the Lord of glory. It is through Him that everything comes to us; it is He and His work alone that guarantee it all. The Apostle has been personifying grace. He has done so, I take it, because he has been contrasting sin and grace as powers in conflict. But that is only a figure of speech, only a manner of speaking. Actually he has been describing what comes to us through and by the Lord Jesus Christ. And, if we would learn anything about grace, what we must do is to look at Him. This is what Isaac Watts puts so well in his hymn:

Now to the Lord a noble song!
Awake, my soul; awake, my tongue;
Hosanna to the Eternal Name,
And all His boundless love proclaim.

See where it shines in Jesu's face,
The brightest image of His grace . . .

And indeed it is! As the author of the Epistle to the Hebrews puts it, Christ is the express image of His Person, the effulgence of His glory, and so Watts proceeds,

See where it shines in Jesu's face,
The brightest image of His grace;
God, in the Person of His Son,
Has all His mightiest works outdone.

All God's gifts are wonderful, but they all pale into insignificance when you look into Jesu's face.

The spacious earth and spreading flood
Proclaim the wise and powerful God;
And Thy rich glories from afar
Sparkle in every rolling star.

But in His looks a glory stands,
The noblest labour of Thy hands;
The radiant lustre of His eyes
Outshines the wonders of the skies.

Have we had a glimpse of that? Do we know anything about it? The Holy Spirit was sent and given in order that we might have a glimpse of this 'glory in the face of Jesus Christ'. Well, then, let us look at Him. Here all the noblest and most glorious aspects of grace are seen most clearly, and if we would grasp what the Apostle is conveying to us with his 'much more', and his 'abundance', and his 'much more abounding' we must turn to the Lord

Jesus Christ. There we shall see the wonders and the triumphs and the glory of God's redeeming grace.

How impossible it is to attempt to summarize such a theme in a few words! I can but give headings and point to the verses in Scripture in which these glories are portrayed most clearly. We should study them and ponder them until we see something of their riches; we must pray God to open our eyes by His Spirit that we may do so. It was God's grace that ever sent Him into the world. It was the grace of God that ever planned all this and decided to send His Son into the world. And it was this same grace that led the Son to come, and to accomplish all He did in this world. It is grace that still prompts Him to perform all that He is still doing for His own, for His people.

What did grace lead Him to do? The Apostle Paul tells us in one verse [2 *Corinthians* 8: 9]: 'For ye know the grace of our Lord Jesus Christ, that, though he was rich, yet for your sakes he became poor, that ye through his poverty might be rich.' 'Though he was rich.' He owned everything, and it was through Him that everything was made. He was Lord of the universe, everything was under His hands. But, wonder of wonders, though He was so rich, yet for our sakes He became poor. It is there we see the real character of grace. We have been talking about the munificence, the beneficence and largesse. It is there you see it all.

Or take another definition of it given by the Apostle in the second chapter of the Epistle to the Philippians in the great statement beginning at verse 5: 'Let this mind be in you which was also in Christ Jesus, who, being in the form of God, thought it not robbery to be equal with God, but made himself of no reputation, and took upon him the form of a servant, and was found in the likeness of men: And being found in fashion as a man, he humbled himself, and became obedient unto death, even the death of the cross.' Or, as Robert Robinson puts it:

From the highest throne of glory
To the cross of deepest woe!

If you want to measure grace, that is how you do so – from the highest heaven down to the cross, and beyond that even to the grave, down amongst the dead. This is the way to see the character of the reign of grace. It was grace, the grace that was in His heart, and in the heart of the Godhead, that led Him to do all this – eventually to give His very life a ransom for us and for our sins. He 'made his soul an offering for sin'. He did not 'hold on to' that glory which He had shared eternally with His Father. He 'made himself of no reputation', 'he humbled himself', He laid aside the insignia of that eternal glory, He came down to earth, He endured the contradiction of sinners, and He went to the death of the cross and all that that involved. It is there you see the bounty, the abundance, the munificence of it all. He gave Himself even unto the death of the cross. So that aspect of grace is seen most gloriously and most brightly in Him.

But come, let us look at the *triumph* of grace as it is seen in Him. There He is, crucified, dead and buried; and the stone is placed on the opening of the grave and sealed, and soldiers are appointed to guard it. But He 'burst asunder the bands of death', and 'rose triumphant o'er the grave'. 'Whom God', said Peter in his sermon at Jerusalem on the day of Pentecost, 'hath raised up, having loosed the bands of death, because it was not possible that he should be holden of it' [*Acts* 2: 24]. The Apostle Paul, writing to the Corinthians in the First Epistle, chapter 15, and dealing with this same theme from a slightly different angle, reminds us of what it was that the Lord had to conquer, what it was that grace eventually had to conquer in Him and through Him. He says, 'The last enemy that shall be destroyed is death' [verse 26]. But He destroyed it. The fifty-fourth verse of the same chapter proclaims, 'Death is swallowed up in victory'; in other words, that 'as sin hath reigned unto death, even so might grace reign through righteousness unto eternal life.' 'Death is swallowed up in victory.' That is an everlasting defeat for death; that is the annihilation of death; it means a taking hold of it and a taking it away. 'Death is swallowed up in victory.' We see that in the Resurrection. Looking at that we can say, 'O death where is thy sting? O grave, where is thy victory?'; and then go on and add, 'Thanks be unto God, which giveth us the victory through our Lord Jesus Christ'. There you see the most glorious aspect of the triumph and the power of the reign of grace, and it is still in Him!

But what has happened to Him since He rose from the grave? We are assured that He ascended up into heaven, and having ascended He has taken His seat at the right hand of God; '... when he had by himself purged our sins, he sat down on the right hand of the Majesty on high' [*Hebrews* 1:3]. In that same first chapter of the Epistle to the Hebrews the author proceeds to an unanswerable argument in the words, 'Unto which of the angels said he at any time, Sit on my right hand, until I make thine enemies thy footstool'. This refers to what is called 'The Heavenly Session of our Lord'.

What does His Heavenly Session mean? It means that He is seated at the right hand of God, and therefore we are able to say that 'He is able also to save them to the uttermost that come unto God by him, seeing he ever liveth to make intercession for them' [*Hebrews* 7:25].

With the old priesthood in Israel, under Judaism, the priests died and they needed new priests constantly, and thus there was always an element of uncertainty, but 'this man, because he abideth ever, hath an unchangeable', an everlasting 'priesthood. Wherefore he is able to save unto the uttermost.' Nothing will be left undone. We shall be brought to that place where we shall enjoy the final consummation of redemption.

The same truth is repeated in Hebrews 10:12 and 13: 'But this man, after he had offered one sacrifice for sins for ever, sat down at the right hand of God; from henceforth expecting till his enemies be made his footstool'. That is a part of the reign of grace. He is there seated at the right hand of God, and He has all power in His hands. He says, 'All power is given unto me in heaven and in earth; go ye therefore and preach the Gospel' [*Matthew* 28:18 and 19]. That was His commission to His disciples. He has all power, He is seated at the right hand of God on the eternal throne, and He is waiting until His enemies shall be made His footstool. And again, Paul says in 1 Corinthians 15:25: 'He must reign, till he hath put all enemies under his feet.' He must! He will! Nothing can ever stop Him, or prevent His doing so.

We see in His Heavenly Session all the aspects of this grace. He is our Advocate with the Father, He 'ever lives to make intercession for us'. He has all power, and He is controlling and directing the entire course of human history. Never worry about the future of the Church, never worry about your own eternal destiny – it is all in His hands. And not only you, and the Kingdom, but everything else is under His power. 'All power is given unto me', he says. He must reign. He is reigning; He is reigning at this moment; let us never forget it. But we see all this by faith; it is not visible at the moment. The author of the Epistle to the Hebrews argues this out for us in the second chapter. The promise is that all things shall be put under Him, but, says verse 8, 'we see not yet all things put under him'. And then the writer adds, 'But we see Jesus' [verse 9]. He is already glorified, and that is the guarantee of the fact that He is going to come back to complete this work.

It is all described so wonderfully in the Book of Revelation, chapter 19: 'He hath on his vesture and on his thigh a name written, KING OF KINGS, AND LORD OF LORDS' [verse 16]. He rides on a white horse, and a sword 'goes out of his mouth'. He is coming to fight a mighty battle against all who are opposed to God and to us who believe in Him. The writer then goes on to give us a glimpse of His final triumph: 'I saw the beast, and the kings of the earth, and their armies, gathered together to make war against him that sat on the horse, and against his army. And the beast was taken, and with him the false prophet that wrought miracles before him, with which he deceived them that had received the mark of the beast, and them that worshipped his image. These both were cast alive into a lake of fire burning with brimstone. And the remnant were slain with the sword of him that sat upon the horse, which sword proceeded out of his mouth; and all the fowls were filled with their flesh.' Again, in Revelation 20: 10: 'And the devil' – the ultimate enemy, the one who first defied God before the creation of the world, that 'Lucifer', that 'Morning Star' that rebelled and withstood God and who has caused all the havoc, 'the god of this world', 'the prince of the power of the air, the spirit that now worketh in the children of disobedience' – 'And the devil that deceived them was cast into the lake of fire and brimstone, where the beast and the false prophet are, and shall be tormented day and night for ever and ever.' And in verses 14 and 15: 'And death and hell were cast into the lake of fire. This is the second death. And whosoever was not found written in the book of life was cast into the lake of fire.' That is what is coming! That is how the Lord is going to accomplish the final triumph of grace over sin!

Such is the picture that is given of Him. And when that happens, when all that will have taken place, then, says Paul, in 1 Corinthians 15: 24: 'Then cometh the end, when he shall have delivered up the kingdom to God, even the Father; when he shall have put down all rule and all authority and power.' His every enemy shall have been conquered and destroyed. 'As sin reigned unto death, even so' shall 'grace reign through righteousness unto eternal life by Jesus Christ our Lord.' 'He shall have put down all rule, and all authority and power.' The devil and all his forces, and all who have been influenced by him, and who belong to him, and all that has come into being as the result of sin – hell, and hades, and death, and everything else – it is all ousted and cast out to be destroyed from the presence of God for ever and for ever.

And then: 'And I saw a new heaven and a new earth; for the first heaven and the first earth were passed away; and there was no more sea.' 'Behold, the tabernacle of God is with men, and he will dwell with them, and they shall be his people, and God himself shall be with them, and be their God' [*Revelation* 21: 1–4]. That is what is coming when the triumph is consummated. Not only the enemy and all traces of him destroyed once and for ever; but this 'new heaven', this 'new earth', and God Himself dwelling amongst His people. We shall know that He is our God, and He will spend eternity with us, and we with Him. That is the glory, and it is the glory to which the Lord Jesus Christ, by the grace of God, is certainly and surely bringing all who believe in Him.

What can we say to these things? I can but urge you to listen to Isaac Watts expressing his feelings about it all, and in the hymn from which I have already quoted –

Grace! 'tis a sweet, a charming theme;
My thoughts rejoice at Jesu's name:
Ye angels, dwell upon the sound!
Ye heavens, reflect it to the ground!

Let us add to that Philip Doddridge's expression of his feelings:

Grace! 'tis a charming sound,
  Harmonious to the ear;
Heaven with the echo shall resound,
  And all the earth shall hear.

Grace first contrived the way
  To save rebellious man;
And all the steps that grace display
  Which drew the wondrous plan.

Grace first inscribed my name
  In God's eternal book;
'Twas grace that gave me to the Lamb,
  Who all my sorrows took.

Grace taught my soul to pray,
  And pardoning love to know,
'Twas grace that kept me to this day,
  And will not let me go.

Grace all the work shall crown
  Through everlasting days;
It lays in heaven the topmost stone.
  And well deserves the praise.

'Grace! 'tis a charming sound, Harmonious to the ear.' Oh that we might spend the rest of our days in this world singing such hymns to His praise and His glory!

Assurance

O for a thousand tongues to sing
My great Redeemer's praise,
The glories of my God and King,
The triumphs of His grace.

'As sin hath reigned unto death, even so' shall 'grace reign through righteousness unto eternal life by Jesus Christ our Lord.'